THE CANDIDATE

THE CANDIDATE

WHAT IT TAKES TO WIN—AND
HOLD—THE WHITE HOUSE

SAMUEL L. POPKIN

OXFORD
UNIVERSITY PRESS

OXFORD
UNIVERSITY PRESS

Oxford University Press, Inc., publishes works that further
Oxford University's objective of excellence
in research, scholarship, and education.

Oxford   New York
Auckland   Cape Town   Dar es Salaam   Hong Kong   Karachi
Kuala Lumpur   Madrid   Melbourne   Mexico City   Nairobi
New Delhi   Shanghai   Taipei   Toronto

With offices in
Argentina   Austria   Brazil   Chile   Czech Republic   France   Greece
Guatemala   Hungary   Italy   Japan   Poland   Portugal   Singapore
South Korea   Switzerland   Thailand   Turkey   Ukraine   Vietnam

Published by Oxford University Press, Inc.
198 Madison Avenue, New York, NY 10016

www.oup.com

Oxford is a registered trademark of Oxford University Press

Library of Congress Cataloging-in-Publication Data

Popkin, Samuel L.
The candidate : what it takes to win, and hold the White House / Samuel L. Popkin.
     p. cm.
Includes bibliographical references and index.
ISBN 978-0-19-992207-9 (hardback : alk. paper)   1. Presidents—United States—Election—History.
2. Presidential candidates—United States—History.   3. Presidential candidates—United States—
Case studies.   I. Title.
JK524.P63 2012
324.973—dc23

2012006845

9 8 7 6 5 4 3 2 1

Printed in the United States of America
on acid-free paper

For Susan Shirk
~~Four More Years!~~
Forever!

CONTENTS

THE CANDIDATE

PROLOGUE

Whatever happened to President Rudy Giuliani?

Throughout 2007, Rudy Giuliani, the former mayor of New York City led the Republican field, at times nearly tripling the numbers of Senator John McCain of Arizona or Governor Mitt Romney of Massachusetts. Giuliani broke all previous fundraising records for a Republican, and GOP leaders from every region of the country and every part of the Republican coalition rushed to endorse him.

Rudy Giuliani won national popular acclaim for the way he guided the New York City government after the 9/11 attacks on the World Trade Center. He became known far and wide as "America's mayor" and was *Time* magazine's Person of the Year. He projected grit and determination, and looked particularly strong compared to President George W. Bush, who was presiding over a weakening economy and seemingly unending, deteriorating wars in Iraq and Afghanistan.

Giuliani was already revered among conservative leaders for his choice of enemies and the relish with which he baited them. New York symbolized Sodom and Gomorrah for many religious conservatives, and liberal excess for many others. Giuliani lowered the crime rate, ridding New York of panhandlers, subway-turnstile jumpers, and especially the squeegee people who descended upon autos at stoplights, wiped windshields with their rags, and waited for tips. California Representative David Dreier (R-CA), a widely respected congressman, endorsed Giuliani, arguing that "If he could [get rid of the squeegee people] we know he can win the war on terror."[1]

What New Yorkers hated, the heartland loved. Giuliani was the man of the hour after Osama bin Laden attacked *his* city. He defended New York police against any and all charges of excessive force or racism. He was a hawk on national defense and a culture warrior.

Giuliani sold more than a million copies of his memoir, *Leadership.* Admirers flocked to his book signing and adoring audiences applauded his core leadership principles—"prepare relentlessly," "communicate strong beliefs," and "surround yourself with great people."[2] He made his "Twelve Commitments to the American people" the centerpiece of his campaign, distributed them at every speech, and promised to keep them before him every day in the Oval Office.

Republicans throughout the country applauded "Mr. Accountability." He was the perfect corrective to the lack of administrative accountability under George W. Bush. Rudy was the strongest Republican when matched with any Democrat, particularly the clear front-runner and likely winner, Senator Hillary Clinton. He would restore the Republican brand name and save the party from ruin.

When the dust cleared, America's mayor, the candidate with the most money, the best poll numbers, and the most endorsements, had set a new record for futility: zero delegates won at a cost of $58.8 million.

And what about President Hillary Clinton?

On November 9, 2007, a *National Journal* poll of seventy-five respected Democratic Party insiders found that Senator Barack Obama was the candidate who had most surprised them—for being a *worse* candidate than they had expected. Senator Clinton, on the other hand, was the candidate who surprised them for being better than expected.[3]

Two days after expert observers thought Hillary Clinton was in control, unnoticed breakdowns inside her campaign paved the way to an eventual, very public defeat.

And before President Hillary Clinton, and before President Rudy Giuliani, there was President Thomas E. Dewey.

Dewey appeared so far ahead of Harry S. Truman in 1948 that George Gallup stopped polling in mid-October to save money. The equally certain editors of the *Chicago Tribune* didn't bother to wait until the results came in and put out an extra evening edition with the famous three-word headline "Dewey Defeats Truman."

Today, all anyone recalls about this, the most stunning upset in American history are the two legends it created: the Truman who "Gave 'em Hell" to save the New Deal, and the complacent, stiff, overconfident Dewey who never knew what hit him.

Why was there no President Rudy Giuliani, President Hillary Clinton, or President Thomas E. Dewey?

The actual story of how an almost incoherent Harry Truman overcame a dashing, crime-busting district attorney–turned–governor is far more revealing. Dewey wasn't complacent or overconfident, and much of the hell Truman tried to deliver was confusing, inarticulate, and garbled. As with Giuliani and Clinton in 2008, critical steps taken *before* the campaign are what made the difference.

INEVITABLE WINNERS

There are two winners in every presidential election campaign: the inevitable winner when it begins and the inevitable victor after it ends. This book explains the difference between them.

It is hard to predict who will win a presidential campaign, whether it is for the nomination of a party or the presidency itself. It is easy, though, to predict the excuses the losers will give later.

When presidential candidates explain their defeat, they generally say they were outspent, or they couldn't get any coverage from the press, or that someone else had wrapped up all the endorsements. Giuliani, Clinton, and Dewey each had the money, the endorsements, and an audience.

Somehow, after the fact, it seems obvious that they never had a chance. Giuliani couldn't win because he was a pro-choice Catholic with a huge ego. Clinton could never win because she was a woman, divisive, and supported national health care. And Dewey was a threat to the New Deal and no match for Truman's populism.

So how did George H. W. Bush, who never managed to win a statewide election in Texas and who championed the Equal Rights Amendment, ever win? How did Ronald Reagan, who started so far to the Left that he was too liberal for the Hollywood Democratic Club to run him for

Congress in 1950, and who had nothing but rich friends, ever win? And how did Barack Obama, an African American with a Kenyan father and an unmarried white mother, ever win?

In every presidential election, there are three possible campaigns any candidate can run: He can run as a *challenger* trying to regain the White House for his party, an *incumbent* trying to stay in the White House, or a *successor* trying to retain the White House for the party in power.

The three campaigns repeat like movie roles: Challengers offer a fresh start, incumbents offer experience, and successors—the toughest campaign—offer continuity. Each role has different inherent vulnerabilities. Each role also experiences different organizational challenges during the campaign.

Candidates who don't understand which campaign they are waging make predictable strategic mistakes. For example, they misjudge how and when to fight. Like boxers, they forget they are facing, in the words of one crisis management expert, "the world according to Mike Tyson." When Tyson was the greatest boxer in the world, reporters would ask him about his opponent's strategy. "They all have a strategy," Tyson replied, "until they get hit."[4]

There are effective attacks and effective counterattacks, even when a candidate is hit by a Tysonlike uppercut on the campaign trail. But counterattacks only succeed when a candidate knows the rules of engagement by which she will be judged. Figuring out how people will frame her fight makes all the difference between the candidate who gets knocked out and the one who picks herself up again. And that is the topic of this book.

It sounds simple...but it is not.

The sophisticated professionals, both strategists and legislators, who endorsed these losing candidates, all paid a price. They lost potential influence with the eventual winner, credibility with their supporters, and status within their party for backing a flop. And they wasted tens of millions of dollars.

Even the most sophisticated observers repeat the common mistake of falling for the person who seems to have all the inherent God-given traits of a leader—like charisma, popularity, and a powerful presence. The problem with this is that time and again we are usually wrong about which qualities a candidate must ultimately have.[5]

Movie producers are "forever searching for heroes" because people look to winners for inspiration.[6] Everyone thinking about running for president looks at the current president to see how he did it, and whether she can measure up to that campaign and use the same strategy and tactics. This is a near-certain road to defeat.

All too often, winners' stories are structured as fairy tales, populated with misleading magic formulas to vanquish enemies and right wrongs before reaching the promised land. There are no magic formulas or silver bullets, but many people claim to have one—that *this* time is different.

Candidates would be better off by examining losers. General William Westmoreland, commander of the American forces in Vietnam, explained to reporters why he had not read any books written by French generals after their devastating defeat there. "They lost," he explained.[7] And so did we.

Losers merit as much study as the flawed, imperfect candidates who win. If the people who began with the most charisma, political glamour, and money got to the White House, the lineup of presidents I analyze here would include those mentioned above. No one would have heard of President Ronald Reagan, President Jimmy Carter—or either of the presidents Bush. Like movie producers, we downplay the nonheroic, implausible aspects of the presidents we remember as heroic.

Many presidents began as improbable candidates—before hindsight rewrote our memories. Richard M. Nixon lost to John F. Kennedy in 1960, then was humiliated in 1962 when he threw a famous tantrum at the press conference after losing the governor's race—and still managed to come back. Carter, a one-term governor of Georgia, started out in fifteenth place in the field of Democratic candidates for the presidency—yet won. Truman's defeat of Dewey is the most famous upset of the twentieth century. Young, inexperienced Senator Barack Obama, just two years removed from the Illinois Legislature, outmaneuvered Hillary Clinton, who had been in two presidential campaigns and two Senate campaigns.

When you write about war, Barbara Tuchman cautioned, write as if you "did not know who would win."[8] Otherwise, as Michael Kinsley cleverly illustrates, what was simply one of many plausible outcomes becomes a predestined result:

> Today, at the frenzied peak of the baroque phase, we debate the wisdom of a candidate's choice of ties—fueled by anonymous quotes from advisers who urged paisley and are damned if they're going down with the ship of a captain who listened to fools recommending stripes.

A week from now, we'll be proclaiming the result as the foreordained culmination of trends since the Pleistocene era.[9]

A presidential campaign, like a military campaign, is what Tuchman is credited with calling "the unfolding of miscalculations."[10] They are always perilous. Charisma, money, and polls are not enough to make it through a campaign.

I have been studying and taking part in presidential elections since 1964. After every election I returned to academia, reassessing the most recent campaign to see what I had missed or misunderstood. Every campaign was a learning experience. What seemed to matter during the campaign always diverged from the predictions of strategists, reporters, and academic researchers about what was *supposed* to matter.

Whether I was working as pollster, strategist, debate participant, or consultant to a network or magazine, I was also absorbing a feel for the rhythms of each organization and the conflicts within and among them. After I processed what I had learned in Clinton's 1992 campaign, I was ready to leave the world of campaigns. Then, having finished a book and some academic articles about public opinion and citizen reasoning, I started preparations for a long-overdue sequel to my book on the political economy of rural Vietnam.

Soon after I returned from a research trip to Vietnam, however, the Lewinsky scandal erupted and I was drawn back into domestic politics, recruited into a group of old hands working with the White House as unofficial advisors.[11] (At the time, I was teaching at the University of California's Washington Center while my wife, Susan Shirk, was serving in the State Department.)

As the scandal was winding down, Robert Squier asked me to be his fly-on-the-wall advisor while he directed strategy for the Gore campaign in 2000. After all I had learned about the complexities of palace politics within Washington, I agreed to stay on as his consultant. When he was diagnosed with terminal cancer I spent time consulting with his partner Bill Knapp while he developed the media for the campaign. That gave me the rare chance to learn about the world of visual imagery I had never appreciated, and see more of the competing claims being fought out in a campaign.

After Squier died, I was asked to stay on and help steady a fragmented research and targeting effort. In comparison with the camaraderie, common purpose, and (mostly) suppressed egotism of the 1992 War Room, the Gore campaign was dysfunctional, incoherent, and low on esprit de corps or unity. I observed White House staffers en route to the private sector more concerned about padding their resume; Gore insiders determined to advance only those issues that improved their chances to get better jobs when Gore won; campaigners protecting their fiefdom to the detriment of adapting strategy; a revolving door of pollsters and chiefs of staff; and a candidate who changed tactics in the heat of battle without telling his staff. As was my custom, I tried to reassess what I had learned from Gore's campaign—but I was unable to achieve closure. For more than a decade I tried to make sense of that disastrous campaign. This book is the result.

As I began to write, I soon realized that there were no standards with which to assess campaigns. To use a golf analogy, did Gore's double bogey lose to George W. Bush's bogey, or did Bush's birdie beat Gore's par? To answer, I had to look at more campaigns. To my astonishment, the boondoggles, blowups, ego clashes, and turf battles I had seen with the McGovern, Carter, Clinton, and Gore campaigns were part of many other campaigns. Slowly but surely I realized that the casts of characters were as predictable as the stock characters in a television sitcom.

I started with the Truman and Dewey archives to see if campaign experience combined with rigorous research would shed new light on this most-examined campaign. From the first day in the Dewey archive I saw there was more to be said. And my initial hunch was confirmed that critical campaign decisions depend not on the technology around the team but on the team around the candidate. I also realized that Dewey and many of his top strategists were brilliant, and that Truman beat him by using the tools of incumbency against the Republican Party, not by being a better campaigner.

That gave me confidence that the first step in analyzing campaigns was the insight that challengers, incumbents, and successors are not playing the same hand; they have different options and different challenges.

The next steps came courtesy of Roger Noll, a policy-oriented economist at Stanford, and Peter Hart, a well-respected pollster. Roger, ever practical, challenged me to explain why campaign strategy wasn't just a standard business school exercise in planning. Peter, a closet academician with a love of teaching, urged me to describe a day in the life of a candidate to show the complexities of his world. Describing a typical day for a challenger, an incumbent, and a successor helped me to explain why planning strategy is harder for a candidate than for a corporation.

Slowly and inevitably I realized that what an intellectually prepared candidate needs isn't a perfect strategy or up-to-date technology, or even the best strategist, speechwriter, or pollster; winning depends upon a candidate's ability to fashion a team that can work with him and his family, and keep them agile and resilient through the next presidential campaign.

This book is my attempt to explain the intricacies of a presidential campaign by examining the winners *and* the losers, the small details and the big picture, the surprising mistakes and the predictable miscues. My goal is to provide a view of what goes on inside a campaign that makes a candidate into a president.

CAMPAIGN JUGGLING

In the beginning there is ambition.

A person who says "I should be president" is claiming the right to be the most powerful person in the world. Normal people do not make this claim. Only the truly audacious can imagine claiming the power of the American presidency. As Barack Obama admitted when he claimed the right to challenge other, more established politicians, "I recognize there is a certain presumptuousness—a certain audacity—to this announcement."[1]

From the first moment anyone announces he is running for president, people size him up in a new way. Candidates face constant scrutiny, the way the men and women sitting around the saloon in old-time cowboy movies eye the new sheriff or the new gunslinger.

The men and women who run have spent years watching other candidates, biding their time, while professing no presidential ambitions. Only after they are in the maelstrom do they realize just how big a leap they have taken. They are on the biggest stage in the world, handling three jobs at once. And they cannot fail at any single one of the three and win.

The candidate has to persuade skeptical voters that she is "one of us," that she understands their lives and shares their values. She has to show everyone a vision of where she wants to take the country during the next four years and how she will lead us there. And the candidate has to oversee her campaign and show people that she can command the ship of state.

Consider a typical day for three candidates: Jimmy Carter in 1976, George H. W. Bush in 1991, and Al Gore in 1999. Each day consists of events and meetings that, when examined in isolation, seem straightforward. Every event and every meeting, however, is related to previous decisions that the candidate has made about what kind of campaign he is running and what kind of team he needs to build, and every event and every meeting will constrain his options in the future.

JIMMY CARTER'S DAY

Wednesday, October 27, 1976. Six days before the election, Jimmy Carter was reeling from a series of personal and foreign policy faux pas. President Gerald Ford, the incumbent, was gaining ground by the hour. Carter had led Ford by more than thirty points in August; now he clung to a one-point lead over Ford in the Harris-ABC and Gallup national polls. Carter needed to carry Pennsylvania and Ohio—both toss-ups.

Carter was so exhausted from nonstop campaigning that he read memos and speech drafts lying on his side, with the pages on the floor next to the bed, so he could read them without moving.[2] His key staff members were just as worn out. The speechwriters were so close to the breaking point that James Fallows said sardonically that the real threat for their secret service detail was not assassins, but the possibility a crazed speechwriter would throw Carter out a window. His press secretary, Jody Powell, was so sick of the press corps "assholes" on Peanut One that he was no longer sure he wanted to *be* in a Carter White House.[3] The pollsters had to have a staffer on duty at night just to read Carter's chief strategist, Hamilton Jordan, the latest numbers to help him fall asleep, like a political version of Bach's *Goldberg Variations*.

Having once been fifteenth in the field of Democratic candidates, Carter had succeeded in the primaries largely by virtue of a personal approach that was moral, plainspoken, and a clear contrast to Washington candidates tainted by the legacy of Vietnam, President Nixon's impeachment, and support for increasingly divisive busing policies. By decrying special-interest groups, he had attracted disenchanted voters but alienated those whose money and manpower were critical for the last days of the campaign.

Carter wanted to finish the campaign with the kind of personal appearances and open, candid discussions that he had begun with, but he had grown ever more cautious, lest he give President Ford more ammunition:

I'm less open now, I know...I don't like it, but I realize it's true. It's just—it's just that I feel so much more vulnerable now than when I started....It doesn't imply dishonesty....It just means the more successful you are in national politics, the more importance is ascribed to what you say—and the more caution you must use....It's unfortunate...but under the circumstances, maybe it was inevitable.[4]

The more liberals and Roman Catholics had seen of Carter during the primaries, the more they realized that he was more than an articulate, fresh, moderate unblemished by Vietnam, Watergate, divisive racial issues, or personal scandal. He was also a devout evangelical Baptist who never seemed to let his hair down.

In trying to show people unfamiliar with Southern Baptist culture that he could be a "regular guy," Carter gave an interview to *Playboy* magazine in which he claimed to have had "lust in my heart" for women other than his wife Rosalynn.[5] When it hit newsstands in September, the interview that was supposed to reassure voters about his tolerance of other lifestyles ended up alarming them about his character instead; what *did* it say about Carter's judgment or sincerity that he gave an interview to a magazine celebrating a sexual lifestyle that contradicted his professed religious beliefs? Two months later, Republicans revived the episode in all the battleground states. Their ads placed the *Playboy* cover next to the cover of a *Newsweek* issue featuring an interview with Ford, inviting readers to read the interviews before deciding how they would vote.

To contrast his foreign policy with the past eight years of involvement in peripheral foreign wars, assassinations, and the overthrow of democratically elected regimes in countries like Chile, Carter repeatedly said, "I would never go to war or become militarily involved in the internal affairs of another country unless our own security was directly threatened." Asked specifically about the potential conflict in Eastern Europe, Carter asserted that he "would not go to war in Yugoslavia even if the Soviet Union sent in troops."[6]

While Carter's general non-interventionist sentiment was highly popular in the abstract, his candor on a specific example raised doubts about his readiness to lead the country during the Cold War. President Ford had already hammered him on it in the previous week's debate—openly promising not to intervene, Ford said, gave the Russians a green light—and the statements were being kept alive by Ford, Henry Kissinger, and columnists from both parties.[7] Carter evoked the need for a fresh start during the primaries; on the last Friday before the election, he needed to revive that desire in the electorate.

Rosalynn Carter had been on *Good Morning America* and *The Today Show* the last two mornings, emphasizing their family's roots in Plains, Georgia, and the difficulties of moving their daughter to Washington for school if Jimmy won. She made sure everyone knew Jimmy was liberated enough to have shared the cooking responsibilities when they married, lest they think his religion made him socially old-fashioned. As First Lady, she would concentrate on mental health and the elderly, she claimed, and she backed it up by visiting mental health facilities in every campaign stop that had one.[8]

Her polyester clothes, natural hair, and always-sensible shoes distressed Washington's elite women when they realized this was the real Rosalynn, not a campaign prop. That was all to the good for the campaign, as it emphasized the difference between the Carters and the Washington elite.[9]

On October 27, Jimmy Carter had to go over plans for a final set of appearances in Pittsburgh and Philadelphia, and decide what to say and where to go during the last four days of the campaign.

His Pennsylvania campaign hung "by a slender thread," his campaign manager admitted, and even that thread looked ready to snap.[10] Carter had made the decision to focus on Pittsburgh and Philadelphia in the homestretch, but that choice led to other choices: what to say in each city, to whom to give interviews, and with which local politicians to be photographed.

Carter's objectives for his Philadelphia and Pittsburgh stops were clear: chat up Mayor Frank Rizzo in Philadelphia and overcome worries about a politically moderate Southern Baptist among union leaders and Catholics. Rizzo and the union leaders had all supported Senator Henry "Scoop" Jackson of Washington in the primaries; indeed, Jackson was the union leaders' "anybody but Carter" attempt to maintain union power in the party by ensuring the nominee was an ally.

Before he could go to Philadelphia and Pittsburgh, however, Carter had to approve plans for the very end of the campaign, decide how to deal with pro-life pickets, straddle a split in the Philadelphia Democratic Party, prepare what else—if anything—to say about Yugoslavia, and figure out how to reassure wary Catholic voters that this Baptist wouldn't resurrect the anti-Catholic animosity of his co-religionists. Simultaneously, Carter had to send the message to his Baptist brethren down South that he was still as devout as ever; rumors had already started that he was not a true evangelical anymore, and didn't believe the Bible was the literal word of God.[11]

The speeches in Philadelphia and Pittsburgh had to fire up crowds with domestic issues and reassure the powerful local political and union leaders whose machines were critical to getting Carter's vote to the polls. Rizzo's machine was as powerful as Richard M. Daley's ever was.

Pittsburgh looked more sympathetic. Mayor Joe Flaherty had supported Carter all along and would be there to help Carter connect with steelworkers and Catholics. But the United Steel Workers Union was highly skeptical of Carter and distrusted him as potentially anti-union. Carter couldn't credibly become a born-again union supporter, so he and his advisors decided he would talk about his running mate, Senator Walter Mondale, a longtime ardent friend of the unions, to assuage concerns.[12]

Moreover, Flaherty would introduce Carter at Irish-American rallies, and Carter could take questions from the crowds to show his authenticity and vision. Flaherty arranged a meeting for Carter with representatives from thirty-seven Irish-American groups belonging to the Irish National Caucus. He didn't know a lot about the history of Ireland or about Irish America, but he knew human rights; when they pressed him on whether his concerns for getting America back to idealistic principles were sincere, Carter won them over. He was back to his comfort zone.

By the end of the meeting, Carter was enthusiastically commended for his "humanitarian concern for Ireland." Earlier in the campaign, Richard Holbrooke, one of the issues staff, had crafted an inspiring human rights speech, and Carter knew how to deliver it with passion and conviction.[13] He was at his best discussing human rights; it gave him the high moral ground and made a powerful contrast with cynical realpolitik and the humiliation of America's first defeat—Vietnam. So when he was pressed about Irish-American concerns for Northern Ireland, he made clear that the U.S. government would not turn a blind eye to Ireland: "It is a mistake for our country's government to stand quiet on the struggle of the Irish for peace, the respect of human rights, and for unifying Ireland." So that there would be no doubt about his sincerity, Carter suggested the establishment of a Commission on International Peace.[14]

For just that one day of campaigning, Carter had to prepare for questions from the press about Philadelphia politics, Yugoslavia, steel imports, union contracts, and whether he promised or merely "hoped for" a tax cut; he had to woo Catholics without alienating Baptists and talk about the role of human rights in foreign policy. He also had to meet with speechwriters and talk with his senior staff about where he and his wife would spend the last four days before the election. And for each stop, he had to learn the names of the local dignitaries he must greet and those he should avoid.

PRESIDENT GEORGE H. W. BUSH'S DAY

December 19, 1991. Forty-four days after the 1990 midterm elections, 61 days before the New Hampshire primary, and 320 days before the presidential election, President Bush was well ahead of every possible Democratic challenger in the national polls—yet scrambling to salvage his presidency and win reelection.

How fast the political climate had changed. In March, after the lightning-quick knockout of Saddam Hussein's army and the liberation of Kuwait, his approval rating had been the highest ever given an American president. He had managed the collapse of the Soviet Union so deftly, and looked so unbeatable after Operation Desert Storm, that Senator Al Gore, Governor Mario Cuomo (D-NY), and all the other top-tier Democrats had decided to bide their time and wait until 1996.

That November 2, just prior to the off-year elections, *Saturday Night Live* had mocked Democratic cowardice with a sketch called "The Race to Avoid Being the Guy Who Loses to Bush." Instead of convincing people to nominate them, the Democratic contenders all tried to persuade voters they would be the worst possible candidate. Senator Lloyd Bentsen (played by Kiefer Sutherland) said that this race would be about ideas, and he had none; Bill Bradley (Kevin Nealon) argued that he, an ex-jock, had even less substance than Bentsen. Mario Cuomo (Phil Hartman) countered that he had pardoned criminals worse than Willie Horton; on and on.[15]

Three days later, the White House was rocked by the blowout victory of little-known Democrat Harris Wofford over Richard Thornburgh in a special election to succeed the late Sen. John Heinz (R-PA) in the U.S. Senate. Wofford had been appointed to the seat after Heinz died that April; the Democratic governor of Pennsylvania could not recruit a prominent Democrat for the seat, as it was assumed that whoever served the rest of Heinz's term would be handily beaten by Thornburgh in November. Thornburgh had been an exceptionally popular governor, cutting taxes and creating jobs, and no Democrat had won a Pennsylvania Senate race in thirty years.

Wofford was sixty-five, had never run for elected office, and was the liberal president of Bryn Mawr College. His entire campaign amounted to little more than one memorable line: "If criminals have the right to a lawyer, I think working Americans should have the right to a doctor." Attacking the much-better-funded Thornburgh for being an insider too close to Bush, he had overcome a forty-four-point deficit.

The Pennsylvania special election was a clarion call to the Republican Party. Suddenly the "stature gap" between Bush and the Democrats didn't seem so big.[16] After Wofford won, Senate Minority Leader Robert Dole told the press he was not sure he even wanted to run for reelection that year, just to return as powerless spokesman for an even smaller and more dispirited group of Republican senators.[17] Family values seemed less important to the voters than jobs and health care, and a sitting president with multiple military and foreign policy triumphs now needed to transform himself from statesman to salesman, from a symbol of peace and security to a mercantilist booster of exports.

Bush's campaign strategists had known since August that his reelection campaign would be more about jobs and foreign trade. While the second-tier Democrats—Senators Bob Kerrey, Paul Tsongas, and Tom Harkin and Governors Bill Clinton and Jerry Brown—all looked beatable, Bush's chief strategist, the pollster Bob Teeter, thought they would have three months to "establish Bush's credentials on the economy."[18]

Wofford's victory, however, forced a new, more urgent timetable on the White House. Patrick Buchanan sensed Bush's vulnerability and decided to challenge him in the New Hampshire primary, and the Senate Republicans scurried to introduce their own health care legislation.[19] The "R word," recession, was in the air, and declining incomes and rising insurance premiums were people's big concerns.

Now Bush's international triumphs suggested a president more concerned about other countries than about troubles at home: Congressional
Democrats showed reporters T-shirts heralding Bush's "Anywhere But
America Tour"; one senior political correspondent cracked that "the only
homeless person he has ever met personally is the emir of Kuwait."[20] The
Tonight Show host Jay Leno mocked the president's sudden turn to the
economy in his monologue:

> 8:30 in the morning I get a call from President Bush....At first I thought
> it was somebody doing an impression of President Bush so I said, "if
> you're really President Bush, tell me about your economic plan: and
> when he didn't say anything I knew it was him."[21]

Putting the focus on jobs and trade was no small task for a sitting president whose schedule was always partially set months in advance. It took
major reshuffling and international diplomacy to begin showing the public that the president's main concern was the domestic economy and not
soft landings in the former Soviet Union or friendly relations with Japan
and China.

The day after Wofford's victory, the White House abruptly announced
the president was canceling his upcoming Asia trip. What had seemed
like a good public relations trip a few months earlier—the visit was built
around the fiftieth anniversary of the attacks on Pearl Harbor, and designed
to reaffirm the friendship that Japan and the United States had forged from
its ashes—now might be criticized as too centered on foreign policy, not
enough on the economy. Two days later the White House announced it
was postponing introducing the North American Free Trade Agreement
(NAFTA) until after the election. American automobile manufacturers
were losing so much ground to Japanese manufacturers that the future of
the American auto industry was in doubt, and workers feared the flight of
jobs to Mexico if tariffs between the two countries were lowered.

The campaign pollsters worried that Bush could end up like a defeated
Winston Churchill, identified so strongly with foreign policy and military security that voters would assume he didn't care about the economy. He couldn't present a credible economic plan until he showed his
concern and involvement with domestic issues. In the latest *Washington
Post*–ABC News survey, 70 percent agreed that Bush "spends too much

time on foreign problems and not enough time on problems in this country."[22]

The lack of an economic program was a serious enough problem that the White House feared Bush would be booed in the economically distressed state of New Hampshire. On December 18, First Lady Barbara Bush had flown to New Hampshire and filed her husband's papers of candidacy for the "first in the nation" primary. She had been tapped because no one—not even the Grinch—would boo her. Her already high popularity had been boosted by her televised Christmas tour of the White House the week before. She showed obvious pride in the handmade decorations she had added to the tree, and she was at her best showing viewers the wonderful work of five hundred volunteer needle-pointers and forty volunteer florists from around the country who had pitched in.[23]

December 19 was the last big news day of the year for the White House before the Christmas season, when Washington pauses. The White House had prepared a barrage of economics events, the centerpiece of which was the announcement of a rescheduled trip to Japan in early January to "make the case that foreign policy successes abroad meant economic prosperity at home."[24] The president was going to meet with the American businessmen who would accompany him to Japan, and then meet with the White House press corps to establish the narrative for the trip as creating jobs by "breaking open markets" and boosting exports.[25]

While Bush was meeting with executives, the First Lady would visit Shaw Junior High School in the District of Columbia to "act as a cheerleader" for her husband's education goals and tell the press she understood that it was tougher now than ever to care for children. The next day she would visit an AIDS facility and tell everyone that she believed AIDS is "a tragedy that affects us all." While socially conservative Republicans emphasized abstinence and considered homosexuality a curable condition, she could at least signal that AIDS victims would not be marginalized by the first family.[26]

But before he could meet with the executives, or brief the press, Bush had to meet with his press spokesmen to get up to speed on the questions both groups would throw at him. Secretary of State Baker had replaced Bush at the Asia Pacific Economic Cooperation (APEC) meeting in Seoul, usually attended by every head of state, and had given a major address on America's role in Pacific security in Japan, the kind seldom given by anyone but the president.[27] Bush needed to know how to respond to what was being said about his sudden aversion to conducting diplomacy.

The president had just flown back from Euless, Texas, where he signed a $151 billion highways bill. Adorned in a hard hat and eating chicken-fried steak, he told the media throng that his domestic priorities were jobs, jobs, jobs. Down the road from Euless, in Arlington, General Motors had just announced that a plant there with 3,800 workers was likely to be closed due to the growing market share of Japanese cars. Bush had to be ready to talk about both the highways bill and the factory closing.[28]

Pat Buchanan had already denounced the president as a misguided internationalist sending "our national wealth to global bureaucrats who ship it off to regimes who pay us back in compound ingratitude." Without mentioning Buchanan, the White House had responded with a threat to raise tariffs on Chinese imports unless China improved copyright protection; China then criticized the United States for the threat. Bush had to be ready to answer questions about China with enough forcefulness to satisfy a domestic audience without setting back any actual progress with the other country.[29]

And now he had to get up to speed on the group of businessmen that would accompany him to Japan in search of jobs. He was going to portray the delegation as a tour to "relentlessly pursue our mission to create jobs and restore prosperity." He was going to tell journalists that he would insist "that our trading partners provide U.S. companies with the same kind of opportunities that their firms enjoy here." He couldn't simply criticize the status quo; he had to know what kinds of steps he wanted Japan to take and what kinds of problems American companies trying to do business in Japan faced. The delegation included auto executives from the Big Three, machine tool manufacturers, and insurance and financial service executives. He didn't want to get into specifics but had to be prepared in case something popped up.[30]

Everything Bush planned to say was aimed at persuading voters he had a viable economic plan for jobs. As president, moreover, everything he said had to be assessed in terms of overseas reactions. He also was the leader of his party, whether he liked it or not, and had to know which prominent allies in congress would support or undermine him depending upon the decisions he made. His cancellation of the trip to the APEC meeting had prompted rounds of criticism in Asia that America was in decline, making it harder for him to pressure Japan and Korea to open up their markets to American manufacturers.

The press conference about the delegation of businessmen accompanying him to Japan required President Bush to anticipate the reactions of Japan, China, and the European Union; prepare for questions about the state of the economy and the feasibility and credibility of his approach; defend the choices of businessmen in his delegation; be ready for questions about the recession; show concern for struggling families; and outline what he would do to keep Japanese auto companies from taking even more market share from their American competition.

Vice President Al Gore's Day

June 16, 1999. A month earlier than he thought it would happen, Vice President Al Gore was in his boyhood home of Carthage, Tennessee, preparing for a midday announcement that would make the obvious official: he would be a candidate for the Democratic nomination for president.

Originally planned for July, the announcement had been moved up thanks to nervous House Democratic leaders who were worried about what kind of coattails they would get from his campaign. They suspected that Gore was taking the campaign for granted by putting off his announcement. Would his campaign help them regain the majority status they had lost after the debacle of the midterm election of the Clinton presidency? Would he run a campaign that would fire up their constituents, or would he ignore the party base and key interest groups, and focus on moderate swing voters living in Republican districts that meant little to Democratic congressmen?

Gore's actual starting point in the polls was as good as it gets within his party, when examined in context and objectively compared to similar situations in the past. In four national polls conducted in June, Gore scored an average of 59 percent, leading Senator Bill Bradley by an average of thirty-two points among Democrats. By comparison, in 1987, then–Vice President Bush was barely breaking 40 percent in national polls among Republicans. Even against the opposition party, Gore looked no worse at this point than did the man who would become the forty-first president.

But without that context, polls sent a wave of panic through the Democratic Party. In all forty-four national polls that year, Gore had trailed the seemingly callow governor of Texas, George W. Bush, by an average of eighteen points. To add insult to injury, he trailed Senator Elizabeth Dole—a woman caricatured as even stiffer and more awkward than he—by double digits in several polls including one in bright blue California. And as dull, monotonic, and uninspiring as Senator Bill Bradley could be in public appearances, he had a war chest that could fund a long and bloody primary.

Gore, his family, and his White House staff were haunted by the specter of Bill Clinton. Gore had been the disciplined, decisive junior partner to the publicly eloquent and privately undisciplined Clinton. Without Gore, meetings would never end and decisions would always be deferred. Yet in the press he appeared as defender in chief, the man who backed Clinton during the tawdry Lewinsky scandal, and the solicitor in chief, the fund-raiser who took the public rap for all the unseemly—legal or not—fund-raising that Dick Morris and Mark Penn convinced Clinton would be necessary to win in 1996.[31]

From the Left and the Right, Gore was being attacked for the shortcomings and scandals of the last eight years. Mary Matalin, one of the top Republican strategists, was framing Gore as a downgraded third term for Clinton, identifying him with none of the achievements and all of the scandals.[32]

Within his own party, Gore was under siege for every unavoidable yet unpalatable compromise, berated by all the interest groups given only half a loaf, and denigrated for all the moderate positions that helped hold the center against a conservative majority in Congress. Even the administration's recent success in defeating the Serbian ethnic cleansing of Kosovo that spring—spearheaded by Gore's ardent, passionate arguments for the bombings that led to Slobodan Milosevic's capitulation—was credited to Clinton by Republicans, while Gore's role was diminished. Republicans now described Clinton as a great president with a moral flaw; Gore was criticized for being too focused on his campaign to contribute to the Kosovo victory.

Clinton saw it all coming that June, telling a friend, "All of a sudden, I'm the master of genius and charm.... They're saying I'm an immoral son of a bitch, but I can jump higher and give a better speech than anybody.

They say I'm Michael Jordan and Gore is pitiful."[33] Clinton badly wanted a Gore victory to preserve his legacy and to deter the possibility of yet more vindictive investigations looking for offenses in his past actions.

With the announcement pushed up and looming larger every day, Gore and his staff had to find the right way to frame the narrative of his campaign. After eight years of public subordination to Clinton, Gore had to begin to assert himself. Was Bill Clinton a lame duck or an albatross? Was the general lack of enthusiasm about Gore among Independents "scandal fatigue" after eight years of Clinton foibles and follies from Whitewater to Lewinsky, or was it "party fatigue" after eight years of a Democratic agenda in the White House?

Gore had to decide which explanation for his low poll standing was correct and what to do about it. And he had to decide whether to focus on Bill Bradley or look ahead to a campaign against the likely Republican nominee, George W. Bush.

The media experts, Robert Squier and Bill Knapp, believed that Gore, while having been in the public eye as vice president for almost eight years, was known mainly by name and media caricatures. Squier told Gore his numbers would improve after Gore stepped up to the plate as a candidate and asserted himself. Then the campaign could fill in the public image. Squier knew Gore had difficulty projecting his warmth, but the legendary filmmaker had worked with Gore for years and assured Gore he would connect with voters when they learned his compelling personal story.[34]

His Vietnam record was particularly important. The epithet "Chickenhawk" has being used to attack Republicans who had avoided Vietnam and were now calling for a stronger, more aggressive military posture. George W. Bush had maneuvered himself into the Air National Guard, for example, and then skipped some of the mandatory drug tests, raising suspicions about whether he was using drugs in addition to his acknowledged heavy drinking. During that divisive war, 234 sons and grandsons of members of Congress were eligible to serve and only 28 were actually in Vietnam.[35] So Gore's service in Vietnam, even as a reporter for *Stars and Stripes*, was no small matter.

The campaign staff agreed that there were three main steps in Gore's launch: a formal announcement speech outlining his vision for the next four years; a long television interview where he finally talked on camera about how he felt when he learned that Bill Clinton had misled him about

Monica Lewinsky; and interviews with Tipper alone or with Al, in which both of them displayed the warmth and intimacy of their marriage and family life. That would provide a triple contrast with Bill Clinton: a Gore agenda, a public rebuke of Clinton, and a warm, monogamous family life with a woman who was kindhearted, spontaneous, and not gunning to be a co-president. Tipper had announced she would host the first-ever White House conference on mental health, a cause she had long championed. She had also given a long personal interview to Diane Sawyer about her past bouts of depression to encourage others to seek help.[36]

Gore believed he had to be ready to respond to questions from AIDS activists pushing him to help end what they called "medical apartheid" against South Africa lest they throw support to Bradley. The South African government wanted to manufacture cheap generic AIDS medicine and the U.S. pharmaceutical industry was vigorously pushing Washington to hold firm; any infringement of intellectual property was piracy as far as they were concerned, whether it was medicine or bootlegged video games.[37]

An unsigned agreement was sitting in the trade representative's office. Until it was signed, the questioning would continue. But the campaign staff could not intrude upon official government work that was the responsibility of White House staffers. And it had to be done without looking like Gore had caved in to protests.[38]

At the same time, Gore had to decide just how much of a threat Bradley was; how far to the Left did Gore have to move? As the probable nominee, anything he did to make himself more palatable to activists would make it harder to hold the center against George W. Bush. He had been meeting with his brain trust, mostly moderates, to come up with new ideas and had endorsed "charitable choice," allowing government aid to religious groups performing social services. This outraged civil libertarians but was important in the general election and in some primary states. He had to decide whether it was safe to stress that theme now or better to wait until later.[39]

For just that one day, Al Gore had to prepare to discuss AIDS drugs, education, farm price supports, high technology, and the environment. He had to be ready for fast-breaking news about Kosovo if the cease-fire broke down. He had to decide how to woo environmentalists and union leaders dissatisfied with eight years of compromises. And he had to decide how far he could go to satisfy them without alienating moderates in the general election. And he had to know the names of dignitaries on all the platforms during upcoming visits to Iowa City and Cedar Rapids, Iowa, and Manchester and Concord, New Hampshire. And he needed to know which of them needed special treatment because they were being wooed by Bradley.

Three Jobs of a Candidate

Three different candidates in three different decades, all facing different decisions, communicating through different media, and targeting different audiences. All three probably believed their situation was unlike that of any previous candidate.

While the specifics of their issues, decisions, and the communications media may differ from those faced by candidates today, there is much common ground. Carter, Bush, and Gore were all juggling the same three jobs that any candidate—then or now—must manage: they were part of a royal family, demonstrating the virtues and values of a leader; a leader of a start-up company, developing and refining his vision of the future; and a CEO overseeing a large organization.

Create a Public Identity

Then as now, candidates all begin by creating a public identity. John F. Kennedy thought of this as building a brand name:

> When you think of the money that Coca-Cola and Lucky Strike put into advertising day after day, even though they have well-known brand names, you can realize how difficult it is to become an identifiable political figure. The idea that people can get to know you well enough to support you in two months or three months is wholly wrong. Most of us do not follow politics and politicians. We become interested only around election time. For the politician to make a dent in the consciousness of the great majority of the people is a long and laborious job, particularly in a primary where you don't have the party label to help you.[40]

Working to develop a brand name years in advance has always been part and parcel of preparing for a run at higher offices. Davy Crockett's image as a larger-than-life embodiment of the self-made frontiersman was built with as much attention to public relations and self-promotion as today's candidates, down to the carefully chosen misspellings and grammatical mistakes in his books.[41]

The candidate's brand name, however, is not designed for the products he produces; he doesn't sell television sets or automobiles or computers. He sells the personal qualities he will put to the service of the country: representing the nation to the world, speaking to the people, and exemplifying the best of the country. He also sells the idea that he can guide legislation and preside over the government and promote peace and prosperity.

These dual responsibilities put stress upon both character and competence. "As national leader the president is expected to walk on water," Fred Greenstein observed, "but as governmental leader he must wade through the swamps of politics."[42]

The candidate cannot campaign only upon past or future legislation, for she—and her entire family—are also the most public of figures. Voters have expectations for how presidents should behave and how they should handle ceremonies of all kinds; candidates must exemplify the integrity, authenticity, and virtue of a president, and their families must live up to the expectations for the First Family.

When President G. H. W. Bush represented his country at international summits and honored war heroes at the White House, and when Barbara Bush decorated the White House Christmas tree with 500 needlepoint volunteers or visited an AIDS facility, they were performing the rites and rituals associated with the First Family.

When Jimmy Carter spoke in a folksy style about his church and upbringing and the legacy of Martin Luther King Jr., and when Rosalynn wore polyester and sensible pumps and visited mental health clinics, they were participating in the uniquely American blend of pageantry and plainness.

When Vice President Gore said he had volunteered to serve in Vietnam because someone less privileged from his hometown of Carthage, Tennessee, would have been sent instead, and when Tipper acknowledged her treatment for depression to help others seek treatment, they too were taking part in these same rituals and showing people what kind of First Family they would be.

Like a royal family, the First Family has an important role in honoring, encouraging, and informing Americans about important groups and endeavors. This is more than persuading voters that legislative commitments are credible, and that the candidate is sincere or competent.[43] Presidents and monarchs confer status on the groups they honor and, therefore, change the relative status of others. The mere act of inviting a world-famous black man, Booker T. Washington, to lunch at the White House in 1901, won President Teddy Roosevelt praise for his "bold stand" in New England and provoked a surge in racial violence across the South. The South Carolina senator Benjamin Tillman raged that "The action of President Roosevelt in entertaining that nigger will necessitate our killing a thousand niggers in the South before they will learn their place again."[44] Seldom are the reactions as dramatic as those to Booker T. Washington, but when Barbara Bush visited an AIDS facility it sent ripples through conservative religious circles.

The rituals, ceremonies, and behaviors of the First Family may be different from a monarch or emperor—monarchs, emperors, and empresses might not eat with their fingers, kiss babies, walk in parades, or engage in small talk with strangers—but they are no less demanding. They are always on display, and people will judge their suitability in part by observing their family and the way the national family can connect with them.

Develop a Vision for the Future

While candidates and their families spend countless hours onstage, auditioning to become or remain First Family, they also must construct and refine a vision for the future and persuade people to invest in this vision.

When Carter worked with his strategy, communications, and polling principals to assuage worried voters and contrast his vision with President Ford's record, his job was selling a vision of where he would take the country. When President Bush decided with his campaign staff how to show voters he was a jobs and economic growth president, and when Al Gore decided how best to establish himself as a leader independent from President Clinton, they too were developing a vision for the next four years and trying to persuade people that theirs was the best available vision for the next four years.

The inner circle around the candidate typically involves a small group of people with their sleeves rolled up, who brainstorm for hours, argue about options, try out numerous formulations, tweak the details, and refine the product. Theodore H. White's *The Making of the President: 1960* launched a new genre of political writing, which chronicled the long, lonely journey of candidates who travel the country with a few close associates on the quest for the White House.[45] There has always been a small group like this that worked directly with the candidate to refine and develop the core message of the campaign.

Preside over the Campaign

At the same time as candidates perform onstage and lead a group to hone their vision, they also oversee a large organization. Many candidates begin as governors, incumbent presidents, or vice presidents. Then, in the midst of the largest campaign of their lives, they become the head of an organization with a rapidly expanding budget, and branches in many states and cities with which the candidate is unfamiliar.

On those three important days before the election—October 27, 1976, December 19, 1991, and June 16, 1999—Carter, Bush, and Gore all dealt with issues similar to those of CEOs, overseeing large groups to whom responsibility for specific issues had been delegated: Carter reviewed drafts of his speeches, discussed travel schedules, prepared to greet local dignitaries, and signed off on advertising campaigns; Bush went over the list of executives that the secretaries of treasury and commerce had assembled for his trip, decided which economic proposals to accept, and where to go and what to say in Asia; Gore reviewed fund-raising plans and briefings from policy experts.

People running large organizations delegate most decision-making to others and spend time only on the tough decisions that no one else can make without their involvement. They have no choice but to delegate. The Nobel Laureate Herbert Simon once compared the job of a CEO to a head chef preparing a gigantic multicourse meal for many heads of state. The head chef relies on other great chefs to prepare each course; he cannot stand at the kitchen door, sniff a sample of all the courses in progress, and know when to intervene. Some parts of preparation can be treated like a thermostat set to a certain temperature, working reliably without further supervision. Otherwise, timing and sampling are essential. Little or nothing about the sauce depends upon tasting the butter, while much about the fish course depends on examining the fish upon arrival from the market. And the closer to dinner, the more the head chef must decide whom can be given great leeway and whom must be kept on a tight leash. Some sous-chefs improvise well on their own when something tastes wrong; others are compulsive perfectionists, willing to hold up the entire banquet to touch up their presentation.[46]

The candidates decide which decisions are too important to be made by anyone else and which decisions can be made well enough by persons to whom they have delegated responsibility. And they decide when to check up on the people to whom they have delegated.

DIFFERING DEMANDS

To be taken seriously, a candidate must excel at one of the jobs: monarch, visionary or CEO. While no one ever excels at all three, candidates must demonstrate competence in each to get to the White House. Part of the difficulty of being a successful candidate results from the vastly different demands of, and the different skills required by, the three jobs.

A monarch inherits standards and can follow a well-defined protocol she has inherited from birth. There is no guidebook for how to look presidential or act like a First Family, just a need to exemplify sincerity and authenticity. Asked how you can prepare to be First Lady, Barbara Bush was typically concise: "I'll tell you in one sentence how you train to be first lady. You marry well. That's all you need to know."[47]

Nor is there ever an ideal vision of the future that any candidate can offer. Start-up companies typically stay out of the limelight until they have an initial design to sell to investors; then they refine their design and produce products before going public. Candidates have no such safety net; their vision (and image) are constantly and publically refined from the moment they declare their candidacy, and they are credible only if their vision is consistent with their image. That consistency is a challenge to maintain. Candidates try to be intimately involved with the inner group developing their vision, but they don't have the luxury of continuous brainstorming because they must be constantly onstage and traveling away from their headquarters.

By the time anyone becomes a corporate CEO, she has been taking part in strategic planning for years; she is familiar with procedures for dealing with risk, deciding when to hedge bets with multiple plans, or when to go all out on a single path. Candidates, on the other hand, begin with little or no personal experience at managing a presidential campaign; many of them have no management experience at all.

Yet at first glance, a candidate's strategic problems seem like those of any large organization, no different from the examples used in business school MBA programs. Years in advance of the campaign, they have to decide what policies will win enough support, what the mood of the country will be, and who will be competing against them.

Strategic plans for corporations do the same exercise regularly. Automobile manufacturers start to plan new models as far in advance as candidates begin to plan their future campaigns. When automobile companies start to plan new models, they don't know what the price of oil will be when the new model is ready; they don't know what the economy will be like; they don't know how changing environmental attitudes will affect regulations—or tastes; and they don't know what their competition will be offering. Will they be producing gas-guzzlers for a public that wants small, fuel-efficient hybrids or practical family cars for a public that wants excitement on the open road? Will they be the only company aiming for a new market—hybrids or electrics—or one of many?

If a candidate's strategic plan was just a political application of MBA planning, campaigning would be easy, and few candidates would end up as unprepared for predictable decisions and crises as Thomas E. Dewey, Rudy Giuliani, or Hillary Clinton. Corporations spend hundreds of millions of dollars hiring outside consultants to refine their planning and strategy; why don't candidates just hire the cream of business consultants themselves?

The reason outsourcing campaign strategy and management cannot work is that candidates face unique contradictions when their three jobs intersect. Seldom does a major corporation suffer if the CEO is involved in a personal scandal. For example, Jack Welch maintained his status as a corporate visionary despite a nasty divorce involving an affair with a Harvard Business School professor. The co-founder and CEO of

Oracle software, Larry Ellison, is well known for his flamboyant lifestyle and the hundreds of millions he spends on yacht racing. Stock analysts, though, never use his personal lifestyle as a reason to buy or sell Oracle stock.

Nor does anyone question the character of a CEO if the company announces a change in the product line. If a candidate who has built her name around isolationism or diplomacy now believes the country should fight a Hitler or search out and destroy the Taliban, her opponents will criticize her for being too slow to face facts or that she was wrong for too long to be president. Did anyone attack Ford or Toyota as flip-flopping phonies for building hybrid cars?

If a candidate states a new policy preference identical to a voter's preference, the voter will wonder if the candidate is just following the polls. When GE or IBM builds exactly the product consumers desire, does anyone call them panderers for listening to the market?

How can a candidate exemplify authenticity and sincerity when they constantly confer with pollsters, writers, and media experts to "decide" what they truly mean? You might tell your spouse that you discussed popping the question with close friends before doing so, but would you ever first ask those friends whether you were really in love?

Authenticity is a claim, not a fact, and the candidate must persuade people the claim is true. Historic Bordeaux wineries go through the same contradictory process to emphasize their claim to prominence and authenticity. No matter how much science and technology Bordeaux chateaux use to manage the harvest and control the acid, sugar, and alcohol levels of the finished product, they emphasize tradition, culture, and craft, and downplay all they are doing to improve their product.[48]

Crafting a vision for the next four years, moreover, invariably raises conflicts between the start-up and the corporation. The new vision may not actually threaten the organization, but it will invariably collide with the worldviews and ambitions of parts of the campaign organization. IBM dominated the world of mainframe computers and decided to enter the market for personal computers only at a late stage. They hid the PC team in a motel, because the executives and engineers in the mainframe divisions saw no reason to build puny desktop computers that would never be as sophisticated or powerful. The executive who built IBM's PC brought the CPU and software outside IBM "because we can't do this within the culture of IBM." Apple went after the market IBM disparaged, and their Macintosh set the standard of excellence in personal computing.[49]

A corporate CEO can control his executives privately and stop them from going to the press or building alliances with the company's board behind his back. A candidate doesn't have the same autonomy; he has to deal with interest groups, appointed secretaries, and his political party, all of whom have a stake in the vision that depends only in part upon whether or not he wins.

Before his first run for president in 2008, former Massachusetts governor Mitt Romney had been a top student at both Harvard Business School and Harvard Law School, made hundreds of millions of dollars buying and restructuring corporations at Bain Capital, and turned around the inept management of the 2002 Winter Olympics—a profitable and highly praised event.

With all that expertise, however, Romney had problem after problem in the 2008 primaries. Afterward he told his close business school friends that campaign decision-making was much harder: "You end up taking into consideration things that wouldn't be important in a business decision."[50]

Conclusion: Rent a Campaign?

Some experienced Washington hands think it is easier than ever to run for president. Bill Moyers, Lyndon Johnson's press secretary and prominent television commentator, has argued that candidates today have it easier and are less accomplished than their predecessors. His argument is that today's candidates win because they buy the best campaign, and not because they are more fit to be president. This is a common refrain. Karl Rove, the strategist for George W. Bush in 2002, was called "Bush's Brain." The speechwriter Robert Shrum was labeled "Kerry's Brain" and blamed for the defeats of Al Gore in 2000 and John Kerry in 2004.[51]

Moyers is wrong to think that it is easy to hire people, and he is still more wrong to think others can do it all for them today. If candidates could just buy or rent a campaign, why do they make so many avoidable mistakes and sometimes make the same mistakes in more than one presidential campaign? Why are they not prepared for the most likely attacks on them or their party, and why are they not prepared for the predictable scrutiny of their past?

The triple demands of royal family, visionary start-up, and CEO, and the contradictions among these roles are only part of the reason it is so hard. Candidates must adjust and adapt faster than actual royal families, bring their new product to market faster than most start-ups, and expand their organization faster than most corporations. Within months their fate will ride upon persons they hardly know with little time to oversee the activities of their staff.

Their entire family must adapt in a few months to the manners and styles and expectations of people from different religions, industries, regions, and lifestyles. In six to eight months the year before the election, the candidates must build a start-up team that will develop and sell their vision, finance their campaign, and manage the central staff. By January of election year they must be putting their organizations into the field and readying them to sell the candidate. Start-up companies work behind closed doors for years before going to their first tranche of financiers. And corporations do not have to capture 50 percent of any market ever to be financial successes.

Anyone audacious enough to run knows already how to bluff. They have to be able to avoid the pitfalls of overconfidence and be ready to back up their claims. They also have to be agile enough to adapt to the luck of the draw. Like athletes, they have to be forward-thrusting, concentrating on the next play, not brooding on mistakes. They have to be tough without a gun, and soft-spoken with one. When they defeat opponents, they must persuade voters they are out to defend them, not destroying others for personal gain. And they must be resilient enough to keep going after public humiliation from defeat or exposure.[52]

Some of the decisions are like chess and others are like poker. Chess has unbelievable complexity, but a chess player knows what pieces he and his opponent have. There is no bluffing in chess, no ambiguous information. In poker there are always budgetary constraints, the luck of the draw, and inaccurate information.[53]

The long chesslike iterations of moves, the bluffs that work, and the wild cards they can play in the poker game all vary by campaign. No matter whether they are challengers, incumbents, or successors, they have no idea what the public mood will be a year later. They are doing the equivalent of packing a small suitcase for the trip of a lifetime, without knowing where they are going or what the weather will be. How can they pack the perfect small suitcase for a surprise journey well in advance? Do they pack beach-wear and end up in ski season, or formal wear and end up at a rodeo?[54]

How do you prepare if you don't know what the issues will be, who your competition will be, what media people will be using, or what they will know?

How do you plan for chaos?

PLANNING FOR CHAOS

The goal for any candidate—challenger, incumbent, or successor—is simple: persuade enough donors, staffers, activists and voters that their vision of where they want to take the country is credible, achievable, and preferable to that of any other candidate.

The very act of entering—or reentering—the presidential arena, knowing they might fail on the biggest stage in the world, induces great insecurity in the most alpha of women and men. To overcome that insecurity, before candidates step into a room to persuade people they should be president for the next four years, they first have to persuade themselves that "Not only should I be President...I am going to be President."[1]

The candidate's security blanket is a message that they feel will persuade others they should be president. In 1988 Senator Joe Biden, for example, couldn't run until he had refined and rehearsed every line of his stump speech and felt confident he would "get the 'connect.'"[2]

As Biden soon learned, a message that connects is only the beginning of an effective campaign strategy; what matters is how voters regard the candidate after the other candidates have responded. It is not what sounds best when the candidate speaks, but what sounds best after the opponents have responded. Karl Rove, the strategist behind George W. Bush's two successful presidential campaigns, credited his high school debate experience for teaching him to look ahead several moves:

> You had to be ready to argue both sides of the question on a moment's notice. So we picked apart our own arguments, anticipated the counter-arguments, and picked those apart, too. Gaming the debate out as many moves in advance as possible was great training for politics.... It taught me that staying on offense was important and that once you were on defense, it was hard to regain control of the dialogue.[3]

Every candidate wants to control the debate so voters focus on the issues and personal qualities most helpful to their campaign.[4] The last thing they want is an open debate on all issues. They know what they want voters to hear about themselves and what they want them to know about their opposition.

There is always an asymmetry between what the two candidates want to talk about. If one candidate wants to accentuate a large difference on an issue, the other will try to minimize that difference and argue that another distinction should be more important to voters. If a candidate stresses his position is in the mainstream of his party, the other will want to emphasize she is actually more extreme. If one candidate underlines how his record shows he is better than the perceived position of his party, the opponent will try to debunk that and show he is no better than the party record. If one candidate emphasizes his personal story, the other will likely emphasize entirely different personal characteristics where she has an advantage, or stresses her actual record of accomplishments.

No matter what jargon, catchphrase, or slogan the candidate uses, no matter what media the candidate uses, no matter which party the candidate represents or seeks to represent, the strategy reflects the lyrics to Johnny Mercer and Harold Arlen's 1944 popular song:

> You've got to accentuate the positive
> Eliminate the negative
> Latch on to the affirmative...

But what accentuates the positives and what eliminates the negatives? Which positives are most persuasive in *this* campaign and which negatives most damaging? What makes the choice between *these* candidates so clear that there *is* no in-between, no ambiguity?

The term "Message Box" has become common usage for strategists describing campaign strategy. It is a simple tool to make sure that the many messages from a campaign are coherent, unified, and account for the actions of the opponent. It is used by organizations such as the National Democratic Institute to train candidates unaccustomed to free elections in countries like Iraq, Afghanistan, and Nepal, and by activists and consultants in campaigns all over Europe and Latin America. It is a square divided into four quadrants:

- What the candidate will say about him- or herself
- What the candidate will say about his or her opponent(s)
- What the opponent(s) will say about him- or herself
- What the opponent(s) will say about the candidate

The goal is to keep the campaign clear and unified. Accentuate your positives, eliminate your negatives, and minimize any unclear "in-betweens" to maximize your advantage over opponents. It might look simple, but nothing could be harder than keeping a presidential campaign consistent and coherent.

A candidate only has unified messages if the campaign makes myriad difficult decisions based partly on fact, partly on analysis of the political terrain, and partly on intuition or experience. And a candidate's messages remain unified only if she can adjust her message box during the campaign.

Each candidate wants to put his best foot forward and say things that make his opponent less attractive. Each candidate also wants to persuade voters she has the best understanding of the country's problems.

Every diagnosis contains an implicit solution. A campaign has to define the nation's problems in a manner that persuades voters one particular candidate is the best solution. It would be a mistake for a candidate to persuade voters they have qualities needed in the next president if a competitor has more of the same qualities.

I have analyzed the strategies and tactics for the candidates since 1948 in both parties. This message box contains the essence of options considered in a typical presidential campaign.

The Message Box

CANDIDATE ON SELF	CANDIDATE ON OPPONENT
Establish Character & Credibility • Personal roots • Milestones • Record of accomplishments	**Undermine Character & Credibility** • Flip-flops • Incompetence • Personal contradictions
Party and Reassurance: Relations to Party • How different from party? • How more like the party than realized?	**Undermine Foundation of Vision—Cheap Talk** • Inconsistencies, "bad" votes • Associates with "bad" advisors or allies • Her donors have "dark" motives
Definitive Difference with Opponent • Goals • Groups • Issues	**Undermine the Difference** • Only good for "them" • Muddle their contrasts • Show contradictions
OPPONENT ON CANDIDATE	**OPPONENT ON SELF**
Undermine Character & Credibility • Flip-flops • Incompetence • Personal contradictions	**Establish Character & Credibility** • Personal roots • Milestones • Record of accomplishments
Undermine Foundation of Vision—Cheap Talk • Inconsistencies, "bad" votes • Associates with "bad" advisors or allies • Her donors have "dark" motives	**Party and Reassurance: Relations to Party** • How different from party? • How more like the party? • How to update party?
Undermine the Difference • Only good for "them" • Muddle their contrasts • Show contradictions	**Define the Difference** • Goal • Groups • Issues

CANDIDATES ON SELF

Two quadrants focus on what the candidates will say about themselves. Each candidate decides what aspects of her past make her vision believable and resonant with voters. Credibility is essential yet hard to ascertain; to paraphrase Justice Potter Stewart's famous comment about pornography, voters may not be able to define credibility, but they "know it when they see it." Credibility is partly based upon assessment of the candidate's motives, partly upon past performance, and partly upon believing that the candidate could, in fact, deliver if she were president.

There is no such thing as a perfect record—there are bound to be votes or policies that were popular in one state and anathema in another, or votes for small interest groups that contradict the candidate's current stance. Records depend upon the eye of the beholder. Does telling voters about wartime heroism make the candidate seem patriotic or militaristic? Do past legislative or executive successes in business or government come across as competence or bureaucratic babble and braggadocio?

People are more sensitive to information about motives than competence. A laundry list of accomplishments doesn't galvanize people who don't know anything about the character of the candidate. Al Gore, John Kerry, and Hillary Clinton all came out ahead on the issues. But as James Carville said, "The human mind revolves around a story....But we're selling a set of issue positions. The same thing always comes back: People always like our positions on the issues, and we always lose."[5]

Character and virtue are like moral firewalls. A good message box always establishes a candidate's values by talking about her personal biography or by demonstrating moral or religious passion.[6] When voters trust a candidate, she can establish competence and dependability by discussing past personal accomplishments or past legislative results. Until trust is established, voters are unlikely to give her the benefit of the doubt.

To build trust with the voters and overcome unpopular policies, a candidate has to rely upon his home style. "Home style" was the term coined by Richard Fenno in his pathbreaking study of what representatives do when they return home from Washington. No legislator, he found, maintained support from constituents solely on the basis of votes in Congress. Every legislator inevitably votes for bills that antagonize some constituents or seem outrageously expensive, unnecessary, or silly. To shore up support, every congressperson worked to build personal trust and assure constituents that he was looking out for them. "Candidates want support, and they offer responsiveness; citizens want responsiveness, and they offer support," Fenno concluded.[7] That exchange of trust could be done many different ways, but it always involved assurances that the politician was "one of us" and not only "of Washington."

What types of assurances persuade voters that the politician is "one of us"? Jimmy Carter highlighted his past as a peanut farmer and small businessman; Al Gore chose to announce his candidacy in Carthage, Tennessee, instead of Washington. Gore's references to his service in Vietnam showed that he had not relied on privilege and education to avoid going—as had his likely opponent, George W. Bush. When Barbara Bush did needlepoint along with hundreds of volunteers throughout America and when President George H. W. Bush put on a hard hat and ate chicken-fried steak with construction workers, they were trying to show that they were still in touch with regular Americans.

Candidates have to decide which past blemishes and failures to address directly and which they should try to ignore. Do they openly discuss their negatives and try to put them in the best light possible, or do they gamble that they can keep them out of the media? Governor George W. Bush had a well-known history of alcoholism and recklessness. He recovered from alcoholism, became a devout Methodist, and talked openly about how his faith in Jesus changed him. He refused to answer specific questions about alcohol or drugs ("when I was young and irresponsible, I was young and irresponsible"), and he demonstrated the authenticity of his conversion with testimonials and personal discussion of scriptures that persuaded voters that his past failures were not relevant to his current character.[8]

Candidates must also decide how to relate to their party. On the key issues of the moment, should they emphasize close connections with party positions or distance themselves from its orthodoxy? On whatever issues the voters care most about, the candidate from the party that voters believe is best at tackling those issues has the wind at his back; the candidate from the party believed to be weaker has a challenge because that candidate has to show she has a background—be it personal or political—that establishes her differences from the party record. Democrats are historically viewed as weaker than Republicans on welfare reform, so Bill Clinton positioned himself as more concerned about work than welfare by pointing to the ways his record in Arkansas made him a "new kind of Democrat." To distinguish himself from conservative congressmen intent on slashing federal welfare and education programs, George W. Bush called himself a "compassionate conservative" and emphasized his focus on education in Texas and his strong personal belief that anyone living in the United States, legal citizen or not, needed education for the good of all.

Opponent on Candidate

The other two quadrants focus on what the opponent—or a journalist—is likely to say about the candidate. Each candidate must decide how to minimize the credibility of his opponent's vision and programs. What kind of attacks on her opponent most enhance her own attractiveness? It is useless, after all, to assail an opponent in a way that hurts the attacker more than the attacked.

Each candidate decides how much emphasis to place on undermining his opponent's personal biography versus trying to persuade voters that his opponent is not acknowledging his "true" record. A candidate will invariably say her opponent is not like the voters, doesn't understand them, and thus cannot be trusted (while the candidate herself is, does, and can). He may find subtle ways to remind voters that the opponent differs from their region, church, ethnic group, or background. Or he might make a straightforward attack on the values of a group the opponent supports, like creationists, environmentalists, hunters, or vegans.

A ubiquitous tactic is to persuade voters that the other candidate is a flip-flopper who turns with the political winds. More than a century ago, President Theodore Roosevelt wrote:

> Our opponents seem at a loss, both as to what it is they really believe, and as to how firmly they shall assert their belief in anything... [they] endorse now what they demanded repeal of earlier [civil-service law] and on the issue of Philippine independence they have occupied three entirely different positions within fifty days.[9]

Highlighting the personal contradictions between an opponent's life and professed commitments is another common tactic. When President Gerald Ford's campaign displayed the cover of the *Playboy* issue where Jimmy Carter had given his "lust in my heart" interview, they were trying to underscore the gap between Carter's beliefs and the decadent lifestyle that magazine celebrated.

Senator Robert Kerrey, a prominent contender for the 1992 Democratic nomination, spent most of 1991 talking about the need for national health care legislation. When the campaign started in earnest, however, it soon came out that he had never provided medical coverage for the employees of his businesses in Nebraska. A strong record as governor and a Congressional Medal of Honor winner from Vietnam provided no cover against the seeming inconsistency between his past behavior and future promises. Kerrey could neither explain why he had not mentioned the health care issue nor why it might not be inconsistent with his current position.[10]

Responding to Attacks

When a candidate is attacked, there are three possible options: push back, attack the attack, or push the envelope.

"Pushing back" refers to rebutting the attack, as in Richard Nixon's famous "I am not a crook" speech. The problem with this tactic, as Karl Rove likes to say, is that "when you're explaining, you're losing."

"Attacking the attack" means labeling the attack as mudslinging or scare tactics—old-style politics from an inferior opponent who has run out of ideas. A standard move has always been, as noted in 1940, "If your opponent calls you a liar, do not deny it—just call him a thief."[11] When Arnold Schwarzenegger was being attacked by Governor Gray Davis during the California gubernatorial campaign in 2003, he said, "Gray Davis can run a dirty campaign better than anyone, but he can't run a state." Still better is having a highly respected ally attack the attack for you. In 1988, when Ohio Senator Howard Metzenbaum voted against a clearly unconstitutional child pornography bill, his opponent, George Voinovich, attacked him for being so liberal that he was not willing to fight child pornography. The single most respected political figure in Ohio, Senator John Glenn, went on television and said, "George Voinovich, you ought to be ashamed of yourself. Get that ad off the air. This is outrageous." Michael Dukakis cited the Metzenbaum attack as exactly what he should have done when he was hit hard on crime. It was "a hellapalooza of a mistake," he realized, to "blow it off."[12]

"Pushing the envelope" means continuing to advance a daring policy while brushing off the attacks as smoke screens, desperate attempts to drown out an issue because an opponent has no alternative. Early in the 2008 primaries, Senator Barack Obama was criticized by Senator Hillary Clinton for his naïveté and inexperience when he said he would meet with North Korean or Iranian leaders without preconditions. Obama, despite criticism from foreign policy experts, continued to vow he would go "toe-to-toe with the leaders of rogue nations." He kept to that position during the primaries and criticized Clinton for voting to brand Iran's Revolutionary Guard a terrorist organization, a move he emphasized could allow President Bush to expand the war against terror into another country.[13]

As simple as these options may seem, the appropriate choice always depends upon knowing what voters have already absorbed, how they evaluate the different responses, and what they care about. Correcting misperceptions and persuading voters is harder than winning a debate scored on logic. People often treat their beliefs like prized possessions they are unwilling to give up. Trying to correct them can backfire and strengthen them. In the heat of battle, it's never obvious whether to send a particular message early or late in the campaign; whether it is better to reply to an attack now or later.[14]

The Plan Is Nothing, the Planning Is Everything

In war, as in political campaigns, "the plan is nothing; the planning is everything." The strategic plan "lasts only until the war starts."[15] Candidates never know what will go wrong or where the miscalculations are most likely to occur.

On any given day a candidate will make simple, straightforward decisions, while other decisions are arrived at only after long, drawn-out staff meetings. Some of the seemingly simple decisions can blow up, and some of the well-planned, thoroughly analyzed decisions will lead to entirely unexamined, unexpected results with lasting repercussions. That was true for each of the three examples from the campaigns of Carter, Bush, and Gore. Seldom does everything go as planned, and frequently the most damaging outcomes were never thought to be remote possibilities.

Plans go out of date quickly. Ken Mehlman, manager of Bush's 2004 reelection campaign, emphasized that a weak planning process means "winging it" and depending upon gut instincts that are often misleading in battle.[16]

Carter

When Jimmy Carter agreed to attend a rally in Philadelphia and meet with Mayor Frank Rizzo, he did not know that former senator Joe Clark was planning to attend the rally. Rizzo was in the middle of a fight for his political life, and Clark was the leader of the anti-Rizzo recall campaign. If Clark was visible when Carter delivered his speech, Rizzo's machine would have sat on their hands on election day. Rizzo was heavy-handed and tough; a Democrat for Nixon in 1972 and a notorious antagonist of radicals and black activists. Carter needed Rizzo, but he also needed the liberal and black voters who happened to be in the middle of a drive to recall Rizzo.[17]

Carter was caught between a rock and a hard place. He had to see Rizzo, but he couldn't be *seen* with Rizzo, lest he enrage constituencies he needed. Liberal and black voters weren't likely to vote for Ford if Carter embraced Rizzo, but they had another option: former senator Eugene McCarthy was running a third-party, spoiler campaign as payback for his party spurning him eight years earlier. If Rizzo failed to rally his troops for Carter on election day, the candidate was almost certain to lose Pennsylvania... and probably the election. The candidate of hope, vision, and tolerance needed help from a divisive, intolerant, old-fashioned, machine politician to become president—and still remain the knight in shining armor.

Rizzo announced he would not attend Carter's rally because some of the blacks and liberals there were his sworn enemies. Fortunately for Carter, Rizzo agreed to meet him on his plane before the rally. Rizzo thus would be first among Philadelphians to meet with him; whatever Carter said to Rizzo would stay between them; and there would be no photos of them together. At the last minute, prominent Democrats with Washington connections persuaded Joe Clark to skip the rally.

Although the Carter campaign managed to thread the needle in that complicated situation in Philadelphia, it ignited a firestorm when Carter addressed the Irish National Congress in Pittsburgh. During the Q&A sessions Carter so loved, he assured his audience that his advocacy of human rights as the centerpiece of American diplomacy applied to Northern Ireland as well as to communist or authoritarian governments. With that innocent declaration, Carter inadvertently made a foreign policy blunder that nearly cost him the election. What Carter thought were uncontroversial moral statements were actually inadvertent endorsements of critical wording favored by the Irish Republican Army and opposed by all other participants in the Northern Ireland peace process. He infuriated cabinet members in England, Northern Ireland, and the Republic of Ireland, and also contradicted the stated position of most prominent Irish-American governors and senators in his own party.

Parliamentarians in Ireland and England condemned Carter's comments. The *Times* of London and the *Irish Times*, among others, attacked him in front-page editorials for remarks that gave "aid and succour" to the IRA and their violent tactics. When Carter attempted to quiet the furor, an angry headline in Ireland read, "Carter Tries to Wriggle Out."[18] If Ford's campaign had noticed and responded to the furor in London and Ireland, Carter probably would have lost enough votes in Ohio (where he won by 11,000 votes out of 4 million) and Wisconsin (where his margin was 35,000 out of 2.1 million) to have lost the election.

Bush 41

President George H. W. Bush wasn't as lucky as Carter. The extensive planning for the trip to Japan failed to recognize a miscalculation that haunted him the rest of his campaign. While the campaign staff worked to portray Bush's trip as part of an economic drive to open doors overseas and create jobs, the executives going on the trip and the proposals offered to Japan were arranged by cabinet officials, Secretary of Commerce Robert Mosbacher and Secretary of the Treasury Nick Brady. The president's export council had urged Mosbacher to bring CEOs from the "Big Three" auto manufacturers and the top auto parts companies. Since autos and auto parts were three-quarters of the trade deficit with Japan, Mosbacher believed that was the best way for the president to win Michigan in November.[19]

Within days of the meeting, Japanese editorials began ripping the American demands. Japan's leading paper, *Asahi Shimbun*, said Bush was waging "gunboat diplomacy" and urged Bush to ask the automakers "Why do European cars sell better in the Japanese market than U.S. ones?" If they looked at their European competitors like BMW, the Americans would see that the Japanese didn't want their cars because the Americans didn't make cars catering to the tastes of their consumers.[20] Attacks from Japanese media hurt rather than helped the president at home because so many Americans agreed that U.S.-made automobiles were inferior to Japanese brands.

The Chrysler CEO Lee Iacocca soon became the most visible and quotable of the CEOs on the trip. This infuriated economic conservatives because Iacocca was a great champion of import restrictions to save U.S. manufacturers. Iacocca had been calling on Japan to save his company by voluntarily selling fewer cars in the United States. The *Wall Street Journal* criticized Bush for failing to stand up to such "America First" isolationism. And commentators everywhere noted that Chrysler, unlike BMW, didn't make a right hand–drive car, and Japan was a right hand–drive country.[21]

Soon the big story became the vast difference in the salaries of American and Japanese CEOs. The American CEOs with Bush were paid an average base salary of more than $2 million each. The Japanese CEOs, in a country with far higher tax rates, earned about one-sixth the amount of their American counterparts. Iacocca alone earned more as CEO of a failing company—over $5 million—than all the delegation's Japanese CEOs combined. Before Bush had met with the Japanese prime minister, the *Wall Street Journal* was so disgusted with the CEOs and their demands for protectionism that they urged Bush to "Give Iacocca to Japan."[22]

Gore

Gore's miscalculations also reverberated through the entirety of his campaign. Instead of establishing his issue themes for the next few years, he generated press coverage that left him more closely associated with Clinton in the press, created serious fissures within his White House staff, and let his family overrule his campaign staff without telling the campaign staff what was happening.

Gore's 1999 Carthage speech announcing his candidacy had been clear and straightforward. He introduced new themes related to working families, education, and values. The speech was well prepared, well delivered…and practically buried in the media by the end of the day.

First, the campaign staff was caught off balance when AIDS activists in the crowd in Carthage caused a ruckus by waving banners and blowing on noisemakers. To make matters worse, the camera angles Gore had approved for his speech were obstructed by the protest banners.[23]

Then the Republican National Committee caught Gore off guard with its replies to his speech. He had expected an attack on him as a leftist, an attack that would be helpful in the primaries to counter Bill Bradley's charges that he was too moderate and conciliatory to the Republicans who controlled Congress. Instead, RNC chairman Jim Nicholson rode to the Westin Fairfax Hotel in Washington in a mule cart to show reporters

"Gore's other childhood abode." Nicholson wanted to minimize any advantage Gore would get from highlighting differences with George W. Bush, who had been part of a more privileged family:

> He's trying to pretend that he was Daniel Boone. Well, Daniel Boone didn't vacation on the frontier, he lived there. And Al Gore isn't Daniel Boone. He is the barefoot boy from Embassy Row.[24]

The guerrilla tactics and Republican ridicule upset Gore personally, but the biggest miscalculation was Diane Sawyer's interview on ABC. First, Sawyer—who happened to be a college sweetheart of Gore's primary opponent, Bradley—threw a pop quiz at him to see if he really knew about farming.[25] Gore passed the quiz but was rattled and discomforted by being put on the spot when he had expected a warm, relaxed interview. Then everything was overshadowed by the way he responded to Sawyer's incessant questions about Bill Clinton.

When Clinton had told the *New York Times* that he would coach the uptight Gore on how to enjoy campaigning more, Gore felt patronized and furious. Nothing stung more than being demeaned in the *Times* or the *Washington Post*. He had spent much of his youth in DC when his father was a senator and always looked up to the papers of record and considered them a friendly part of his world. Gore could barely contain his resentment over Clinton's comments. When asked about Clinton's role in the campaign, he tersely told *Newsweek* "He's got a full-time job being president—and he's doing extremely well." He marginalized his chief of staff Ron Klain for deciding that the *New York Times*'s interview with Clinton would probably help him, thus stripping his most campaign-savvy White House staffer of a role in the campaign.[26]

Over and over, Sawyer asked Gore about his comments about Clinton: Was he still a great president? What did he think during impeachment? Had Clinton lied to him? and the like. In response, Gore used the word "inexcusable" five separate times in referring to the Monica Lewinsky affair.

As his media specialists had predicted, Gore's decision to announce his candidacy and separate from Clinton on the same day turned the spotlight away from his campaign and onto his views of Clinton and whether Gore would stand by his earlier praise of him.[27] Instead of making Gore more attentive to the advice of his media advisors and pollsters, it made ~~him less trusting of anyone except his family and their close friends.~~

All Strategies Are Misleading

A well-constructed message box purports to provide a map of the campaign. It should relate strategy (which battles to fight) and tactics (how to fight the battles). The only problem is that *all maps are flawed*. Maps are useful precisely *because* they are inaccurate. They provide a selective view of reality in which the critical information is highlighted by leaving out irrelevant details, like the names of every school, store, and back road.[28]

Strategies are also valuable only when they make the relevant features prominent and leave out the others. However, campaign strategies go out of date much faster than maps because any hour can bring changes in the political landscape that make once-minor features critical and once-important features irrelevant. The features to exaggerate and the features to minimize in a political strategy are only partially predictable.

When they start their planning, candidates cannot know with certainty how to portray themselves in their campaign and must prepare for uncertain futures. In each of their three jobs as royal family, head of a start-up, and CEO, they have to adapt to ever-shifting political terrain, and they have to take account of changing media. And challengers, incumbents, and successors all deal with voters applying standards different from those by which they were judged in their last campaign. And they all confront new organizational challenges in following their strategy.

The Political Terrain

The political terrain is determined by the public's views of the president, the political parties, and the current state of the nation. Each candidate has developed a public reputation for specific issues or traits. Suddenly, in an instant, the terrain can shift under their feet. The politician who has spent years lauding the virtues of deregulation might have to talk about bank fraud and financial crisis; the proponent of amnesty for immigrants might face an outbreak of anti-immigration referenda dividing the party. And there are unexpected issues in every campaign that change the terrain: an invasion of an oil-rich country; a terrorist attack; a major natural disaster; the toppling of a dictator; a successful nuclear test in a hostile country.

No Democrat planning to run for president in 1976—before Watergate exploded—could know that Richard Nixon's resignation would heighten voters' emphasis on personal morality. All the top Democrats stood on the sideline in 1992 after Operation Desert Storm made President George H. W. Bush look invincible. Eight months later, they all regretted their prudence. No Republican planning to run for president in 2012 will know sufficiently in advance of the election whether President Obama's calls for creating jobs through investments in infrastructure will make him look strong or naïve.

Changing Media

Candidates also face media that have changed since the last campaign—including new technologies, new channels, or new types of programs. These changes create new ways to reach audiences and, in turn, what kinds of information and issues might matter to voters.

Candidates are audience-seeking missiles, but they cannot respond instantly to new media opportunities. It takes time and work to figure out how to connect with new audiences. Every time new forms of media emerge, every time new channels or web pages are created, every time the cost and availability of access changes, people find ways to create new audiences, build followings, challenge their party's power structure, and overturn old political bargains.

Television and radio provided an opportunity for candidates to use brief messages to reach those not interested enough to read long newspaper articles. In 1952 the advertising maven Rosser Reeves persuaded a skeptical Eisenhower to take advantage of the big audiences created by others to send inexpensive messages, such as:

BIG ADVERTISERS SPEND MILLIONS WITH TOP TALENT AND GLITTERING NAMES—TO BUILD A BIG AUDIENCE. But—between the two shows—comes the humble "spot."...For a very small sum YOU GET THE AUDIENCE BUILT AT HUGE COSTS BY OTHER PEOPLE. It's a form of jujitsu.[29]

New technologies also provide candidates opportunities to send longer, more detailed messages to potential supporters. George McGovern and George Wallace were the first two candidates to use direct mail to raise money and lay out their agendas. In the 1980s, Newt Gingrich began building a following using CSPAN, a minor cable network ignored by most politicians because it had a small audience.[30]

In 1992 James Carville's rule was "In politics, you haven't said anything until you've said it on television."[31] Two decades later, his statement is as outmoded as earlier statements about the glamour and magic of getting reported in newspapers, movie newsreels, or radio. When Carville asserted the necessity of getting on television to communicate to voters, email was not widespread. In 2000 there was no YouTube or Facebook. In 2008 Barack Obama was the first candidate to place *real* campaign messages on *virtual* billboards in video games. New media can throw even seasoned pros like George Stephanopoulos off balance. In 2008 he confessed, "I wouldn't know how to run a campaign in this environment."[32]

Communication technologies have always been in constant flux. But changes in the media also create opportunities for new messages from new people, which alters the policies that can be promoted, the boundary between public and private, and the relative importance of endorsements from important people and groups. Each time the audiences change, there are new audience-makers with whom to consider alliances and new issues that can be raised.

These potential gains are always gambles. Candidates can easily miscalculate which parts of a detailed promise to a specialized audience will alienate broader audiences, or which parts of broad promises will alienate new audiences that care about the details. Congresswoman Michelle Bachmann became a darling of the religious Right and the Tea Party with her outspoken attacks on President Obama. She also did enough damage to her reputation that her candidacy self-destructed. After he resigned as her campaign manager, Ed Rollins implicitly blamed Bachmann's failure on her overreliance on shocking, poorly thought-out pronouncements:

When you raise small-donor money, you go on Fox and say something more or less outrageous and that's what people contribute to.... You throw a hand grenade, and people respond. [To win] you've got to be a serious candidate with serious solutions.[33]

There will be new audiences in new places interested in learning hitherto unreported details about the candidate's record. The candidates cannot be sure in advance where the audiences will be or who will control access to them. Even eating new ethnic foods can land a candidate in trouble. On a visit to New York in 1972, George McGovern tried to order a kosher hot dog with a glass of milk. In 1976, at a "Viva Ford" rally in Texas, Gerald Ford famously tried to eat a tamale without removing the corn husk in which it was wrapped. In 2003 John Kerry ordered a Philly cheesesteak with Swiss cheese instead of the traditional Velveeta.[34] In each case, the media delighted in portraying the candidate as a fish out of water.

Candidates have always sought ways of appealing to one side of an issue without losing voters on the other side. In 1948 President Harry Truman wanted to signal his support for civil rights in order to mobilize black voters outside the South and wean liberals away from Henry Wallace's left-wing campaign. He also faced a major rebellion from southern democrats who opposed civil rights and integration. Truman's secret research team (kept away from the party machinery) learned that he could safely include civil rights in the middle of a speech on a different subject; as long as civil rights was not the lead, southern newspapers would overlook it.[35]

After the 1992 Republican convention, President George H. W. Bush spoke before an evangelical convention in Dallas to shore up support. He was going to say that the Democratic platform left out the letters G-O-D. It was risky to use that line; while it was red meat to the evangelicals, it was anathema to many more voters. His campaign staff calculated it was a risk worth taking, since Bush would speak way past anyone's deadline, so the press would not cover the speech. This time, however, the press *did* cover the speech, and the resulting coverage reinforced the view that the religious Right was calling the shots for Republicans.[36]

Senator George Allen was thought to be a Republican hopeful for the 2008 nomination—until comments that played well in one part of Virginia were put on YouTube for the rest of the state and the country to see. Noticing an opposition campaign staffer videotaping his rally, Allen referred to S. R. Sidarth, a dark-skinned, South Asian man, as "Macaca." Allen's smirking, derisive use of this North African racial slur—used by colonials to equate dark-skinned people with monkeys—stimulated researchers and bloggers to investigate deeper into his past. His casual use of the "N-word" in college was soon all over the news. Reporters then discovered that Allen's mother was from an ancient, distinguished North African Jewish family. Allen had always campaigned as a born-again Christian—in no way incompatible with having a Jewish mother—yet had never mentioned his mother's roots.[37]

Before the final unraveling of a strong presidential hopeful ended, Allen defended his Christianity by claiming to have eaten a ham sandwich for lunch; apologized profusely for wearing a Confederate pin in a yearbook photo, and having a hangman's noose in his law office; and alienated the Sons of Confederate Veterans by disavowing his Confederate heritage.[38]

Every time the media change, candidates have to reconsider how they present their personal and political past. Boundaries shift between "what happens here, stays here" and the stories that get coverage elsewhere. New media transform yesterday's private indiscretion into tomorrow's exposé. Today's off-color comments are tomorrow's evidence of poor character or bad judgment.

THE WAR ROOM

In 1988 Vice President George H. W. Bush's campaign destroyed Michael Dukakis, making the Democratic candidate look weak and passive. Bush assailed Dukakis for seeming to care more about rehabilitating violent convicts than about deterring violent crime, and being more concerned with defending the rights of protesters than about standing up for the country. The attack ads were bad enough, but the real problem was the way Dukakis organized his campaign. No campaign could stay "on message" if it were constantly either defending against charges—spurious or legitimate—or ignoring them, thereby looking too weak and clueless to defend themselves.

Mandy Grunwald, Clinton's key media person in 1992, persuaded the Clintons that reorganization of their campaign was necessary to avoid the paralysis that had undone Dukakis in 1988. She urged the Clintons to put James Carville in charge of the campaign; they needed a leader who would "wake up every morning trying to figure out how to fuck the competition."[39] Hillary Clinton got it at once. "What you're describing is a war room," she said, providing "both a name and an attitude."[40]

Sticking to a strategy involves far more for a candidate than knowing a message and sticking to it. Candidates need a small group of campaign leaders—usually no more than five or six people—that works together with the candidate to develop, revise, and refine strategy while the candidate is raising funds, giving interviews, and speaking to voters around the country. The nature of the small group and the kinds of decisions made, however, change as the nature of competition changes in response to the political terrain and forms of communication used.

The war room was developed to cut through traditional campaign bureaucracy. It reorganized the presidential campaign to provide the speedier responses needed to communicate in the era of twenty-four-hour news cycles, with the goal of controlling the national conversation about where the country should go and who should lead it there.

In the era of nonstop news on television, a message box could guide a campaign only if there was a group that could monitor public opinion and adjust the campaign's message fast enough to deflect, turn back, or preempt moves by the opposition. Only continuous face-to-face contact among principals would make it possible for the campaign to alter its strategy and tactics rapidly enough to keep up with the pace of the news media.

Rapid response required extensive advance planning to be ready for the opposition's most likely tactics. The goal was to evaluate every message and ad as part of a debate; a message was never used just because it sounded good or tested well on its own. This meant evaluating messages on the basis of how persuasive they were *after* people had seen a countermessage. This could not be done without the kind of planning and replanning the military emphasizes.

Neither campaign, of course, can totally control the dialogue with the public, so each tries to throw the other off its chosen message. Just as an army moving across the countryside can stay on course only if the flankers and advance parties prevent ambushes, detours, and blockades, a campaign can stay on course only if it can suppress ambushes and diversionary actions by opponents.

Bill Clinton's campaign designed its responses to deflect and minimize the attacks on him in the eyes of voters, not just to hit back. While the leaders of the war room talked frequently about attacking the Republicans to reassure

Democrats that Clinton would not be immobilized like Dukakis, many of its most effective moves were designed to minimize or duck the attacks so that President G. H. W. Bush looked like he was tilting at windmills. During the 1992 primaries, a small number of close friends of the Clintons worked with core strategists to plan the rehabilitation of Bill Clinton from the attacks already under way on his character. Then the Democratic Convention was structured to show people other aspects of Clinton's life that put the questionable episodes in perspective. When people learned that he had grown up without indoor plumbing, the fact that he had avoided the draft during the Vietnam War looked like good fortune, not family connections. Attending Georgetown, Oxford, and Yale signified merit, not privilege and wealth.

The 1992 War Room's success was such that it is still the base of the family tree for presidential campaigns today. The goal then, as now, was keeping the campaign on strategy. Rapid response is necessary but not sufficient for a strong campaign. A candidate has to be agile enough to maneuver through the media and sudden changes in the political climate. A candidate has to be resilient to get back up and keep going after setbacks or feeding frenzies from the press. Planning and coordination are necessary so that each battle is fought with an eye on how the tactics affect future battles.

Teamwork and the Politics of Strategy

The central existential problem for a presidential candidate is: How does someone with enough ego and audacity to run deal with their personal weaknesses? Stuart Stevens was a media specialist for George W. Bush in 2004 and 2008, and directed strategy for Mitt Romney during the 2012 primaries. One of his favorite axioms for candidates is "If you don't enter this process humbly, you will leave it humbly."[41] But how can anyone asserting they are the most qualified to lead the nation acknowledge that someone else might know more about some parts of the job than they do?

Lawyers like to say that no one should ever ask a witness a question in court if they don't already know the answer. For a candidate, the equivalent is thinking through and preparing for the best response to every move they make. That is one of the hardest parts of building and updating a team. They cannot do it if they do not face their weaknesses and their opponents' strengths—if they only play half of the message box.

In 2006, members of Hillary Clinton's nascent campaign were sure that Barack Obama would not run in 2008 because he was too inexperienced to persuade voters he could be a good president. Clinton dismissed the idea that personal shortcomings would deter an audacious politician: "You don't think about your weaknesses. You think about your strengths."[42] Candidates also have a hard time acknowledging the strengths of their opponents.

It is also hard to summon the bravado to run without believing you are better (and your opponents are weaker) than others have yet realized. If a candidate won't think about her own shortcomings or her opponent's strengths, it is up to her to build a team that will.

Every step of the campaign is harder than the one before because the pace always quickens. Paul Maslin, a veteran pollster with experience in a number of presidential campaigns, compares presidential candidates to mountain climbers scaling a high-altitude peak:

> You make your plans in the fresh, oxygen filled air of sea level. You gradually journey up, working as a team, dealing with each challenge as it presents itself. But in a campaign's final days, when the key decisions must be made, you're in the equivalent of the death zone, harried and short of time and breath. If you do the wrong thing, the consequences are fatal.[43]

As the pace of campaigning increases near Election Day, candidates have less time and energy for decision making and meetings. Either the team does more before the candidate joins the meeting, or decisions are deferred and less gets done.

Since time is limited, so too is new information. There are some things candidates don't want to know, some they don't need to know, and some they need to know. During the Watergate hearings, Senator Howard Baker's mantra about President Nixon was "What did he know and when did he know it?" A more appropriate question for objective analysis of campaigns is "What should he or she have known and when should he or she have known it?" If candidates didn't know what they needed to know, when they needed to know it—because they were wasting time reopening old decisions, or trying to make more decisions than time permits—it means they didn't build an effective team.

STRATEGY IS POLITICAL

No campaign needs a strategy for deciding how to tell the temperature or time of day. Whenever the answer is clear and easy to determine, no strategist need apply. But campaign information is always confusing. There is never time to wait for better information, and it is often unclear what information is most relevant.

Changing strategy is just as political as changing the tax code; it redistributes power, status, and resources among members of the campaign. Moreover, the redistributive effects that the strategists care about—their status or profits or causes—bear no necessary relation to the outcome of the election. As Pierre Sprey has shown repeatedly for new high-tech weapons, "Their importance is unrelated to their cost."[44] It is easy to dazzle observers with glamorous demonstrations of the newest technologies that are irrelevant in an actual campaign.

Just as in warfare, the people who decide which battles should be fought and what weapons are required have strong personal stakes in the decisions. Every change in strategy or tactics creates winners and losers among the team members. Strategists, Steven Walt has shown, "are unlikely to favor strategic proposals that undermine their own positions.... [They have] a greater interest in defending their positions than in pursuing truth."[45] Many will naturally lose perspective on what is good for the candidate; some will fight mainly to preserve their seat at the table, others for their time with the candidate, and others for attention for their pet issues, profits, or fame.

The late Richard Holbrooke, who served Presidents Carter, Clinton, and Obama with distinction, was one of the most talented foreign policy specialists in the Democratic Party and an ambitious, hard-driving person whom his best friends called high maintenance. Reporters and diplomats considered him a self-aggrandizing master of bureaucratic infighting who would whisper, pester, bluff, threaten, throw fits, or leak information as the issue—or his reputation—demanded.[46] When he died, world leaders gathered together to pay homage to things he accomplished that no one else might have been able to do.

One of Holbrooke's first heroic accomplishments was for Carter. He single-handedly rescued Carter from condemnation in Dublin for Carter's inadvertent support of the IRA in Pittsburgh. Holbrooke spent forty-eight hours on marathon international phone conversations, persuading Irish cabinet members that any formal censure of Carter would backfire whether he won or lost the election.[47]

Every campaign contains women and men almost as ambitious, strong-willed, and audacious as Holbrooke. Candidates need people who can handle the pressure and intensity of governing and of the campaign.[48] With so many strong-willed people, moments of harmony are few and far between. Leaders of winning campaigns might claim they were one big, happy family to contrast themselves with the finger-pointing, buck-passing losers, but in fact no one succeeds with shrinking violets or docile followers unwilling or unable to fight for more resources.

Candidates cannot eliminate the conflicts; they can only manage them. Any candidate who assumes that mild-mannered policy wonks and specialists are somehow less ambitious than other, more aggressive presidential advisors is confusing a lack of personal ambition with self-control. As David Halberstam noted of the reserved, reticent, highly controlled secretary of state Warren Christopher, "He was a ferociously ambitious man, a good deal of whose energy went into concealing how ambitious he really was."[49]

Family members will argue about their roles and schedule, and voice strong opinions about what is good for the candidate—and themselves. Friends will vie to be useful and will intervene frequently to try and preserve their influence by undermining newcomers and by claiming they know what is best for the candidate. Issue specialists will push their issue, and strategists will always argue that their own particular expertise and techniques are superior. And all of these people will be looking for ways to use each other to have the last word with the candidate.

"What Got You Here Won't Get You There"

Carter, Bush, and Gore struggled with very different campaign issues. The biggest contrast among them, though, was not the result of differences in political terrain or the changes in media. The biggest difference between them was the type of campaign they were running.

Every candidate is judged by different standards than she was in any prior campaign. Carter's previous campaign had been for governor, Bush's was as a vice president seeking to be a successor, and Gore's was for vice president leading the cheers for the president and leading the attacks on the other party. In their presidential campaigns, each slowly came to realize that they couldn't campaign the same way as in their last campaign.[50]

Carter, the challenger, campaigned on the promise of change and was being judged by his campaign, not his little-known record in Georgia. He had to show an understanding of complex issues and new cultures and localities he had never dealt with before. He did not have to defend years of messy decisions in Washington as President Ford did. He could issue policy papers and defend them without having to get the rest of the executive branch on board. He could turn his campaign in a new direction overnight.

President G. H. W. Bush, as the incumbent, had the power and majesty of the government behind him and was hailed as the chief. He was also closely connected to foreign policy, an issue that no longer mattered much to voters. Bush now wanted to avoid his former area of strength and establish a new image—which was far harder than establishing a first image. Moreover, when Bush wanted to talk about a policy he had to coordinate between the campaign and the government. Each side thought it should have control of policy pronouncements and schedules. Every speech was a battle between campaign staffs wanting thematic clarity, and bureaucrats and cabinet members wanting pet details and important caveats covered. Campaign staffs worried about the voters' reaction to policies advocated during the campaign, while the executive-branch denizens worried about the ultimate impact of the policy on their policy careers.

Al Gore, the aspiring successor, had been cheerleader and defender of someone else's agenda for eight years. His challenge was to convince people he was not responsible for the failures and compromises of the last eight years and claim some credit for the successes. He had to prove he could be an independent leader after being a follower. His campaign also struggled with more acute organizational problems than an incumbent president because he had to deal with the conflicts between his staff and the president's staff, as well as the conflicts between government and campaign.[51]

Since challengers, incumbents, and successors are viewed by voters differently, have different relations with Congress and different organizational problems, a candidate's last war will always be the wrong war.

3

CHALLENGERS: THE SEARCH FOR AN EXPERIENCED VIRGIN

In 1980, voters were so frustrated by a choice between the lesser of two evils—balancing Ronald Reagan's frightening "dark side" against President Carter's failings—that many of them considered voting for a poorly known, barely examined third-party candidate: Congressman John Anderson. While Anderson had never accomplished anything of note, he looked better to many voters than Reagan and Carter, with their well-known flaws and shortcomings.

During the Anderson boom, Ellis Weiner penned a satirical *New York Times* piece in which he proposed a superior alternative for the presidential race. His candidate was the ideal combination of everything people yearn for in a president: someone who was clean and above the battle, yet experienced in political combat and able to right the wrongs in Washington.[1]

He nominated Yoda.

An ideal challenger must be known as someone with the skills to resolve the current crisis and who excels personally in the areas where the incumbent falls short. George Lucas's animated, two-foot-tall creation was clearly the one to rally people, no matter the crisis and no matter the shortcomings of the incumbent.

Yoda didn't have to develop a public reputation or worry about name recognition; his legend was already known far and wide. He was imbued with the intelligence of Einstein, whom he resembled, and was supremely skilled in light saber combat.[2]

He also had moral glamour. People knew he led an order dedicated to peace and justice. Yoda was totally credible and competent, so Weiner believed he could—and would—deliver on his promises. People could trust in him without worrying about the details and fine print. There are no devilish details with a saintlike, pure candidate.

As we now know, Yoda turned out to be fallible. Yet the dream lives on: the quadrennial contest to lead a party in a presidential election inspires people to look for a real-world Yoda.

BELIEVING IS SEEING

The ideal challenger is an experienced virgin.

That oxymoron reflects the contradictions between the two responsibilities of a president: the candidate should be unsullied and never compromise her (and your) principles, and also be ready to end messy politics as we know it and solve previously intractable problems—from day one.

Stendahl (Marie Henri Beyle), whose pioneering nineteenth-century novels were among the first that combined realism and psychology, noted that in love, "Realities model themselves enthusiastically on one's desires." As with the passion of new love, the initial passion an exciting challenger inspires is a mixture of "revived memories, old fantasies and perennial needs."[3]

Rather than looking realistically at the records of experienced candidates, which are always a mixture of virtues and flaws, people still hope for a new challenger who can rise above politics and provide simple, direct solutions to complex problems. The best campaigns inspire us to dream the impossible dream, to accept the illusion that one challenger alone is speaking the truth. When a new challenger connects with people, the voters believe wholeheartedly in his promises to go beyond politics as usual.

Of course, Richard Reeves noted, this is all a fantasy: "The American political system doesn't produce anti-politicians, even if the best campaigns produce the illusion of anti-politics."[4] To paraphrase John Kenneth Galbraith on speculative bubbles, the dream of a heroic challenger reemerges as soon as people have forgotten the last disappointment.[5]

Some politicians want to campaign as the anti-politics outsider, who inspires people with dreams of a brighter future. Others want to run as the powerful can-do politician with legislative accomplishments, who knows how to twist arms, build coalitions, and deliver. Winning challengers all end up a blend of the two roles: the sincere, idealistic, inspirational moral leader, and the hard-nosed, pragmatic executive. The American president, after all, is at once the chief executive and the public face of the government. Presidents are judged partly by results and partly by their vision for the country.

Frustrated voters yearn for a challenger they can be sure is truly committed to them and their goals, not just pandering to them. They doubt the sincerity and honor of challengers with personal flaws, so the ideal challenger should be pure and untainted.

To stay this way, a challenger cannot compromise her ideals with ambiguous behavior. Since legislation eventually requires coalition-building—and coalition-building necessitates compromises—the ideal challenger should be isolated from the current partisan battles.

When politicians battle over the details of policy, the charges and countercharges blur into cacophony and the policy debates look like mudslinging. There are no white suits in a mud fight. Only an outsider can get away with wearing a white suit, because only such a challenger can appear above the political battling and remain pure in the eyes of the voters.

HOPE AND CHANGE

When an unknown, youthful challenger to the established party leaders wins the all-important caucus in Iowa, she uses her victory speech to interest others in joining the growing movement against the "old order." The newcomer will claim that there is a new identity, a community coming together behind him. The press will attribute the candidate's success to new technologies. Moreover, the candidate will be credited with the revolutionary idea of having supporters in the network offer their own ideas and visions.

A typical upstart speech, for example, credits the movement, not the candidate:

When I announced my candidacy, I said that this candidacy was not just mine, but the people's—a candidacy for all those who are about America but who feel that America's politicians don't care about or speak to them. This campaign was staked on a fundamental belief that the majority of Americans are not apathetic, just ignored.... By the thousands, Iowans in every town and community from every walk of life...have sent a clear message to America's leaders who have lost touch with and confidence in the American people.

This could be from the Obama campaign of 2008, the Gary Hart campaign of 1984, Jimmy Carter in 1976, or Wendell Willkie in 1940. It is actually from a manuscript by Patrick Caddell, written just before the Iowa caucuses of 1988. The major strategist behind George McGovern in 1972, Carter in 1976 and 1980, and Gary Hart in 1984, Caddell was looking for someone to follow his script in the " '88 campaign."[6]

Caddell's idée fixe was the outsider who would rid alienation and discontent to the White House. His generation, he believed, was one "with a collective social conscience, a collective sense that they can do great things, yet they are leading a life right now that's fairly mundane...in terms of changing the world."[7]

Lee Atwater, who headed the Republican National Committee and ran George H. W. Bush's successful 1988 campaign, feared Caddell more than any other Democratic strategist. Atwater felt that no one was better than Caddell at helping a candidate persuade voters that it was time for a change, or leading that candidate to make the right changes.[8]

There is an existential dilemma at the core of democracy: the "hope and change" candidates who can follow a script like Caddell's are often more appealing than candidates who offer more experience but less uplifting rhetoric. Successful compromises, solid accomplishments, and experience are seldom as exciting as ideals and visions of uncompromised successes. The newcomers, however, have to show that they are more than a pretty face and that they have the substance to defend their ideals. They have to show that they are both fresh and able to stand up to the enemies of progress.

Take a sound bite like "It must be so sick and so depressing in Washington, where a man's word no longer counts." This would be laughable coming from a senior senator or an incumbent president. But in 1999, George W. Bush spoke it as a man from Texas, where a man's word—people believed—was always good.[9] In her 1969 commencement address at Wellesley College, Hillary Rodham called upon her classmates to "practice politics as the art of making possible what appears impossible." She still has those ideals, yet people would scoff at her for speaking those words as a seasoned politician.

Lines such as these blame the fights in government on the people who are there, not on the inevitable entanglements of conflicting partisan coalitions or fiscal reality.

From 1948 to today, the sentiments have varied little, although they have been spoken by challengers with little in common.

"We the People"		
The American people can solve their problems only by united effort...I shall try to build up understanding...	1948	Thomas E. Dewey
This is not a job for any one of us or for just a few of us. It will take the best of all of us....As we launch this crusade we call to go forward with us the youth of America.	1952	Dwight Eisenhower
The times are too grave, the challenge too urgent, and the stakes too high—to permit the customary passions of political debate. ...[time] for a new generation of leadership—new men to cope with new problems and new opportunities.	1960	John F. Kennedy
We shall light the lamp of hope in millions of homes across this land in which there is no hope today.	1968	Richard M. Nixon
Together we can restore a government as good as the people.	1976	Jimmy Carter
It's the people's contest. It's much larger than me.	1992	Jerry Brown
The Man From Hope	1992	Bill Clinton
It must be so sick and so depressing in Washington, where a man's word no longer counts.	1999	George W. Bush
This campaign is not really about me, it's about a movement to take back the country.	2004	Howard Dean
This campaign cannot be about me. I am an imperfect vessel for your hopes and dreams.	2008	Barack Obama

The challenger of hope and change calls upon people to join together in a quest. No politician fits every quest, and no quest fits every terrain. Even if every politician could play the outsider role, not every year is ripe for such a candidate. The un-politician outsider is most appealing when people are distrustful of insiders and doubt the value of their experience and judgment. When Gary Hart was the young senator running amid a group of graying, old-fashioned, orthodox Democrats, he made that point succinctly in a critique of Walter Mondale: "He thinks I'm his problem. I'm not his problem. He's his problem."[10] Much of Hart's appeal, in other words, was that he was not Mondale.

When people are alienated from both Democrats and Republicans, they will turn to an outsider unencumbered by the kinds of alliances and votes that make regular politicians look unpalatable at a time of hard choices or clashing principles.[11]

Hope for new, easier answers to old problems wears thin as surely as water runs downhill. Inevitably and predictably, people initially attracted to a desirable candidate begin thinking about feasibility. Like children going to Disneyland, excitement over the thrills of the destination give way to more practical questions: Where will we eat? How much will everything cost?[12]

When Walter Mondale asked Gary Hart in 1984, "Where's the Beef?" quoting a then-popular burger chain commercial, he touched on the inevitable questions about ways and means. He pushed Hart to define the "new ways" he was calling for. Hart had no good answers and faded, as did Ross Perot, John Anderson, and Jerry Brown—the man who had seemingly limitless presidential potential when he became the young, iconoclastic governor of California in 1975.

For a brief moment in 2011, Herman Cain was among the front-runners for the GOP nomination. He had no political experience but was likable and had simple clear solutions to offer for all the country's current ills. When Peter Hart conducted one of his quadrennial focus groups for reporters in Ohio, he asked the participants to think back to fifth grade and characterize each of the candidates with the same descriptors they used on their elementary school classmates. A majority described Texas governor Rick Perry as a bully, Mitt Romney as the "rich kid," and Cain as an "all-American, " a "hard worker," the "kid everyone respects." But when Hart asked, "Is anybody willing to raise your hand and say, 'I would be comfortable if he became the next president of the United States?' " not one responded.[13] Without the beef, Cain's brilliant first impression was not enough to carry him once stories about his alleged sexual harassment and extramarital affair surfaced.

All of these men were once attractive candidates of hope and change; without experience and concrete qualifications, they could win early popularity and attract enough followers to win some state primaries. Without "the beef," however, these challengers failed. It is not enough to keep promising hope and change. Challengers must also be able to fill in enough details to keep the vision credible.

POSITIONING

On the road to winning their party's nomination and going on to the general election, candidates have to decide how they want to position themselves: which issues and personal traits will they emphasize, and which voters will they target. To position themselves, they have to decide whether to campaign as the front-runner or inevitable nominee, or get down off their pedestals; prepare for new voters in new places; and decide how to rectify old, indefensible, or inconsistent positions. After they decide how they will position themselves, the terrain will inevitably change suddenly. Some of their targeted voters will not like them or their message, or they will find that they prepared for the wrong rival. Then they will have to reposition themselves.

The traits and policies that show a candidate to best advantage depend upon the other candidates. Anyone with a reasonable chance of getting the nomination will try to avoid positions on the Far Left or the Far Right that make it harder—after the primaries—to reach 50 percent of the entire electorate. But a dark-horse candidate with nothing to lose may be willing to seize upon a position that ignites intense passion among her base while alienating large numbers of moderates.

The traits voters most desire depend as well upon the incumbent. People do not have fixed views of an ideal president; what they want depends upon what they like and dislike about the incumbent. That makes it easier for challengers to persuade people they have a clear philosophy without being specific by contrasting themselves with the incumbent.[14]

When long shots try to get the nomination by mobilizing passionate minorities, it becomes harder for other challengers to hold positions that less passionate and engaged voters will also accept later. In 2004, John Kerry's Iraq War inconsistencies would not have been so attention-grabbing were it not for the ways he responded to support for Howard Dean at the beginning of primary season. Dean faded fast, and Kerry's hard swerve to the Left lived on into the general election.

Dean had raised money faster than any previous candidate in history on the basis of a single issue: opposition to the War in Iraq. Dean's absolute, unequivocal opposition to the war—"the wrong war at the wrong time"— made him an overnight sensation, a hero to everyone for whom the war was unalterably wrong. He stood up for their moral imperative and soared past cautious rivals who believed that most Americans would never elect a candidate who held that position. He led the primary field in 2003, broke every fund-raising record, and was endorsed by former vice president Al Gore. It was downhill from then on.

The position and passion that got Dean a plurality of Democrats in a few short months—in the year *before* the primaries—made it harder for him to ever get beyond the single-issue passions on the Left. The closer Dean got to 40 percent of the country, the farther he got from 50 percent.[15] Dean's antiwar position was not troubling for people who believed all wars are bad, or those who knew enough to believe this particular war was bad. Dean, however, had trouble convincing people that he would fight *some* wars and was only opposed to *this* aspect of the "war on terror." How do you separate opposition to one war from pacifism, when you have pacifist supporters?

Dean is not an isolated example. Barry Goldwater in 1964 and George McGovern in 1972 won their respective nominations with strategies that ignited partisan passion while alienating too many others. On the days they were nominated, few of their supporters would have preferred a more moderate Republican or Democrat with a greater chance of victory in November; a year or two later, those same supporters might well have regretted not settling for either a moderate Republican when they saw Lyndon Johnson's civil rights policies, or a moderate Democrat when they saw Richard Nixon's enemies list.

Before candidates know who their competitors will be, they have to plan what kind of Democrat or Republican they want to be if they are to put together a credible record of effort and commitment. Candidates with established reputations plan for years how they will position themselves to show commitment to some parts of their party's heritage and differences in other areas. Bill Clinton and Al Gore, for example, were active in the Democratic Leadership Council, which was an important forum for moderate Democrats (particularly from conservative states) to push for policies on jobs, taxes, and crime, which would have broader appeal after the Republican victories in 1980 and 1984 and nullify the erosion of support for any Democrat in parts of the South and Midwest.

Talk is cheap; a candidate can only make credible claims to being a different kind of Republican or Democrat by picking the right fights and showing that they care enough about a principle to do more than talk. John McCain prepared for 2008 by standing up to his party's president, fighting against torture, and then investigating and exposing scandals involving, among other things, Republican fund-raisers that defrauded Native American tribes of millions of dollars.[16] Hillary Clinton co-sponsored legislation with Republicans—including some of her husband's chief antagonists during his impeachment—which improved medical care for National Guard soldiers.

PEDESTALS

All challenger candidates have followers who place the candidate on a pedestal. It is easy for candidates to bask in this admiration and assume other people also share the admiration and respect.

Candidates start out thinking they are important, admired, and deserving because of accomplishments in their last position, or because they are ahead in polls, or an acclaimed hero. While they are on the pedestal, voters look at candidates in terms of how much they deserve an honor or how likable they are. Admiring and liking someone for his past accomplishments is different from preferring him for the next job.

Put anyone on a pedestal and she is evaluated against the viewer's subjective standards, particularly personal traits and feelings related to likeability. Put that person next to someone else and the viewer will choose between the two people using different standards. A choice and an evaluation are particularly different when a candidate has personal negatives and policy positives. In a lineup of candidates, the policy differences dominate; on a pedestal, the personal strengths—or flaws—are magnified.[17]

By definition, all candidates claim they deserve to be president. Yet they must claim to be deserving without acting entitled to the job. They must persuade voters they are working for them and do not take their vote for granted. That cannot happen when the candidate is talking down to voters from a pedestal, telling them why she is the best candidate. As one screenwriter noted, "In the old westerns, the fastest gun in the West never said he was the fastest, others said it. And if the gunslinger said he was the fastest? That was comic relief."[18]

PAROCHIALISM

All candidates are parochial, and so are the teams and organizations from their last campaign. Senators have to convince people that they are not out of touch, that they are not more Washingtonian than their part of the homeland. Governors have to demonstrate that, while in touch with regular people, they are not unprepared for foreign policy. Heroes have to show people that they can cope with areas other than the ones in which they've already succeeded.

Each candidate has to show people of different ethnic, religious, economic, and cultural backgrounds that he understands and cares about their problems, too. Each candidate has to perform specific forms of political and cultural triangulation. Political triangulation refers to the process by which a candidate adopts some of the other party's goals, policies, or values to win support. By "cultural triangulation," I extend the analogy to include the ways candidates go beyond stereotypical positions associated with their race, gender, region, or religion to build bridges with other groups.

Triangulation requires planning and preparation. Candidates from California or New York might have to convince midwesterners that they have a feel for rust belt woes or the agonies of farmers. Midwestern candidates, whose constituents include deer hunters and avid fishermen, might have to convince coastal voters that support for deer hunting is not support for concealed weapons. This not only requires knowing what the voters want to hear and saying it; it also means showing them evidence that the candidate truly *believes* it.

Many candidates have to deal with cultural triangulation, too, and those stereotypes can be more difficult to overcome than stereotypes based upon region. Until a member of a racial or ethnic group has done well in presidential campaigns, candidates from the group have to persuade party leaders that voters will accept them.

John Kennedy had widespread prejudice to overcome in 1960 to become the first Roman Catholic president, as did Barack Obama, Hillary Clinton, and Mitt Romney—potentially the first black, woman, or Mormon president—in 2008. More than 40 percent of respondents answered "religion" when asked what they liked or disliked about the candidates in 1960. Despite Eisenhower's bipartisan appeal, moreover, Richard Nixon received a larger share of the vote from Protestant Democrats than Eisenhower received in 1956 when he defeated Adlai Stevenson 57 percent to 42 percent.[19]

Jacqueline Kennedy told friends she was mystified by concerns about her husband's religion, because "Jack is such a poor Catholic." In eleven years together with Kennedy, Theodore Sorenson never heard him pray aloud, muse about God, or express any cares about theology. None of this would help him triangulate, though, because being a bad Catholic would reflect bad character and alienate Catholic voters.[20]

Kennedy spent years planning his cultural triangulation before running. He worked on ways to minimize fears about Catholicism and maximize the positive associations with Catholics. The spectrum of doubters ranged from anti-Irish bigots and cross-burning Ku Klux Klansmen to intellectuals and theologians concerned about Catholicism as an institution for whom "error has no rights."[21] He developed a separatist position on church and state more stringent than what was traditionally espoused by Protestants—"I believe in an America that is officially neither Catholic, Protestant, nor Jewish"—and emphasized the common Judeo-Christian tradition of the country.[22]

Kennedy's strong anti-communism streak and his charges of a "missile gap" were tent poles for an argument he had been making since the early 1950s: Catholicism's well-known antagonism to communism and communist oppression of Catholicism in Eastern Europe would make up for the belief of many that the Democratic Party was "soft on communism." It is difficult to see Kennedy's silence when the Senate censured Senator Joseph McCarthy as anything other than an attempt to avoid any vote that would blur his position or hint at weakness.[23]

Anyone running for president as the "first" of any group also has to persuade members of that group that they are not wasting their vote on a hopeless candidate. The party leaders Kennedy had to persuade were mainly Catholics themselves. And anyone running for a hitherto unachievable office will have some leaders openly hostile to his bid, or at least quietly trying to impede his way to preserve their own status as a leader. Many among the American Catholic Church hierarchy resented Kennedy's statement that the oath of office took precedence over one's religion; the most prominent Roman Catholic leader in America, Cardinal Francis Spellman of New York, treated Richard Nixon warmly and went out of his way to be seen with him.[24]

RECTIFICATION

Positioning includes deciding if and when an old stand must be revised to rectify past errors, or to explain discrepancies between what was practiced then and what is being preached now.

Politicians do that, after all, on far larger issues. When the serial presidential campaigner George Wallace first ran for governor of Alabama in 1958 as a moderate, he proudly accepted an endorsement from the National Association for the Advancement of Colored People and rejected an endorsement by the Ku Klux Klan. After he was soundly defeated, he vowed never to be "out-niggered again." Running again as a segregationist, he became one of the single most prominent opponents of integration in the South. Chided by friends for turning his back on his early commitment to helping poor blacks get equal treatment, he explained: "You know, I tried to talk about good roads and good schools and all these things that have been part of my career, and nobody listened. And then I began talking about niggers, and they stomped the floor."[25]

Rectified errors can make a hero out of a senator on the most divisive issues of the day. Senator Arthur Vandenberg is a brilliant example—indeed a master class—in the political uses of rectified error.[26] Vandenberg was one of the most passionate, ardent opponents of preparation for World War II; he minimized the threat of Hitler and regarded every security policy of FDR as a ploy to strengthen the government and build socialism, not to make America secure. Like Robert A. Taft, the most powerful Republican senator of the era, Vandenberg considered Roosevelt a greater threat to America than Hitler. After Hitler had conquered France, though, Taft still argued that foreign dangers to the country paled in comparison with the danger from an enlarged national government. Just weeks before Pearl Harbor he warned that "long before we have dealt with armed autocracy in Europe, our liberty will be swamped by excessive Executive authority, and we will see here a completely totalitarian government."[27]

Vandenberg's passionate conversion to internationalism earned him enough popularity to make him a presidential contender after the war. Through what Richard Rovere called "vicarious atonement," he made it possible "for lots of other isolationists—who knew, if not that they were wrong, at least that they were licked—to make an honorable peace with the administration."[28] Announcing his change of heart—called a "Speech Heard 'Round the World"—Vandenberg said that the world had gotten smaller and now "I do not believe that any nation hereafter can immunize itself by its own exclusive action."[29] This made it impossible for Taft and the remaining isolationists to unite their party against the Marshall Plan, NATO, or the United Nations.

Repositioning

Primaries test candidates' agility because they must reshape their brand name to fit current ideas about their political party and adapt to unexpected challenges from within their own party. The candidates inevitably must reposition themselves because they have misjudged voters' concerns or opinions over their (out-of-power) party, or they miscalculated their rivals and are offering the wrong policies for the voters they need to persuade.

In 2000 George W. Bush prepared for a major challenge from Steve Forbes, the wealthy publisher, and ignored Senator John McCain. Forbes had a one-note 1996 campaign composed of a flat tax proposal, where everyone paid the same tax rate and entrepreneurs would be freed from the shackles of taxation and regulation. Forbes had no political experience before 1996 and still managed to win over 10 percent of the votes in Iowa and New Hampshire—and actually carried the Arizona and Delaware primaries. While no one ever expected Forbes, an ordinary speaker with no leadership qualities and very limited presence, to win the 1996 nomination, his high-profile attacks on Senator Bob Dole forced Dole to spend time and money counterattacking Forbes.

George W. Bush began his campaign assuming that Forbes would be his major opponent, so Bush prepared a tax-cut plan to prevent Forbes from attacking Bush as a big spender.[30] Bush beat Forbes in Iowa, but only by 41 to 30 percent. He might have lost without these preparations, despite the fact that he was governor of Texas and Forbes had never held office.

While Bush campaigned in Iowa, McCain skipped that state and spent all his time travelling New Hampshire on his bus, "The Straight Talk Express." He campaigned on his "maverick" brand name, and positioned himself as a reformer who thought for himself and didn't toe the party line. McCain trounced Bush badly in New Hampshire, 49 percent to 30 percent, and suddenly Bush was fighting the last war.

In a few weeks, Bush changed his focus and described himself as a "reformer with results," implicitly contrasting a governor who delivered reforms with a senator who talked about change. Eighteen days after Bush lost New Hampshire, he beat McCain in South Carolina, 53 percent to 42 percent.

If Bush had not been prepared to talk about reforms and what he would change in Washington, his campaign might have ended in New Hampshire. He still needed the tax cut to placate distrusting conservatives and make sure that Steve Forbes didn't attack him. So he put the tax cut deeper into his speeches, after education and Social Security.[31]

THE RIGHT ENEMIES

One of Hollywood director Roger Corman's rules was "A hero is only as strong as the villain." Nothing makes a candidate look more heroic than choosing the right enemy.[32]

Enemies clarify what a candidate stands for—"My enemy's enemies are my friends"—and provide a way for voters to assess the candidate's courage and willingness to fight for others, not just for profit.

Senators have interest groups and constituencies for whom they have battled for years, and the leaders of those groups can endorse them, testifying to those battles. This means they have some constituencies whose members know unambiguously whose side the senators are *really* on in those legislative battles. This is a double problem when moving from a passionate interest to a majority coalition: How does a challenger allied with a specific interest group or constituency convince others that they are fighting their own agenda and not blindly following the orders of others? After years championing the auto industry, how do you convince people you can also be serious about global warming or renewable energy?

Walter Mondale was unambiguously dedicated to the advancement of unions throughout his career. He did not believe it was ethical to criticize political allies in public, so he refused to criticize unions when he had strong disagreements with them. During a critical early debate in the 1984 primaries, Gary Hart challenged Mondale to "Name a single time you have ever differed with the AFL-CIO." Mondale obfuscated and never did persuade people he stood up for his own beliefs instead of following someone else's lead.

Voters always worry about the character of consensus builders, focusing on whether the candidate's support for a cause represents a genuine personal commitment or merely a campaign tactic. Challengers don't have warranties, and there is no product-testing lab to tell voters whether they deliver on promises.

So how does a challenger persuade voters that he will do what he claims? For a few challengers, their credibility is guaranteed. What demonstrates patriotism more than being a prisoner of war and enduring torture rather than denouncing your comrades in arms in the "Hanoi Hilton" like John McCain? It is not easy for any candidate to question the defense policies or patriotism of a John McCain, who followed a father and grandfather to Annapolis, then tried to hang himself so that he would not crack under torture and betray his family and his country.

But for challengers who are not heroes, enemies are one of the easiest ways of establishing credibility and proving that their positions are more than cheap talk. If an army wants to signal to the enemy that they are never going to retreat, they burn their bridges behind them. Making an enemy is the political equivalent. It is a credible way to persuade suspicious voters that a candidate is not playing both sides.

Bill Clinton believed that crime—and white fear about black crime—was a critical obstacle for any Democratic challenger, even a moderate southern one. Speaking before Revered Jesse Jackson's national Rainbow Coalition convention in June 1992, with Sister Souljah, a renowned rap singer, in attendance, he stunned everyone by charging that her lyrics were racist. Souljah had written and recorded, "If black people kill black people every day, why not have a week and kill white people?" Clinton charged her remarks were "filled with a kind of hatred you do not honor. If you took the words 'white' and 'black' and reversed them, you might think David Duke was giving [her] speech."[33]

It takes costly actions like that—which anger people and make enemies—to show that a challenger is making a stand. Clinton's speech embarrassed and infuriated Rev. Jackson and many other black leaders, and clearly demonstrated to voters that Clinton was paying a price for his stand, not just mouthing pieties about tolerance. This persuaded many skeptical white voters that Clinton was as sincere about fighting crime as about supporting civil rights and minority progress.

THE THREE TYPES OF CHALLENGERS

Challengers begin their quest for their party's nomination as senator, governor, or hero—a person who has developed public reputations for accomplishments on battlefields, athletic playing fields, or corporate boardrooms. (While some former vice presidents have run—and won their party's nomination—well after their term is up, they still have to deal with a presidential legacy in unique ways. These examples—Richard Nixon and Walter Mondale—will be examined alongside other vice presidents in chapter 7.)

Whatever their last campaign was, they will have to adjust to the role of challenger for the presidency, on new terrain, with changed media.

Senators

The Senate is the best place to build a platform, formulate positions on national issues, build alliances with powerful constituencies, and raise money. Yet no great sitting senator has ever been elected president. In 1957, a special committee chaired by Senator John F. Kennedy selected the distinguished former senators whose portraits should hang in the Senate Reception Room: Henry Clay, Daniel Webster, John C. Calhoun, Robert M. La Follette Sr., and Robert A. Taft Sr. In 2000 Arthur Vandenberg and Robert F. Wagner were added. Every one of those men (save Wagner, who was born abroad and thus was ineligible) sought the presidency. All failed.

If more portraits were to be hung in the reception room, Lyndon Johnson, Robert Dole, and Edward Kennedy would be considered. All three ran from the Senate and failed, and only Dole managed to win a nomination—on his third try. Only LBJ ever became president, and he was running as an incumbent—not a senator—when elected in 1964.

Senators have to prove that they have not forgotten ordinary people. They have powerful staffs filled with world-class experts on the issues around which they build their reputation. Senators have constituencies based on their issues and their expertise. The specialization and expertise of their staff is a hindrance to change, causing them to stumble while moving from their trademark issues to the concerns of the day. The details that matter in legislation are not easily connected to the dreams and experiences of ordinary people throughout the country.

Senators have a hard time adjusting to campaigning around the country because their staff works on national issues, and they think they know how to speak to the nation. It always is something of a shock for them when they realize that they are indeed parochial when they leave Washington, where they are considered cosmopolitan, accomplished, and respected.

Senators have Washington experience (known to DC insiders as "Hill experience"). Once they have established themselves in the Senate they command enormous power. Without the support of a majority of the president's party, no treaty, bill, or potential judicial appointment is ever given a hearing. Without support from sixty senators, no bill, treaty, or judicial appointment passes. Senators have as much control on public policy as most cabinet members, and most of them know as much about their assigned legislative area as the cabinet members who come and go every few years.

Senators also have valuable experience raising large amounts of money from groups partial to their legislation. They know how to talk to the national press about their Senate agenda and committees. They all have some familiarity with national television and the Sunday talk shows critical to political elites.

On any issue where the senator meets with the president, the senator probably knows more about the bill than does the president. A senator only deals intensively with a few bills in their area of expertise or critical for their constituents and key supporters, while the president must deal with *all* bills. That only misleads the senators into thinking that they can impress voters because their grasp of issues and legislation is superior to that of the president.

When running for president, being a powerful member of the Senate becomes a liability. Shortly after being sworn in, Barack Obama realized the Senate "is paralyzing...and designed for you to take bad votes."[34] Major legislation involves compromises, side payments, and least-bad choices. How does anyone who compromises in order to build a majority demonstrate their core values and "true commitments"?

The wisdom and respect for adversaries necessary to legislate means a person has made compromises. These compromises necessarily obscure a legislator's true values: it is not easy for voters to distinguish *respect* for the other side from *support* for the other side.

The inescapable dilemma for a senator is how to be a successful legislator and still persuade voters that he is sincere. Much of what senators do involves redistribution—giving to some and taking from others. This means there are always winners and losers. There is no way anyone can be a great senator without accumulating difficult votes, and every vote is a potential taint. Free trade, judges nominated by the other party, legislation with something your supporters like and something they despise, treaties that go too far or not far enough—all are part and parcel of being a senator and making democracy viable.

Every Democratic senator who had a chance to win the party's nomination for president voted in 2003 to give President George W. Bush authorization to use force—if diplomacy failed—against Saddam Hussein. Obama, the sole dissenter among all the contenders, had not gotten to the Senate yet, so he could afford to hedge his bets. By contrast, in 2006 he had turned downright equivocal on the subject when the *New Yorker* editor David Remnick gave him a golden opportunity to draw a sharp contrast with Hillary Clinton. Obama hedged:

> People might point to...our different assessments of the war in Iraq, although I'm always careful to say that I was not in the Senate, so perhaps the reason I thought it was such a bad idea was that I didn't have the benefit of U.S. intelligence. And, for those who did, it might have led to a different set of choices. So that might be something that sort of is obvious. But, again, we were in different circumstances at that time: I was running for the U.S. Senate, she had to take a vote, and casting votes is always a difficult test.[35]

In addition to taking tough votes, senators' successes are narrow, specialized achievements that matter a great deal to intense, passionate specialized interests. This makes it easy to raise money from the environmental, religious, financial, industrial, or ethnic groups who care deeply about the fine print in the legislation, but they hardly register with most of the public. Until, that is, a rival for the nomination advertises that the industry the senator protected from "undue regulation" poisoned a river, moved its plant to China, took away contracts from a factory in Iowa, or overcharged the government for defective weapons.

When a legislator spends enough time in Washington to learn about the details of their legislative assignments, it is seen as a disease—Potomac Fever. It is as if the legislators are the political equivalent of missionaries or Peace Corps volunteers. Once they learn how to manage government, solve problems, and deal with the details that are an inescapable fact of life, they are vulnerable to the charge they have "gone native" and are no longer on the side of the regular people.

Senators run for office every six years and don't always have tough reelection campaigns. They achieve their finest legislative victories brokering compromises between powerful persons with opposing interests. They are not brokering the deals between a manager and a factory worker, but rather the deals between the president of a giant corporation and the head of a union. They are not renegotiating a mortgage conflict between a loan officer and a homeowner; they are mediating between bankers and investors earning millions of dollars. They can easily lose touch with what ordinary people understand about the details and intricacies of their accomplishments.

Senators are rightfully proud of the legislation they pass and the deals they broker. But when they run for president, they show very little understanding of the elemental fact that few collective actions are viewed as individual accomplishments. Senators like to say, "I wrote...," "I passed...," and "I held a hearing..." These are obscure concepts not easily connected with changes in people's actual lives, so it is hard for one of the one hundred senators to receive special credit for the passage or defeat of any bill.

Senators are legislators, not executives, and they have a difficult time adapting their staffs to national campaigns. Edward Kennedy and Robert Dole's staffers were supremely competent on every issue with which they dealt as senators. When they ran for president, their Senate staffs were ~~fish out of water, possessing the wrong skills for a conversation with the~~ American people.

When Edward Kennedy challenged President Carter in the 1980 Democratic primaries, his Senate staff included superstars like Steven Breyer, now a Supreme Court Justice, and Dr. Larry Horowitz, a renowned expert on health policy and medical ethics.

Nothing better demonstrates the problems a great, experienced senator faces than the power struggles between policy experts with enormous expertise and people skilled in communicating with ordinary people. The result in the Kennedy case was a campaign mired in a power struggle. The campaigners viewed the experts as self-promoters with cushy offices and secure jobs. The policy experts saw the campaign consultants as poorly educated rabble-rousers who did not understand government.

The staffers believed that the senator's ads and speeches should highlight specific legislative accomplishments. The campaigners wanted to persuade voters that Kennedy would do better than Carter with the problems of the day— inflation, unemployment, energy shortages, Russia's invasion of Afghanistan, and the fifty-five American hostages in Iran. No one on Kennedy's staff had built their careers on a single one of these issues, so highlighting any of them displaced—and potentially demoted—a powerful staffer.

The policy experts had the senator's ear for the first months of the campaign. None of them thought to prepare Kennedy to answer obvious, predictable questions from reporters. At Kennedy's first appearance, a reporter asked him about the most important problem facing the country— inflation. All Kennedy could say was, "I would devote my full energies and effort to deal with it in every respect of American public policy."[36]

Months before Kennedy announced his candidacy, Congressman Tip O'Neill, an old and trusted family friend, warned him to prepare for the "moral issue."[37] His Senate staff never followed up, although stories of Kennedy's womanizing, his recent separation from his wife, Joan, and her personal battles with alcoholism and her awareness of his womanizing were all public knowledge. And then there was Chappaquiddick: ten years earlier, a young staffer, Mary Jo Kopechne, had drowned in the backseat of his car when he drove off an open bridge. The senator pled guilty to leaving the scene and later investigations determined he was driving recklessly. The questions about Kennedy's behavior—the length of time it took him to summon help or call police, why he left the scene, where he was going, etc.—were probably as well known then as when the death of Princess Diana, the trial of O. J. Simpson, or the Monica Lewinsky scandal were at their peaks.

In Kennedy's first national TV interview, on *60 Minutes*, Roger Mudd asked him what should have been an extremely basic question for a candidate: why he wanted to be president. The senator's answer became the emblem of everything wrong with his campaign:

> I have a great belief in this country, that it is, there's more natural resources than any nation of the world; there's the greatest educated population in the world; greatest technology of any country in the world and the greatest political system in the world. And yet I see at the current time that most of the industrial nations of the world are exceeding us...and the energies and the resourcefulness of this nation, I think, should be focused on these problems in a way that brings a sense of restoration in this country...I would basically feel that—that it's imperative for this country to either move forward, that it can't stand still, or otherwise it moves back.[38]

No one on a senator's staff asks a senator why he wants to be president. And it may not dawn on them that ordinary people will find that question crucial. The policy experts on the Kennedy staff all knew why he *should* be president—no one in the country could be better on their issues than the senator for whom they prepared legislation. The mistake was assuming everyone else appreciated their work and cared more about the senator's specialties than the major problems of the day.

The key Senate staffers were all friendly with the Kennedy family and allied themselves with family members and old JFK campaigners to make sure the campaign staffers did not take control away from them. They packed the Washington campaign meetings with Senate staffers and 1960 campaigners—identifiable by the tiepins JFK's friends wore to commemorate his heroism while commanding PT Boat 109 during World War II. Some of the planning meetings ended up with more than sixty-five people in the room, a clear sign of fragmentation and disaster.

In an interview years later, one of Kennedy's key Senate staffers disparaged the books about the campaign: "I was in every meeting that mattered," he said, "so I know what really happened." That is another way of saying that he wouldn't let anything matter unless he was there.[39]

Kennedy had the problem that all great senators have in learning how to move from a world-class legislative powerhouse to a presidential organization. As a senator, he had separate experts for each of his Senate committees and issue areas. But senators typically speak to specialized audiences: passionate environmentalists or oilmen, ministers or scientists, military veterans or nurses. When they campaign for president, senators either learn—or else they flop—that explaining a policy to the grass roots across the nation is entirely different from mediating between opposing elites.

At one of Kennedy's first stops he was asked about health care and gave a sound, coherent, twenty-minute answer. One of his speechwriters, Robert Shrum, chided him after that his answer was "Everything you ever wanted to know about health care—and a hell of a lot more besides."[40]

Governors

As challengers, governors have a very different set of strengths and weaknesses from senators. Whether it is better to start as a senator or governor depends upon the nature of the times and the popular images of the two parties.

Governors are executives and are more experienced with selling visions and results instead of advocating on behalf of specific legislation; they begin with executive experience and a staff organized for and familiar with state life and politics; they are accustomed to setting issue priorities, and they are intimately involved with education, jobs, and crime. Unlike senators, governors are only remotely involved with national defense and foreign policy.

Senators usually make themselves into brand names by establishing strong, distinct positions on issues: for Jesse Helms, it was opposition to the United Nations; for Phil Gramm, removing any and all regulations on investors; for Rick Santorum, the sanctity of life; for Sam Nunn, national defense.

Governors only get distinct trademarks for particular issues in very unusual circumstances (such as southern governors who stood in schoolhouse doors, vowing segregation forever). That gives them more flexibility to adapt to changes in the economy. When the Great Depression gave

Democrats and FDR national power to change the role of the government in providing jobs and infrastructure, Senate Republicans defended their trademarks and opposed most of the New Deal. Republican governors, however, had to worry about jobs and schools and roads, and were far more likely to take moderate positions on the New Deal. Governors like Thomas E. Dewey of New York spearheaded the reform movement within the party that eventually, after decades of battles, led to the Eisenhower breakthrough and, later, the Nixon presidency.[41]

When inflation, unemployment, and energy crises all hit the United States in the 1970s, Democratic senators—whose trademarks were attached to the Great Society era of increased spending on programs for poor and minorities—maintained their identities. Democratic governors, particularly those, like Bill Clinton and Jimmy Carter, from southern states became champions of a more moderate approach to spending and an increased emphasis on job creation. Whereas governors who wanted to become president once visited the three I's of Democratic politics—Ireland, Italy, and Israel—Clinton made four trips to Taiwan trying to bring jobs and investments to Arkansas.

Governors also have the advantage that they have never raised taxes on voters in the other forty-nine states. They can defend any taxes they raised as a special case owing to the peculiar circumstances in their state.

When a disaster strikes, governors direct the rescue in front of news cameras, while senators introduce a bill to eventually provide assistance for the fire, flood, earthquake, or hurricane victims. Disasters are for governors what wars are for generals, a time when the politically uninterested will pay attention. Otherwise, national attention is rare for governors. While they have more contact with the grass roots, they are far less experienced with national media scrutiny and typically end up making big mistakes as presidential candidates.

When Bill Clinton was governor of Arkansas, he was proud of his ability to outsmart the press when they talked to him about subjects ranging from pot smoking to ethics, when looking ahead to a possible presidential run. When people asked him about his experience with marijuana, Clinton—who had tried pot in England—had been able to satisfy Arkansas reporters by saying, "I've never broken the drug laws of our country."

Ray Strother, then his media consultant, warned Clinton that national reporters smelled blood when they heard cute, evasive answers.[42] Indeed, when Clinton used his pet Arkansas answer in one of his first national interviews, Don Imus saw the loophole in his answer and immediately asked him about England. Clinton's answer: "I've never broken a state law....But when I was in England I experimented with marijuana a time or two, and I didn't like it. I didn't inhale it, and never tried it again."

"I didn't inhale" became one of the most memorable, oft-repeated lines of his presidency, a source of endless jokes and an easy way for other politicians to disparage his sincerity by highlighting his evasiveness.[43]

The biggest obstacle for governors is their staffs; their parochial local team, no matter how good they are in their own state, often cannot transition to a national-level team with the know-how to run a presidential campaign. It is difficult to let go of close staffers and create the kind of team necessary to succeed nationally.

Governor Howard Dean's Vermont chief of staff, Kate O'Connor, claimed for herself the right and experience to be the all-around troubleshooter for Dean's presidential campaign, fending off anything she personally believed was out of character for Dean. "I can sort of look at something and know whether he'll like it or not," she bragged to the press. "We've seen each other so much, for so long, that I can sort of sense his moods. I know every position he's ever taken on every issue."[44]

Anytime a staffer protects their role by keeping the same gatekeeping authority when new issues, new campaign production schedules, and new states are in play, a disaster is waiting to occur. How could O'Connor possibly know what a Vermont governor needs to know in Iowa or California, or about nuclear issues, or the time it takes to produce an ad and get it on the air?[45]

Soon O'Connor was overloaded, exhausted, and near collapse, trying to control all contacts and communications. A senior deputy, David Bender, suggested she take a few days off. O'Connor turned ferocious and snapped, "I know they want to get rid of me....I will do this job if I have to do it from a hospital bed hooked up to an IV because I'm the only one who protects Howard. Everyone else wants something from him."[46]

Howard Dean saw early that "When you're running for president, you have to put your fate in other people's hands."[47] Dean realized O'Connor was a bottleneck and that her piles of unanswered letters and unreturned phone calls were so disorganized that important donors and media were not given priority.[48] He never broke the logjam that loyal, intelligent—and overloaded—O'Connor created. She had never dealt with national media, international issues, or campaigns, yet she tried to return more calls herself than one person could return, while simultaneously deciding who merited face time with Dean.

Every campaign has a conflict between personal staff, passionate volunteers, and professionals. Dean's inner circle clung to more power than they could efficiently handle by allying themselves with young, inexperienced (and nonthreatening) volunteers, dividing the campaign between true believers and mercenaries. Anyone who looked like a threat, Joe Trippi lamented later, was dead. One manager was forced out solely for questioning the monopolistic power of O'Connor.[49]

The Vermont inner circle claimed to know everything about Howard Dean—but they did not know about remarks he made in 2000, in which he disparaged and ridiculed the Iowa caucus. Unfortunately for his team, these comments were explosive—worse, they were on videotape. When they aired eight days before the caucus, Dean's vote fell twelve points in a single day.[50] If the campaign had known of the remarks and Dean had acknowledged them well in advance, a good-natured, groveling apology would have sufficed. Instead, Dean lost the Iowa caucus, leading to the infamous "I Have a Scream" speech that cost him enough support in New Hampshire to effectively kill his campaign.

To this day there are Dean true believers who blame the media for his downfall because his election-night speech, still known as the "Dean Scream," was replayed 633 times on various network and cable shows in the next four days.[51] The Deaniacs will correctly argue that Dean did not understand that he was using a particularly sensitive microphone that made his shouts sound harsh and unpresidential.

But there were bigger problems at play in the speech; it was directed entirely at the young volunteers in the room, ignoring the biggest television audience any of the candidates had yet drawn. Every other Democrat that year (indeed, any candidate in either party in any year) came to the podium in Iowa—win, place, or show—to speak to the national audience and to the New Hampshire audience for the next primary, most of whom are tuning in for the first time. Dean was so overwhelmed by this time that he could not process, listen to, or trust anyone trying to prepare him for the evening.

More than 3,500 young volunteers came to Iowa to make the caucus "The Perfect Storm." Leaving the auditorium after his concession speech, Dean saw one of his volunteers with the trademark orange Perfect Storm stocking cap. Dean sighed, turned to his pollster, Paul Maslin, and said, "They may have fucked up Iowa, but they sure changed America." Maslin later wrote that Dean "could just as easily have said 'we' instead of 'they.'"[52]

Heroes

A century ago, a party could put a silent, unexamined, victorious general on their ticket—like Helen of Troy on the bow of a ship—and attract additional voters to the heroic face on a coalition of disparate regional groups. Today, heroes have to show that their heroism is relevant to the issues of the day and the office of president. Douglas MacArthur, John Glenn, and Bill Bradley all won vast initial audiences, enthusiastic volunteers, and adequate financing for their past exploits as heroic general, legendary astronaut, and world-class scholar-athlete, respectively. In the end, none of them ever won a single primary.

Just as those challengers who excite voters with fresh ways of articulating highly desirable goals eventually have to deal with feasibility and show content, heroes have to show that their old heroism matters for new problems. While it is easy for a hero to excite, it is rare that a hero can still look heroic when talking about new problems in a new arena.

Throughout American history, the challengers or incumbents who managed to win the most support outside of their party were victorious generals: George Washington in 1792, Andrew Jackson in 1828, William Henry Harrison in 1840, Zachary Taylor in 1848, Ulysses S. Grant in 1868 and 1872, and Dwight Eisenhower in 1952 and 1956.[53]

Victorious generals have two advantages over other challengers. First, they are typically better known than other contenders. People with little or no interest in politics usually pay attention during a war. Second, they have proven that they care about the common good and not just their own personal fortune. Seldom if ever would anyone dare claim that someone risked his life for others just to embellish his reputation.

When the times call for a hero, it is easier to envision a hero rising to the challenge once more than to imagine someone who has never been heroic doing so. Victorious generals, however, are few and far between, and all heroes still have to connect their past heroics with the new office and challenges.

RUDY GIULIANI

Despite celebrity backing and major support from conservative pundits and southern governors and senators, Rudy Giuliani broke John Connally's 1980 record for spending the most money for the fewest delegates in a presidential primary contest.

The conservative *New York Post* columnist John Podhoretz promoted Giuliani as the one Republican who could save America from a Hillary Clinton presidency. Both John McCain and Giuliani showed leadership and both had baggage, but Giuliani had not been part of Washington politics the last few years, so he also could promise to clean up Washington.[54]

He loved claiming special powers beyond those of mere mortal candidates. He would beam at his audience and feign humility while gushing, "I'm trying to say this in the most humble way possible. I'm very good at doing the impossible."[55]

With all the right enemies, he looked great to Republicans everywhere. He was invited to address a session of the Alabama legislature and received a standing ovation. They knew what Governor Bob Riley meant when he told Rudy, "One of these days, you have to tell me how you *really* cleaned up New York."[56]

Although Giuliani attracted big crowds throughout the country, he epitomized the principal failure of heroes as challengers: he could not both receive accolades as a hero and acknowledge the need to prepare and learn new subjects.

Rudy's national coming-out party in spring 2007 was the Conservative Political Action Conference in Washington. The conference is singularly important; it is where Republican candidates court all the major power brokers with conservative constituencies. The speaker who preceded Rudy, Wayne LaPierre of the National Rifle Association, called for a "new Boston Tea Party," and the feverish ideologues were "looking for a battle cry" from Rudy.

George Will introduced him, itself a signal that Will thought Giuliani could revive the party and the conservative cause. Will described him as a "Margaret Thatcher conservative" whose political philosophy was pugnacity. Giuliani's reception befitted a man who had cleaned up New York and titled his *Foreign Policy* article about "terrorism's war on us" "Defending Civilization."[57]

Giuliani then destroyed his own claims of competence by being totally unprepared for the obvious. He did not apply his core principles on which he had expounded to adoring audiences during the book tour for *Leadership*—"prepare relentlessly," "communicate strong beliefs," and "surround yourself with great people"—in his own campaign.[58]

A man who had worked day and night to master every previous job from U.S. Attorney to New York mayor never learned how to discuss his own commitments, let alone explain how his New York policies would change as president.

Giuliani's speech paid the obligatory homage to Ronald Reagan and then was so disjointed that he deflated the energized crowd waiting for a battle cry, or at least a little red meat. All Will could say the next day on ABC's *This Week* was that he was informal and meandered. Peggy Noonan, the *Wall Street Journal* columnist and former speechwriter for Reagan and G. H. W. Bush, was equally disappointed in him. Giuliani's performance, Noonan felt, was ad hoc and bush-league, "as if he hasn't thought it through."[59] Podhoretz agreed. He still thought Rudy had the best chance of stopping Hillary, but he was "failing to execute on key fundamentals." It was time to "get real" and put his intellect to work.[60]

Giuliani made his "Twelve Commitments to the American people" the centerpiece of his campaign, distributed them at every speech, and promised to keep them before him every day in the Oval Office. When a woman in New Hampshire asked him how he would proceed on commitment number six—"I will lead America towards energy independence"—all he could do was crow about his past accomplishments: "This is where we really need a leader....We need somebody who can do the impossible. Now, I say that because I did this a lot in New York."[61] Asked an obvious question—on a topic of his own choosing—America's mayor had neither a prepared "home-run" answer nor an evasive platitude nor an attack on liberal orthodoxy. It is possible to be a successful candidate without having thoroughly developed plans; in fact, Ronald Reagan won cheers discussing the values underlying his unfinished plans in 1980. But Giuliani was not prepared to avoid the question. He simply had no answer.

Giuliani's strong beliefs attracted a plurality of his party, and his willingness to take on liberals and clean up the city resonated widely. But while traveling as a hero with a staff designed to support a hero, he could not pay lip service to his own leadership principles. He could not prepare relentlessly or surround himself with great people while striding the stage as a hero for yesterday's feats nor look heroic discussing new problems.

When Peter Boyer noted that Giuliani's feeble showing at the Conservative Political Action Conference showed he hadn't figured out the difference between "celebrity and candidacy," he thought he was talking about Giuliani's idiosyncrasies.[62] In fact, he was putting his finger on a problem characteristic of heroes campaigning on their heroism.

Heroic greatness impedes candidates from working with experts and learning their way through new issues and new constituencies. Heroes become accustomed to veneration and looking and acting noble. How can anyone receive acclaim for yesterday's acts, then learn the details of what he will do next without yielding his invulnerable air? How long can anyone enjoy acclaim without swaggering? And how can anyone act invulnerable without diminishing those around him?

Since 1948, General Dwight Eisenhower is the sole heroic candidate to succeed. He was willing to get off his pedestal, conduct Q&A sessions with regular people and reassure voters he wasn't out of touch. He avoided any missteps that detracted from his reputation and made sure that everything he said "would make [good reading] at the Quai d'Orsay or at No. 10 Downing, [and] sound good to the fellow digging the ditch in Kansas."[63]

CONCLUSION

While many people believe they would be great presidents, few are willing to make the sacrifices and spend the thousands of hours it takes a challenger to get there. No matter what assets a candidate begins with—hopeful rhetoric, concrete experience, financial backing, endorsements, a respected brand name—there will always be new terrain, new media, and new competition. As we see in the next chapter, audacity, experience, followers, and money are just the entry ticket. No one wins who cannot adjust strategy and stay on course.

THE CHALLENGER WHO COULDN'T LOSE: HILLARY CLINTON IN 2008

The Democratic primary of 2008 was a fight to the finish between a well-known, powerful, and successful woman, and an inexperienced, barely known African American raised in Hawaii and Indonesia.

Hillary Clinton began with majority support in every poll, a massive war chest, a team of stars, and national campaign experience. Barack Hussein Obama began with little experience in competitive elections and a glowing yet thin reputation based on a legendary speech at the 2004 Democratic convention.

Clinton had what it takes to stand up to national media; she had withstood vicious attacks from the Far Right and conservatives time and again. When Obama declared his candidacy, no one could be sure that he could take a punch or whether he had the stomach to keep going; in the only statewide race he had run, his leading opponents in both the primaries and general had been undone by revelations of personal scandals.

But this primary didn't come down to Clinton and Obama as candidates. This was a battle of teams, of campaign organization and adaptation. And in that battle, Obama's team came out ahead. Clinton lost because she set up a team whose planning mistakes and obliviousness in 2007 put 2008 in jeopardy from the beginning and because her team was glacially slow to react to the obvious, recurring signals about media, the issue terrain, and her competition.

She tried to make all the decisions, structuring her team in a way that all but guaranteed they would be unable to function without her in the room. Her management style enabled crippling turf battles and created an environment where vetoing changes in strategy was always easier than implementing them.

The Obama campaign mistakenly thought they would have to be near perfect to win. They were nowhere near perfect; their campaign was riddled with major miscalculations and erroneous assumptions. Clinton could have conceivably pulled out of the nomination at numerous steps along the way. That she *didn't* makes the 2008 Democratic primary essential for any examination of how challengers begin their run for the White House.

CLINTON: SHOCK AND AWE

Of course, running as a challenger works best when you campaign like one. And with a commanding lead in the polls, an extensive Rolodex of fund-raisers and donors, an experienced stable of issue experts, and a campaign team that had worked with her in either her husband's presidential campaigns or her two winning Senate campaigns, Hillary looked—and behaved—like someone already a nominee rather than someone trying to convince voters to choose her as their leader.

With no opponent close to her in the polls, Clinton focused on avoiding any positions that would endanger her chances later. Her campaign manager, Patti Solis Doyle, called their strategy "shock and awe": deliver a quick knockout blow with big endorsements, early primary victories, and a commanding lead in fund-raising. Their message to major fund-raisers was "this candidacy is inevitable because we'll have more experienced consultants, more political insiders, more money, and more of every resource that is vital to being nominated."[1]

Hillary's team concluded there were only two candidates with any chance of slowing the Clinton juggernaut: former Senator John Edwards and Barack Obama. Edwards had had been camping in Iowa seemingly forever. If they beat Edwards in Iowa, New Hampshire would win the race. If Edwards won Iowa, she still could win in New Hampshire, then finish him off for good on or before Super Tuesday when he ran out of money.

Obama, with his lofty words and lack of legislative accomplishment, seemed less of a threat. He inspired hope, but Mark Penn, Clinton's pollster and strategist, was confident that Obama had no staying power; once "voters think about him five minutes they get that he was just a state senator and that he would be trounced by the big Republicans."[2]

With the nomination all but guaranteed, Clinton's goal was to position herself to capture moderate and independent swing voters in the presidential election. Penn believed "swing is (still) king." His viewpoint was that elections are always won by concentrating on moderate swing voters, not by energizing the base, and certainly not by mobilizing nonvoters—particularly if they are young.[3]

Clinton was campaigning in the primaries as if she were already the nominee of the party working to capture enough additional votes to defeat her Republican challenger. She was running as an experienced insider so that no Republican opponent could claim she wasn't ready to be commander in chief, and she was campaigning to woo swing voters so no Republican could say she was too far to the Left.

Obama: The Long March

In December 2006, two years before a single vote would be cast in the primaries, the editorial board of the *Chicago Tribune* asked Obama how the Republicans would run John McCain versus him. He answered, "War hero against snot-nosed rookie."[4]

Obama's multiracial, rags-to-Harvard story was like a modern-day version of Abe Lincoln's log cabin. Democrats of every persuasion were intrigued. One pollster told *Rolling Stone* it was like having Bobby Kennedy walk in your door, something you waited all your life for. Bruce Reed, the president of the centrist Democratic Leadership Council, saw the hope he inspired: "People don't come to Obama for what he's done in the Senate," he said. "They come because of what they hope he could be."[5]

The snot-nosed rookie didn't know how much money he could raise; his team didn't know if he would be ready for more pressure and scrutiny than anything he could imagine. What the campaign *did* know was precisely who their competition would be.

For a passionate minority of Democrats, his extraordinary speeches and résumé sufficed to evoke visions of greatness. Everyone else needed to see some evidence. David Axelrod, his chief advisor, and David Plouffe, the campaign manager, believed Obama's only chance was to focus on the handful of small states where caucuses or primaries were held before February 5—Super Tuesday—the Tuesday in February or March when the largest number of states hold primaries. In the small states—Iowa, New Hampshire, Nevada, and South Carolina—they could practice retail (small group, person to person) politics and show their home style, meeting with every reporter, visiting every county, talking to every possible group. That would give them a chance to go around Hillary's elite endorsements and persuade voters to support Obama.[6]

The only way they could win against the established brand, they believed, was by attracting new buyers. It would be easier to recruit new voters than to persuade people to switch from Clinton, particularly before Obama had won anything. Then, if he won in Iowa, he could get in position to dislodge voters who had started with the safer choice.

Whereas Clinton's team planned for a blitzkrieg, Obama's team planned for a long march. They had to chip away at her delegate by delegate, state by state. Primary delegate selection rules were extremely complicated, and they had no expert like Clinton's friend and ally Harold Ickes to sort things out, so they had to set up a committee just to figure out how to maximize their delegate yield state by state and dollar for dollar.[7]

The difference in approaches went far beyond the obvious distinctions between a front-runner and a newcomer. Axelrod believed a campaign needed a single overarching theme, which could work with disparate groups. Based upon his experience in 1996, Penn was the direct opposite of Axelrod in strategic approach, searching for discrete programs and policies that could appeal to small microslices of voters.[8] Both approaches were a mixture of faith and reason, and at this point no one could say where the reason ended and the faith began.

TERRAIN

The 2008 campaign began against a backdrop of impatience with the war in Iraq and disenchantment with the Republican Party and President Bush. It was clear that competence and experience were on voters' minds.

The results of the 2006 midterm elections, in which Democrats had retaken majorities in both houses of Congress, suggested that 2008 would be a "change election," like 1984 and 1992. This was likely to be a year when voters were turned off by politics as a whole, not just by a president or a party. Peter Hart, the dean of political pollsters, found three-quarters of the country wanted the next president's *approach*—not just his party—to be different from Bush, and more people wanted a domestic focus rather than a focus on Iraq and terror. Hart sensed that this would be a year where authenticity was particularly salient.[9]

The two campaigns came to very different assessments of how best to navigate the environment. Clinton's view was that the toxic atmosphere was due to Republican control and the moral certainty of the White House; what the country needed was pragmatism and competence. Obama saw the rancor as the result of excessive partisanship on both sides; what the country needed was less ideological rigidity.[10]

CLINTON'S MESSAGE BOX

A woman who wanted to be president, Penn wrote, had to persuade people that she was "man enough" to be commander in chief:

> They do not want someone who would be the first mama.... There is a yearning for…someone who can combine the toughness they are used to with the negotiating adeptness they believe a woman would bring to that office. They are open to the first father being a woman.[11]

A lightning rod for conservative attacks during her husband's administration, Clinton was regarded by many as insincere—a panderer. Penn argued that the way to build trust was to "convince people of the seriousness of your convictions." Her record would establish the credibility needed to be trustworthy.[12] Above all, she should emphasize the strength of her convictions by remaining steadfast: "Avoid anything that even smells like a position change and stick to criticism of current policy as much possible." She referred with pride to the attacks she withstood, urging people to "kick my tires [to] see whether or not I'll collapse."[13] To show her competence and experience she emphasized her pride in working the system and getting things done.

The decision to focus solely on her political experience was highly contentious within the campaign. Mandy Grunwald and Howard Wolfson, her media and communications directors, respectively, wanted to show more of Clinton's character so that voters would understand where she was coming from. Grunwald produced a biographical ad in which Clinton told about her mother's pioneering spirit, and how the mother had to take a train to California and move in with an aunt when she was ten. At Penn's insistence, the ad was shelved. His interpretation was that middle-income and middle-aged voters were "grounded in facts, values, and experiences"; the 90 percent of the country who were taking pay cuts were "not at all about personality."[14]

While some voters did love her, others disliked her intensely. Peter Hart had conducted focus groups about the primary candidates for reporters in May 2007. Clinton was viewed as cold and determined, and her image was far more sharply etched—and problematic—than the image of any other candidate in either party.[15] Hart had been Walter Mondale's pollster in 1984 and knew there was room for candidates to gain at Clinton's expense. What Hart told Mondale in 1984 was true about Clinton in 2007: "I said to him … 'You're well known, but not known well.' So there was not much flesh there for people. There was just bare bones."[16]

There was plenty about Hillary to assure Iowans that she was "one of us" and not only "of Washington." She may have seemed thoroughly modern and secular through the media filter, yet she was an old-fashioned, staunch Methodist who carried a daily prayer card everywhere—and used it. She was part of a women's prayer group in Washington before joining the Senate, where she became part of a more devout bipartisan prayer group. "Whenever I think I am like her," Grunwald said, "religion is the part that I know is most different about Hillary. It really is a comfort for her and sustains her in a way that's hard for the rest of us to understand."[17]

As the campaign began and Obama drew big crowds and positive press coverage, Penn was still certain that Obama was no threat: "He is all sizzle and no steak." He also interpreted the press coverage about his personal story—his childhood in Indonesia, his years in Hawaii—as a liability: "I cannot imagine America electing a president during a time of war who is not at his center fundamentally American in his thinking and in his values."[18]

Obama's Message Box

The Obama campaign had to offer voters a persuasive critique of Bush that went beyond competence and party. If the problems with Bush were his incompetence and Republican ideology, then the "solution" was a competent Democrat, hardly an obvious way that the inexperienced Obama was preferable to Clinton or Edwards. They needed a critique of Bush that also implicated Clinton, an outsider campaign tailored to Obama's unique strengths and Clinton's weaknesses.

Obama's biography and demeanor gave him a potential edge over the others at changing the tenor of Washington. His writing and his style were detached from partisan politics, and he was not associated with the bloody battles between Democrats and Republicans during the Clinton years and after. He could argue that getting anything done in Washington required changing the hyperpartisan tone of government and restoring civility. But while Obama needed to stand for change, he also needed to make change more important than experience, not an easy case for a country at war with a president who had been overwhelmed.

Axelrod devised three rhetorical tactics to persuade voters that Obama was a credible candidate of change—and make it hard for Clinton to trump or match him. First, talk of new politics. Second, talk about fighting special interests. Third, say things people don't want to hear.[19]

Clinton's shock and awe approach was the perfect counterpoint for Axelrod's approach. Inevitability reminded voters that she was an experienced insider, acting as if the nomination was already hers. And running solely on issues left any doubts about her character unresolved. Axelrod knew that voters had doubts about Clinton's character. He drew two conclusions from this. First, Obama should level with people and say unpleasant truths—proving he wasn't pandering and telling people only what they wanted to hear. And above all else, if Clinton was going to run as the candidate of experience, they had to make her pay a price for it.[20]

Their strategy was to contrast Obama with Hillary in terms of his conviction against her calculation; his determination to change the system with her skill at working the system; and his bipartisanship with her partisan trench warfare.[21]

Voters would judge Obama's competence by how well he handled his campaign and whether he could take punches, stay on his feet, and keep his cool. The campaign, Axelrod assured him, would be a proving ground for strength."[22] Obama had to prove his strength, however, without any evocation of the "angry black man" stereotype so lethal in much of the country. If Obama acted "tough and gritty," he would undermine his image. He had to "wear ambition lightly, and to allow toughness to be taken for granted."[23]

Obama was candid with audiences about their legitimate doubts that he was ready. He talked about the importance of competence and substance, and told Iowans in his speeches to "kick the tires and be clear that I have a grasp of the issues."[24] Obama crafted his attacks to emphasize that Clinton was continuity and he was change. The implication was clear when he talked about people who "spent so long in Washington that they didn't believe change was possible."[25]

To remain as "clean" as possible, Obama would deliver his criticisms of Clinton in person during debates and speeches. Obama's phrasing—calculation versus conviction—usually made the contrast without using her name.[26] That defused and flummoxed the Clinton campaign. They were prepared only to answer fire with fire; when Obama criticized her only indirectly, they were unable to run their negative ads without becoming the candidate who destroyed civility in Iowa.[27] Obama had to manage a doubly difficult job of cultural triangulation. He had to persuade African Americans he was "black enough" to understand them and care about them despite growing up in a white household in Indonesia and Hawaii. He also had to persuade white Americans he was "white enough" to be more than a great orator or a "niche candidate" fighting to redistribute more of the pie for minorities.

Near the beginning of the campaign, he met with "the Colored Girls," an informal club of the most powerful African American women in his party. Obama was contradictory, presumptuous, and arrogant. On one hand, he acted "as if he owned the table" because he was black. On the other hand, he offended some of them by saying race would not matter in the election because he was not going to campaign that way—as if no one would care that he were black unless he talked about it. In other words, blacks should vote for him because he was (silently) black, but whites would not vote against him if he was (silently) black.[28]

Cornel West, the Princeton professor and prominent public intellectual, was openly derisive at the beginning of the campaign. Obama had white support because he held blacks at arm's length; "What are you willing to sacrifice for?" West wanted to know. Julian Bond, chairman of the board of the N.A.A.C.P., made it clear to Obama that it wasn't only public intellectuals who wanted more: "A portion of black voters want Obama to give them some raw meat."[29]

Many established black community leaders resented him as a perceived threat to their leadership. A black candidate who could build a multiracial coalition might marginalize leaders—like Al Sharpton—who could only work the black side of the street. Part of Obama's attraction was precisely that he was *not* a vociferous agitator but a highly intelligent, well-educated mediator.

Saturday Night Live parodied the growing tension between established black leaders and Obama while also raising the question of how black a candidate could be and still win. In a February 2007 skit, Jesse Jackson (Darrell Hammond) and Al Sharpton (Kenan Thompson) introduced their own "blackness" scale:

JACKSON: Barack, at this point and time, you're right about here: above Will Smith, but just below Bill Clinton.
SHARPTON: But this could change as the American people get to know you better. For instance...
JACKSON: You were raised by a single mother and your grandparents.
SHARPTON: Moving up.
JACKSON: In Hawaii.
SHARPTON: Moving down.
JACKSON: You have an African name, Barack.
SHARPTON: Moving up.
JACKSON: But in high school, you went by "Barry."
SHARPTON: Moving down.
JACKSON: You married a black woman.
SHARPTON: Moving up.

JACKSON: But in the past, you dated white women.

SHARPTON: Still moving up.[30]

OBAMA: PLANTING SEEDS

The two campaigns took vastly divergent approaches to utilizing new media and the information available as Internet usage soared. The Obama campaign changed the very organizational structure of their campaign, reallocating resources and authority. The Clinton campaign concentrated on using new information to do more refined top-down targeting of messages.

Both Plouffe and Axelrod had been involved in the 2004 and 2006 campaigns, and saw how people of every age were going online for news or political blogs. Axelrod's takeaway from 2006 was that the Internet was going to turn political communications into a two-way exchange:

> As more and more people become wired to the Internet and fluent in it, it becomes a greater and greater tool for organizing the grass roots and the democratization of politics. It's not just a tool for delivering messages to people but a tool for people to deliver messages to you.[31]

This was a major rethinking of the standard campaign, where messages were sent from campaign to voter. Plouffe and Axelrod changed the organization of the campaign to take advantage of the Internet to use peer-to-peer communication for persuasion, Get Out the Vote (GOTV), and fund-raising.

Julius Genachowski, a law school classmate of Obama's who built a career in information technology, persuaded them to take a corporate approach to the Internet, bringing metrics and software design into the campaign. They invested more than two million dollars on building the hardware infrastructure for their website and another half a million for data and software.[32] Plouffe also had the IT group report directly to him.[33]

Obama was one of the first senators to have a Facebook page, and his account was handled by Chris Hughes, a Facebook founder interested in politics. Hughes excelled more at engaging people and making user-friendly software than at writing code, and he left Facebook to join the campaign-built MyBO.com, a political version of Facebook.[34]

Plouffe gave the team permission to develop streaming videos without waiting for approval so that they would be timely—and open—with their supporters.[35] Organized like a start-up and doing all the work in-house, they could tweak and change their online content in a schedule attuned to the twenty-four-hour news cycle.

Penny Pritzker, Obama's chief fund-raiser, worked with the online operation to democratize "bundling," where one person gets friends, contacts, and colleagues to donate to the campaign. This was usually done by big donors, and the bundlers were given special status, like George W. Bush's Rangers in 2000 or the "Hillraisers" for Clinton in 2008. Obama's team set up the software that made it easy for small donors to invite friends to visit their website and contribute on their page.[36]

The most radical gamble the Obama campaign made was shifting money away from traditional campaign patterns into local organization and local media. Presidential campaigns worked harder and harder to match different ads to different audiences, but even with all the clever microtargeting, the same number of exposures still was producing declining effects in polls.[37] The Obama campaign spent a larger share of the total budget on GOTV and organizing volunteers, and more of the media money, particularly in the primaries, on local media.[38]

Between 2001 and 2004, Karl Rove had been developing improved methods of GOTV. Rove commissioned research that showed—as academic research confirmed—that contacts from people who knew the targeted person, or were affiliated with the same church or group, were vastly more effective than calls from anonymous people.[39]

Obama's campaign gambled that they could build a secular church utilizing social connections between people. They developed a bottom-up approach that combined grassroots organizing and social media. By May 2007 the campaign was already running a three-day school, Camp Obama, to teach unpaid enlistees how to use personal stories and examples to engage people with Obama and the campaign.[40]

They lowered the barrier to entry for all supporters with a user-friendly website. Then they used rallies to get people connected to the website. Obama rallies always began by asking the crowd to text 62262—OBAMA—on their cell phones and enter their zip code if they wanted to hear about events in their neighborhood. Then they were asked to call or text friends or neighbors and tell them where they were. There was nothing new about friends calling friends; the Obama campaign just made it a more integral part of being a supporter.[41]

Their software made it easier for supporters to do more. Supporters could download an iPhone app, which would organize their existing contacts according to the date of each state's primary or caucus, and then would send reminders when it was time to call their friends and talk about voting for Obama. Volunteers uploaded information about the friends they had called, how firm their opposition or support was to Obama, and how certain they were to vote. The information didn't have to be perfect—friends can mislead friends—it only had to be more useful than the existing demographic and attitudinal sorting.

The Obama campaign assumed that many of their supporters were occasional voters who didn't know where or when to vote in a primary, or how to caucus. So they used Google to help them. Whenever someone Googled for a polling place, an Obama ad popped up offering a voting place lookup tool for that area.[42]

The campaign was determined to understand *how* the voters were processing and using the information, rather than what stories and information voters wanted.[43] Campaign staffers tracked every detail including which MyBO. com pages were visited, which campaign emails were read or forwarded, as well as which ads at what times on which channels got the most views. They had clear evidence early on that their system was ahead of the others. Visitors to Obama's site spent three times as much time on each visit as did visitors to Edwards's, Clinton's, or any other major contender's site in either party.[44]

Although they expected a drawn-out battle if they won Iowa, the campaign dared to budget only five million dollars for all activity in states after Iowa and New Hampshire—not enough to open offices. All Hughes could do was help volunteers connect with each other and tell them, "Get busy on your own. Take the campaign into your own hands."[45]

CLINTON: MEDIA

The Clinton campaign took a much more traditional approach to media and communication, and a much more restricted view of what kind of feedback from voters mattered. Her website was designed to inform supporters, not to build community, and her campaign concentrated on testing messages with polling and monitoring the national media.

Clinton's media operation focused on the national press as the drivers of the stories that filtered down to local media. This too was in contrast to the Obama campaign's belief in a new world of media where "Internet drives cable; cable drives networks." They saw that they could get many stories into circulation if they started at the other end of the pecking order; if a story took off it would eventually make the national press.[46]

Penn interpreted the 2004 and 2006 media changes differently from Axelrod and Plouffe. Voters were more informed thanks to the Internet, but Penn dismissed the notion that "a bunch of twenty-something bloggers really mattered." He had a traditional top-down perspective in which the Internet was "one more place to pitch a brand."[47]

Clinton's 2006 Senate campaign had been one of the most expensive races on record—forty-five million dollars spent on a runaway victory against a poorly funded, weak challenger. Much of that money was spent on improving voter targeting technologies so that the 2008 campaign would know where to advertise for maximal effect and what messages to send to each group.[48]

Penn's specialty was finding and naming new demographic groups in intuitive, appealing ways—"soccer moms" in 1996, "waitress moms" in 2007—that made the next steps obvious: find the right small demographic groups and inform them about issues via media or mailing. Penn started with the premise that people are what they buy, that "You could find out what people thought without talking to them" by studying their consumption patterns. Chris Hughes and the Obama team thought the whole enterprise was ridiculous. "We have a social network for a particular goal, and that's electing Barack Obama," Hughes said. "We don't need to know if you like chocolate ice cream."[49]

CLINTON'S MANAGEMENT STYLE

Paul Begala described the differences between Bill and Hillary Clinton by explaining which he would want for his lawyer if he faced the death penalty: "If there was a jury, I'd want Bill. If it were a judge, I'd want Hillary."[50]

This difference was reflected in the way Hillary worked with her strong-willed principals. Whereas Bill would have long meetings, ruminating and chewing over issues, listening to others, and then deferring decisions,

Hillary wanted all meetings to be "transactional," so she could make all key decisions herself. She was also extremely disciplined and prized loyalty and discretion above all else.[51]

Clinton had a team of stars who had worked with her for years. Penn was the main pollster in the 1996 presidential election, working side by side with both Clintons through the impeachment battles, and providing polling and strategy for her two Senate campaigns. The former head of the Democratic National Committee, Terry McAuliffe, had raised more money for the Clintons than any other Democratic fund-raiser. Grunwald handled media in the 1992 presidential campaign and both of Hillary's Senate campaigns. Wolfson was her spokesman for eight years. Ickes had been her friend and ally for decades, ran the 1996 reelection campaign, and was an acknowledged master of the arcane and intricate delegate-selection rules. Her chief of staff for the campaign, Solis Doyle, had been with her for seventeen years, starting as her scheduler and then managing her Senate campaigns; after all those years together they were like a mother and an adopted daughter.[52]

Disagreements within her team were often hostile and abusive, but Hillary was unperturbed; she would listen to their arguments and then make her decision. This discord didn't hamper her Senate campaigns because, she told people, "everyone stayed in their own lanes."[53]

In a sign of trust in his competence and judgment, Hillary made the unprecedented move of giving Penn the dual roles of strategist and pollster. He exuded certainty and was discreet, putting sensitive findings in separate reports labeled, "for your eyes only."[54] His dual status raised the level of animosity among her principals, and screaming matches erupted regularly on conference calls and in person. None of the others trusted Penn; he seldom showed them more than a few tables from any survey. Solis Doyle's nickname for Penn was "fat fuck"; she and Ickes warned Hillary three separate times about the danger of letting the same person both make and evaluate strategy.[55]

The infighting and rivalries within the Clinton campaign (between Penn on one side, and Grunwald and Wolfson on the other) created an either-or power struggle over how to portray her to voters. Penn emphasized the importance of showing strength, of proving that a woman candidate would be a plausible commander in chief. Ickes and Wolfson, on the other hand, were sure she had turned around her first Senate campaign in New York only when her charm, humor, and genuine empathy were allowed to come through.

On policy fights among issue specialists, Clinton was confident in her ability to settle disagreements and establish positions. She was less certain in her ability to decide arguments over messaging and strategy; those, she deferred to Penn. Her abdication killed teamwork. Penn so frequently went directly to the Clintons to override choices with which he disagreed that his colleagues considered discussion futile.[56]

There was so much conflict about where one staffer's lane ended and another's began—not to mention their profits and status as campaign professionals—that the interservice rivalry choked off cooperation and innovation. No one was willing to shift money or authority. The activities that matter more in a primary than in a general election were given short shrift. Minimal attention and resources were allocated to the staffs in Iowa and New Hampshire, and little attention was paid to delegate selection.

Anyone who gave unpleasant news to her in front of the others risked being undercut by rivals or—even worse—being cut off by Hillary. The rivalry also choked off innovation from below. Principals were so busy defending their own turf that no one ever presented innovations from junior staffers in front of the others. Staffers confessed to reporters that they held back because "I don't want to get spanked by Mama."[57]

Praising Clinton and attacking Obama became the easy options. For most of the campaign, her staff never tried to prepare her to counter the predictable attacks because to acknowledge there might be things about Hillary to attack could possibly land someone in trouble.[58]

Obama's Management Style

Inside the Obama campaign, senior staffers nicknamed him "Black Jesus." The blind faith and passion he aroused was so strong that senior staffers worried that it would further inflate his already robust ego.[59]

Obama did not grasp just how limited his time would be and how much he would have to delegate decisions about his daily life and future to people he did not know. "You just have to let go and trust," Plouffe counseled him. "Your staff will inevitably screw up. But...you have to be the candidate. Not the campaign manager, scheduler, or driver."[60]

Plouffe and Axelrod proposed early on, and Obama concurred, that there should be a salary cap in the campaign. The salary cap helped solve two major problems: (1) it gave the campaign credibility with Obama's friends, family, and fund-raisers by eliminating consultants after big fees, and (2) it also reassured Obama that they were being careful with the money he raised and limited the number of decisions Obama spent time on. They desperately needed him to spend his time improving delivery, raising money, making alliances, and getting used to the rhythms of being a presidential candidate.[61]

Obama's major concern was having a communications process that would not break down under stress. By January 2007 Axelrod saw he could not manage communications and develop the message at the same time. To keep everything working smoothly, he recruited Larry Grisolano to take over his administrative control and manage the pollsters, research, and advertising. That left Axelrod free to concentrate on strategy and message with Plouffe.[62]

Plouffe and Axelrod had been willing to change the power structure— and give up some control to utilize the full possibilities of new media and the Internet. For instance, by bringing in the technology officer Joe Rospars, who had worked on Dean's 2004 campaign, they were effectively agreeing to decentralize part of the campaign. Without that earlier restructuring they would never have attracted Chris Hughes or been able to take advantage of his breakthrough innovations.

Hughes joined the Obama campaign only after they showed him that his group wouldn't be marginalized: "just a couple Internet guys in a corner."[63] Again, organization triumphed. Plouffe and his deputies soothed whatever egos needed soothing, and slowly but surely Hughes gained the authority and budget to build his online operation.[64]

IOWA: ADAPTATION AND TEAMWORK

Iowa and New Hampshire are the ultimate in retail politics. The two long and deeply intimate first campaigns are emotionally and physically exhausting—and different from anything else candidates have ever done in their political careers. They are the ultimate test of whether a candidate can take her public reputation and organization into new terrain and adapt quickly.

Iowa depended on which alternative to Bush would draw more people to the caucuses—and that, in turn, depended as much on both national and local organizations as it did upon the candidate and his or her message.

In a primary election, voters step into a booth, mark their ballots in private, and leave; delegates to the national nominating convention are then allocated based on state and congressional district-level returns. The Iowa primary is a caucus, where voters gather together for several hours in a large room, typically a school auditorium, church basement, or library. Supporters of each candidate then try to persuade other people to join their group. The persuasion period is often critical because no candidate can win any delegates unless 15 percent or more of the attendees at that specific caucus site are in their preference group. This threshold places a premium on recruiting activists willing to devote time and energy into both mobilizing supporters to attend and attracting attendees who support nonviable candidates.

Every election cycle there are legitimate gripes and complaints from other states that Iowa and New Hampshire are too rural, too white, or too secular to be representative of the country or the base of either party. And the Iowa caucuses are not representative of Iowa because they require more time than ordinary voting.[65] All the criticisms miss the big point: the states are small enough so that candidates can do intensive retail politics—if they have the mind-set and endurance to woo local activists.

Candidates might know intellectually what Iowa and New Hampshire entail, but it is still hard for them to get off their pedestals and overcome their parochialisms. Activists take their role in vetting candidates seriously; they don't mobilize their friends before grilling the candidates personally and making sure they have what it takes.[66]

Candidates learn the routine of speaking before huge crowds fairly quickly. You need to know the name of the town, the politicians and activists to praise by name, the name of the local teams, and a local example of a national problem. Even when facing a hostile crowd, you don't have to pay attention to the individuals.

Small groups are more grueling for candidates. Suddenly they sit in church basements and coffee shops for countless hours of retail politics and small talk about new issues and personal questions. The activists all want to be heard and see if the candidate can connect with them personally. Taking the process seriously means the activists take themselves seriously too.

Obama in Iowa

Having an ego big enough to run for president makes it very easy to underrate opponents, and Obama had not appreciated how hard it was to be as articulate and competent every day as Hillary Clinton was. He had the physical stamina but did not realize how much campaigning depended upon psychological stamina and experience. The highs were fewer and the hours longer than he had imagined. Inspiration and celebrity were only part of the job; there was a long distance between inspiring people and winning votes.

The frequent debates among all the challengers—at least one a month—were not helping him either. His modus operandi was to impress people with his brains, not with leadership or solutions. At one forum he was so vague when moving beyond talk about changing the ways of Washington that *Time* magazine's Karen Tumulty finally asked him point-blank, "What really are your top issues?" Obama faltered badly.[67]

He simply had not grasped that campaigning was neither intellectual nor cerebral nor anything at all like a former law professor's fantasy of the ultimate Socratic dialogue. Obama was learning that only professors can be long-winded and Socratic. After all, a professor rewards those students who listen carefully and learn the right answer; in an election, it is the other way around. And there are far too many problems on which the candidate must be knowledgeable for long seminars; instead, the candidate must learn to delegate more and more of the analysis to staffers and match the time available to the amount of information they can absorb.

Obama always wanted to show he understood both sides of a debate before explaining why he was right. His exasperated aides stopped holding mock debates with surrogates for Clinton and Edwards, a standard practice in every campaign. Instead, they blitzed him with questions so that he would "sharpen his answers irrespective of what others were saying."[68] Obama started avoiding debate prep and began to leave early when they wanted him to improve his delivery.[69]

For all the energy Obama projected and the passion he aroused at his rallies, his campaign headquarters felt cold and soulless. The Obama who always engaged with his audience and talked about "we" instead of "I" could be aloof. When he returned to Chicago, he would head for the gym or go out of town again without checking in to cheer up his staff.[70] Obama's sour moods were getting the campaign down.

Finally, Axelrod, Plouffe, and Pete Rouse, his Senate chief of staff, took Obama out to dinner. After Obama had said his fill, he realized he was the actual subject of the meeting. "Is this an intervention?" he asked. It was. The inner circle laid it all on the line for him: he needed to change his attitude.[71]

Obama's increasingly peevish attitude, though, was a direct result of his unease with the strategy at the core of his campaign: devoting as much time and money as possible to Iowa, and spending no time or money courting black voters. Axelrod and Plouffe could not devise a single scenario that did not begin with victory in Iowa, and they could see no way to win black voters *unless* they first won Iowa. If Clinton won Iowa, she would win New Hampshire—a much stronger state for her. That would persuade most black voters to stick with her because Obama did not have enough white appeal to go the distance.[72]

But Axelrod's Iowa-centric campaign was not so much about avoiding blacks as it was about using "third-party authentication" to nudge skeptical whites—less-educated, older ones in particular—to feel they had permission to vote for a black candidate, regardless of their general feelings about other black men and women. Axelrod needed to make Iowa do for Obama what winning anti-Catholic West Virginia had done for John Kennedy in 1960.

But what if Obama lost—a possibility far more real after seven months of campaign hell with little progress to show his family and friends? What would it be like to live with the aftermath among his friends?

If he spent time and money in black communities and lost, at least he would face fewer recriminations after the campaign. But minimizing regret only made defeat more inevitable. He needed to go all out instead of hedging his bets.

Obama called Plouffe on the way home from the intervention dinner. He was in "one hundred percent agreement with the strategy.... But if you want me to perform in Iowa, I need to have this burden lifted."[73]

Finally Axelrod and Plouffe and a few others worked out a solution that strengthened the campaign and assuaged Obama's worries. They brought Valerie Jarrett, a brilliant and successful black executive, into the inner circle to take part in all meetings and communicate regularly with black leaders around the country.

The inner circle now had a key ingredient. Jarrett was smart enough (Stanford and Michigan Law School), political enough (a former Chicago official and now a highly successful developer), and close enough to the Obamas that she could say things to the family that only a longtime personal friend could provide. That she could court black constituencies the white guys couldn't court was a bonus.[74]

The intervention led to a counterintervention. His feathers ruffled by the dinner, Obama called his old friend Christopher Edley, one of his Harvard Law professors, to visit the campaign. Edley had worked on policy in other presidential campaigns and had been in charge of President Clinton's Affirmative Action Review. He was an African American whom Barack and Michelle trusted, and they wanted to hear what he would say.

Edley didn't like the Iowa strategy, concentrating on white voters, or leaving the women's vote to Clinton. He disparaged and insulted Axelrod and Plouffe for their focus on message over content and the lack of time for Barack to do "deep-think." Edley's lengthy discourse gave Obama a chance to listen and watch while a family friend from the black intelligentsia made a loud, passionate argument for "letting Obama be Obama."

None of Edley's suggestions for changing the Iowa-centric strategy were ever put into effect, yet the meeting was as important as the intervention by the senior staff. Obama felt like Big Brother was controlling him, and pushing back made him feel more comfortable and less constrained. When Edley later worried whether he had gone too far, Jarrett reassured him that he had performed exactly the role Barack wanted: clearing the air between family and friends, policy advocates, campaign staff and minority communities.[75]

Obama called a third meeting to go over process and strategy in September, in order to sharpen the contrast with Clinton and tap the Clinton fatigue they believed was bubbling along below the surface.[76] They had to bring it to the surface indirectly, though, without Obama being aggressive. Their last chance to do this would be at the Jefferson-Jackson Day dinner in November.

CLINTON IN IOWA: CAN A ROCK STAR DO RETAIL?

In December 2006, a few power players from New Hampshire met with Hillary in Washington. Terry Shumaker, a longtime Clinton supporter and an activist who had been in the trenches for eight New Hampshire primary campaigns laid out Clinton's challenges in a detailed memo. The key question, he emphasized, was "How does a 'rock star' do retail?"[77]

Shumaker was acutely aware of how easy it was for prominent, successful politicians to avoid retail. He wanted to make sure that other local activists knew Hillary would not be haughty: "If she runs, she is very committed to campaigning in New Hampshire in the traditional way, as she did in New York," he told the *Manchester Union Leader*. "She very much wants to do retail politics."[78]

It had seemed at one point that Iowa was solidly in the Clinton column. In February 2007, she visited a high school auditorium in Des Moines, Iowa, on a near-arctic Saturday morning. Despite snow flurries and a high temperature of twelve degrees, three thousand people packed the gym to hear her. She strode in to Jesus Jones's "Right Here, Right Now," entering on the line "There is no other place I want to be." The crowd erupted into deafening applause.[79]

In the two months since that initial outpouring, Hillary had limited herself to two overnight trips to Iowa, while Obama had spent more than twice as much time there. Michael Whouley, a high-powered political consultant, visited the Clintons in their New York home to drive home the importance of following up: Iowa required time as well as money; staff and media alone would not win Iowa.[80]

Whouley saw at once that Hillary thought Iowa felt strange and that she was uncomfortable there. She didn't understand or like going to out-of-the-way places to meet with small groups of activists. She resisted phone calls. Hillary had great "phone style"—when she made phone calls to activists she was amazing at engaging them in "real conversation" about kids, and so forth—but she hated it because she had trouble getting off the phone.[81]

Clinton blamed Iowa, but she was no longer used to doing the kind of retail she had done with her husband in Arkansas or nationally in 1992. As a senator, she had learned how to do ten minutes with a treasury secretary on debt, or fifteen minutes of refereeing a debate among advisors over Afghanistan; now she had to make the psychic change to withstanding an hour of talk about the local pharmacist's troubles with Medicare reimbursement and act like she hadn't heard it before.

Meanwhile, "shock and awe" was not working on the donors. In January, four of the party's top fund-raisers had committed to Obama. In April,

Clinton's campaign trumpeted the best fund-raising quarter any Democrat had ever had, only to be outshone by a bigger Obama total within days. One of her advisors realized that she was in a long fight, that no blitzkrieg could end the election: "It belied our arrogance that nobody else could meet her on the field of battle."[82]

Clinton was avoiding Iowa and her national staff was not building a statewide organization there. No one understood that Iowa was essential to Obama and that Obama knew it. After the first quarter of 2007, Obama had spent $633,000 in Iowa—more than all the other Democratic candidates combined, and more than five times what Clinton spent. He had hired a local fund-raising firm and was staffing offices all over the state. Clinton, in contrast, had not shelled out $100,000 for a copy of the Iowa Democratic Party's list of past caucus attendees. This list was both the starting point for all political organization and a goodwill builder; the local party's main source of revenue was selling this list to all the candidates every four years.[83]

Mike Henry, realizing they were going to face a well-funded opponent, wrote a memo forcing the issue: Iowa would cost at least fifteen million dollars, so play to the hilt or save the money for later. He summed up his fears for Iowa in a memo: "This effort may bankrupt the campaign and provide little if any political advantage."[84] When Henry's memo was leaked, Clinton had to publicly respond: should she skip Iowa or inevitably drop. She decided to compete in Iowa.

At the end of June she was farther behind Obama in fund-raising. In the second quarter he beat her by $10 million, and without salary caps, she was spending money much faster than Obama. She was relying on the big donors from past campaigns, and the new limits on donations made them much less valuable.[85]

When she went back to Iowa for the Fourth of July, she knew that she was fighting against an opponent who would have as much money as she did and who had real appeal. Fortunately, Hillary's own appeal reemerged during that July trip. Everywhere she went, crowds gave her powerful outpourings of support. She breakfasted with three hundred potential supporters at the Iowa State Fair, ate a Snickers Blizzard, chatted with folks at a Dairy Queen, and marched in parades in Mason City and Clear Lake, where she walked behind a float with a woman dressed as a golden Statue of Liberty. After one of the parades, Clinton joked to reporters, "Everyone waved at me...and I'm just happy because all five fingers were showing." She looked like a candidate working for the nomination.[86]

Hillary's trip rattled Peter Giangreco, who did the direct mail for Obama. Giangreco, who was passionately committed to Obama, believed that Obama almost lost Iowa—and the election—during her trip.[87]

ADAPTATION VERSUS RIGIDITY

By Labor Day 2007, the three key assumptions about Clinton at the heart of Obama's strategy were way off the mark. They thought that Democrats would find her too divisive to win. They incorrectly presumed she would get little positive executive credit for her time in the White House; if vice presidents got no credit, why would a First Lady? Her one quasi-executive policy attempt, derisively dubbed "Hillarycare," had been an abject failure. Voters didn't seem to care.[88]

Most surprising of all, they never expected her "remarkable" transformation on Iraq. In the face of growing anger and widespread belief among a majority of Americans that the war was not going to succeed, her vote to give President Bush authorization for war if diplomacy failed was now very hard to justify. The Obama campaign assumed that his 2002 antiwar speech would give him a clear advantage on questions about defense or foreign policy.[89]

Hillary managed to neutralize the Iraq issue by talking about how to get out of Iraq as fast and safely as possible, using forward-looking language and distributing a DVD in Iowa with her plan for withdrawal. While Clinton could be crisp enough for sound bites and still show enough sense of competence—talking of brigades, logistics, secure highways. Obama could only talk vaguely of getting the troops out.[90]

Obama's team was right, however, about voter's thirst for change in Washington that went beyond putting a Democrat in charge of the partisan process. And they were right to bank on the role of social media and the Internet. By the end of 2007, half of all Internet users were using video-sharing sites, and there was little or no age or race divide. In 2006 only 5 percent of Facebook users were older than thirty; in the next twenty-four months the proportion of over-thirty grew to half. Moreover, 42 percent of all eighteen to twenty-nine-year-olds were getting campaign news on the Internet. And one in six Americans had email exchanges with friends or family about candidates![91]

The general campaign interest also augured well for their assumptions about mobilizing young voters. Political communications between friends and family about politics were expanding, another clear indication that people were unusually interested in the 2008 election. A March 2007 *Washington Post*–ABC News poll found that 65 percent of voters already said they were following the election closely, compared to only 37 percent at that time in 2003. Indeed, there was so much interest in change that Republicans were disengaged from their own primaries; in a Pew poll in the fall of 2007 more of them could recall the names of Obama and Clinton than could recall the name of any single Republican candidate.[92]

Campaigns would only know that the electorate was likely to expand, however, if they paid attention to communications patterns or were sophisticated about the way they screened calls on their surveys. Obama's campaign knew that this was going to be a high-turnout year because they were recruiting volunteers everywhere and getting a higher than usual response rate.[93] They saw the rate at which people were volunteering and that high school students had an unusually high level of interest in the caucus.

Iowa state law allows anyone to vote in the caucus who would be eighteen years old by Election Day. In 2004 only about 250 high school students had caucused, yet Obama's campaign had organizers in two-thirds of Iowa high schools. They also planned to ask many college students to vote at home and not on campus—gaming the system to place supporters where an additional vote was most likely to lead to an additional delegate. Facebook was an important part of that effort, because social networking was so central to everyday life for these young people.[94]

Still, for all their accurate predictions about the importance of change, the role of volunteers, the organizing and fund-raising value of new media, and the declining value of traditional media, Obama's campaign wasn't making much progress against Clinton.

INTERSERVICE RIVALRY

When Plouffe and Axelrod first laid out "Change versus Experience" as the contrast between the two campaigns, Obama was skeptical that Clinton would run on experience. He found it hard to believe that her experts wouldn't figure out that this was a change election: "I gotta believe Hillary has people just as smart as our team all around her....Aren't they going to realize this and try to take our message?"[95]

Obama's pollster, Joel Benenson, had worked for Penn. He and Axelrod tried to persuade Obama that Penn was the opposite of a team player. With Penn in the dual role of pollster and strategist for Clinton, they had no doubt that Obama would have better teamwork and would adjust faster. Penn, they told him, stayed close to his clients by playing to their strengths and never pushing them to deal with any weaknesses that took them out of their comfort zone.[96] That gave him a leg up on anyone who pushed Hillary to do something she didn't like doing. And it kept the campaign on his turf—top-down targeting and media.

Voters consistently have one of three general views of front-runners: some strongly opposed voters are in the "anybody but (Hillary)" category. Some strongly committed voters are in the "(Hillary) no matter what" category. The third group consists of voters in the "(Hillary) because there is no one else" category. It is extremely hard to sort out the latter two groups, but her campaign operated as if the third category was inconsequential. That flew in the face of presidential primary history.

When proclaiming inevitability was first discussed, Ickes was characteristically blunt, asking, "How many of you ever shook hands with President Ed Muskie?" Peter Hart was just as dubious: "Inevitability is not a tune that people can march to."[97]

In the fall of 2007 the campaign still emphasized Clinton's inevitable victory, and their talking points kept referring to polls and endorsements. They were so confident that they brushed aside any concern with firewalls, delegate selection mechanics, or the so-called superdelegates.[98]

On September 29, 2007, Penn told the senior staff that victory was in sight. The "Obama fantasy" was fading, and the myth that Hillary was unelectable was exploding. Moreover, Obama's strategy "makes no sense": Obama was in third place in Iowa, yet upping his Iowa media buy at the same time he held a 24,000-person rally in New York, a state he was sure to lose.[99]

Obama did have a strategy, and his tactics made complete sense. His team had figured out the critical differences between primaries and general elections; managing losses intelligently was as important as winning Iowa. It is not surprising that the media missed some of Obama's strategy and most of the critical changes in tactics and organization. The puzzling aspect is why a presidential campaign like Clinton's didn't get it.

Penn was right: New York was obviously a state Hillary Clinton was going to win in the primaries. In a general election—where the winner gets all of the electoral votes—it would have made no sense at all for Obama to campaign there. But this was a primary, where three-quarters of the delegates are allocated at the district level and one-quarter according to statewide results. In each district, and at the statewide level, the delegates are awarded by proportional representation—with a threshold that is critical to strategic planning. Clinton's strategist did not understand that all states were proportional.[100]

Obama's campaign defined victory in terms of delegates, not votes or polls or money raised. The campaign's director of delegate selection, Jeff Berman, spent the summer of 2007 with seventy-five lawyers, going through the complicated and arcane rules for each state. Delegates in Democratic primaries are allocated on a basis of "winner take most." Any candidate with 15 percent of the vote in any district or state receives at least one delegate. The bonus for getting the most votes in a district or state was actually so modest that the primaries should have been called "winner-gets-slightly-more."[101]

In March 2007 Obama's campaign also started courting superdelegates—party leaders or elected officials who receive their vote because they are governors, senators, congressional representatives, or members of the Democratic National Committee. More than half of these delegates were appointed when Clinton's campaign chair, Terry McAuliffe, headed the DNC, and Obama's team did not want any delegates committing to Clinton because Obama ignored or slighted them. Yet the Clinton campaign had neither a superdelegate nor delegate strategy.[102]

In fact, before Obama's New York rally, his campaign had already eliminated a Clinton firewall without leaving their fingerprints behind. Two states, Michigan and Florida, tried to move the dates of their primaries so they would be just after Iowa and New Hampshire, and before Super Tuesday—a violation of the rules the DNC had set for 2008.

After months of charges and arguments, on August 25 the DNC voted to strip the Florida and Michigan primaries of all delegates. Plouffe was ready for the decision; he dispatched a senior staffer on a secret mission to the state party chairs in the four states scheduled before Super Tuesday—Iowa, New Hampshire, Nevada, and South Carolina. The staffer suggested that the chairs ask all candidates to sign a pledge stating they would not campaign in any states that broke the rules and moved their primaries. Then the Obama and Edwards campaigns both said they needed time to decide. After interest had built, both campaigns announced the next day they would sign the pledge. At that point, the trap was sprung; the unprepared Clinton campaign had no choice but to go along.[103]

THE "OH, SHIT" MOMENT

While Penn saw a (primary) mission nearly accomplished, Clinton's Iowa staff was pleading—more and more frantically—for additional resources to manage the ground war. The national staff, lacking any familiarity with Iowa and busy with polls, messages, and media, had no "Iowa Desk" to handle immediate problems and timely decisions. Though they would have preferred to speak with someone who at least owned a map of Iowa, desperate Iowa staffers eventually tried to settle for "anybody with a pulse…Anybody!"[104]

Just three days before Penn's September 29 "mission nearly accomplished" memo, all the candidates were in New Hampshire for a major debate. Obama's Iowa team had events scheduled all over the state to coincide with that night's debate, many organized by volunteers recruited and trained through his website. John Edwards had fifty-four debate parties in Iowa. Clinton's website was silent—almost no Iowa events of any kind were listed. The *Huffington Post's* Zack Exley wondered what was going on with the Clinton campaign—surely the Clinton campaign couldn't be passing up such an opportunity. Did they not know how much Iowans, and particularly activists, went online for political news and blogs?[105]

On October 15, after months of urgent prodding, Hillary's Iowa staff had a Chicago meeting with the top advisors. This time Ickes came. Penn opened the meeting by presenting polls that showed Clinton still doing well in Iowa. It was exactly what Hillary liked to hear: she didn't have to do more retail in Iowa. By the time of the meeting, Obama had already run 4,372 local ads in Iowa, compared to 1,972 by the Clinton campaign.[106]

The Iowa staff had just gotten together the funds to do some focus groups, and what they found were scores of befuddled Clinton supporters. They called it an " 'Oh, shit!' moment"—not only was Obama ahead of them in sewing up activists and organizing supporters to shepherd people through the caucuses, he was also way ahead of them in teaching people how to caucus.[107]

Ickes went to bat for the Iowa staff and made sure they finally got the money they needed to go all out the rest of the way. The Iowa campaign asked for money to hire another one hundred people whose only job would be to go door to door, sit down in homes with voters identified as Clinton supporters, show them a DVD about how caucuses operate, and give them a pep talk about how important it was for them to show up for Hillary on January 3.[108]

When the Clinton senior staff finally poured out the resources, it was three weeks until the Jefferson-Jackson Day dinner and just under three months until the caucus. In every Iowa or national poll Clinton was still ahead of every Democratic candidate on strength, experience, and nearly all of the issues. Yet Obama was close enough in Iowa to make anyone who understood caucuses uncertain about the outcome, especially given the difficulties of predicting caucus results from surveys.

Organization is never effective without message.[109] Obama had the organization, but he had not turned the corner from promising to presidential. Clinton had a less active Iowa organization but had been able to return fire from the other candidates without reviving worries about her calculation and lack of conviction.

When Clinton decided to forgo talk about her roots, religion, personal values, and her mother's pioneer spirit, she left herself vulnerable to reopening old doubts about whether she was after power for herself or for the common good. It came back to haunt her ten days before the Jefferson-Jackson dinner at a televised debate on MSNBC. The other candidates came prepared to take the fight to her—no matter the subject, the answer had to be a critical contrast with Hillary.

Asked about drivers' licenses for illegal immigrants, and wanting to show sympathy for their plight without taking a very unpopular stand on an emotional issue, Hillary tried so hard to wheedle her way out of the question that, in one reporter's words, "she nearly invented a new yoga position." Her imprecise, meandering response suddenly gave candidates a chance to criticize her double-talk.[110]

The Obama campaign had been trying all year to contrast Obama's conviction with Hillary's calculation. In one convoluted debate exchange, she made their case for them. Suddenly many people who had been for Hillary when there wasn't anybody else were reassessing the field.

Another crack came to light at an energy forum in Newton, Iowa. Despite the antiwar sentiments of college students, Hillary's team announced a "Students for Hillary" campaign. But they were so worried about student criticism of her in any Q&A that they organized an elaborate operation to be sure that the right kinds of people asked Hillary the right kinds of questions.

A Clinton staffer asked a Grinnell student, Muriel Gallo-Chasanoff, if she would like to ask a question. Gallo-Chasanoff wanted Hillary to compare her energy program with those of the other candidates. The staffer replied, "I don't think that's a good idea, because I don't know how familiar she is with their plans." Opening a binder to a page with preprinted questions, the staffer tore one out labeled "College Student," which the student agreed to ask. The staffer gestured to Clinton to call on Gallo-Chasanoff, who then asked the stiltedly worded question she had been handed: "As a young person, I'm worried about the long-term effects of global warming. How does your plan combat climate change?" Clinton's pitch-perfect response began by noting that it was always young people who asked that question.[111]

Within days the story bounced from Gallo-Chasanoff's friends to the Grinnell College newspaper to CNN, the other candidates, and voters all over Iowa, amplifying doubts about whether Clinton was too calculating.[112]

"Plantgate," as it became known, was one more distraction for an overloaded campaign visibly crumbling under pressure. They were understaffed and having a terrible time getting ready for the Jefferson-Jackson Day dinner. Teresa Vilmain had to keep calling and badgering people for money to purchase tickets before they were all gone; when she finally got the money, the best seats had already been sold to Obama.[113]

Four days before the most important event of the entire Iowa campaign, the speechwriters hadn't finished Hillary's speech—a speech she would have to deliver without a Teleprompter, in front of the national media and all Iowa.[114] Since Penn insisted on signing off on every draft of the speech, Hillary saw them only at the end of long, exhausting days.[115]

THE JEFFERSON-JACKSON DAY DINNER

The Jefferson-Jackson Day dinner unfolds more like college basketball's March Madness or a Super Bowl than a day of high-stakes politics. It is a test run of a campaign's organization, a chance to see which supporters will actually participate, and an opportunity to impress national media. For Iowans it is as important as the Iowa results are for donors, voters, and press elsewhere. The main storyline was always the same: Who could take down the front-runner or become *the* alternative?

In November 2003 Hillary had visited Iowa to emcee a raucous, animated Jefferson-Jackson Day dinner for the Iowa Democratic Party. Before dinner, she drew larger crowds to her book signings than the other candidates could get. Then, in front of a record Jefferson-Jackson dinner crowd, Hillary fired up the audience with her keynote address. "[Bush] has no vision for a future that will make America safer and stronger and smarter and richer and better and fairer," Clinton said. "We have to have a vision of where we want to lead this country." Political veterans all understood that her call for vision—indeed, her very appearance at the dinner—meant she would be back.[116] Now, in 2007, she had to respond to her own challenge with her vision of how she would lead her party and where she wanted to lead the country. The 2007 crowd shattered the 2003 attendance record. Nearly 10,000 people jammed into the gym for the long evening. It was obvious at once that Obama's mostly young supporters far outnumbered Clinton's more middle-aged crowd.

Penn immediately tried to spin the differences in age by derisively suggesting that Obama had bused in kids from other states—a tactic he himself had tried (and failed) to do for the same event. Penn scoffed that Obama's supporters "look like Facebook.... Only a few of their people look like they could vote in any state."[117]

Dinner began at 6 p.m.; the speeches at 7. Presidential candidates are limited to ten minutes each, with windy local politicians making the most of their moments in the sun in between. It took more than four hours to get to the main event: Clinton and Obama were the last two speakers.

Each had three audiences for their speeches. They had to keep their supporters fired up and energized to work the caucuses, bringing friends and persuading neighbors to join with them; they had to convince the undecided and the supporters of the minor candidates to join them now or later; and they had to take advantage of the massive national media presence.

Clinton had had less than twenty-four hours to revise and learn her speech, but she had crisp, clear, fiery delivery. The entire speech was a cry to take it to the Republicans:

I know that as the campaign goes on it's going to get a little hotter out there. But that's fine with me, because, you know, as Harry Truman said, if you can't stand the heat, get out of the kitchen. And I'll tell you what: I feel really comfortable in the kitchen. So we have to ask ourselves what is this election going to be focused on? Well, I'll tell you what I want to do.... I believe we should be turning up the heat on the Republicans! They deserve all the heat we can give them![118]

Four years earlier on this same stage, she had criticized the other candidates for a lack of vision, for attacking Republicans without an alternative path for the country and the party. Now she ignored most of her own advice.

Axelrod texted his instant response to Plouffe, back in Chicago: "Other than her supporters people are stone silent." She had not connected with the undecided Democrats in the room, let alone supporters of the minor candidates whose goodwill could matter at the caucuses.

Plouffe's reaction was a mixture of bewilderment and relief. The speech featured no attempt to make a clear contrast with Obama or to strengthen her personal relations with Iowans. She emphasized her political credentials and ignored her personal biography.[119] Had she talked about starting out in Washington with a cooperative approach and getting attacked anyway by Newt Gingrich, or explained why Democrats could be more ambitious now that they controlled Congress, Obama would have been one side of a two-sided argument about how to restore civility and change the tone. Instead, Hillary took the toxic atmosphere as a given and offered no hope of changing it.

It was a speech she could have given a year later in Denver, if she had won the nomination. At that point, talking as if she were the nominee leading her party into battle, the contrast with the Republicans would have appealed to Democrats who had supported the other candidates. Speaking to activists and young voters with no memories of the Clinton White House, it put her on a pedestal and framed the caucus as a referendum on Hillary.

She left the door open for Obama, and he strode right in. Without using anyone's name he contrasted insiders and outsiders and called for change:

The same old Washington textbook campaigns just won't do in this election...not answering questions because we are afraid our answers won't
be popular just won't do...telling the American people what we think
they want to hear instead of telling the American people what they need
to hear just won't do. Triangulating and poll-driven positions...just
won't do.[120]

Obama thrilled his supporters, impressed the rest of the audience, including the press, and reassured anxious donors and activists.[121]

Clinton's staff all praised her performance, but she sensed they were sugar-
coating their comments. She asked Vilmain why Obama's supporters outnumbered hers so badly; she thought this was more than a financial screw up over
tickets, but she could also see that Obama had scored at her expense.[122]

Ten days later, a *Washington Post*/ABC Iowa poll confirmed that Obama
was making important progress. The African American from Hawaii, by
way of Indonesia, was well ahead of the midwesterner from Illinois on
"understanding the problems of people like you" (30 percent to 20 percent) and "most honest and trustworthy" (31 percent to 15 percent). And
while three-quarters of likely attendees believed Obama and Edwards were
willing to say what they think, only half the voters believed she would say
what she thought.[123] She was back where she started at the beginning of
the campaign.

THE IOWA ENDGAME

Days after the Jefferson-Jackson dinner Penn reported that Clinton was
now in trouble. Her negatives had risen sharply in the poll after the dinner,
and he blamed the trouble on positive press for Obama, as well as attacks
from Obama and Edwards.[124]

All of her team—particularly Hillary and her husband—resented
Obama's ability to look clean while his campaign fought dirty.[125] Obama
explained away his campaign's irregularities as innocent mistakes while
claiming—in nonattack attacks—that her hardball tactics were evidence
of overweening ambition and entitlement.

At a dinner with the editorial board of the *Des Moines Register*, the board
praised the Obama and Edwards campaigns for their efficiency and asked

Clinton why her campaign, in contrast, was so lackluster. The reporters wanted a good fight and succeeded at getting under her skin. The next morning she exploded on the staff conference call:

> We're getting outhustled here...not a field problem, it's not a political problem, it's a messaging and communications problem. Their message is beating us here, their press team is beating us here, their overall communications is just better than us here, and we have to do something.... This is all about Iowa, we need to win there, decision makers need to go do Iowa.... Everybody's got to go.[126]

Hillary's next press conference became a much bigger story. She was still steaming when she took on Obama directly. She questioned his "ethics, character" and "courage," and said she would spend the next month alerting Iowa voters to "a troubling gap between Obama's high-minded rhetoric and his political performance." Her examples of his Chicago-style opportunism—a sweetheart deal on his home from a corrupt developer; his slush fund; his dodging tough votes in the Illinois legislature; his lack of specificity on many topics—were all overshadowed by her preamble: "Now the fun part starts."[127]

That sentence was a "cringe moment" for campaign consultants who liked and respected Clinton. When she called intraparty combat "the fun part," she became a "warrior woman" in a suit of armor—not a person revealing her personal warmth.[128]

The campaign threw everything they could at Obama. The lack of strategic planning and coordination in her campaign was glaringly obvious. Some of the charges were easily turned or deflected, and some hurt Clinton more than Obama. When Bill Clinton called Obama a "roll of the dice," Obama had an answer—from an unlikely source:

> The truth is, you can have the right kind of experience and the wrong kind of experience. Mine is rooted in the real lives of real people and it will bring real results if we have the courage to change. I believe deeply in those words. But they are not mine. They were Bill Clinton's in 1992, when Washington insiders questioned his readiness to lead.[129]

Five months after Wolfson, Solis Doyle, and Grunwald had argued to air Hillary's personal story, the campaign aired the ad about her upbringing and her mother. She started talking about her mother in stump speeches, and then—another first—appeared with both her mother and her daughter on the campaign. But how were the two story lines supposed to fit together?

ELECTION

In the days before the delegates were selected in Iowa, no one knew for sure what would happen. Penn estimated that turnout would be about 90,000, 25 percent lower than in 2004. By fall he upped his estimate to 150,000. The Obama field operation expected a turnout between 167,000 and 180,000. Gordon Fischer, a former Iowa state party chairman, thought the turnout could reach 200,000, but no one else took that prediction seriously.[130]

A few hours before midnight on New Year's Eve, the single most important public poll of the campaign was placed online—the *Des Moines Register*'s final poll. Joann Seltzer, their pollster, had two bombshells. First, there would be a historic, astronomic influx of independents and young voters that suggested a turnout of at least 220,000. The other bombshell was her numbers: Obama, 32 percent; Clinton, 25 percent; and Edwards, 24 percent.

The *Register* poll kept count of people who said they would not caucus as well as those who said they would. After studying their results Penn went back and did a new poll himself but with a broader sample than usual. The poll confirmed the basic *Register* findings: Obama at 41 percent, Clinton at 30 percent, and Edwards at 24 percent.[131]

After Penn went over the numbers again, he sent Clinton a last-minute email hedging his predictions: if turnout was "radically different" from 2004, "the outcome will be radically different" for Clinton. Clinton went "apeshit." They had spent a fortune on developing scientific targeting in the 2006 campaign, and now Penn was saying they might be operating on the wrong assumptions about the electorate![132]

The Democratic candidates had just spent 50 million dollars and much of a year in one small state competing for 1 percent of the delegates to the nominating convention. And not one of them came close in their predictions. Everywhere in Iowa, attendance soared; twice as many people attended in 2008 as in 2004, a total of 250,001.

After supper on the big day, the former Iowa governor Tom Vilsack, a key Clinton supporter, walked into his hometown caucus site in Mount

Pleasant (pop. 8,751) and saw a roomful of people he didn't recognize. The sheer size of the crowd unnerved him.[133] None of the candidates had opened a field office in Henry County, working instead from field offices in Burlington, twenty-nine miles away. The Orange Bowl was on TV. The temperature was -2 °F. And yet, in a county of 20,000 people, 1,400 people caucused, compared to 605 in 2004.

Vilsack had no reason to think the crowd in Mount Pleasant was bad for Clinton...until he saw supporters of the minor candidates—the ones who didn't have a hope of getting to 15 percent—move to their second choice. Very few chose Clinton as their second choice. By the time he got back to Clinton's headquarters in Des Moines, he was certain she would lose.[134]

Hillary's senior staff started the day believing she would clinch the nomination within thirty days—win or lose; staffers in the Clinton boiler room were turning green. Vilmain had been sure Clinton had the numbers; now she urged Terry McAuliffe to prepare the Clintons for a third-place finish. McAuliffe minced no words: "we're going to get our ass kicked."[135]

Hillary had never expected to finish third. She had never lost an election; she had never had a tough primary. She was completely unprepared. When she made the obligatory congratulations call to Obama she managed one sentence: "Great victory, we're three tickets out of here, see you in New Hampshire."[136]

Clinton now had to get over the shock and make a most unexpected speech. A huge national audience would be watching her performance. Jerry Crawford, her Midwest coordinator, was in the room, and he marveled at her resilience. She was the "ultimate prizefighter who has taken the ultimate punch and pulls herself together and doesn't get knocked off stride and goes downstairs and performs."[137]

She dumped the prepared concession speech and spoke extemporaneously—with her customary precision. Addressing the local and national audiences, she stressed there was a long road ahead and thanked everyone in Iowa.

Before she made her concession speech she looked at her key aides and said: "I'm doing what you all asked me to. Every time you ask me to do something, I've done it. Would you just give me a clear understanding of precisely what my mission is here?"[138] That was damning whether it was true or not. Either her team was offering her poor advice or she was not listening to them. While Hillary *may* have done everything she was asked to do, she didn't hear what she needed to hear when she needed to hear it.

Later, after her speech, when they were discussing whether to attack Obama, she sighed and said, "Maybe they just don't like me."[139] That poignant comment by a spurned candidate is another indictment of her campaign management. How much voters liked her depended upon which Hillary they were allowed to see.

Obama had money, a plan, an electrifying stump speech, and proof he could be "enough like us" to win in Iowa. He had spent eighty-three days in Iowa, and his team had spent an entire year building an organization neighborhood by neighborhood to connect him with persons totally unused to thinking about voting for an African American—at any level. What would happen in states where he had nothing but paid media and a few visits? None of his team had any illusions that one expensive victory would necessarily convince white and Hispanic voters he was both electable and enough like them to be more reliable than Clinton.

If Obama won in New Hampshire, it would all be easy the rest of the way. If not, it would depend upon grinding out delegates state by state.

New Hampshire

At four o'clock the next morning, Clinton arrived in New Hampshire for five days of nonstop campaigning. Her day began with a critical conference call with her senior advisors. Wolfson, Grunwald, and Penn were still in Iowa. For the first time in the entire campaign, her husband also sat in on the call. The team was in total disarray, too beaten down to rise to the occasion. They were tongue-tied and depressed. Penn sounded like he was drugged, with thick and sluggish speech. Solis Doyle wasn't there; overwhelmed, she had gone back to Washington without telling anyone. The silence on the call was deadly.

Hillary took the lead; she was ready to get a new game plan in order. She had analyzed Iowa and decided what was wrong: they had "ceded people under thirty," neglected younger women, and had underestimated Edwards's Iowa strength. "We need to do things differently....We need to mix it up," she said, throwing out some possibilities for the next step. Again, there was only a long silence.[140] Finally Clinton spat out, "This has been very helpful talking to myself," and hung up.

Any explanation for defeat contains an implicit plan for victory. Hillary had to figure out why she lost in order to know what she should do next. The senior staff all had ideas about what to do next, but they were incompatible, and no one could lay out the options clearly for her to decide. She had to decide if the problem was Iowa, her strategy, or her team. Wolfson, Solis Doyle, and Grunwald all thought the personal biography she showcased at the end—six months after it had been prepared—helped her get back into the game. Was the answer to change her message, change the way she campaigned, or—as Penn and her husband fervently believed— attack Obama?[141]

Hillary overruled Penn and her husband: "Where are we going? It's just throwing stuff against the wall."[142] She had never had any compunctions about going for the jugular. Yet at that moment, she saw no benefit to assaulting Obama. Attacks would help her only if they made a contrast, which left her looking more like the president people wanted.

She had campaigned upon inevitability and thirty-five years of experience; was she so few people's second choice because of her policies or her presumption? Only 8 percent of the caucus participants thought electability mattered when they made their choice. No longer inevitable, how should she change her message? While 20 percent of the caucus participants were looking for experience, 52 percent said that their priority was change. What to say now?

When she got to her first event that morning at 8 a.m., she went backstage with her New Hampshire team and a group of longtime supporters, including Shumaker, the man who had asked her whether a rock star could do retail thirteen months earlier. Now she was ready. She immediately decreed a style befitting a challenger. The campaign had become "too imperious, her events too much like White House events," she said. "I want to take questions at every single event."[143] Hillary began campaigning for the nomination, asking for a chance to lead the party.

Her trump cards were still her experience and the best grasp of the issues. New Hampshire voters knew little about Obama; he had spent far fewer days and run far fewer ads there. Hillary, on the other hand, had been coming there for sixteen years of campaigning, and spent four years at Wellesley College just sixty-one miles away. New Hampshire was a state where she already had connections everywhere.[144]

Clinton started hammering Obama about the difference between inspirational rhetoric and legislative results in New Hampshire. She called him a talker, with no accomplishments, in contrast to the president who should be a doer that could pass legislation.

The personal animosity between Obama and Clinton was so intense by now that both candidates were having trouble controlling themselves. This time it was Obama who went too far. At a Saturday debate in New Hampshire, he was unable to contain his resentment. Gene Spradling, the WMUR (Manchester) news anchor, asked Clinton about experience and likability:

What can you say to the voters of New Hampshire on this stage tonight, who see a resume and like it but are hesitating on the likability issue, where they seem to like Barack Obama more.

"That hurts my feelings," she said, drawing laughs. "He's very likable. I agree with that. I don't think I'm that bad." Before she could move on to talk about experience Obama cut in with, "You're likable *enough*, Hillary."[145]

Obama's remark, delivered, he later realized, in a rude and condescending manner, was repeated over and over on local television. Independents and wavering voters were already moving back to Clinton, and the debate had not slowed the movement.[146]

On Monday, less than sixteen hours before the first votes would be cast, Clinton went from trying to *appear* open to being so open that she unnerved both campaigns. At a coffee shop where she was talking with sixteen women, a middle-aged woman from Portsmouth asked, "How do you do it?...How do you keep upbeat and so wonderful?" Clinton couldn't keep her guard up. Her voice wavered, and her eyes were moist as she answered, "It's not easy and I couldn't do it if I didn't passionately believe it was the right thing to do....I don't want to see us fall backwards. You know, this is very personal for me." The women applauded her and some of them, including the woman who had asked the question, got teary themselves.

Only twice before had a candidate gotten teary in public, and both moments were enshrined in political lore as disasters. In 1972 Ed Muskie had a tear on his check when denouncing a particular slanderous story in the *Manchester Union Leader*. In 1987 Congresswoman Pat Schroeder burst into tears when she announced that she "Couldn't figure out a way to run."

Clinton and her campaign staff all thought she had just blown the election with what she called a "Muskie moment," but they soon concluded it was playing well. At Obama headquarters, Plouffe assumed that anything so unexpected from a calculating opponent must have been "deviously contrived and staged," but Axelrod saw it as a "moment of humanity from someone who badly needed to show one."[147]

In the last two days before the election there were five major public polls of New Hampshire. Obama led by an average of 8 percentage points. Hillary knew how bleak it looked. She asked Patti Solis Doyle what all the options were if she lost, and Solis Doyle laid them out, ranging from fighting on until the last dollar was spent to withdrawing at once.[148] The polls were off by an average of ten percentage points. When the final vote had been tallied, instead of Obama by 8 it was Clinton by 2.

Winning in New Hampshire was at least as good as winning Iowa. Like Ronald Reagan in 1980 or George H. W. Bush and Michael Dukakis in 1988, she could come out of New Hampshire with the wind at her back. She started to call herself the "comeback kid," just as her husband had after his second-place finish in 1992 saved his campaign after three months of tabloid frenzy.

Before the early wave of leaked, partial exits polls trickled in, Hillary had already shaken things up by demoting Solis Doyle and bringing in Maggie Williams, her former White House chief of staff, to run the show. The last straw was Solis Doyle *mentioning* that withdrawing was one of the options if Obama won New Hampshire—Clinton considered that an act of supreme disloyalty.[149]

With or without Solis Doyle, her team still could not work together or agree on what worked in New Hampshire. Bill Clinton was now acting more like a doting spouse or a deposed monarch than a skilled politician. He believed that they had to go after Obama; after all, he had gone after Paul Tsongas and Jerry Brown in 1992. The other advisors thought that his advice was wrong but hadn't figured out how to tell that to a former president.[150]

SEEDS THAT SPROUTED

All the concern about developing a workable process and mutual trust between Obama and his family, friends, and the campaign staff was starting to pay off, and so were all the innovations and gambles on new technology and organization.

In late 2007 their wildest projection was that they could raise $10 to $15 million online in January if they won Iowa, but they ended up raising $36 million that month. Obama's campaign had made it clear that they wanted to keep the people involved. They didn't ask supporters for money very often, and they didn't give big donors and fund-raisers a special elite name. While most of Clinton's major donors had already maxed out at the $2,300 ceiling, wave after wave of Obama donors started signing up for subscriptions, giving a few dollars every month.[151]

They saw at once Hillary's retail campaign was hurting Obama. "[Clinton] looked like she was fighting for it and that she was very much on ground level," Axelrod noted. "We looked like we were sailing above...hoisted on people's shoulders."[152] She had reversed the contrast: now Obama was on a pedestal, while she was on the ground close to the people.

Iowa and New Hampshire yielded a combined sixty-seven delegates and twenty superdelegates. In exactly twenty-eight days, there would be nearly 1,700 delegates up for grabs in sixteen states and seven caucuses. Before then, though, there were two other states that could provide the momentum needed to steamroll into Super Tuesday: the Nevada caucus in eleven days and the South Carolina primary in eighteen days.

Obama immediately moved to try stilling doubts about his experience with endorsements. Two days after losing in New Hampshire, he played his John Kerry trump card, the endorsement he had saved for a rainy day. Kerry stressed that Obama was experienced enough to be president and called for passing the baton to a new generation—an implicit dig at both Clintons. Endorsements started coming in from important Democrats who feared that Clinton would be a drag on their ticket. The campaign shined as much light as possible on Senator Claire McCaskill of Missouri, and Governors Kathleen Sebelius of Kansas and Janet Napolitano of Arizona, whose endorsements helped Obama with white, college-educated women who liked both Obama and Clinton.[153]

Peter Hart equated Obama's challenge with Gary Hart's in 1984: balancing credibility with generality. Obama's appeal, like Hart's, was the pledge of rising above party to seek a new consensus. He could persuade people that he could forge a consensus around new ideas only if he were deliberately vague about what he would do. Voters were united in the belief that the American house needed repairs, but "half want to shore up the floorboards and the other half wants to fix the roof. They may all want to unite, but unite around what?" Obama could only attract both groups—floor first and ceiling first—if he wasn't forced to say which he would do first.[154]

Nevada

The campaign was now a protracted battle, but Clinton's aversion to caucuses was so intense after Iowa that she wanted to ignore the eight remaining caucuses. However, since Florida primary was off the map, she realized that she would have to win *somewhere* in the month between New Hampshire and Super Tuesday. Since more than half the South Carolina voters would be African American, she agreed to spend time in Nevada.[155]

In contrast to her Iowa staff, Clinton's Nevada team was disciplined, adequately funded, and seldom obstructed by the central command.[156] Consequently, Clinton won the caucus easily, 51 percent to 45 percent.

South Carolina

No one had ever tried to use volunteers to mobilize black voters in a state like South Carolina before. Democratic candidates all relied on giving "walking around money" to local black politicians for them to use for GOTV. Obama's local supporters worried that they would be left high and dry by the nontraditional way Obama ran his campaign. "There are no volunteers in South Carolina politics," one told Plouffe. "You need to pay for your help—and your turnout." Iowa campaigns just wouldn't work here.[157]

Plouffe sent two white men to build their organization because they couldn't afford the local politicians. The irate local black elite told Plouffe, "Now you are telling us to do it a different way—you people who have no idea how to win our elections."[158]

The local staffers immediately changed from stylish, modern campaign buttons to buttons with pictures, so the rural and less educated residents would know Obama was black. Michelle was featured prominently because she was much darker skinned; people needed to know Obama wasn't "putting on airs" by marrying a light-skinned woman.[159]

Most of the black leaders seldom had tough primary challenges and had rusty organizations with limited capacity. Most of them were male and traditionally patriarchal about women. African American women and younger blacks flocked to the Obama campaign. The Obamas were as glamorous and exciting to them as JFK and Jackie were to young Catholics just earning acceptance from Protestant America.

On primary day, 13,000 Obama volunteers were on the streets of South Carolina, 11,000 of them from that state. Hillary Clinton received 140,000 votes, enough for an easy win in 2004—only enough for a very distant second in 2008. Obama more than doubled her vote, capturing 55 percent of the total vote and 8 percent of the black vote.[160]

When Bill Clinton realized that Obama would win in South Carolina, he decided to highlight Obama's dependence on the black vote to downplay the implications of the win for later primaries. When a reporter asked him if it took two Clintons to beat Obama in South Carolina, he reminded the reporter that Jesse Jackson Sr. "won South Carolina twice."[161]

It's a standard practice to point out that a rival's victory in a state is due to a high concentration of some ethnic or religious group. Bill Clinton's racial references, however, hit raw nerves among many Democrats. In arguing that only his wife was electable, many voters thought he was trying to *make* Obama unelectable. He outraged many Obama supporters and made it harder for hard-core Democratic Party regulars to support Hillary despite their doubts about Obama's commitments to the party.

Obama was getting under the skin of Clinton's black supporters in Congress and their allies in the black establishment. Charges of racism cut to the soul and threaten identities. "The people who don't like the Clintons have found the Clintons' worst nightmare—a very dynamic, talented black man to run up against them," one of Hillary's most powerful black supporters, Black Entertainment Television founder Bob Johnson, told reporters. Johnson had fought hard—and had done well while doing good—and he did not think Obama's heart was in fighting for blacks. He considered Obama a "guy who says, 'I want to be a reasonable, likable Sidney Poitier in *Guess Who's Coming to Dinner.*'...For the uninitiated, that's how you call someone an Uncle Tom in an age that has not read *Uncle Tom's Cabin*."[162]

These statements mitigated Obama's problems with the party establishment. Black congressional representatives supporting Clinton started to get angry calls from constituents calling them "house Negro" and "handker-chief head."[163] The angry rhetoric from the Clinton campaign also angered Senator Edward Kennedy, who had wanted to stay neutral. Hillary's staff, supporters, and strategists in New England desperately tried to convey Kennedy's unhappiness to her top staff, but there still were no good communications between the top staff and any teams on the ground.[164]

Caroline Kennedy had never endorsed a candidate in the primaries, but she and her Uncle Teddy were getting pressure from their children and both endorsed Obama now.[165] The one-two Kennedy endorsement bonanza on the two days after South Carolina was manna from heaven.

SUPER TUESDAY

A true test of any campaign organization is its ability to keep the right metric—delegates—in focus. In an economics textbook, the right metric might be obvious, but keeping it in mind is seldom easy when so many important people rely on the press for their assessments of how a campaign is doing.

The Obama campaign had been working on evaluating the expected value of campaign visits in terms of the delegate haul, not the size of the state or the total number of delegates. They had targeted all the caucuses—very expensive per voter but inexpensive per delegate—and now were focusing on delegates, not headlines.

The comparison of delegate hauls for Idaho and New Jersey symbolize the folly of a primary strategy that didn't focus on delegates. Before Super Tuesday, reporters, fund-raisers, and Obama all kept asking Plouffe why Obama was visiting Idaho when he was only visiting California twice. If they skipped Idaho en route to California they could make one or two more stops. And a stop in Delaware?[166]

Plouffe explained that it was the difference between the importance of a state and the value of a visit—the delegate "bang per buck."[167] The benefit in delegates they could expect from the visit to Boise far outweighed the value of a few hours in California.

Obama's campaign had already spent $5.6 million in California, and over one-third of all voters had voted early by mail. Clinton would win there but not by enough to get a delegate bonus. Meanwhile, the huge rally in Delaware would receive massive media coverage in parts of

New Jersey, whereas yet another California visit would not get much media coverage—locally or nationally.

In Idaho, Obama's 16,880 votes to her 3,652 votes earned him fifteen delegates to Clinton's three—a net gain of twelve.[168] In New Jersey, Clinton beat Obama in the popular vote 613,500 to 501,372, which got her a fifty-nine to forty-eight edge in delegates. Thanks in part to his Delaware visit and the coverage it earned in neighboring New Jersey, Obama outdid her for the price of one visit each to Idaho and Delaware and one paid staffer in Idaho for six weeks.

On the day Clinton thought she would clinch the nomination, Obama won twenty-one more delegates. The visits to Delaware and Boise, the money spent in New York in 2007 when he was third in Iowa and doubling down, and the close attention to the rules all were on the money.

After Nevada, Clinton never contested another caucus. She left Obama to get the bonus from big wins and tried to win the election while ignoring the caucuses and the delegate selection rules that placed a premium on losing efficiently.[169] Without the caucuses, the election would have been nearly a dead heat.

ENDGAME

After Super Tuesday Obama gave her two big openings, but Clinton was unable to capitalize without inflicting damage on herself.

A week after Super Tuesday, ABC News aired a story about Obama's preacher, Rev. Jeremiah Wright. The excerpts from videotaped sermons were incendiary and as angry, anti-white, and anti-American as a 1960s Black Nationalist. Wright called the United States the "U.S. of KKKA" and after September 11, 2001, he preached that "America's chickens...are coming home...to roost."[170] Obama couldn't brush this off; Wright figured prominently in his autobiography and inspired both the theme of his legendary convention speech and the title—"The Audacity of Hope"—of his second book. As *Rolling Stone* wrote in February 2007, for the son of two atheists to choose Wright as his sounding board and bridge to Christianity gave Obama "as openly radical a background as any significant American political figure has ever emerged from, as much Malcolm X as Martin Luther King Jr."[171] Later, Obama was videotaped at a fund-raiser making disparaging comments about "bitter" whites who had nothing but religion and guns to console them.

Clinton—and her husband—asserted that Obama did not have enough white support to beat the Republicans in November. "Hardworking white Americans" supported her, she pointed out in speeches.[172]

A year earlier, the videotaped sermons on sale at the church could have derailed Obama and Clinton would have been inevitable. Now that voters had been following him for a year, it was hard to persuade many voters that Obama agreed with Rev. Wright, and that Clinton would be a better president than a man with a racist pastor.

The woman who had dubbed the war room just flailed away. She had been present at its creation when the 1992 campaign deployed state-of-the-art technology, always trying to anticipate the opposition's counterattack before making a move, while striving to keep strategy and tactics in line. In 1992 one of Carville's major rules was to stay out of the way when your opponent is self-destructing. As she pounded Obama, her own ratings dropped. Fewer people considered her trustworthy or honest. Democrats now regarded Obama as more honest, more trustworthy, and more electable.[173]

In response to Senator Clinton, Obama managed to send simultaneous "black enough" and "white enough" signals while offending no one. He told a crowd in North Carolina that "when you're running for president, then you've got to expect it." He then brushed his shoulders as if flicking dust away.

It was a simple gesture, but it spoke volumes. And it did so in completely different ways for different demographics. For older white voters, Obama was dismissively brushing off Senator Clinton's claim about electability and race. For black voters and younger white voters, he was making a loud and clear cultural and racial reference that implied she was putting him down. They were familiar enough with Jay-Z's song "Dirt Off Your Shoulder" to know the line "If you feelin' like a pimp nigga, go and brush your shoulders off."[174]

CONCLUSION: TOO LITTLE, TOO LATE

The night after Barack Obama clinched the nomination, an African American mother tucked in her children. "You know this is a big deal, right?" she asked them. Her daughters assured her they did. "But it would have been a big deal if Hillary Clinton had won," ten-year-old Malia Obama told her mother, "because women couldn't vote for a long time, either."[175]

Hillary Clinton did not lose because she had insurmountable negatives, limited appeal, or an unbeatable opponent. And she did not lose because she had a fatally flawed strategy. All candidates have some insurmountable negatives, limits to their appeal, tough opponents, and flawed strategies. She morphed into a stronger candidate after New Hampshire and was the personal equal of Obama on the campaign trail. While she was personally resilient, her campaign was inflexible and rudderless. She put pollster Penn in charge of evaluating strategist Penn and assumed that bitter dissension over strategy would not matter if everyone kept to his own lane. But the dissension made it nigh impossible to build the new lanes that are critical in a national primary, the ones that never mattered in her husband's 1996 reelection or in her statewide Senate elections.

If she had been quicker to recognize the move toward the Democrats among Independents and young voters, she would not have based affirmation of her character upon policies at the expense of her personal biography. Presidents have a brand name with all voters, but challengers must expand theirs, and she did not.

Voters always care about personal character in a challenger, and primary voters always want to know the direction in which a challenger will take the party. The rhetoric Clinton used in debates throughout 2007 was more self-centered and credit-claiming—and less inclusive and unifying—than that of Obama. Whether she was trying to act above the fray and project inevitability, or even Thatcher-like strength, she used self-centered "I-words"—I have, I am, I will—50 percent more frequently than she used "we" words.[176] While she was asserting her preeminence, he was trying to build relations with the audience.

Late in the campaign when new senior advisors were brought in, Geoff Garin, the pollster brought in to balance Penn, found "There were lots of people who spent a lot of time thinking about what to say about Barack Obama and not enough people waking up every morning thinking about how to make the case for Hillary Clinton."[177]

The supreme irony is that the person who ignored the polls and defended her legislative record looked more political than the person who paid attention to pollsters and strategists, and told people unpleasant truths to persuade them that he was authentic and not political.

Not coincidentally it was voters under thirty and Independents who provided Obama's entire Iowa margin. In fact, the turnout of young voters and

Independents there was not that different from 2004, when there was already a surge in turnout of both groups that was overlooked by Clinton's campaign. They scoffed at a Facebook-looking Obama crowd, but in reality 12,500 high school seniors participated in the caucuses, where the entire Obama margin over Clinton was fewer than 20,000 votes. Indeed, if the same proportion of voters by age and party identification had voted in 2004 as in 2008, Obama would still have won, albeit by a much narrower margin.[178]

When it was over, Penn acknowledged that inevitability resulted in a referendum: "Is Hillary perfect or not?" Later, when asked to rethink the strategy, all he could offer was attacking Obama sooner and raising more money to send a message. It never dawned on him that ignoring her weaknesses was a mistake, or that inevitability might have limited her appeal to new donors and voters. The campaign never managed to put Obama on the spot and force him to take sides, and the attacks they did launch lowered her ratings on trustworthiness and honesty.[179]

Looking back on the campaign, Geoff Garin credited Obama for tackling his weaknesses head-on: "Just as experience was Obama's unique burden, the question of what makes Hillary tick was her burden. Obama faced up to his; the Clinton campaign never faced up to hers."[180] She began her campaign as if she were a leader in exile, not someone with a vision for the future seeking to unify the opposition behind that vision and lead them to the White House.

INCUMBENTS: REGICIDE OR
MORE OF THE SAME

I knew that my first one-on-one encounter with President Jimmy Carter would be disconcerting. What I didn't know was that the president would end up disconcerted.

On October 26, 1980, three days before Carter's critical debate with Governor Ronald Reagan, I was at Camp David—where Roosevelt and Churchill planned the invasion of Europe and where Anwar Sadat and Menachem Begin agreed to a peace treaty—for final preparations and "war gaming." I had studied Reagan's speeches and interviews, and devised ways to counter his folksy arguments with intuitively appealing counterarguments instead of trying to deflate him with statistics.

I arrived after dark in a White House car. Everything was different from the way I had imagined it. The grounds were heavily forested, and the driver had to be careful to avoid the ubiquitous deer roaming the woods. Other than guards and the Secret Service, there were no signs of power, prestige, or modernity. I knew that there was a little three-hole golf course put in for President Eisenhower, but by daylight it was barely noticeable amid the wooded walkways. The small guest cottages scattered around the main buildings and meeting rooms were more like national park campgrounds than a prestigious retreat, and the meals prepared by navy cooks were suited more for a military base than a state dinner.

I didn't realize that the buildings at Camp David—renamed by Eisenhower for his grandson—would be so rustic. It felt like a place more for meditation than mediation. Only years later did I come to fully appreciate why isolation, spartan quarters, and a total lack of ostentation and luxury were the attraction of Camp David. The total change of scenery and the absence of any pomp gave the busiest, most heavily pressured and burdened person an opportunity to recharge his batteries. Even before the Internet and cell phones, there was never a moment without important calls to be returned, decisions to be made, and jobs to be delegated.

The next morning, I walked into the main building to join the communications team. Carter's pollster and press secretary, Pat Caddell and Jody Powell, took me aside. They were going to try again to persuade Carter to have a mock debate, and since I knew Reagan's material backwards and forwards, I would be assuming the role of the former governor of California. Before we rejoined the others, they told me to do a "full Reagan"—I was to hold nothing back.

Flushed with adrenaline, I started to get nervous and confused. I was on both sides of the battle. Which part of me did I want to win: the pollster/writer or the debater? I wanted Carter's lines, which I had helped to write, to lead him past Reagan, but I also had to try and beat Carter with Reagan's lines so that the president would be ready.

The day before, while we all discussed preparations, the president had been calm and composed; now, while the camera crew was preparing to record the first debate session, Carter was on edge. Before we began he said, "Let's put a time limit on this."[1]

He would talk without notes, of course, while I had copies of Reagan's actual utterances. As I was shuffling and organizing the sheaves of paper, the president quipped, "If Mr. Reagan is not going to get ready for the debate, maybe we should postpone it again. He's done it six times already."

As soon as the session began, I dug in, going after Carter with the exact attacks Reagan was using. I spoke of worried Americans wondering why the president could not do more, and recalled presidents who had rallied the country through military and economic challenges bigger than those Carter had not been able to overcome. The attacks were powerful yet indirect; rather than calling the president weak or ineffectual, Reagan resorted to more subtle, coded criticisms that were harder to defend against. He appeared respectful of the office and the president, suggesting that Carter was hamstrung by defeatist Democrats in Congress. The genius of this tactic was forcing Carter to choose between rebutting the premise or the conclusion: Should he say "I am not weak" or "Democrats are not defeatists"? Contesting one point left him tacitly conceding the other.

The room was silent. People started to tense up; his staffers averted their gaze. I could see that Carter was bewildered. When I spoke he would alternately feign a smile or wrinkle his nose in disgust; look away from me in embarrassment or glare at me in anger. Then I noticed red spots on his cheeks, and hostile looks on the faces of Marine guards and Secret Service agents around the room.

After only eleven minutes of practice—time enough for only one question, plus a response and follow-ups—Carter looked away and muttered, "Why don't we stop?" This worried me—with only nine days left before the election, the race was neck and neck. The debate could be decisive.

Why was the president so tense and irritable? I had said nothing that Reagan had not been saying for months. Yet many of the people in the room—including, I realized, Carter himself—didn't know what Reagan was actually saying. Standing ten feet away from the angered president, I quoted what Reagan had said and would continue to say about America's declining stature under Carter:

> Weakness and vacillation have been the trademarks of the Carter foreign policy. How many other countries boycotted the [Moscow] Olympics, when our athletes, who had trained for four years, were forced to stay home? How many of our allies sold wheat to the Russians and technology to the Russians when we tried to impose an embargo on them?

The president looked lonely and vulnerable when he heard Reagan's critique in front of his wife, his closest friends, and his inner circle. He had lost his presidential aura. Everyone was uncomfortable. His chief domestic policy advisor, Stuart Eizenstat, an understated southern Jew who was nonetheless central to this group dominated by Southern Baptists, tried to dispel the discomfort and reassure the president everyone was still with him by singling me out as a Yankee Jew. "You didn't know Governor

Reagan was Jewish, did you?" Eizenstat said. "Well," I quipped, "Governor Reagan *is* from Hollywood."

Fighting the Last War

How could Carter be surprised by Reagan's everyday rhetoric? Why was he thrown off balance against an opponent whose lines he should have already known?

Carter was a veteran speaker and a strong debater, but he was doing terribly because he was trying to approach the debate the same way he did in 1976, when as a challenger he could contrast his personal values with President's Ford's results. He had not fully grasped that the landscape had shifted under his feet. Now *he* had four years of results. He didn't realize that this time, as the incumbent, he had to respond to Reagan's blows. He expected to get through the campaign talking only about his strengths and Reagan's weaknesses. But he could no longer simply attack; he had to defend the policies of the last four years, and he was not prepared to do so.

Carter tried to explain that the terrible economic times were easing. Reagan looked at Carter and rattled off the different groups Carter had blamed for the economic crisis: the American people (for being cynical and distrustful of government), Congress (for not supporting enough of his bills), the Federal Reserve Board (for its monetary policies), and OPEC (for raising oil prices). "The symbol of this administration," Reagan said, "is the president pointing his finger at someone else."

Reagan was trying to narrow the deference zone, the extent of "benefit of doubt" accorded the president. To preserve this zone, incumbents highlight their invisible accomplishments: all the bad things that *didn't* happen, and the good things that *did* while voters weren't paying attention. Challengers want incumbents to be debited for all the bad things that *did* happen when voters were attentive.

Challengers all claim they are speaking truth to power, on behalf of "the people" they listened to and learned from during their campaign, while the incumbent was in Washington. In 1976 Jimmy Carter campaigned everywhere saying, "I am not a politician." In his debates with President Ford, challenger Carter had said, "We won the nomination by going out into the streets, barbershops, beauty parlors, restaurants, stores, in factory shift lines, also in farmers' markets, and livestock sale bars—and we talked a lot and we listened a lot. And we learned from the American people."[2] In 1980 it was Reagan talking about what he had learned from the people, and what they thought about government waste and mismanagement.

Carter's uncertainty about how to criticize Reagan and defend himself reflected his lack of readiness for his new debate role as the incumbent. Whereas challengers offer hope and change, the incumbent has no alternative to offering, in James Carville's perfect phrase, "more of the same." Carter wanted to talk about his character and virtue, and he was not ready to explain why his last four years were a stepping-stone to four better years. Like so many candidates before and after him, Carter was fighting the last war.

Fighting the last war is fighting the wrong war. As the legendary executive coach Marshal Goldsmith tells CEOs, "What got you here won't get you there."[3]

Early in the second debate-preparation session, the subject turned to Reagan's simplistic energy policy. "Listening to Gov. Reagan," Carter said, "I was reminded of myself four years ago. I've been in the White House now for almost four years as president, and I've learned to appreciate more and more a statement that H. L. Mencken made, that 'for every difficult question there's a simple answer: easy, glib, and wrong.'"

No one in the room saw the deep irony of what he was saying. When Carter compared Reagan's simple and naïve claims to his own statements in 1976, he was criticizing Reagan for using rhetoric that Carter had used successfully when he was a challenger.

A scene like Carter's debate preparation has occurred in every incumbent president's campaign before a debate. The reasons vary, but the one constant is that presidents resent debate practice. Presidents typically feel that their challengers are unworthy, and having their motives questioned in mock debates unsettles them.[4] From Ford in 1976 through George W. Bush in 2004, every incumbent president has fidgeted and insisted that he didn't need to go through mock debates. For example, in his first practice session, Ford suddenly looked at his watch and announced, "I think this is enough." Former senator George Mitchell "clobbered" Bill Clinton in an early mock debate in 1996. In 2004 Bush was so irritated and distracted that aides finally moved the sessions to Crawford, Texas, so Bush would have fewer reasons to interrupt.[5]

Presidents believe they are still in touch with the country because they hold town meetings, chat with championship teams and Olympic medalists, visit with important constituents, read the polls, and hold press conferences. In fact, they are as out of touch as Hans Christian Andersen's naked emperor. They do not realize just how insulated they are in the presidential bubble. "[A president] never leaves the White House," White House staffer Michael Berman said, "I don't care where he is, he is [in the White House]…and the intimidation of people by being in the presence of the president is extraordinary."[6]

George Reedy learned from serving in the Kennedy and Johnson White Houses and spending time in others as a reporter that White House life is the life of a royal court. The White House is organized to relieve the president of anything that gets in the way of his concentration or comfort. As a result, "it is only a matter of months until they become part of an environment which he necessarily regards as his just and due entitlement—not because of the office but because of his mere existence.…No one ever invites him to 'go soak your head' when his demands become petulant and unreasonable."[7]

The military term "campaign" is derived from the words for open country (*nella campagna* or *dans la compagne*) and is an apt metaphor. After wintering in its barracks, the king's army would take to the field. In a reelection the elected leader must expose himself, defend his administration's policies, and justify his right to continue in office. No president has an easy time having his authority challenged, but it forces him momentarily out of the bubble in which he has no choice but to live, given the pace and demands of the office.

Psychologically and organizationally, this simple point is difficult for incumbents and their staff and family to grasp. A victorious challenger enters Washington like a conquering hero, believing he is ready to govern at his inauguration. Challengers have spent years getting there, adjusting to the terrain and competition, and winning the support first of their party and then a plurality of the electorate. They all promised to change Washington, and they all think they are ready to enact it.

Every president believes people know more about what he has done than they do. Part of having a sizable enough ego to run (to say nothing of the ego boost that comes with winning), Joe Napolitan observed, is believing despite evidence to the contrary that "The whole country knows what you said and what your position is."[8]

As George W. Bush wryly noted when a victorious Barack Obama proclaimed he would change Washington, "When I campaigned for office, I said I was for change.... Everybody who campaigns is for change." Change, Bush pointedly added, is "a very effective slogan."[9] He might as well have said "*just* a slogan."

Challengers talk about the presidency as if the president *were* the government, as if the values and policies they espouse would become the values and policies of the entire government. The vanquished congratulate the victors and pledge cooperation and comity. But all the talk of a honeymoon and bipartisan cooperation is simply talk. "The good news for Bill Clinton is that he's getting a honeymoon in Washington," Senator Robert Dole said after the 1992 election. "The bad news is that Bob Dole is going to be his chaperone."[10]

Incoming presidents quickly become overwhelmed by the enormity of the job and the limits of their control. After four years of on-the-job training, they have a very hard time believing the public can take seriously a challenger who is naïve enough to claim he is ready to be president (as they themselves claimed four years earlier).

No president yet has accomplished more than he promised in his campaign, nor more than he actually *expected* to accomplish. And no president has found the job of president easier than he expected.

Presidents are surrounded by rivals who wanted to be president themselves. "Anybody like myself who has once made the decision that they want to give a State of the Union address... never ever permanently surrenders that," Senator Bob Kerrey told Bob Woodward.[11] These rivals do not cede legislative power, no matter how effusive their public pronouncements of cooperation. Just as Kerrey bumped heads with Clinton, members of the president's party always work to protect their personal reputation and prerogatives when they conflict with the president's national agenda.

General Dwight Eisenhower's 1952 landslide carried Republican majorities into power in the House and Senate, the first time in more than two decades that the Republicans had achieved unified control of the federal government. Despite all his expectations for his unified government, the newly elected Eisenhower lamented that "Republican Senators are having a hard time getting through their heads that they now belong to a team that includes rather than opposes the White House."[12]

Eisenhower campaigned as an avowed internationalist, was not an isolationist, and was committed to continuing America's international role with NATO and the United Nations. The Republican Senate old guard, on the other hand, considered the internationalism of the post–World War II era an aberration to be ended as soon as possible. Many conservatives feared that international organizations and treaties would strengthen the federal government at the expense of the states and possibly nullify southern segregation laws. Once in power, they were determined to use their newfound majority status to dismantle international security agreements like NATO, with or without support of the president, who had been NATO commander.[13]

The day after Eisenhower's inauguration, Senator John Bricker (R-OH) opened the first session of the Republican-controlled Senate with Senate Joint Resolution 1, known as the Bricker Amendment, a call for a constitutional amendment that weakened the power of the president by shifting most treaty-making power to Congress and state legislatures. Eisenhower privately considered it "stupid, blind isolationism." He was able to defeat it only with the legislative skills and support of Senate minority leader Lyndon B. Johnson.[14]

Bill Clinton came to Washington so confident about what he could accomplish with Democratic control of both houses of Congress that his transition team planned for a second 100 days to implement after the standard "first 100 days" plan was finished. The assumption was that the new budget and the health care overhaul would both be finished within three months. Clinton did not get a budget passed until August, and the health care initiative was an infamous failure.[15]

President George W. Bush and his strategist Karl Rove had fewer illusions about their ability to pass legislation, but they did have a sophisticated plan for making the Republican Party the majority party. Rove's plan included raising the Republican portion of African American voters by at least 4 percent and then implementing immigration reform that would court middle-class Hispanic voters who supported Republicans on economic grounds. Opposition within their own party derailed their attempts to build a Republic majority.[16]

During the 2008 campaign, Barack Obama time and again condemned the Bush administration's use of "enhanced interrogation techniques" used against detainees suspected of terrorism and vowed to close the Guantánamo Bay prison where many detainees had been held for years without any formal charges having been filed. In his first three years of office he neither closed Guantánamo nor ended use of the interrogation techniques he had vilified during the election.

In 2008, Obama contrasted his ability to change the system and restore bipartisanship with Hillary Clinton's ability to withstand partisan combat. After his first year in office, the polarization between Republicans and Democrats was greater than for any new administration in the last seventy years.[17] The Tea Party movement channeled the anxiety of middle-aged, middle-class voters that their Medicare and social security would be spent on undeserving poor and illegal immigrants, or bailing out banks and corporations.[18] In the 2010 midterm elections the Republicans regained control of the House of Representatives. Democrats worried that Obama would be another one-term president who left the party badly weakened. The party faithful debated whether Obama should act like Bill Clinton or Harry S. Truman to rescue his presidency and revive his party.[19]

In fact, by 2012 Obama was acting like both Clinton *and* Truman, trying to divide and conquer the opposition by putting Congress on the spot in the style of Truman, and "working the system, not changing it," in the manner he had criticized the Clintons for using.[20]

HARDER THAN IT LOOKS

All presidents come to power surrounded by the people who helped them produce and refine their vision of the future. In the campaign world, George Stephanopoulos wrote, the mortal sin is to be "off message."[21] In government, though, the very size and complexity of the administration make a unified message virtually impossible.

Early in his administration, President Obama had to leave a meeting on whether to rescue the Chrysler Corporation before he had gotten the information he needed to make his decision: he had to rush to a meeting on Afghanistan strategy, then decide how to react to North Korea's threatened launch of a rocket near Japan, and then respond to a major flood in Fargo, North Dakota. David Axelrod, tasked with developing a coherent message for the administration despite the crush of events, asked others, "What is this, a 'West Wing' episode?"[22]

If only a White House could be as harmonious as the one portrayed on *The West Wing*. The reality is less personal, less coherent, and less harmonious.

Everyone is operating with partial information. The people close to the president never have enough time to gather information. Lloyd Cutler, for example, served with distinction in several Democratic White Houses as senior counsel. Lawyers like to learn all the facts before making a decision, he noted, "But you don't have time to do that in the White House."[23]

Martin Anderson served in Nixon's and Reagan's White Houses and worked closely with four Republican presidential campaigns. When people come to the White House, he realized, they have no idea how the sheer size of government affects coordination among the key people around the president:

> People don't realize the extent to which the President of the United States is forced to delegate enormous authority.... The pressures that come in are incomprehensible. So when he says, "Do something,", he usually thinks, "Well, maybe it will get done". Most of the time, it doesn't get done, but he says, "Maybe it will get done." And he doesn't have time to follow up.[24]

Presidents have no choice but to delegate. This dilutes their attempts to shape and control the public messages from administration officials. Presidents and senior staff learn through painful experience that they cannot speak openly in any meeting of more than three people without someone leaking the comments to advance his own agenda. This presidential discretion does not rein in opportunistic staffers from trying to claim advantage over people not in the meeting.[25]

Few people ever get one-on-one time with a president, and many important people don't ever meet with the president except at picnics, state dinners, or public occasions. Peggy Noonan never met Reagan before she drafted his famous D-Day anniversary speech at Pointe du Hoc, France. Reagan didn't waste time articulating his ideas in person because his themes were clear enough for speechwriters to create a draft and leave the editing to him. President Clinton, at the other extreme, spent hours with the speechwriters going over their drafts. Speechwriter and communications director Don Baer nicknamed drafts of Clinton's speeches "fire hydrants" because "There's a physical act he essentially performs upon them."[26]

Face time with the president is the most valuable currency there is inside an administration. So many persons want "just a word or two" with the president that elaborate protocols develop in any White House for talking to the president. George Reedy, experienced with administrations from the inside and outside, saw the critical importance of rationing out the president's face time with others: "No one interrupts presidential contemplation for anything less than a major catastrophe somewhere on the globe. No one speaks to him unless spoken to first."[27]

In the Reagan White House, female reporters wore red dresses to press conferences because they were more likely to be called on. When President Clinton praised a particularly garish tie a reporter was wearing, other reporters started wearing similarly gaudy ties. To be the target of insincere presidential flattery, Michael Kinsley wrote, "is even more flattering than sincere flattery since it demonstrates a recognition that the recipients are powerful people who need to be kissed up to." In George W. Bush's White House, nothing bestowed more prestige than a nickname given by the president, caustic and derisive though they often were. Karl Rove had to endure being known as "Turd Blossom," the Texas name for a wildflower that sprouts in a cow patty.[28]

When the Obama family moved to the White House, its closest friends hoped to give them the same timely solace and support they had provided during the campaign, support that grew out of thirty years of shared life. After the election, one of their closest friends, Dr. Eric Whitaker, realized they hadn't grasped "how isolating this whole experience would be."[29]

The former *New York Times* reporter Todd Purdum, whose wife Dee Dee Meyers was a Clinton White House press secretary, saw that every White House is designed to keep a president distant "from friend and foes alike." If a very close friend is on the short list of *known* presidential friends, he might get the direct number to the Oval Office. The call will go through either the personal secretary or the director of Oval Office operations, and from there to the president's personal aide. If the timing and the president's mood are right, the call *might* go through. More often, they will arrange a call back when the president is in his limousine en route somewhere.[30]

Presidents have so many ceremonial duties or meetings that nearly all of the drama and passion occurs between their chief of staff and the rest of the government. It is in the chief's office, former Bush press secretary Marlin Fitzwater wrote, that toppled officials "shed their tears of goodbye.... Supreme Court nominees plead and appeal for more time, wars were planned, and petty arguments were held by the fistful over egos out of control."[31] The chiefs themselves are so busy that all but the most senior staffers never get to talk to them unless they get to the White House around 5:45–6:00 a.m. and catch them for a loose moment before their every moment is structured.[32]

The chief of staff's job description, as Carter's chief of staff Jack Watson reflected, is partly a javelin catcher. They take the heat to protect the president and they deliver as much bad news as possible. The functionality of a White House depends upon whether they know when messy debates require a meeting with the president, when a bruised ego needs presidential stroking, or when an irritated, overworked, or angry president has given an order he will regret later.[33]

When James A. Baker was appointed chief of staff to Ronald Reagan, he interviewed former chiefs about the job. The only way to protect a president, Dick Cheney told him, was with "an orderly paper flow." That meant a chief should "Be an honest broker. Don't use the process to impose your policy views on president." The other danger, Cheney learned, was the casual "oh by the way" decisions, made when someone wheedled something out of the president over drinks or dinner or as a meeting was breaking up.[34]

Given the importance of presidential statements on any imaginable subject, every presidential speech becomes, in Peggy Noonan's words, "a battle in a never-ending war…when the smoke cleared there was Reagan, holding the speech and saying the words as the mist curled around his feet. I would watch and think, 'That's not a speech, it's a truce. A temporary truce.'"[35] Every presidential speech has to have a paper trail so that no elegant phrase upsets delicate alliances, spooks Wall Street, overturns budgetary agreements, offends a powerful constituency, or rattles the wrong sabers. This, in turn, gives speechwriters good reason to stall on drafting a speech to protect their prose from lexical mutilation over endless "mere" policy concerns.[36]

A forum of former presidential press secretaries all nodded knowingly when Jody Powell said that one of the biggest jobs of the senior staff is to "know when the president really means what he is saying." And he stirred memories of past nightmares for all of them when he noted that the most dangerous people on the whole staff were those who ran off on their own and later used "the president told me to do it" as an excuse. When something went wrong, Powell continued, it was hard to know what had actually happened before he briefed reporters. "People, instead of telling me what happened, would try to tell you what they thought you ought to say about what happened."[37]

In an administration, not only is the number of critical people involved in every imaginable issue far greater than in a campaign, but so is the influence of the First Lady and close friends. In a war room, top staffers usually learn what the candidate is hearing from his family and close friends. Rosalynn Carter, Nancy Reagan and, of course, Hillary Clinton became valuable conduits for anyone in their good graces. Just as important are a president's friends: Harry Truman's poker pals, Ronald Reagan's "kitchen cabinet," nearly every president's golfing partners, or Gerald Ford and Richard Nixon's drinking partners.[38]

Media scrutiny of every moment of the First Family's day is more exhaustive than during the campaign. Eleanor Roosevelt, raised amid servants and governesses, was active in the first wave of feminist politics and was clueless about cooking. In the White House she had to become what the *Washington Post* called the "first housewife of the nation" and showcase "economy menus" to raise spirits of Americans struggling through the Great Depression. The only way she could endure the role of First Lady was to live her White House years "impersonally: ... It was almost as though I had erected someone outside myself who was the President's wife. I was lost somewhere deep down inside myself." Michelle Obama, a Harvard law graduate in an administration dealing with another severe economic crisis, became the champion of school nutrition and family garden plots.[39]

THE PRESIDENTIAL MESSAGE BOX

Every administration comes to power giving too much weight to the attractiveness of its message and not enough to the importance of the failings of the last administration. Once a new president is in power, he forgets that voters who preferred him to the alternative did not necessarily comprehend or support all of his intentions. He believes his victory was due to his vision and goals; he underestimates how much the loss of credibility for the previous president helped him and overestimates how much his own party supports him.

Slowly but surely, incumbents realize that they are not conquering heroes but commanders in chief whose views are worth as much as seventeen senators. If presidents agree with a bill, it takes a simple majority of senators or congressmen to pass it; when they disagree, it takes two-thirds of the legislators (17 more senators than a simple majority) to override the veto.

As incumbents prepare for their reelection, they must deal with the same issues they dealt with as challengers: positioning, avoiding parochialism, rectification, repositioning, and choosing the right enemies. But in each case, they have less latitude than the challenger. Challengers have the luxury of second-guessing incumbents; the incumbent's decisions cannot be reversed.

A president's message box is the polar opposite of the message box he used as challenger. The president will argue that the country should not "change horses in the middle of the stream," as FDR said, because he is safe and the challenger is risky. In 1976 Carter asked "Why not the best?" but in 1980 he tried to leave footprints and use definitive language that emphasized authority: terms like "strongly believe," "firm commitment," and "I have always stood for." In 2000 George W. Bush was a "compassionate conservative" decrying the depravity and decay of Washington, "where a man's word no longer counts." In 2004 his campaign argued that things were difficult but America should "stay the course" and that Bush was a strong leader whose bold actions made America safer and stronger.[40]

Once they have been elected, the role and rhetoric change. Incumbents want deference and the benefit of the doubt. They all want to emphasize things that only a president can preside over: Supreme Court appointments, treaties, summit conferences, and wars (both hot and cold). It is no accident that the specter of "the three a.m. call"—exemplified by an image of the red telephone connecting the president with a nuclear decision against shadowy enemies—is thrown in the face of every inexperienced challenger by the incumbent. Presidents have to convince voters that "mere reality" is better than hopeful promises of change.

The terrain will always be different in a reelection because the focus of voters will be on whether the incumbent's policies are working—and if not, why they should be continued.

All over again, incumbents must show that they have not been captured by Washington and lost touch with the ordinary people. They must decide which positions must be revised to rectify past errors, or how to explain discrepancies between what they preached then and they practiced in office. And above all, they must decide how to respond to the ways that current ideas about their political party are affecting them. As challengers they planned what kind of appeal would work best with centrists without alienating too many in their base. They worked to show commitment to some parts of their party's heritage and differences in other areas. Now they have to deal with their entire party, whether it is the majority or minority in Congress.

Since they are the bird in the hand that people have been watching for four years, it is far harder for them to reshape their image or to appear as free of inconsistencies as they were in the previous campaign. A challenger can promise less pollution and more jobs, or lower taxes and more services. Now the contradictions are apparent, and incumbents have disappointed supporters who got less than they expected on at least some issues they cared about.

Unlike challengers, presidents do not have to show a common touch and persuade people they can represent them. They don't necessarily have to campaign if they decide they are better off running *from* the White House. In 1972 Richard Nixon hardly campaigned at all, staying in the White House to deal with negotiations in Paris to end the war in Vietnam, and speaking during managed events in the Rose Garden. Infuriated journalists claimed that Nixon's Rose Garden strategy undermined the American system. It may have undermined the ability of journalists trying to get more coverage for their stories, but it was a reasonable decision on the part of Nixon to stay out of the way while his opponent was in trouble and unable to explain his policies.

Nixon, in fact, was following a strategy that Turner Catledge, editor of the *New York Times*, considered to be one of the most effective "stunts" an incumbent could use in his campaign—simply dramatizing himself in the job. In 1940, when President Roosevelt stayed in the White House, Catledge wrote that "He is lying low in the hope that his opponent will run himself to exhaustion around an open track or at least bark his shins against the fences built up out of some closely drawn controversial public questions."[41]

Bold Moves

Despite the difficulties of adjusting to a new war, incumbents have major options not available to challengers.

First, incumbents can use their veto power to differentiate themselves from Congress—particularly when the government is divided. Truman,

Nixon, Reagan, Clinton, and George W. Bush all found it easier to capture moderate voters when they were in the position of defending the center against the other party's extreme, instead of fighting with their own party.

Second, if the country is threatened or attacked, they are, as Lyndon B. Johnson said, "the only president you've got." They are the indisputable commanders in chief, the ones addressing a rapt nation from the Rose Garden or from behind the desk in the Oval Office. It is harder to criticize a wartime president, particularly early in any war.

Finally, incumbents have the power to undertake bold moves, like Nixon's world-changing visit to China. To this day, when Democratic strategists think about dramatic moves a president can make, they ask each other how to finish the sentence "If only Nixon could visit China, only a Democrat could..." Nixon's 1972 visit to China was a key part of his reelection strategy and made the rest of his foreign policy credible. When that trip was announced, liberals and conservatives alike were stunned. The defense of Taiwan and the total isolation of China were pillars of Cold War strategy among anti-communists in both parties, while antiwar liberals assumed that Mao Zedong would never deal with a hawk like Nixon. No one on the left could criticize the move to open talks with China. This bold move, in combination with voters' increasing belief that Nixon would honorably end the Vietnam War—the most important issue at the time—took the wind out of George McGovern's sails.[42]

McGovern had repeatedly pledged to end the war and get all the troops home immediately. But now voters didn't see Nixon as the unadulterated hawk. In one of the Watergate tapes, his chief of staff, Robert Haldeman, went over strategy with the president:

So little is known about McGovern, you'll have a better chance of changing people's mind about him...to start with, you got 40 percent of the people who will vote for you no matter what happens. You got 40 percent of the people who will vote against you no matter what happens, so you have got 20 percent of the people left in the middle who may vote for you or may not and that 20 percent is what you've gotta work on....You're so well known, your pluses are clear, clear as well as your minuses; that getting one of those 20 who is an undecided type to vote for you on the basis of your positive points is much less likely than getting them to vote against McGovern by scaring them to death about McGovern: and that, that's the area that we ought to be playing.[43]

DIVIDE AND CONQUER

In 1996 President Clinton was at risk. His first two years had been a string of failures and excesses, and Democrats had been soundly thumped in the midterm elections in 1994.

Senator Bob Dole's campaign to win the Republican nomination had two important elements. First, to win the nomination without a divisive fight, he had to stay close to Speaker of the House Newt Gingrich, one of the main engineers of the Republicans' midterm success.

Second, Dole needed a clear contrast to Clinton on welfare reform. This strategy would work only if the Republicans sent Clinton such tough conservative legislation that he refused to sign it. Ever since he had failed to pass health care reform, Clinton had been on shaky ground with centrists.

To Dole's horror, neither element panned out. Riding high from the midterm elections, Gingrich overreached on a game of brinksmanship with the executive branch, forcing a government shutdown and allowing Clinton to move ahead of Dole in the polls. The freshman Republicans, George Stephanopoulos recognized, "had become Newt's Frankenstein monster—and my new best friends. The more they dug in, the better off we were. Even pragmatic veterans adopted their kamikaze spirit."[44]

The Dole campaign tried all summer to keep the Republican-controlled Congress from passing a welfare reform bill that Clinton would sign into law. Dole sent Senate emissaries to Senate Majority Leader Trent Lott, asking him to defer the welfare compromise Clinton was amenable to so that he could use the veto against Clinton in the fall campaign. The Senate Republicans up for reelection, however, were desperate for a bill to pass, so Lott chose to pass the bill—and help Clinton. Once it passed, Dole's strategist Tony Fabrizio knew the campaign was sunk: "they aimed the torpedoes at the hull and then started throwing water at it."[45]

When Clinton signed the welfare reform months later, he angered parts of his base but persuaded many moderates he had Republican support. He put his challenger on the spot and showed voters that important segments of the out-of-power party supported him.

By his 2012 State of the Union address, Obama had taken a page from Truman's playbook. Instead of trying to work with Republicans and proposing bipartisan, moderate, post-ideological, legislative solutions to national problems, he called on Congress to act on behalf of popular goals without giving it a chance to shred or mock his proposals. His speech was filled with irrefutable lines like:

> This Congress should make sure that no foreign company has an advantage over American manufacturing.
>
> Send me a bill that bans insider trading by members of Congress; I will sign it tomorrow.
>
> Congress needs to stop the interest rates on student loans from doubling in July.
>
> I ask the Senate to pass a simple rule that all judicial and public service nominations receive a simple up or down vote within 90 days.[46]

RALLY ROUND THE FLAG

Facing a recession in late summer 2001, President G. W. Bush gradually morphed his 2000 campaign pledge to honor the sanctity of the Social Security funds—popularly called a "lockbox"—into a conditional pledge of sanctity "except in the event of recession, war, or a national emergency." After 9/11, he grimly joked, "Lucky me—I hit the trifecta."[47] In 2002, Bush began a push to expand the war on terror to Iraq on the premise that Saddam Hussein was accumulating weapons of mass destruction.

By 2004, there was very little reason to believe that any WMD would ever be found in Iraq, and no one in Bush's administration stood by its initial claims that the war would be fast, the occupation brief, and the costs covered by oil revenues from the revived economy of a newly democratic Iraq. Bush won none of the three 2004 debates with Senator John Kerry. He still won the election, albeit narrowly.

Unlike Clinton, Bush couldn't run against Congress and Democratic legislation because his party controlled both the House and Senate. But the country was at war, and it isn't easy to salute the flag while attacking the commander in chief.

Any time a president protects the country from an enemy, whether it is military or a natural disaster, the president gains prominence. Any reminder of death or danger heightens the amount of confidence and trust people are willing to place in national leaders. Even brief mentions of death prompt people to instinctively turn toward their leader and see him in a more charismatic light.[48] And unlike redistributive programs that take from some and give to others, defense against natural disasters or physical threats can provide benefits to all. The public viewed Bush as their defense against terrorists; criticism of their defender could easily appear to increase that threat.[49]

Many believed that Bush had mismanaged the war and grievously underestimated its costs. But no matter how a war is proceeding, the president is still the commander in chief. Rove grasped the major themes of the reelection campaign before they knew who the Democratic nominee would be: Bush was a Strong Leader who Leads a Strong Team through Bold Action. When the opponent turned out to be a senator who voted for the war and now criticized the decision, Rove gloated: "You're looking at the same intelligence the president is and arriving at the same conclusion, and if you accuse him of misleading the American people, what were you doing? Are you saying, I was duped?"[50]

When things are going badly, challengers can argue that the president is wobbly or weak, but it is hard to vehemently denounce the president. The best that experienced Democratic pollsters could find for congressmen and senators to use during a war was that the president was not up to the job. Rove, now a columnist and the head of an independent funding operation for conservative causes, laid out the line for 2012 in mid-2011: "Obama, frustrated and increasingly unsteady, is losing his cool. On his recent Midwest bus trip, for example, the president tried making a virtue of impotence, blaming others—including the GOP House—for his failures." Former governor Mitt Romney used similar language: Obama was well intentioned, but "out of his depth" and didn't understand "what makes America work." Romney's premise, his chief strategist Stuart Stevens told reporters, was that "this is a referendum on Obama, the economy is a disaster and Obama is uniquely blocked from being able to talk about jobs."[51]

DEWEY'S REAL HELL

To this day, incumbents from both parties invoke Harry S. Truman when they are far behind in the polls, promising to give their opponents as much hell as Truman did during his stunning, unexpected 1948 comeback. But while people remember his pithy and fiery stump speeches, his sophisticated Washington strategy played a far bigger role in defeating New York's governor Thomas Dewey.

The real hell Truman gave Dewey was in Washington, where he accomplished the legislative equivalent of Nixon visiting China—a combination of bold legislative confrontations and wily political cooptation of vainglorious Republicans—by exploiting two splits within the Republican Party to isolate and disarm Dewey.

First, Truman negated Dewey's ability to attack his foreign policy vulnerabilities by co-opting the Republicans Dewey needed to draw a credible contrast with Truman. Second, the president took advantage of a Republican-led Congress to establish his relevance. Rather than giving Congress specific bills that the GOP would immediately kill (while blaming Truman), he grabbed hold of general goals that voters heavily supported (e.g., ending rampant inflation) and challenged Congress to address them. Third, Truman redefined himself as organized labor's only hope by defying popular opinion and vetoing anti-union legislation, even though he knew his veto would be overridden. Fourth, he managed to throw a spotlight on the Republican Congress's lack of support for Dewey's moderate agenda. Finally, Truman outmaneuvered Dewey and effectively tied the Republican Congress to an agricultural crisis. And in the end it worked because Truman's campaign detected a change in terrain and responded forcefully before Dewey's team knew what was happening.

Before the 1948 campaign, Truman was as reviled as he is revered now. Union leaders called Truman the "number one strike breaker," and his friends and cronies were implicated in graft and corruption. People struggled with inflation plus shortages of meat, bread, and housing. Tired of waiting to return home, overseas troops mutinied, and there were hundreds of "bring back Daddy" clubs organized by servicemen's wives to force faster demobilization.[52]

In 1946, running on the slogan of "Had Enough?" the GOP took control of the Senate and House for the first time in sixteen years. The jubilant Republicans promised that every session of Congress would open with a prayer and close with a probe, while they cut taxes 20 percent, balanced the budget, and trimmed the national debt.

Until the last weeks before the Democratic National Convention, prominent union leaders like the head of the United Auto Workers Walter

Reuther, Minneapolis mayor Hubert Humphrey, Eleanor Roosevelt, Congressman Claude Pepper, and others were desperately trying to find a candidate to replace Truman, whom they described as "incompetent, unappealing, and unelectable."[53]

There was little or no sense of "we" in his fragmented party. A southern rebellion over the tough civil rights plank Hubert Humphrey had pushed through inspired Senator Strom Thurmond to run as the candidate of the Dixiecrat Party. On the Left, the former Democratic vice president Henry Wallace was the Progressive Party candidate for president, challenging Truman's domestic policies and arguing that communist moves in East Europe were defensive responses to American antagonism toward the Soviet Union. If that were not enough, some of the biggest unions intended to punish Truman, whom they denounced for breaking their crippling strikes after the war.[54]

Truman had to unite the party and persuade them not only that the Republican Party was wrong but that Dewey would govern like the conservative majority controlling his party in Washington, not the moderate Republican he was in New York and certainly not like the reasonable party platform his allies in the party had written.

Tying Dewey to the Senate majority leader Robert Taft was essential because Dewey differed in practice and ideology from Taft, whom he had defeated easily in the primaries. Known as "Mr. Republican," Taft was isolationist, anti–New Deal, and anti-union. The old guard supported him while the majority of Republican voters preferred Dewey, moderate by the standards of the time, a brilliant public speaker, a reformer, a civil libertarian, and a tough politician.

When the Republicans captured both houses of Congress in 1946, Truman began implementing the strategic advice of James Rowe, who had been an assistant to the president under Franklin D. Roosevelt. Rowe's now-famous memo stressed the importance of standing for goals instead of advocating specific programs. That strategy would avoid getting trapped and looking weak when the Republicans buried or shredded his programs. Instead, Truman should paint the Republicans into a corner: call upon them to pass legislation dealing with inflation, housing shortages, and the like. Then he should veto legislation that went too far. Truman kept that memo in his desk and relied upon it for the next two years.[55]

The Taft-Hartley Act placed severe limits on a union's right to call strikes, organize secondary boycotts, or expand, and it gave states the right to outlaw union shops. After the postwar strikes, Truman's veto was easily overridden with the support of nearly half of all Democrats in the House and Senate. From that moment on, the former "number-one strike breaker" became most unions' last line of defense in Washington; for the public, he became "anti-strike," not "anti-union."[56]

FOREIGN POLICY

Truman had to be certain that Dewey would not look preferable on foreign policy, or any domestic advantages he gained by charging Dewey with guilt by association with Taft would be useless. In 1948, 50–60 percent of the country considered foreign policy or the threat of war the most important problem facing the country, and a plurality of the country thought Republicans could do a better job of handling it.[57]

Truman got little credit for being president during the ongoing crises. Instead of a Truman Plan for rebuilding Europe after the war, Secretary of State George Marshall became the father of the Marshall Plan. After the Russians blocked access to West Berlin in June 1948, over half the country was willing to send troops to France, Italy, Greece, or Turkey to prevent a Russian takeover. A major war could begin at any moment, yet only one in ten Americans thought Truman had done the most to form the present foreign policy. Dewey was preparing to attack Truman on mishandling the Communist threats in China, Eastern Europe, and Russia.[58]

The Truman administration was vulnerable to charges of mismanagement of foreign policy only if Dewey could credibly claim he would be a better interventionist. Taft and many other senior GOP isolationist senators were unwilling to go along with a change in a general principle of their party, even if the change could win the White House in 1948.[59] Senator Arthur Vandenberg and John Foster Dulles were essential to Dewey's campaign because they were the only two Republicans with the stature to assure voters that Dewey, a staunch interventionist, could both stand up to Stalin and have support in his party.

Vandenberg's public conversion to internationalism was hailed as "The most important speech to come from the Senate Chamber in the last 80 years."[60] Truman's under-secretary of state, Robert Lovett, played upon

Vandenberg's vanity, telling him that his leadership was essential in helping create NATO. After that, Vandenberg was no longer willing to risk his
enhanced stature and a national stage upon which he could perform and
pontificate.

Through a series of canny manipulations, Truman disarmed Dewey so
he couldn't deliver any of the hard-hitting speeches that Dulles had written for him on the weaknesses and failures of Truman against Stalin and
the growing strength of the communists in China. Dulles was invited to
secret meetings with Marshall and Lovett, and asked to apply his diplomatic expertise to the ongoing negotiations over the Russian blockade of
Berlin. Then they asked him to attend the UN General Assembly meeting
in Paris that fall.[61]

All the bipartisanship, Acheson recalled later, was a "magnificent fraud." It
was always good for the president to say "politics stops at the seaboard, and
anybody who denies that postulate is 'a son of a bitch and a crook and not
a true patriot.' Now, if people will swallow that, then you're off to the races."
Vandenberg knew it was at least partly a sham, but he swallowed it to further
his prestige, and when Dulles also was reeled in, Truman silenced Dewey.
After Dulles died, Dewey simply noted that after the election, Truman never
met with Dulles again, he "just put him into the outer darkness."[62]

Spotlight on Taft

Dewey had the support of Republican moderates, and the 1948 GOP platform reflected this. It called for continued price support for farmers, loos-
ened immigration controls to help war refugees from Europe, and many
other progressive programs that were in line with Dewey's record in New
York. Moderate Republican governors needed the New Deal programs for
their states and had helped Dewey derail attempts by Senator Taft, a fer-
vent anti–New Dealer, to get the party to call for a rollback of the federal
government.

Strike two on Dewey was Truman's call for a special session of Congress
after the Democratic National Convention. When Truman called upon
the Republicans to pass their programs for the good of the country, he
put Dewey's fate in Taft's hands. Taft could pass the programs, ensuring a
Dewey victory—if he also publicly supported legislation that contradicted
his personal brand of conservatism.

Truman's move was high-stakes poker and Truman knew it. It was risky because the Republicans could begin with a civil rights bill guaranteed to produce a filibuster by southern Democrats. Or they could pass bills that sounded good yet were toothless.[63]

Dewey saw at once what Truman was proposing, and dispatched his most experienced associate, Herbert Brownell, to negotiate secretly with Taft. If Taft would pass any one small item and say that the rest was too complicated to rush through during a special session, the illusion of unity could be preserved. All Brownell needed for Dewey was a revision of the very restrictive Displaced Persons Act or a modest expansion of Social Security. All that Taft would agree to do was ask Senator Chapman Revercomb of West Virginia whether his committee would be willing to hold hearings on immigration, making it easier for mainly Catholic East European refugees to come to the United States. Revercomb, a staunch Baptist, refused to hold hearings and Truman won a major victory.[64]

Dewey had no good option available. Denouncing Taft, who ran dismally in the primaries against Dewey, was problematic; it would only prove that Senate Republicans did not support his foreign policy. Dewey ran away from Taft while Truman, as he had wanted to do all along, ran against Taft and the do-nothing Republican Congress. After Taft lost the nomination, Truman crowed, "Taft didn't have to carry on his pretense of caring about the needs of the people. He could act in his real character—as a cold-hearted, cruel aristocrat."[65]

Strike Three

The special session did not immediately dim Dewey's star, but it prepared the way for Truman to use Taft against Dewey later.

The former Ohio governor James Cox, the Democratic Party's losing nominee in 1920, sent the Cox Newspapers' Washington bureau chief, W. McNeil Lowry, to see Clark Clifford, a young, ambitious, and politically savvy member of Truman's staff. Lowry tipped off Clifford that a barely noticed provision in the last farm bill was likely to destroy the farm economy at harvesttime if there was a good crop.[66]

The Republicans had stipulated that the government could build no more grain-storage facilities, which meant that if the government storage was full, farmers would either have to pay for private storage or build certified storage facilities of their own. In an ordinary harvest year this change would have been a noticeable—but manageable—cost to the farmers. However, 1948 was the biggest corn and wheat harvest in history. There was also a countrywide shortage of the lumber and chicken wire farmers needed to build their own facilities.

No certified storage meant no government certified price for the crop; by October, panicked farmers were forced to sell their corn at distressed prices because they could not build the proper storage bins on their farms. When no more storage was available, corn prices fell by almost half.

Dewey was strongly pro–price supports, but there was a "smoking gun," proof that one Republican motive for refusing to build more storage was to depress grain prices. Lowry had found proof that the Republican committee's expert witness was getting a payoff on every bushel of cheap wheat from exporters.[67]

Dewey was not implicated in the scandal in any way. But the Republican Congress *was* responsible, and that made it plausible that Taft and the other Republicans would overrule Dewey and do away with all price supports next.[68]

Early on in Dewey's first run for the presidency in 1944, his campaign manager Herbert Brownell learned that midwestern farmers were suspicious that Dewey's East Coast–based agricultural advisors had backed policies that favored consumers over farmers. In 1948 Brownell, now managing the Republican National Committee, grew more and more concerned with the farmers' suspicions and tried repeatedly to persuade Dewey to include a prominent midwestern farm expert into his campaign to reassure them.

When Dewey refused, Brownell wired Dewey and offered to resign, but Dewey never saw the telegram. While Dewey's inner circle was "blissfully unaware" of the crisis, Republican congressmen in the states hit by falling grain prices went on the war path over the issue.

After he lost, Dewey told a reporter, "I never quite understood what the farm situation was to cause all that trouble." Only when it was over did Dewey's advisors understand how the Democratic vice presidential candidate Alban Barkley had spread the word—via an airplane financed by union contributions—through the rural areas that were once safely Republican.[69]

When the election was over, a Truman strategist told national columnists Joseph and Stewart Alsop that Dewey probably would have won, "If the Republican National Committee had only spent a few of its millions supporting the corn market in the last half of October." Dewey ran stronger than other Republicans had in urban areas from coast to coast, and he carried New York, Pennsylvania, New Jersey, Michigan, Connecticut, and Maryland. But he lost Iowa, Ohio, and Wisconsin, states he had carried in 1944 against Roosevelt. Later, a University of Minnesota student, Walter Mondale, found that Dewey ran as strong as ever among dairy farmers but had lost enough support among grain farmers to cost him the critical votes.[70]

The *New York Times* columnist Arthur Krock called Dewey's loss the "greatest whodunit of the century." Republicans quickly turned the whodunit into a "hedunit," blaming Dewey for a bland, uninspiring race. He was ridiculed as "the little man on the wedding cake" by Alice Longworth Roosevelt because he looked just like the formally attired figure on cakes at fashionable weddings. Dewey was actually a far better orator than Truman; he could be as tough and fiery a campaigner as Truman or Barkley, and he was almost dashing enough to be a matinee idol. Dewey had been working with polls since 1939—testing messages, issue positions, and alternate phrasings of positions, whether to criticize Hitler or ignore him. He thrashed Harold Stassen in a debate with his eloquent attack on outlawing the American Communist Party—it was "un-American" and "futile anyhow to try to shoot an idea with a law." And he was so electrifying when fighting the mob in New York that Dutch Schultz hatched a sophisticated plan to assassinate Dewey, only to have other mobsters kill Schultz to save themselves from the full wrath of the FBI.[71]

This stunning comeback, however, was due to Truman's strategy, not Dewey's personality—or Truman's fiery speech. Truman muffled Dewey by using the tools at an incumbent's disposal, thwarting his challengers' attempts to use an incumbent's inherent weaknesses against him.

Truman was only able to defeat Dewey by recruiting a campaign staff that made rapid responses and long-term planning compatible, one organized outside the control of the hidebound and sluggish Democratic National Committee. Equally important, Truman's campaign minimized toxic interstaff conflicts by designating a White House staffer with enough authority to ensure that the White House and campaign were working together for reelection.[72]

TEAMWORK AND STAFF CONFLICTS

Decisions are never made quickly, nor are they revised easily for incumbents. There are two staffs—the White House staff and the campaign staff. There is constant friction—or open conflict—between them, and a president's failure to manage relations between them can be fatal.

There are two sets of competing speechwriters, and a president's speeches must be vetted carefully lest they panic Wall Street, provoke unexpected reactions abroad, or contradict a presidential policy. The provocative statements of a challenger often can be explained away, while every presidential statement has ramifications at home and abroad.

There are two chiefs of staff, and each has his own turf to protect and his own constituencies. The campaign chief focuses on press and voters in critical states, and passionate minorities who contribute money and volunteers; the White House chief pays attention to negotiations with Congress and not upsetting legislative apple carts or starting public fights with federal agencies.

The policy staffers in the campaign are focused on emphasizing accomplishments and promises that resonate with the current interests of voters, while the policy staffs inside the government want to trumpet the accomplishments they were responsible for. And when cabinet members or key staffers are attacked by the challenger, they are determined to defend themselves when the campaign would prefer they stay out of sight.

Every incumbent's campaign is slower to adapt its message to changes in terrain, media, or competition. It takes time for campaigners who have worked only for challengers to grasp that voters now look more at results and less at promise and character. When voters judge incumbents, there is more "What have you done for me lately" and less "How have you looked to me lately?"

Teamwork and the control of staff conflicts are more difficult—and crucial—for a president because every single word matters. Everything takes longer. Campaign strategists love bold, clear strokes, but with presidents they are seldom successful without extensive planning and time. Before Truman accused Republicans of sticking a pitchfork in the farmer's back, Clark Clifford did extensive research to find evidence that would stand up before the public and made sure the files were protected from destruction.[73] Before Nixon went to China, he had been communicating with the Chinese and planning the trip for more than two years.

White House speechwriters and the campaign communicators will fight over language and content. Speechwriters still want eloquence, but now accuracy matters more. When Martin Anderson wrote speeches for President Nixon, Bryce Harlow, a senior aide, warned him, "you will be forgiven for not being eloquent or brilliant, but you will never be forgiven for being wrong." Harlow was Nixon's most trusted aide, responsible for "taking the zingers out" before the president got in trouble.[74]

There are fights over scheduling between the White House staffers concerned about their policies and the campaign staff concerned about visits to battleground states. For presidents, a "spontaneous campaign stop" is an oxymoron. No president can make an impromptu visit without days of planning and security checks, and if a scheduled visit is canceled, it earns bad press and bad blood.

When a policy is unpopular with the public, the policy advocates within the White House and cabinet members will insist the problem is the delivery, not the content. In 1994, Bill Clinton's health care advisors kept assuring him that it was the spokesman and the ads that were the problem, a diagnosis that appealed to Clinton. Paul Begala, who was a Clinton White House advisor and strategist, noted, "Every politician who gets in trouble thinks it's how they're saying things instead of what they're saying." In the case of Clinton's attempts to reform health care, the midterm election wipeout ended that debate. "Guess what? It was the content," Begala said. "So we changed. We had to."[75]

Jimmy Carter's pollster and campaign strategist, Pat Caddell, fought to have the same influence in the White House that he had had in the campaign. Caddell's idée fixe was the outsider who would ride alienation and discontent to the White House. His generation, he believed, was "a generation with a collective social conscience, a collective sense that they can do great things, yet they are leading a life right now that's fairly mundane...in terms of changing the world."[76] When Carter's economic policies were not reviving the economy and Democrats were alienated from Carter's moderate spending programs, Caddell convinced him that the problem was a crisis of confidence, not a failure of policy.

Carter met with philosophers, spiritual leaders, and professors to discuss the crisis of confidence and then gave a very well-received speech known forever after as the "malaise" speech. Carter told the country that "All the legislation in the world can't fix what's wrong with America....We've learned that piling up material goods cannot fill the emptiness of lives which have no confidence or purpose."[77]

Instant reaction to the speech was overwhelmingly positive; Carter's ratings went up eleven points overnight. They crashed soon after. After a moralistic analysis attacking the shallowness of modern culture and asking everyone to say something nice about his or her country, he shuffled his cabinet, introduced a technocratic policy to end dependence on foreign oil...and did absolutely nothing to address the problem he had just identified as the root of all other problems.

Jody Powell later realized, "If you make a bold stroke like that, you do have to think about how do you follow it up? What [does] day 3 and day 4 and day 5 look like. How do you translate that into additional steps?"[78]

Even after the message is fully vetted it remains harder for an incumbent to keep his administration's principals in the White House or cabinet on message. The best contrast with the opponent is seldom the policy triumph most important to White House staffers. In the Reagan White House, for example, the campaign staff wanted a campaign where the incumbent went after the Democrats aggressively. The White House policy staff, however, wanted a "these-are-our-triumphs" approach. It was, after all, a chance for them to shine a light on their pet policies as they began to scramble for better positions next term or a cushy outside job.[79]

It is always hard to control policy specialists tough enough and smart enough to work in a presidential environment, but it is much harder to keep them in sync for a reelection campaign than for a challenger's. If a headstrong policy expert goes too far with the press, the candidate can dismiss him or say that he doesn't speak for the campaign, and the promise of a future job within the administration is usually a strong incentive to keep ambitious people inside the tent. After a candidate wins, the foreign policy, economic, defense, and environmental appointees all have their own budgets, platforms, and audiences.

President Ford's secretary of the treasury, William Simon, traveled the country ostensibly to help Ford but was in fact doing more to promote himself. No one on the inside was willing to butt heads with Simon, so the White House sent the campaign strategist Stu Spencer to speak with him:

> I go in there. We chat. He tells me all these wonderful things he's doing. "I gave 115 speeches, blah, blah, blah." I let him go through all this and then I said, "I understand that, Mr. Secretary, but you never mentioned Gerald Ford." I thought he was going to come across the desk at me. He really flipped out. It got worse from there, but I'd made my point....Ford was great that way. He said, "Good, tell the rest of them that."[80]

Presidents as overwhelmed as Truman can turn an election around, but they cannot do it with clever ads and memorable phrases unless they have planned their moves and established their credibility in advance. By the time incumbents—or challengers—say they will fight like Truman the rest of the way, it already may be too late to fight like Truman.

It takes many more months for an incumbent to develop a credible defense of a half-full glass than it takes a challenger to remind people that the president promised to fill the half-empty glass all the way. With a concrete record and dueling staff, it is much harder for a president get everyone on the same page to fight the same war. But it is not enough to fight the same war; they have to fight the *right* war.

THE UNBEATABLE INCUMBENT:
GEORGE BUSH IN 1992

Japan was the tip of the iceberg for the Bush/Quayle '92 campaign. When he returned from Japan, the president faced growing cultural and fiscal divisions within his party. His White House staff, which had worked so well on foreign policy crises throughout the world, was misfiring on domestic policy. And he couldn't get a straight story from his staff whether the economy was getting better.

The Democrats were in disarray; Bush's most dangerous rivals had been spooked by the triumph of Desert Storm, so he faced only second-tier candidates: less-well-known outsiders and senators with limited name recognition or support. Still, he still had not developed a vision for his next term that could hold his party together and create a contrast with the Democrats, that would justify four more years.

Since 1980 Republicans had relied on two major issue advantages against the Democrats: maintaining a strong national defense and lowering taxes. Through skillful, effective diplomacy, Bush had presided over the dissolution of the Soviet Union's "evil empire," the beginning steps of democratization in East Europe and in the fifteen states of the former Soviet Union, as well as the unification of Germany. He built a twenty-six-nation coalition to help beat back Saddam Hussein's regional threat to the Mideast. Two of the top three Democratic primary contenders—Senator Paul Tsongas and Governor Bill Clinton—had never served in the military.

But the contrast between a strong national defense under a Republican president and a weak national defense under a Democratic president was suddenly less important. The most salient contrast would now be domestic policy and the economy.

A Tale of Two Bushes

Time magazine's Person of the Year award goes to the man or woman who has made the biggest impact—*for better or worse*—on the year's events. For 1990 the editors decided that President George H. W. Bush was the first person uniquely qualified to earn the distinction by both standards—for better, because he guided foreign policy with "resoluteness and mastery," and for worse, due to the "baffling," "ludicrous," and "truly embarrassing" manner with which he managed domestic policy—particularly taxes.[1]

Repudiating his cynical "read my lips" pledge to never raise taxes was not what *Time* considered ludicrous about his domestic performance. It was his mismanagement of negotiations with the Democrats. In three days he had four different bargaining positions.[2]

In his acceptance speech at the 1988 Republican National Convention, then–Vice President Bush told Democrats: "Read My Lips: No New Taxes." Bush and his closest friends and advisors believed it was a pact with the devil. His future secretary of state, James Baker, acknowledged as much to Rep. Dan Rostenkowski: "We're going to elect a President of the United States," he said. "We'll talk about *that* after he's elected."[3]

"Read My Lips" was a natural progression from the antitax campaign Bush had run throughout the Republican primaries. The GOP of 1988 was far more opposed to taxes than in 1980, when Bush had campaigned as the moderate alternative to Ronald Reagan, attacking Reagan's fiscal policy as "voodoo economics." Bush's 1988 campaign was on the ropes until New Hampshire's governor John Sununu, his New Hampshire campaign chair, used an antitax pledge to attack Senator Robert Dole. When Dole refused to sign a meaningless, irresponsible pledge that would only bring on more pledges, Bush—who had happily signed—attacked Dole as "Senator Straddle." Then Bush trashed a presidential commission designed to provide bipartisan cover for the next president. His television ads showed him saying, "If it doesn't recommend a tax increase, I'll not only eat my hat, I'll eat Bob Dole's hat."[4]

From the moment Bush was elected he knew his decisions about taxes could make or break his reelection. Could he get away with the same kinds of "magic asterisks" and "rosy scenarios" as David Stockman? Stockman, Reagan's budget director and fiscal guru, had used the asterisk for "additional budget reductions, to be announced by the president at a later date" and optimistic assumptions about future growth rates to generate "rosy scenarios" underestimating future deficits under Reagan. Or had the soaring deficits gotten so far out of hand that he could have a healthy economy only if he could slow the growth of the deficit? Either way, he would anger part of the Republican Party unless he could persuade people that he had fought to the end for his principles and had been dragged kicking and screaming to raise taxes.[5]

Since late in 1989, reporters and columnists had been asking whether Bush knew what was going on in the domestic side of the White House. George Will had accused Bush of conducting an "unserious presidency" and the *New York Times*'s R. W. Apple wondered if Bush was passive and timid.[6]

There was near-unanimous private consensus among Bush's budget analysts and treasury officials, as well as finance committee members in both parties, that the deficit had to be controlled or he would be a one-term president. In March 1989, after discussing the budget with his economic team, Bush wrote in his diary that he would need to raise revenues:

[Richard] Darman [director of the Office of Management and Budget] conducting a good briefing. His message: we can get by this year and perhaps get a deal with no revenue increase, but after that we're going to have to raise revenues—there's no way to get around it—there's no way around it given the sharp cut in the Gramm-Rudman. I tell him that I can't raise taxes this round and it will be very hard in the future, but I want to see the options and I'm not going to be held up by campaign rhetoric....If the facts change, I hope I'm smart enough to change, too.[7]

It is never easy for any politician to get credit for saving money *tomorrow* by spending money—or raising taxes—*today*. Anyone who pushes for action risks getting ahead of public opinion and getting attacked for crying wolf. When Martin Feldstein, chair of Reagan's Council of Economic Advisors (CEA), accurately forecast that budget and trade deficits would be more than double the year before, Secretary of the Treasury Donald Regan testified that Congress could throw the report in the wastebasket.[8]

Bush's political advisors were unanimous in their opposition to raising taxes in 1989. Ed Rollins, in charge of the Republican National Committee, warned him that the pledge was politically sacred. Bob Teeter, Bush's pollster, told him that he did not have enough credibility to break the promise so soon. Bush also worried that breaking the pledge would cripple him internationally: "How will any foreign leader ever trust me abroad?"[9]

His financial experts thought Bush should do something immediately: the sooner he acted, the healthier the economy would be in 1992. There was also another Republican gambit from the 1980s that made it harder to wait any longer to reduce the deficit: the Gramm-Rudman-Hollings Emergency Deficit Control Act required a balanced budget by 1991 and included a draconian clause: if the 1991 budget was not declared "balanced," there would be immediate cuts of over 40 percent to the defense budget and 25 percent to domestic spending. Michael Boskin, chairman of the CEA, believed that they had run out of alternatives; they were at a point where any further manipulations to hide the deficit would be "blatantly obvious."[10]

In 1990, the Democrats controlled both houses of Congress and refused to negotiate with the White House until they were sure that Republicans shared in the blame for any tax increases. Bush would have to take his lumps for new taxes or for massive cuts to defense and domestic spending. Democratic congressmen reminded each other that Republicans needed to move first: "if we agree to taxes, we're political idiots of the first order."[11]

Bush had to decide whether to do public battle. He could play a game of "chicken" with the Democrats: refuse to accept any new taxes and veto their budget until taxes were forced upon him in exchange for cuts in the Democrats' pet programs. Then, if Gramm-Rudman kicked in, he could attack them for threatening the safety of the country. Treasury Secretary Nick Brady and Darman both believed, however, that a delay in lowering interest rates or a slowdown of the government if Gramm-Rudman kicked in would threaten economic health in 1992.[12]

June 26, 1990

Talks between the White House and congressional leaders of both parties stalled; the negotiators agreed on the outline of a budget agreement, but Democrats would not sign off without Bush's public commitment. After the way Bush had used unsustainable pledges to attack Dole and then Mike Dukakis, they were in no mood to settle for vague assurances that could be turned against them.

Bush's aides drafted a statement for him to sign that began: "It is clear that both the size of the deficit problem and the need for [passage] require...[spending cuts and] tax revenue increases." That left open whether Bush was accepting responsibility for the "tax revenue increases" or simply acknowledging the passage given to him would raise taxes. The Democrats adjourned to discuss the statement and came back insisting that two words be added to the first sentence. It needed to read: "It is clear *to me*."[13]

Press secretary Marlin Fitzwater was told to release the amended statement. When he saw the phrase "tax revenue increases," he was stunned. He looked at the Democratic leaders sitting in the room; they were staring back with two different looks: "One was of the cat who ate the canary. The other was frozen fear, as if I might blow their cover and expose their victory. They said absolutely nothing."[14]

Fitzwater saw that the game was over; the Democrats "had taken us to the cleaners...[and] demanded that the statement be issued before they left [the White House], because they knew that if anyone with smarts and balls saw the statement they might talk the president out of it."[15]

Fitzwater managed to catch Sununu's eye as he left the room so he could talk to the chief of staff privately before issuing the statement:

"What do you want?" he demanded.
"Sir," I said. "This says we support raising taxes. This breaks the pledge."
"No it doesn't," he said curtly. "It says 'increased revenues.'"
"Nobody will be fooled," I said.
"It says 'revenue increase,'" he repeated as he turned to go back into the room. "Issue it."[16]

In the narrowest technical sense, Sununu was right. There were no new taxes, just increased tax *rates*. But such nuanced points didn't jibe with the explicit concreteness of "Read My Lips." Teeter had warned Bush that governors who made firm tax promises they couldn't keep got in big trouble later, but Bush's media advisor Roger Ailes argued that after eight years as a vice president, Bush needed "the Clint Eastwood factor" and the famous line from the "Dirty Harry" movies would be an unforgettable sound bite.[17]

It was all up to Sununu to prepare for any fallout, because the president had a typically hectic day ahead of him where every minute was metered carefully. In the next three hours alone, Bush had meetings with his National Security team (twice), his secretary of state (twice), the foreign minister of Egypt, the head of the National Jewish coalition, his White House counsel, and the director of presidential personnel. He also participated in a U.S.-Egypt discussion of the suspension of talks with the Palestinian Liberation Organization, and he spoke about education and immigration with a group of Hispanic reporters. His afternoon and evening were just as full.

Sununu, however, had made no political preparations because he thought no promise had been violated. The chief of staff, Elizabeth Drew wrote, was "a walking example that someone can have a high IQ and be a fool."[18] He was also as arrogant and dismissive of congressmen and cabinet officers as he was of Fitzwater.[19] Sununu did not understand that adding those two small words would start a firestorm—which it did. News programs and talk shows replayed the original RNC footage over and over. Conservative newspapers used monster headlines like "READ MY LIPS...I LIED," "FLIP-FLOP," or "Bush Bites His Lip." Television shows reminded viewers that Bush had savaged Walter Mondale (in 1984) and Michael Dukakis (in 1988) for saying tax increases were necessary to cover the growing deficit. Newt Gingrich told reporters he was "enraged," and a majority of Republican congressmen signed a letter opposing any change in tax rates. And if that wasn't enough, Mondale and New York's governor Mario Cuomo both went public to praise the president for seeing the light.[20]

Five weeks later Sadaam Hussein occupied Kuwait, and Bush began to assemble an international coalition to liberate Kuwait. Oil prices shot up, and Bush spent all his time on the crisis while his domestic staff dealt with the budget.

Democrats in Washington were not about to make it easy for Bush. They could now pay him back for his "Read My Lips" pledge—and restore some credibility with their base if they extracted gains from him. The Democratic budget submitted that October, not surprisingly, raised taxes more (and cut entitlements less) than the White House expected.

Sununu, and therefore the president as well, were unprepared. Bush tried to regain his balance by attacking the Democrats for raising the marginal tax rate on individuals earning over $200,000 and vetoed a continuing resolution that shut down the government for a few days. This resurrected the fairness issue, and Democrats immediately unleashed commercials attacking Bush for favoring the rich when middle-class families were hurting.[21]

Ailes and Teeter advised Bush to veto the budget that was now worse than the original budget. Darman and Brady argued a deal was needed to get the economy moving by 1992. Without a deal, interest rates would not drop. It was also possible that Bush's international coalition to deal with the Persian Gulf Crisis would collapse if the defense budget were cut by Gramm-Rudman.[22] Bush ended up making the worst of a tough situation. In a move that alienated his Republican colleagues—and signaled political impotence to everyone else—he decided to sign the budget without demanding a better deal from the Democrats.[23]

A plurality of the country opposed the plan, and Bush's favorability rating fell thirteen points during the October negotiations. The drop in his popularity was particularly strong among voters over the age of fifty, who opposed the budget deal 50–29 percent. Republican voters were almost equally divided over whom they trusted to make wise decisions about the deficit: the president (36 percent) or congressional Republicans (39 percent).[24]

Now Bush had the worst of all worlds: he raised taxes to reduce the deficit, but whatever good deficit reduction might have done was not enough to counteract rising oil prices.[25]

DOWN WITH THEM ALL

While the president had been concentrating on the ongoing foreign crises, populist anger toward the federal government was hurting both parties.

Within months of his inaugural, the full force of the changing world of talk radio and cable television had hit. Congress was about to simultaneously ban all honoraria and raise their pay 50 percent, to $135,000, a reform endorsed by President Reagan to reduce dependence on speaking fees from special interests. Ralph Nader persuaded a talk-show host in Boston to campaign against the move, and overnight a loose national alliance of talk radio hosts were beating the drums.[26]

A caller to a Detroit show suggested that people demonstrate their outrage at the pay increase by sending a used tea bag to their Congressman.[27] Soon hundreds of thousands of used tea bags were being dumped in front of the White House, or sent to congressmen and senators.[28] Mainstream media supported the pay raise and the reforms, but the tea bags and angry voters successfully spooked Congress into dropping the reforms.

When the 1990 budget negotiations were stalling, Jack Gargan, a Florida retiree, took $45,000 from his retirement account and started a group called THRO (Throw the Rascals Out). He ran newspaper ads urging everyone to vote against incumbents to punish them for failing to solve the deficit problem. Retirees and older workers were all concerned that Social Security and Medicare would disappear—all for wasteful spending, tax cuts for the wealthy, and congressional pay raises. They didn't trust either party. Soon Gargan received two million dollars in contributions and placed ads in more than 100 newspapers throughout the country. When Bush started final negotiations with the Democrats, Gargan appeared on *ABC Evening News;* when the president agreed to raise taxes, Gargan went on *Larry King Live,* showing off a bumper sticker that read, "This Fall, Fire 'em All—Re-elect Nobody."[29]

WHAT DID BUSH KNOW AND WHEN DID HE KNOW IT?

The time between the midterm elections and reelection year is critical for incumbents; the planning that does (or doesn't) happen can make or break them. For most of 1991, the fights about strategy in the Bush White House were divorced from reality. Before the defeat of Saddam Hussein, the Bush White House was already confident about reelection, so confident that no one was focusing on very clear signs of potential trouble. After all, the reasoning went, the president was named Man of the Year *before* the lightning-fast military victory.

No one inside the White House bubble was grappling with the rapidly changing nature of the facts on the ground at home. No one was telling the president how fast the terrain was changing. Nothing about the exceptional display of American power during Desert Storm distracted the public from worries about the current economy, the future of the country, or the belief the United States was falling far behind Japan. The euphoria was merely relief that at least America could still do *something* right.

The pessimism about the future that had been growing during Reagan's second term was still there: a month after the war, only one-third of the country thought the next generation would be better off. Unemployment and inflation were low, but potential voters had a pervasive sense of stagnation. The long-term economic future looked uncertain compared to their own past, and they doubted whether their country would remain a world economic leader. In the immediate afterglow of victory, a plurality of Americans believed that the world's leading economic power of the next century would be Japan.[30]

Inside the White House, business proceeded as usual. Sununu was serenely confident that Bush would roll through 1992 on the "Three Ks": crime, quotas, and Kuwait.[31] Democrats were still soft on crime, still supported affirmative action, and they had voted against authorizing the use of force in Kuwait.

A former engineering professor who was proud of his IQ, Sununu believed that the 1990 budget deal had taken deficit problems off the agenda, and he was persuaded by Nick Brady that the economy was improving and the fundamentals were sound.[32] Voters, however, vote on their subjective opinions about their welfare. And from the voters' perspectives, the fundamentals at home—and abroad—were not sound. By March, 79 percent of the electorate believed the United States was in a recession and 61 percent of those felt that Bush had inherited the mess from Reagan.[33]

Since so many voters still clung to the belief that spending cuts would be enough to right the ship, Bush could bring the public along only if he persuaded them that he, too, wanted no new taxes, that he had reluctantly decided that *this* time was different. In other words, if he decided taxes were unavoidable, he would have to pander, siding with the public while preparing them to see that there was no other alternative—this time.

While Sununu was extremely good at processing critical memos and making the trains run on time, he also acted as if he were the deputy president. Instead of making sure the president always knew about conflicts on which he needed to weigh in, Sununu used his control of presidential access to enforce his opinions about the correct presidential decisions.[34] It was hard for Bush to hear a realistic assessment of the economy, because changing his assessment affected the standing of people close to him in the White House—including Sununu. Teeter turned down an appointment as deputy chief of staff because Sununu refused to agree to allow him private time with the president; Teeter was experienced enough to know that if his polls contradicted Sununu's assessments—or if there were unpleasant truths Bush needed to hear—he would never get on the president's calendar.[35]

There was nobody in the White House to think full-time about political strategy, no one with any sophisticated understanding of public opinion. The Republican National Committee was operating in the dark. Its chief of staff, Mary Matalin, thought Sununu had "the political sensitivity of a doorknob." As long as he was controlling access to Bush, the political team "didn't even know what kind of information was getting to [him]."[36]

Bush was aware of the problems with Sununu: he was arrogant and controlling, alternately alienating and undermining powerful senators and cabinet members. At one point, it was so bad that the president had to install a special post office box at his summer home so he could get correspondence from cabinet members with whom Sununu disagreed.[37]

By the summer of 1991, there was no denying it any longer: Bush knew Sununu had to go before he could start organizing his reelection campaign. But Sununu was well-liked by ardent antitax conservatives. If Bush replaced Sununu, he would lose an important pipeline to the Republicans who most distrusted him—and a valuable lightning rod against attacks from the right.[38]

Sununu was too proud—or tone deaf—to see that he was no longer on good terms with the president. He was not invited to a critical meeting at Bush's home in Maine, but he showed up anyway, only to leave at once after being denied time with the president. Bush arranged for his son George to talk with top players about the organization of the campaign, so that he could then tell Sununu how everyone felt about him; but even that didn't get the message through to Sununu. Only months later, on December 4, 1991, did Sununu finally resign in the wake of a scandal over his personal use of government planes and White House limousines.[39]

Bush's rationale for waiting so long to remove Sununu was that campaigns were just "a two-month sprint" beginning after Labor Day of the election year.[40] It was a fatal rationalization premised upon his partial, rose-tinted recall of his defeat of Michael Dukakis in 1988. His closest allies were anxious. Fred Malek, the campaign's future COO, urged Bush to start on the economy to reassure panicky businessmen. Ailes was so worried that he came to Washington to tell Bush that people couldn't understand why the economic team was not more like the widely respected Gulf War team.[41]

Sununu's departure came too late for Bush to repair much of the damage he had caused. For months the president had been misled about the economy. The polls showing all the public concern had been dismissed. It had taken months of shouting matches—and, finally, a threat to resign—before Michael Boskin, chairman of the council of economic advisors, got an audience with the president.[42]

Fred Steeper, Teeter's longtime associate and now the pollster, worried that Bush would end up like Winston Churchill, the hero of Great Britain in World War II, who immediately lost power when voters turned from war to peace. Bush's problem was the opposite of Truman's. Truman neutralized the Republican advantage on foreign policy so he could battle them over the contrast in domestic policies and priorities. Bush's strength was foreign policy, but that would be decisive only if he had a domestic political strategy that took away the Democrats' domestic advantage. What Steeper wanted Bush to call for a few popular solutions, which Democrats could not support.[43]

Five days after Steeper's memo emphasizing the need for a domestic economic contrast with the Democrats, a move designed to remove an unfavorable, odious contrast with the Democrats was sabotaged by leaks within the White House. With unresolved internal conflicts and a chief of staff spending more time on his own survival than the president's, no one was coordinating legislative politics and political communications, and a planned move to take civil rights off the table blew up inside the White House.

Bush had carefully negotiated a bill on minority hiring in cooperation with Senators Edward Kennedy and John Danforth to soothe moderates and minorities infuriated by the Clarence Thomas Supreme Court confirmation hearings. The White House scheduled a Rose Garden signing ceremony with prominent civil rights activists present to publicize the signing and thus reassure moderates that the president was committed to minority progress. Some, but not all, conservatives were furious because the bill was not tough enough. To reassure them, Bush's counsel, Boyden Gray, drafted a presidential directive ordering all federal agencies to make sure they used no racial quotas or preferences in hiring. Young Turks in the White House immediately leaked the draft directive. It was the worst of all worlds for Bush. Three cabinet members opposed the directive, which had to be scrapped, and the civil rights leaders all canceled their participation in the signing ceremony.[44]

In 1988 that kind of contrast had been easy—Democrats were divided on tough anticrime measures and wanted to raise taxes. Now Bush was president and needed to campaign on much tougher terrain, the economy. And by default, the Japan trip ended up being the last and only game in town for Bush.

A trip that was supposed to reinvent a war president as the leader of the country's economy ended up setting back Bush and the Republican Party. The trip is best remembered for the state dinner in which the tired, flu-stricken president vomited directly onto the Japanese prime minister before collapsing with his head in the lap of his appalled host. The president's illness launched a wave of jokes, editorials, and metaphors. On *The Tonight Show*, for example, Johnny Carson had a field day:

> President Bush is doing just fine....If you had to look at Lee Iacocca while eating raw fish, you'd barf too. [Afterward] the president got some more bad news: Japan also bars the import of Kaopectate....At first they thought everyone at the dinner had the stomach flu because all the American auto executives were on their knees too. Turns out they were just begging.[45]

But Bush's ill-timed (and very visible) illness was only the icing on the cake. The trip was a disaster from every standpoint. The American auto executives were making *six times* what their counterparts in Japan earned; Iacocca alone was paid more than two million dollars in a year when he had fired 74,000 workers. The U.S. automakers tried to persuade Japan to import American cars, and yet they didn't make a left-hand-drive car. Bush was promoting corporate fat instead of industrial muscle or farm products; the auto executives were arguing against free trade.[46]

Immediately after the trip, 63 percent of the respondents in a CBS/ *New York Times* poll considered the trip a failure, while 18 percent said it was a success.[47] The perception that Americans were going hat in hand to Japan, with a president seeking economic help to stay in office, triggered more than one hundred editorials about "begging."

The trip damaged the Republican Party as much as it did the president. Throughout the first three years of the Bush presidency, Republicans came out ahead when voters were asked which party would be better dealing with the nation's problems. When the economy faltered the gap had narrowed, and now, after the Japan trip, there was a 42–29 advantage for the Democrats.[48]

BUCHANAN

In addition to the Democratic hopefuls on the Left, Pat Buchanan was going after Bush on the Right.

Buchanan was a superb talk-show pugilist. He all but declared the Gulf War a Jewish conspiracy, saying repeatedly that "There are only two groups beating the drums for war in the Middle East—the Israeli Defense Ministry and its amen corner in the United States." In his columns he talked about a war led by men with names like Perle, Kissinger, Krauthammer, and Rosenthal, a war that would be fought by "kids with names like McAllister, Murphy, Gonzales, and Leroy Brown."[49] Buchanan was just as strident and passionate about protectionism as he was about isolationism. He called for a new nationalism that stood up for America, and attacked Bush relentlessly for spending more time on world crises than on the plight of American workers.

From the beginning, Buchanan drew crowds in economically distressed New Hampshire. After Bush's Japan trip flopped, Buchanan was polling over 20 percent in January; on the day of the primary, he surprised the White House by snaring 37 percent against Bush's 53 percent. That made Bush's woes front-page news: maybe the unspeakable—an incumbent losing the election—was not impossible.

Buchanan raised the ante by going south and attacking Bush on cultural and social issues, charging that he was soft on religious values. He began attacking Bush over the National Endowment for the Arts, with an ad showing men dressed in chains and leather harnesses, which an announcer called "pornographic and blasphemous art, too shocking to show." Within a few days, the head of the NEA resigned, and Buchanan proudly proclaimed "the scalp."[50]

It was a no-win situation: Buchanan had neither the money nor the support to win the nomination, so Bush could not stoop to Buchanan's level without lowering himself. The White House sent Vice President Quayle to attack Buchanan, but it backfired badly, opening the floodgates for recycled 1988 attacks that Quayle was unfit to be a heartbeat away from the presidency. When Quayle said Buchanan was unfit to be president, Buchanan asked, "How would he know," before adding that he wouldn't attack Quayle because "I don't want to be charged with child abuse."[51]

Perot

Though he was a thorn in Bush's side, Buchanan posed no real danger. The real threat was the growing middle-aged, middle-class anxiety. Their anger was about their future, not unemployment or inflation. Unlike the 1960s, older people were more critical of the state of the country and more likely to think a "major shakeup" was the only solution.[52]

On the weekend in 1991 before Harris Wofford shocked the White House with his bellwether Senate victory in Pennsylvania, Ross Perot, introduced as "the guy who should be the next president of the United States," spoke to 2,000 alienated taxpayers in a Florida high school gym. The rally was sponsored by THRO (Throw the Hypocritical Rascals OUT). Perot had called Jack Gargan to cheer him on a year earlier, and they had stayed in touch. The crowd waved "Ross for President" banners, and Perot electrified them:

> The junk bond frenzy and buyouts of the 1980s have paralyzed the economy and the United States is no longer a world economic power. Politicians aren't listening to the will of the public, and taxpayers feel helpless to change a government that no longer appears to be "By the people, for the people."[53]

Perot was becoming a household name in 1991, an important billionaire taken seriously by the *New York Times* and the *Washington Post*, and respected by Democrats like Mario Cuomo. Perot's was a name to cite when appealing to commonsense truths about the need to get Washington's house in order.[54] Bush had no plan, and centrists were disenchanted with traditional Democratic policies; Perot appealed to those who had jobs but were worried about the economic future.

Three days after the New Hampshire primary, at a time when the economy was sluggish and more than half of all Americans said they did not have a favorable opinion of any of the candidates, Perot appeared on *Larry King Live*, announcing that he would consider running for president if volunteers placed his name on the ballot in all fifty states. His offer spread throughout the country as viewers telephoned their reactions to local talk-radio shows. When he appeared on C-SPAN a month later, the network received 2,000 phone calls and 70,000 letters requesting a transcript of the segment, smashing Perot's own record from when he spoke out against the Iraq war a year earlier.[55]

While the Bush White House focused on keeping taxes as low as possible without shutting down the government—and Democrats debated and how to strengthen the safety net and provide health care—a third constituency, focused on the deficit as a symbol of mismanagement and decline, had coalesced around Perot. Perot voters were concerned about economic insecurity, fearing that international trade was somehow sending the good jobs overseas, and that the soaring deficit would leave them without Medicare or Social Security later. Above all else, these were voters who were weakly attached to either political party and did not trust the system.[56]

MEANWHILE, BACK AT THE WHITE HOUSE

Bush's White House was still divided between people whose careers depended upon never violating the main tenets of Ronald Reagan and pragmatists concerned about the national economy.

One of the biggest challenges faced by incumbents is negotiating the conflict between their administration's staff and their campaign staff. Mary Matalin, a highly valued member of Bush's 1988 campaign who worked with the White House, "discovered that the English language was heard in two different ways. We heard it politically and they heard it governmentally."[57]

The White House staff didn't like campaigners interfering in their domains; they resented yielding any turf to the "dopes, Neanderthals, and thugs" who claimed their ideas would benefit the president's campaign.

And with an incumbent, the policy people have power they don't have in a challenger's campaign. A challenger can fire staffers or deny they are speaking for the campaign; cabinet members and White House staffers, however, cannot be fired without unwanted publicity.[58]

New laws governed how campaigns were run, and Bush—wary of getting hamstrung with any ugly investigations—instructed Boyden Gray to be certain that the laws were carefully observed. Gray ruled that the campaign laws required such a strict separation of policy and politics that the only communication between campaign and White House would be between Teeter and Malek (on the campaign side) and Samuel Skinner, the new White House chief of staff. That guaranteed near paralysis; Matalin had to find a way to run a campaign and keep Gray from impeding any attempts at a popular message from the president: "In the beginning everybody complied. No one wanted to create an ethical problem for President Bush by violating these rules, so we remained hamstrung...that's not how campaigns work; they've got to be instantly responsive." Eventually the campaign learned to "Commit the sin and ask forgiveness if you get caught....We didn't do anything illegal, or even unethical, just insubordinate. We figured the free world would survive our insubordination."[59]

Marlin Fitzwater tried to resolve some of the problems by meeting with the scheduling, communications, and speechwriting staffs, so that as soon as Teeter and Skinner had set the president's schedule they could be sure that press announcements, invitations, speeches, and scheduling would mesh. Skinner considered this a power play and reversed most of the decisions to let everyone know who was in charge. Fitzwater held no more meetings, and the chaos continued.[60]

Skinner was overloaded and had, at best, partial control of the paper flow, but was too concerned about his own status to delegate to Fitzwater. The White House was still floundering. Even before he had disrupted Fitzwater's attempts at efficiency, the new chief had scared potential new hires away from the White House by scapegoating and firing the director of communications in order to protect Bush after the Japan trip.[61]

"Our Worst Political Nightmare"

As bad as the president's troubles were, campaign strategists were still confident that the savvy and expertise they had used in 1988 to roll over

Dukakis would work just as well in 1992. This confidence, from Fred Steeper's vantage point, was bordering on delusion.

In early March it was clear that Bush's Democratic opponent would be Governor Bill Clinton of Arkansas. "Slick Willie," as Clinton was called by his Arkansas detractors, had the kinds of negative stories that opponents regarded as manna from heaven. His first national television appearance was on *60 Minutes*, where Bill and Hillary tried to refute stories about an alleged affair with a would-be nightclub singer named Gennifer Flowers. The next thing most Americans learned about Clinton was a letter he wrote in 1969 to the head of an ROTC unit he had promised to join, apologizing for not joining the unit, and thanking the officer for "saving him from the draft" because that reprieve allowed him "to maintain my viability within the system."[62]

Despite a very heavy load of personal baggage, Steeper told the others that Clinton was "our worst political nightmare...a Southern Conservative Democrat. If the election were held 30 days from now we would lose."[63]

Charlie Black, a sidekick of Lee Atwater known for hard-nosed campaigns, thought Steeper's claim was "Bullshit....In 30 days we can run a better campaign than they can...the people in this room are better and smarter than Clinton's people." But Steeper was worried enough to write a follow-up memo: the country was in a twenty-month recession, 78 percent thought the United States was on the wrong track, and voters wanted change. The campaign needed to take some risks, "to do some things we would not normally do."[64]

Both Clintons were controversial and the entire Democratic Party was suspect on spending and taxing, but Bush was still in trouble. Clinton had an economic plan he could contrast with Bush's record, one in which voters could "find hope." Still, the game was far from over, and there was far more support for conservative solutions than for liberal ones. Voters blamed Congress more than they blamed Bush for the lack of a recovery, and by four to one, they preferred downsizing government over raising taxes to "meet the growing needs of the American people."[65]

By April, Steeper reported that Clinton looked like the lesser of Bush's problems. In focus groups with 1988 Bush voters, Clinton was described as "scum," a "liar," or "slick." The Bush voters were mainly disappointed with the president; they felt he was out of touch, or didn't care about their sense that their dreams were fading and the country was in decline.[66]

To cover for his lack of an economic plan, Bush's campaign tested the theme "This man who changed the world will change America." Steeper's focus group dismantled that theme: first, his 1988 voters didn't believe he *had* changed the world. And if he had, "he should have changed America first." They also asked, "He's taking credit for changing the world? Is he taking credit for unemployment? Is he taking credit for the economy?"[67]

The exciting candidate now was the billionaire Ross Perot, who was becoming more than a "none-of-the above" choice: "Voters [conclude] that since Perot built a $2 billion fortune from a $6,000 [*sic*] stake, he can handle the country's financial troubles.[68]

Perot's credibility as a self-made man persuaded many voters that he knew enough about government to fix things. Furthermore, he told interviewers that no tax increases were necessary if common sense were applied to the problems: "we've been taxed to death."[69]

The White House and the campaign couldn't agree on whether this was a two-way race with Clinton or a three-way race with Perot. It wasn't until after exit polls showed Perot's strength in California that they went into action. Perot would have beaten them both in a three-way race with 39 percent against 29 percent for Clinton and 25 percent for Bush.[70] After several weeks spent analyzing how to attack him, the campaign decided their best option was a "surgical strike" against Perot. Trigger-happy strategists, however, turned it into a full-scale assault.[71]

Campaign strategists started going after Perot one by one. The RNC chair Rich Bond described Perot as "a wild-eyed purveyor of reckless lies." Stories started coming out about Perot alleging he was psychologically unfit for public office. The White House reporter George Condon summarized the message: "Scary, paranoid, eccentric, goofy, wild, reckless, bizarre, way out there, frightening, and temperamental—all were used to describe Perot in the last 48 hours."[72] Perot held his own, though, doing much better at attacking Bush's negative campaign than if he had been left on his own to answer questions about his past. The only thing Bush is good at, he reminded audiences, is "political assassination."[73]

FREELANCING AT THE WHITE HOUSE

Regardless of who emerged as Bush's main competitor, a three-person race meant moderate voters were more valuable than ever. Still, whether the issue was taxes, race, religion, or family values, Dan Quayle was determined to concentrate first and foremost on the conservative base of the party.

On April 29, a Los Angeles jury acquitted the policemen whose lengthy and severe beating of Rodney King had been captured on video. Rioting broke out in several parts of Los Angeles and went on for days. Unlike the 1960s, the national reaction was more understanding of the anger and less outraged over the destruction of property.

Bush personally approved a statement that called for calm and acknowledged the "frustration and anguish" anyone who saw the videotapes must feel. William Kristol, Quayle's chief of staff, immediately objected to the line because it suggested disagreement with the verdict; when the statement was released anyway, he made sure columnists knew that conservatives within the White House opposed it.[74]

Three weeks later, Quayle gave a speech on the "poverty of values." The body of the substantive speech had been initially prepared for the president to deliver at Notre Dame's commencement and had been toned down by the campaign in order to be inclusive enough to reach beyond the party base. Quayle wanted to steer the speech back to the Right and throw some red meat to the values-oriented conservatives, so he had Kristol insert a line calculated to have "shock value." At this time, *Murphy Brown* was the most popular sitcom on television; its fictional hero, an unwed news anchor, was about to have a child. The day that 38 million viewers watched Murphy give birth to a son, Quayle picked a fight with the show:[75]

> It doesn't help matters when prime-time TV has Murphy Brown, a character who supposedly epitomizes today's intelligent, high-paid professional woman, mocking the importance of fathers by bearing a child alone and calling it just another "lifestyle choice."[76]

As Quayle had hoped, the furor roused the base and enhanced his support by social conservatives. It also contradicted his boss's attempt to look less strident and narrow-minded. Murphy Brown, Mary Matalin pointed out to the men, was the second most popular woman in America after Barbara Bush.[77] Decrying a "poverty of values" might have been a winner after the urban riots of the 1960s, but attacking a fictional character made Quayle sound more like Pat Buchanan than Richard Nixon at a moment when the campaign was targeting moderates.

Slick Willie

When Clinton finally clinched the nomination on June 2, he was damaged goods. It was hard, if not impossible, for the Bush strategists to imagine a Clinton comeback.

As long as he was seen as Slick Willie, his economic expertise and programs were irrelevant. Bush's strategists had been preparing since 1990—when Lee Atwater had identified Clinton as the most potentially dangerous candidate to face Bush in 1992—to contrast Clinton's toxic persona with the president's admirable personal character. Atwater had visited Arkansas to recruit the candidate most willing to savage Clinton in the 1990 gubernatorial election, and used that candidate "to throw everything we can think of at Clinton—drugs, women, whatever works. We may or may not win, but we'll bust him up so bad he won't be able to run again for years."[78] Atwater's candidate lost in the primaries, but all the material from that campaign made the national press and had turned Clinton into a caricature of a country snake-oil salesman.

The Republicans had more weapons at their disposal. There couldn't be an easier year to run against welfare- and entitlement-oriented, "tax and spend" Democrats than 1992, when middle-class worries were so high. Clinton might try to duck the kinds of promises that had sunk Mondale and Dukakis, but Jesse Jackson—who had run from the Left in the 1984 and 1988 primaries—could make demands that would make Clinton look bad to moderates. "Jesse Jackson," summarized *New York* magazine's Joe Klein, "may well stand between the Democrats and presidency for the next 20 years." Jackson's focus was on redistribution, entitlements, and economic justice, and he was violently opposed to any compromises for the sake of electoral expediency. Leaders of the women's groups were no more interested than Jackson in promoting policies that would attract moderates and men at the expense of their own agendas.[79]

Another Republican attack was already set for after the Democratic convention. The Bush campaign had already prepared the same line of environmental attacks that they had used on Dukakis in 1988. Few rivers anywhere in the country were dirtier than some of the rivers in Arkansas—a major state for poultry production. The commercials were ready to roll.[80]

If this was not enough, Bush—with help from Roger Ailes—had brought the single most powerful radio talk-show personality in America,

Rush Limbaugh, into the fold. Although conservative, Limbaugh had not been a wholehearted supporter of any candidate, nor had he ever invited—or needed—guests on his show. Roger Ailes courted Limbaugh and brought him to the White House for dinner with Bush and an overnight stay in the Lincoln bedroom. The charm worked; Limbaugh was a full-fledged Bush supporter from June on, welcoming both Bush and Quayle on his show that fall.[81]

The assumption that Clinton could not resurrect himself flew in the face of Reagan's 1980 comeback, and Bush's own triumph in 1988. Bush's campaign was only prepared to fight the last war—with the weapons from the last war—and paid no attention to the possibility that Clinton could fight any different war from the one they wanted...and needed.

SLICK WILLIE STRIKES BACK: MANHATTAN PROJECT AND THE RHETT BUTLER BRIGADE

Clinton's own campaign knew their candidate was on life support. He would win the nomination, but he would arrive at the convention badly wounded. When focus groups saw spots in which Clinton talked about issues, his articulate discussions of personal responsibility, jobs, and so forth reinforced the image of a polished, insincere politician.[82]

As the saying goes, mud makes good paint because it doesn't wash off easily. But it can wash off. Top campaign strategists, and a few strategically chosen friends, spearheaded the effort—nicknamed "The Manhattan Project"—to retool Clinton and move beyond the considerable mud he collected from charges of adultery, draft dodging, and marijuana use.[83]

Instead of endless rounds of rebutting all the charges about evasiveness and lack of core values, the campaign would emphasize what they wanted voters to know, and in so doing, fill in the story of Clinton's personal and public lives. If it worked, the negative baggage would be isolated incidents in his trajectory, not the centerpiece.

Since 1984 Clinton had been working to develop more market-driven economic policies and more realistic expectation of the role of government and the importance of incentives. While his evasive answers implied that his policies were pandering, no one could accuse him of shifting with the winds. Ben Wattenberg reviewed his policy speeches and concluded that "tapes of Clinton's speeches of five or ten years ago could have been used in the 1992 campaign."[84]

In a three-way race defined by middle-class anxiety, campaigning on traditional entitlements would make Clinton easy prey for Republicans. "We need to mention work every fifteen seconds," emphasized James Carville. "By the end of the convention, what do we want people to know about Clinton," Mandy Grunwald elaborated. "That he worked his way up; that his life's work had been in education and investing in people; that he values work; that he had moved people from welfare to work; that he has a national economic strategy to put America back to work."[85]

Clinton could overcome hostility and skepticism in person, but his TV exposure was useless. Voters discounted his ads as words lacking commitment; traditional news shows only wanted to talk about his indiscretions and evasions. Grunwald convinced the others that the only way to go was an alternate, wholly unconventional route.

Clinton's first appearance was on *The Arsenio Hall Show*, a hipper version of the standard late-night shows. Decked out in shades, Clinton played his saxophone before joining Hall for a long talk about riots, urban gangs, and work. He followed up with appearances on an MTV special with an audience of young voters and did long call-in segments on *Today*, *CBS This Morning*, and CNN's *Larry King Live*.

Republicans and Democrats criticized Grunwald for this strategy, which they felt was beneath Clinton. The criticism missed the point, for more of the discussion was about his policies than his electability. He finally got the chance to talk—without looking scripted—and reach a bigger audience than he ever could in person.[86] And it was free.

If Clinton could rehabilitate his character, the election would be a battle between competing economic programs...and Bush had none. If Clinton could restore personal credibility, the only way left for the Republicans to take him down would be by tying him to welfare, redistribution, and left-wing identity politics.

Unlike Bush, Clinton was prepared to separate himself from the most stringent demands of the party's base to stay within reach of the center. Clinton had been one of the earliest and most ardent members of the Democratic Leadership Conference (DLC), founded by Al From, a Democratic strategist, after Mondale's defeat to provide an intellectual home for centrist and conservative Democrats. Their emphasis was on combining opportunity with responsibility and the need for government to take an active role in job creation, moving beyond false dichotomies pitting family values against aid to poor children, or merit against quotas. In his 1991 keynote address, Clinton said that "Family values will not feed a hungry child, but you cannot raise that hungry child very well without them" and that "work is the best social program this country has ever devised."[87]

As a leading figure in the DLC, Clinton had been in conflict, open or not, with Jesse Jackson for years. Jackson dismissed the centrist DLC as the "Rhett Butler Brigade" because many of the founders were senators and governors from southern states like Georgia, Virginia, and Arkansas.[88] What Jackson disliked, the Republicans feared. When James Pinkerton, Atwater's crack researcher and issues man from 1988, heard Clinton's 1991 DLC speech, he smelled trouble:

I remember thinking to myself, *they're on to something here*. This is a lot of our stuff or what should have been our stuff....I said, "oh-oh, we better not let this guy get nominated, because we can handle Cuomo and Gephardt and whoever else."[89]

The White House was too consumed with infighting and their own campaign to notice during the primaries when both Clinton and his wife started to clarify their differences with the party's Left. Hillary's approach to abortion (namely, that it "should be safe, legal, and rare") outraged many activists, but others quieted down when an African American woman defended her, saying there were other, more salient issues at play in her community: "They don't wake up in the morning and say, 'my goodness, there's a threat to my right to have an abortion.' They wake up saying 'My kid's going to get shot or I need a job or I need health care.'"[90]

Clinton made sure he was consistent, no matter whether his audience was working- and middle-class whites or African Americans. During the primaries he gave the same speech in Macomb County, Michigan—famous as a home of disenchanted white Democrats upset over welfare going to minorities—as he did the next day in Detroit. He was asking whites to end their racial animosity, and blacks to fight welfare dependency; both groups responded.[91]

Clinton's big surge, however, came when he stood with Senator Al Gore of Tennessee and introduced him as his vice presidential running mate on July 10. The Republicans were caught off guard.

On his own, Clinton was viewed by his own distinctive features—many of which were so negative that they made it nearly impossible for many to believe he had any commitments. Clinton and Gore together changed the way people viewed Clinton. Once Clinton-Gore was facing Bush-Quayle, the common traits of Clinton and Gore dominated while Clinton's own albatrosses receded from the foreground.

Gore's persona, his record on armed services–related issues, and his involvement with nuclear and defense issues highlighted again the lesser stature of Vice President Quayle. Plus, with a prominent environmentalist like Gore on the ticket, Republicans couldn't attack Clinton on chicken waste.[92]

REPUBLICAN CONVENTION

In mid-August James A. Baker finally agreed to return from the State Department to run his good friend's campaign. From the moment Baker arrived, the bickering between White House and campaign staffs ended and everything moved fast. The unmanageable, circus-like meetings of forty or more were now held to no more than ten people. There was one decision point—Baker. That freed up Matalin, Black, and the others to get things done, and Matalin saw that it boosted Bush's confidence because he didn't have to "look over his shoulder."[93]

But there was still no economic plan; there was still no way a president's campaign could move as fast as a challenger's; and there was no way that Bush could unify his party before the convention.

Pat Buchanan would openly, loudly, and clearly endorse Bush only if he got a prime-time spot for a convention speech. The overloaded staff was so concerned about the endorsement that they did not look carefully at the contents of the speech.[94]

Buchanan's was the opening night's prime-time speech, and it set the tone like no other Republican convention since Goldwater's in 1964. The campaign had gambled that Buchanan in prime time would boost ratings, but that was about the only thing they got right. Buchanan proclaimed "a religious war going on in our country for the soul of America. It is a cultural war, as critical to the kind of nation we will one day be as was the Cold War itself." There was an "insidious plague," Buchanan spat, with which the Democrats were infecting America. Buchanan's campaign manager, his sister Bay, was looking ahead to her brother's next presidential run and was thrilled about a platform with "none of that big tent garbage." Even the professionals got carried away. The RNC chairman Rich Bond told the convention "We are America.... Those other people are not America."[95]

The reaction to the convention was so negative that Baker shifted into damage-control mode to recover some of the moderates turned off by the fiery rhetoric of Bush's opening acts. Bush's own speech was hardly better—it was cobbled together without a coherent frame, nor did it include the economic plan that had been eluding them for years.

In the absence of something substantive to offer voters about the economy, the battle plan against Clinton shifted back to attacks. Ironically, their vilification and demonization of Hillary Clinton turned her into a sympathetic figure.[96]

The cocky strategists who thought they could take Clinton down divided the responsibility with Baker to protect their reputations. Charlie Black joked to Baker, "You get the President's positives where they need to be and I'll get Clinton's negatives where they need to be."[97] Black still hadn't figured out just how different an incumbent campaign really was. How can you attack "change" when all you can offer is "more of the same"?

Right after Labor Day, Steeper dropped a bombshell: the public now thought it was riskier to stay with the president than to give Clinton a chance. "If there are no substantial changes in government policies on domestic problems," he reported, 18 percent of the country think "things would get better" and 54 percent thought "things would get worse."[98]

Desperate, Baker and his deputies tried to put together a coherent economic plan to present the next week at the Economic Club of Detroit. They couldn't call it a "plan," though, because Bush's credibility was so low that focus groups hooted at the word.[99]

Black wasn't faring much better on the attack side. Clinton's negatives were never that far from the surface, but an incumbent's attacks are harder to pull off if they've been used in the past, or look like a smoke screen. The press was also quick to remind voters how negative Bush had been in 1988.[100]

By October the Bush campaign tried to attack Clinton for attending a rally in London against U.S. involvement in Vietnam. It was such a haphazard, last-minute desperation move that the frantic Bush campaign had not realized that its own chair of Bush's CEA, Michael Boskin, had spoken at the rally, too.[101]

CONCLUSION

Mike Piazza was one of the greatest catchers in baseball history. A few years after he retired, a reporter asked the twelve-time all-star if he missed playing major league baseball. "You never lose the desire to play," Piazza told her, "but you lose the desire to prepare to play."[102]

George H. W. Bush still wanted to be president in 1992. He might have had trouble articulating his specific goals for a second term to his aides, but he truly believed himself "best suited to handle what crosses that desk."[103] He still wanted to preside, but he had no particular concern over what he would preside. Like Piazza, Bush had lost the hunger and drive to prepare. He believed he was entitled to remain president on the basis of his international efforts.

In 1988, he had the credibility and stature to make untenable promises, and split Democrats by raising issues on which they were not prepared to compete. But when the Soviet Union collapsed and the Democrats nominated a governor who could give the same speeches about jobs and welfare to white and black audiences, Bush couldn't rest on his international laurels or his frayed connections to Ronald Reagan.

Several phrases and moments from the campaign became staples of political culture in the United States: Bill Clinton's "I didn't inhale"; Bush calling his opponents "Waffle Man and Ozone"; the president looking at his watch during a presidential debate as if he were anxious to get off the stage; and James Carville's clear and concise credo, "the economy, stupid," which continues to be used in campaigns throughout the world.[104]

As memorable as each of these discrete phrases or events is, none of them swayed the outcome on their own. Bush didn't lose the election—or even many votes—because he looked at his watch, or because Carville's line raised the salience of the economy and lowered the salience of social issues. Bush lost because he was unwilling to plan ahead for an unavoidable budget showdown over taxes and entitlements. Without advance planning, he couldn't look like he was jobs-oriented in the international arena, where he was most comfortable. And when you "lose the desire to prepare to play," the decision about whether you *get* to play leaves your hands very quickly.

After Lee Atwater's death from brain cancer in March of 1991, Robin Toner wrote that "Whenever President Bush stumbled, or the White House botched a deal with Congress, or a Democrat drew blood, some Republicans would sigh and say, 'This would not have happened if Lee was still around.' "[105] The nostalgia, while understandable, is as naïve as the president's memory of 1988 as "a two-month sprint." It fails to distinguish the ways a campaign *in* the White House differs from a campaign *for* the White House.

It also ignores all the problems inside the White House that Atwater could not solve while he was alive, and all the advice he gave that was ignored—like building in time for right-wingers to ventilate if you're going to displease them, or knowing that "Quayle will have to go" if Bush got into too much trouble in the race. Nor did the president take Atwater's advice to veto the infamous budget deal.

It wasn't as if there was no one to take Atwater's place. Ailes thought Charlie Black was every bit as tough. He was "the kind of guy who, if he came home and found somebody making out with his wife on a rainy day, he'd break the guy's umbrella and ask him to leave, then have him killed a year later," while "Lee would blow the house up."[106]

The White House, Fitzwater realized after the defeat, had allowed "bitterness or anger about the press" to cloud their judgment and believe the economy was doing fine:

> We distrusted the press and believed the traditional economic indicators, thus totally misreading the growing anxiety in the country about jobs, careers, corporate restructuring, and foreign competition. We believed it would be enough to talk about caring and about creating jobs, without actually developing an economic message of action.[107]

When Bush was at his home in Houston preparing his acceptance speech for the convention, he urged friends to get David McCullough's new biography of Harry Truman, telling them to "Start reading at page 653"—the section where McCullough's depiction of Truman's whistle-stop campaign begins. "That is what I'm going to do," Bush told them.[108]

Bush had forgotten Atwater's analysis of 1948—the analysis that had highlighted the four years of planning that had gone into the two-month sprints in 1988...and 1948. Atwater thought 1948 marked the first "permanent campaign" inside a White House and considered Truman's strategy of confronting Congress to be the key to his success. Truman's strategy memos were "So deep and original," Atwater said, "one can scarcely believe [they were] not produced by a full-time political consultant with years of experience and study."[109]

Hamstrung by a two-month sprint not set up by years of advance planning, Bush grew increasingly frustrated—and outraged—that the country might evict him for those "two bozos" as he neared judgment day for his reign. The night of the election, his concession speech said all the right things but his last line revealed the pain of being deposed: "So we will get behind this new President and wish him..."—there was a notable pause before he concluded—"wish him well."[110]

SUCCESSORS: LAPDOGS OR LEADERS

In 1932 Franklin Delano Roosevelt asked John Nance Garner to be his running mate. Garner was the Speaker of the House at the time, a man liked and respected by his constituents—he was elected for fifteen consecutive terms—and his colleagues alike. He played poker regularly with Roosevelt and used his ample connections on Capitol Hill to ease the way for passage of the New Deal legislation. The *New York Times* proclaimed that FDR had broken with tradition by naming a truly important man, not a nonentity, to be vice president. While Garner was portrayed as powerful and central to the administration, he still felt demoted and enervated in his new role. He had been the second most powerful man in Washington; once ensconced as the VP, he called himself "just a spare tire." After he was out of Washington, he was more candid: "Worst damn-fool mistake I ever made was letting myself be elected vice president."[1]

Whatever party a candidate belongs to, the most challenging route to the White House is that of a successor: a candidate—either the sitting vice president or another governor or member of Congress—who attempts to retain the White House for their party after two terms of a sitting president.

The vice presidency is now worth more than in Garner's time, when he dismissed the job as a "bucket of warm piss" (the newspapers changed the quote to "spit").[2] Today's vice presidents have it a bit better: they have more policy responsibility than in the past, and participate more in the selling and defending of the administration. Still, it is a tough road to the White House if the president lives out his term.[3]

Since 1945, Richard Nixon, Hubert Humphrey, George H. W. Bush and Al Gore all won their party's nomination while serving as vice president. Only Bush succeeded—the first sitting vice president to do so in more than 150 years. (Nixon lost as a sitting VP in 1960 and won the presidency as a challenger to Humphrey—who ran as Lyndon Johnson's successor—in 1968.)

Succeeding an incumbent president is no easier for governors or senators from the ruling party. Only three times since 1900 has there been an election without a sitting vice president or president on the ballot: 1920, 1952, and 2008. In each case, the candidate of the party in power (Governors James Cox and Adlai Stevenson, and Senator John McCain) lost.

There are a couple of reasons for this. First, voters become fatigued with the incumbent party after two terms. Second, vice presidents—despite having a great job for developing name recognition, doing favors for politicians, and raising money—have all the organizational problems of an incumbent, plus an added layer of challenges regarding their character, vision, and credibility. Successors, therefore, have the hardest time of all candidates figuring out the difference between what got them there and what will keep them there, and then developing a manageable campaign strategy.

AIR FORCE TWO OR A CONSTITUTIONAL INCONVENIENCE?

When vice presidents travel the world on White House assignments, be it to a foreign leader's funeral, an international meeting not quite important enough for the president, or a "fact-finding trip" to give them exposure or soothe a rankled constituency, they are treated as the second most important person in America. They can build up countless IOUs by making detours from their official business and lending glamour and stature at a favored politician's fund-raiser, their presence heralded by the arrival of Air Force Two, a traffic-stopping motorcade, and a full retinue of secret service agents, aides, and press.

But from the moment a person is picked as a running mate, he is already a source of contention and power struggles within the presidential candidate's inner circle, and is regarded by some of the political elite as a compromise (at best) or the lowest common denominator (at worst).

The eventual choice is never the choice of the entire party. Unlike the winner of the primary, a vice-president did not earn her place via electoral combat. In addition to facing resentment from the power players within the campaign, there is the scorn and enmity from those passed over for the position.

When the nominee's campaign screens potential running mates, the list of potential nominees includes those just on the list for their name to be leaked as a quid pro quo for an endorsement; people included to acknowledge needed constituencies; and contenders whose inclusion might actually help the candidate seal an electoral victory. (Of course, candidates will always say that their only criterion for choosing someone is that he or she is qualified to be president should the need arise.)

There are always staff conflicts within the nominee's camp about whom to choose because the evidence about who can help with which demographic or constituency is never clear-cut. The murky data estimating which running mate–in–waiting helps the ticket gets so convoluted that Bob Teeter "used to look for 28 electoral votes or some demographic bloc. Now, the crucial question is how the press and public react in the first 48 hours."[4]

Indeed, the choice almost always obscures the campaign's message while the press digs deeper into the running mate's past and finds covered-up slush funds, statehouse corruption, electroshock treatment, secret payments to party officials, a spouse's tax problems, use of family influence to avoid active military duty during Vietnam, inconvenient votes against legislature designed to court needed voters, or a pregnant, unmarried daughter.[5]

When Governor George W. Bush asked Richard Cheney to screen his candidates for vice president, Cheney prepared detailed, exhaustive questionnaires that only proved, as former VP Dan Quayle put it, "Everybody has negatives." Cheney, who became Bush's eventual choice, never filled one out himself, and his own negatives came to light before the campaign had a chance to prepare for them. No one in the campaign saw his corporate, tax, or medical records in advance.[6] They weren't ready to talk about Cheney's votes against programs Bush strongly supported as "compassionate conservatism," or that while Cheney was CEO of Halliburton Oil, they defied U.S. rules against trade with Iraq. Halliburton refused to disclose

Cheney's role in controversial decisions, and the result, the campaign's press secretary told Bush, was that "We're getting our asses kicked in the media because we're not prepared."[7]

The candidate's staff has a vested interest in the choice of a running mate, too: the Washington hands and the strategists all know their roles and positions will be influenced by the potential VP's staff and consultants. The professionals nearly always favor candidates with whom they have worked over the candidates they don't know, and the policy specialists are interested in candidates whose expertise and issue areas are likely to make their role more central.

"It's a lot easier to kill legislation than pass legislation," Quayle noted when looking back at his own experience. "So it's a lot easier to knock off VP candidates than to actually get one through the mill."[8]

Once inside the administration, vice presidents suffer fresh rounds of humiliation at the hands of the president and his staff, to whom the VP has become a constitutional inconvenience. When they fly around the world representing their country, it provides great footage if they run for president, but only rarely do vice presidents actually handle sensitive negotiations unless someone besides their own staff—a cabinet member, say, or a senior aide to the president—is present to give the final word.

Not until Franklin Roosevelt died did his staff bother to tell Harry Truman any details of their negotiations with Churchill or Stalin, or that the government was developing nuclear weapons. The newly inaugurated president was "totally uninformed" about crucial events. Lyndon Johnson was one of the country's most powerful, accomplished senators, but he spent three years being mocked by Robert Kennedy and all the cool, sophisticated friends of the family. Kennedy told everyone that he thought Johnson was a mistake, that his brother's offer had been a courtesy offer Johnson was supposed to turn down. Johnson didn't even have an office in the West Wing of the White House; he conducted his business from his Senate office. Now, however, his old colleagues did not even let him attend the democratic caucus; he was part of the White House—albeit a lonely one—and no longer one of them. When Vice President Spiro Agnew tried to buttonhole senators on behalf of Nixon, he was publicly rebuked by the Senate majority leader Mike Mansfield for meddling; Agnew was not entitled to do business on the Senate floor: "He's a half-creature of the Senate and a half-creature of the executive."[9]

Vice President Bush was an outsider, even a heretic, in the Reagan White House. Few of his friends, other than James A. Baker, the chief of staff, got jobs in the administration, and when he entered a room for a meeting, all the conversation stopped and the subject changed. No vice president can argue—or even politely differ—with a president in front of staffers without a leak revealing rifts in the White House, so Bush kept silent in front of staffers or in cabinet meetings. Then he was further belittled by stories that he "had nothing to contribute."[10] At least Bush, thanks to Walter Mondale's office in the West Wing, wasn't banished to the Old Executive Office Building where previous VPs had been relegated.

Every president does his best to have smooth relations with the vice president, but staff tension and backbiting are part of the job. When presidents don't want to accept a proposal or do someone a favor, they instruct their staff to do it in such a way that *they*, not the president, take the heat. Whenever President's Ford's staff analyzed a proposal by Vice President Nelson Rockefeller and told the president that Rockefeller's ambitious proposal wouldn't fly in a belt-tightening season, the chief of staff Donald Rumsfeld was the designated "bad cop." Rockefeller was certain that all the animosity was motivated by Rumsfeld's ulterior motivation—to persuade Ford to dump Rockefeller for a better candidate (him).[11]

Who Are You?

The conflicts within the administration are one thing, but once a vice president decides to run for president, the way voters perceive him is quite another. Until the public sees evidence to the contrary, vice presidents are not leaders but followers with questionable strength. They are no longer powerful senators or a successful governors; they are cheerleaders for someone else's agenda. If a president is worth seventeen votes in the Senate (the difference between a simple majority and a veto-proof majority), then the vice president is worth only one—the tie-breaker.

Vice President Bush was the youngest war hero of World War II, an all-American first baseman, and Phi Beta Kappa at Yale. He was also ambassador to China and head of the CIA. Still, as vice president he was lampooned in Garry Trudeau's *Doonesbury* comic strip as having placed his "manhood in a blind trust."[12] George Will gibed that "the unpleasant sound Bush is emitting…is a thin, tinny 'arf'—the sound of a lap dog."[13]

Vice presidents are all suspect, then, both on leadership and autonomy. Are they tough enough to stand up for what they believe if they were willing to cheer for someone else's agenda and defend policies inconsistent with their prior record? Do they even have core beliefs anymore?

Vice President Hubert Humphrey's friends were always confused when Humphrey defended President Johnson's Vietnam policy. Humphrey compared the problem to "being naked in the middle of a blizzard with no one to even offer you a match to keep you warm—that's the vice presidency. You are trapped, vulnerable, and alone." Since the vice president "cannot make policy or propose new solutions.... Pretty soon you're sounding like the administration cheerleader, and the public ridicule sets in."[14]

The only way a successor can prove they can take a punch is to take a punch and hit back. That is hard for successors. Many of their party's base will be disappointed by the inevitable compromises the president has made in order to pass legislation and secure enough votes from moderates to win reelection. If the VP fights with the base and stands up to their demands for ideological purity, how does he or she win the primary? A VP cannot even attack the other party as easily as his other primary opponents, because he has been defending some of the compromises the other party demanded from the president.

Vice President Nixon had the great luck to encounter the perfect enemy at the right time with the media present. In 1959, when Cold War tensions were very high, Nixon represented his country at an American exhibition in Moscow. As he was showing the Soviet premier around, Khrushchev stopped at the RCA television studio exhibit and launched a tirade of propagandistic invective about the superiority of communism and the failures of capitalism. Nixon initially maintained diplomatic calm and looked weak.

However, immediately after the communist leader's harangue, William Safire (then doing PR for a home builder) maneuvered the two into his employer's cutout model of a typical American home. Crowds blocked the way out, so they sat at the Formica kitchen table. With a reporter from the *New York Times* looking on, Nixon was forceful, firm, and effective at standing up for the United States and letting Khrushchev bluster without ever backing down or losing his cool. Safire then managed to smuggle out an embargoed photo of Nixon jabbing his finger in the chest of Khrushchev. The story and photo ran immediately across the United States and the "kitchen debate" established Nixon as a forceful defender of the American way of life. President Truman always said "if you cannot stand the heat, get out of the kitchen," and Nixon showed he could literally stay in the kitchen and go against America's toughest opponent.[15]

No successor, not even Nixon, ever has an easy time assessing what kind of shape he is in as he approaches the campaign. Successors cannot prove they are autonomous enough to be leaders until they show they can defeat challengers and win the nomination. The president's lowest common denominator now has to prove he is actually the best choice to lead the party.

Vice presidents all start as tainted insiders. Unlike governors, they cannot claim they are outside Washington and uncontaminated by the national problems du jour, be they gridlock, taxes, scandal, or military stalemate. And they cannot easily claim leadership and autonomy after defending someone else's choices for eight years without any public disagreements. They *are* the system when they begin the campaign.

Voters start the primary season with only one style of leadership firmly on their minds: that of the current president.[16] It takes time for the vice president to establish his own personality and identity, and for the public to get accustomed to an alternate style of leadership. Every vice president struggles with the decision about how to achieve separation without alienation: defining a path for the next four years different enough to meet the new terrain and competition, yet not offensive to the president or his supporters.

Ironically, nothing a president says in public can help prove a successor's autonomy. If voters suspect a successor is merely a puppet, an endorsement from the puppeteer solves nothing. This creates another dilemma: If you are trying to persuade people to ask you to be their leader, how do you claim superior experience and competence without sounding entitled to inherit the nomination?

Albatross or Legacy

When presidents from a new party take power, they first deal with the easy issues—matters that unite their party, or which the other party cannot afford to publicly oppose. Soon after his inauguration, President Clinton signed the family medical legislation that President Bush had vetoed to placate the business community. President Reagan immediately issued an executive order to freeze all hiring of new federal employees, and to show he cared (despite the budget cuts), he began a series of weekly orders proclaiming what his counsel called the "disease of the week."[17] By the end of the incumbent party's second term, however, the low-hanging fruit had all been picked, satisfying some of their supporters and diminishing their fire.

Presidents also slowly but inevitably alienate some other constituencies whose demands are inconsistent with staying in office. Clinton thought he could allow gays to serve openly in the military with an executive order, only to be informed by senators that they would pass legislation overturning the order.[18] Reagan promised further budget cuts and found that it was always easier to cut taxes than cut spending, alienating deficit hawks.

With some constituencies satisfied and complacent, and others turned off by inaction, an erosion of support—some fatigue—is inevitable. On average, a candidate from the incumbent's party can expect to lose about half a percent of the national vote every year, or about 4 percent after eight years.[19]

The question facing a successor is this: Are voters feeling incumbent fatigue or party fatigue? The answer a successor chooses settles the question of whether the incumbent is an albatross or a legacy. And that, in turn, is a critical part of campaign planning. The explanation for fatigue is an implicit plan for victory.

If the incumbent is an albatross, the successor has to decide how to separate himself from the incumbent while remaining close to the party. If the problem is the party, the successor must decide how to remain close to the incumbent and avoid being too closely identified with his party's unpopular core beliefs. Whatever the successor decides, other candidates will challenge the decision in the primaries.

Hubert Humphrey wanted and needed to separate from Lyndon Johnson on Vietnam in 1968; it was the overriding issue holding Humphrey back, overshadowing even civil rights. Walter Heller, chairman of the Council of Economic Advisors, thought Johnson treated Humphrey "like a staff sergeant might treat a private." LBJ had control over most Democratic campaign money and used his power of the purse to force Humphrey to support his war policies. In the last weeks of the campaign, a desperate Humphrey stood up for himself, called for a bombing halt, and Johnson went along. He made up fourteen of the fifteen points by which he trailed Richard Nixon. It was too little, too late. Humphrey lost by just over 500,000 votes, or seven-tenths of 1 percent of all votes cast.[20]

He had not dared to separate when he needed to. "After four years as Vice President...I had lost some of my personal identity....It would have been better that I stood my ground...I ought not to have let a man who was going to be a former president dictate my future."[21] Yet Humphrey also realized the reality inherent in attempting to assert one's self from the VP's office: "Anyone who thinks that the vice president can take a position independent of the president...has no knowledge of politics or government. You are his choice in a political marriage, and he expects your absolute loyalty."[22]

John McCain had always been a "maverick," reform-oriented senator, willing to criticize President George W. Bush over policies with which he disagreed. Despite difficult relations with him, a McCain defeat in 2008, when he ran as successor to Bush, would be a repudiation of Bush, so the president's staffers tried to believe that "McCain was the hope of the world because, well, because he chose to be a member of our party."[23]

When the financial crisis exploded in 2008, McCain asked President Bush to call a summit meeting so he could show leadership on an issue the incumbent party had to address during the campaign. McCain had to figure out which conflicting Republican position to take. The Republican president he wanted to succeed believed that a massive bailout was needed at once to prevent collapse of the U.S. economy. A majority of Republican congressmen were opposed to spending the money. McCain had to decide whether this was an ideological fight between a moderate president and a conservative base or a fight between the politician responsible for the economy and politicians whose constituents didn't understand or like government spending.

Bush was an albatross, but he was also an incumbent Republican president. Suddenly McCain had none of the advantages of a vice president and all of the problems.

Secretary of the Treasury Henry Paulson later wrote that McCain didn't even have a strategy for using the meeting to score political points, let alone handle the crisis. He had so little to say, according to Paulson, that he turned the meeting into a farce. McCain mostly sat silent until pushed hard to say what he thought of Paulson's three-page proposal. McCain wanted to gain some credit for the bailout instead of being left out when Bush negotiated with the Democrats, but he couldn't handle it. The Democratic congressman Barney Frank finally got so frustrated with McCain's stalling that he began to shout, "What's the Republican Plan?" Vice President Cheney laughed out loud.[24]

Even when the president is a positive legacy, the successor still will have to defend how the in-party is dealing with current problems without breaking with the president. Nobody accused Eisenhower of being militarily weak, yet in the first 1960 debate between Senator John F. Kennedy and Vice President Richard Nixon, Cuba was mentioned thirty-five times. Fidel Castro had led an armed revolution the year before and anti-communist concerns were inflamed by a prospective Soviet outpost ninety miles from Florida. Over and over Kennedy criticized Nixon for the fate of Cuba and the administration's inaction in the face of this security threat.

Kennedy knew that the administration was planning an invasion of Cuba; that summer, Alabama's governor John Patterson had told Kennedy he had approved a CIA request to send 350 Alabama Air National Guardsmen to train Cuban exiles for an invasion of Cuba. But Kennedy also knew that Nixon could say nothing to rebut his criticisms without destroying the secret plan.[25]

While the base of the party in power inevitably is less hungry and united, the out-party and their supporters get increasingly anxious to return to power. After eight years, it is easier for the "outs" to rally around a candidate who is "anybody but the opposition."

TEAMWORK

Teamwork within the campaign is much harder for vice presidents than for incumbents or challengers. Whereas incumbents must reconcile the differences and conflicts between their administration and their campaign, successors must manage the damage caused by *three* staffs: the president's staff, their own staff, and the campaign staff. There will always be two inside staffs jockeying over policy while the candidate tries to coordinate his campaign with his policy staff.

When a president runs for reelection, he has staffers he has known well over time. Their future depends upon leaving the White House as winners. In the second term, George Reedy notes, the people who know the president well are mostly gone, either burned out by the pressure or moving on to cash in on their various reputations.[26] The new second-term staffers will be leaving when the president leaves office, so their future depends more upon establishing their own credentials than upon establishing a relationship with a vice president trying to win the next election.

While the president's second-term staff is focused on their own résumés, the vice president's staff has been waiting patiently, enduring slights real and imagined from the president's staff. They are intent on using the campaign to their advantage, to show their value and move up in the next administration.

VICE PRESIDENT BUSH IN 1988

George Bush had been an inept campaigner in 1984: his speech had been awkward, and he looked like a bully when he faced off against Congresswoman Geraldine Ferraro in the vice presidential debate. Trying to sound macho afterward—and not realizing he was being recorded—Bush bragged that he had "kicked a little ass."[27]

His political standing and his organization were inadequate for a presidential run—which is why Bush began planning his 1988 presidential campaign shortly after the 1984 election. That far in advance, Bush couldn't know who his Republican opponents in the primary would be nor who the Democrats would nominate. Still, there were steps he could take independent of that knowledge, all of which served him well by the time the campaign began in earnest. Among them were building a campaign-ready organization to develop a strategy that maximized the benefits of his office; ignoring the personal and public humiliations he and his wife endured because of their status inside the White House; making it appear as if there was no distance between them and the private, shy president and the socially domineering First Lady who resented Barbara Bush's popularity;[28] staying personally close to the president, and quietly using his office to collect IOUs from the elected officials and interest group leaders who would be most useful in his 1988 campaign; using the primaries to reestablish his identity and let the separation from Reagan occur naturally; and exploiting divisions within the Democratic Party to unite Republicans and force the Democrats to defend unpopular, divisive policies. None of this would have been possible if he had not also developed a way to control the conflicts between his campaign staff and the two White House staffs.

Bush identified his critical task as separating from Reagan without alienating him—or his wife Nancy. He needed separation to "demonstrate he was his own man, and set out a clear direction and goals." He also needed Reagan's blessing to hold the party together and quell mutinies that could be launched by true believers attacking him for revisions. He would have to figure it out himself "in his own way and on his own timetable."[29]

He also had to build a national organization and use the vice presidency to get a leg up on his primary rivals. That meant strengthening his political action committee, Fund for America's Future, and upgrading his White House staff.

When he interviewed Lee Atwater to chair the Political Action Committee (PAC), he was looking for managerial competence along with positive relations with Reagan.[30] Atwater was acceptable on both counts, and he was also expert at mobilizing the types of critical voting blocs most culturally distant from and distrustful of Bush. Atwater was from redneck country, played blues guitar, and had no qualms about doing anything and everything to help a candidate win.

Atwater's analysis of the terrain and competition for 1988 was that Bush's two biggest political threats were a centrist Democrat like Gary Hart, already attacking stale orthodoxy, or a "new ideas" Republican like Jack Kemp. If Hart opposed Bush by arguing "it is finally time for a change," Bush would have low odds of winning. While Kemp had no base, he was quick to grab simple, clear ideas—tax cuts, the gold standard, religious freedom for Christians in Eastern Europe—and run with them while they were in fashion.[31]

Atwater was fascinated with the new ideas and "new generation of leadership" themes that Hart and his pollster and advisor, Pat Caddell, had used to challenge the reigning orthodoxy of the Democratic coalition. Atwater had concluded that the terrain had changed for both parties and the Republican right wing was no longer the "nominating wing of the party."[32] Bush had to flirt with them but only move far enough toward them to win 25 percent of their votes. Such a feint to the right would sucker the other candidates to move farther to the right. At that point Bush's quarter of the Right's votes plus a majority of the moderates would get Bush the nomination without making it too hard to reach the center of the electorate in the general election.[33]

SUBSERVIENT AUTONOMY

Bush may have been the butt of White House jokes and silent during cabinet meetings, but all the while he was improving his relationship with

Reagan. Reagan was a shy loner with so little talent for friendship that he normally connected with others only through jokes. At his weekly private lunch with the president, Bush used his own talent at friendship and brought Reagan jokes he could use instead of policy papers to discuss. Bush's staff knew "the way to earn a stripe...was to give him a *Joke for the President*."[34]

While remaining subservient to the president inside the White House, Bush slowly established a basis for his autonomy, building bridges within the party and collecting IOUs. By 1985 Bush was actively courting evangelicals, the group most culturally distant from a preppy, Episcopalian Yale man. Using his foreign policy expertise, he began to identify himself with below-the-radar projects like the plight of Ethiopian Jewry and their return to Israel. Powerful evangelists like Pat Robertson were using their religious media to mobilize evangelicals to help return the lost tribe descended (according to legend) from Sheba to Israel. Until they were all back in Israel, Robertson preached, Jesus would not return.[35]

By helping leaders like Robertson, Jerry Falwell, and Ed McAteer, Bush built a southern firewall for the primaries. He just had to be acceptable to the religious Right if there were no evangelicals remaining in the race; at that point, favorable coverage on the Christian Broadcasting Network (CBN) and his elite connections would be enough.

By helping them help Israel, Bush courted two constituencies for the price of one: Israeli leaders were also thrilled with the political support and tourism from the religious Right.[36] In 1986 he had glorious, well-choreographed visits to Israel and Jordan; the Israeli government even lent the Jordanians helicopters to help Bush transport his entourage and get the photo opportunities he wanted for the campaign.

The success in Israel was followed by trips to other foreign countries. By 1987 Bush got a wild reception from cheering crowds in Poland, visited European heads of state, and made a videotape with the British prime minister Margaret Thatcher for later use. While the trip was, of course, entirely official business, a Fund for America's Future–financed camera crew was there, too.[37]

Bush started using his PAC and his White House aura to visit fundraisers around the country, signing up governors as co-chairs of his PAC, and inviting them back to the White House for breakfast, so they could tell their constituents back home they had pressed critical issues there. A former head of the RNC, Bush concentrated on governors because they knew their local media and issues far better than senators, and they had the staffs to put the events together.[38]

Working with governors and Israel to solidify support on the Right put Bush in good shape for the elections. He was making no commitments to the Right for which he could be savaged after the primaries—who could criticize him for rescuing Ethiopian Jews? Atwater's analysis that a post–New Deal candidate was the only serious Democratic threat to Bush was on the money: In May 1986, polls showed Hart leading Bush by four percentage points, while Bush crushed conventional, big-ticket liberals like Mario Cuomo by thirty points.[39]

NOVEMBER 1986

Then the bottom fell out for the party and for the White House. By September 1986, just ahead of the midterm elections, Republicans had lost its party advantage on all the big issues: deficits, strong defense, and social policy. Top Republican strategists met secretly in Washington to determine the best way to hang on to control of the Senate. There was near-unanimous consensus among them that the only topic Reagan could talk about without hurting the candidates was drug abuse and his belief that "just saying no" would do more than any government spending.[40]

The Republicans still lost control of the Senate with Reagan on the sidelines. Democrats picked up two of the three open seats and knocked off seven incumbent Republicans, six of them hard-core Reagan adherents elected in 1980.

The election was not even the worst news that month for Bush. The rest of the year was dominated by the revelation that the Reagan administration had been selling arms to Iran in exchange for the release of hostages held in Lebanon. The deal sent advanced weapons to an embargoed enemy of the United States. The weapons were sold at a substantial markup, and the profits were used to fund the contras, the guerrillas fighting the Marxist government of Nicaragua—a direct violation of U.S. law. If that weren't enough for a media circus of hearings, investigations, and indictments, there were explosive allegations that the White House and the CIA knew that the contras were smuggling cocaine and heroin in the planes delivering the weapons.[41]

For most of the next year, Bush was dogged by questions about what he knew and when he knew it. He was not indicted, but there was enough lingering suspicion to hurt him inside the party and in matches against Democrats. In January 1987, his lead over Robert Dole for the nomination had dropped from forty-four points to fifteen.[42]

Nevertheless, thanks to the governors he had recruited, particularly New Hampshire's governor John Sununu, Bush survived the declining popularity of Reaganomics in good form. Bush got the nomination, but his campaign was still sputtering and the Republican Party was losing support. The Republican analyst John Petrocik was candid about the party's problem: "The Republican coalition has some indigestible elements.... There isn't a coherent vision of the party or its policy agenda that is going to hold these people together."[43]

Before he developed a vision, he needed a coherent campaign. State by state in the primaries Atwater managed to keep things moving. But the campaign was inefficient, and relations with the White House were slowed by turf battles and well-meaning friends of Bush and his family.

Bush and his family shared Reagan's distrust of hired hands like Atwater; a profanity-laced interview that Atwater had conducted with *Esquire* (in his underwear, no less) didn't help matters. Bush's younger son, George W. Bush, chewed out Atwater and decided to keep his eye on him.[44]

Atwater understood the conflict of interest inherent in his role and made certain that W could look over his shoulder any time he wanted to. While W's oversight helped establish Atwater's credibility, it didn't help him speed up decision-making enough for a national campaign.[45] Atwater couldn't cut the number of decision points and limit second-guessing. He didn't have the clout to change the power structure, and the bickering was destroying efforts to develop consensus on a message.[46]

Bush's pollster Bob Teeter was famously slow and cautious. When he would finally reach an agreement with Atwater and Roger Ailes, they were constantly second-guessed by Bush's good friend Nick Brady. Brady was a wealthy Wall Street investment banker from an old family well-known in thoroughbred racing circles. Supremely confident, Brady liked to remind everyone he had been a senator, even though he was appointed by the Republican governor of New Jersey to finish the remaining seven months in the term of a Democrat, Harrison Williams, who resigned to avoid an expulsion vote after a bribery conviction.[47]

No one was following up on key decisions; far too many people were reporting directly to Atwater; and decisions were being made on a short-term basis without any consideration of how they affected future options or how they related to media and the VP's performance.[48]

Atwater finally reduced the delays with help from a peer of Bush's family and friends, Gary MacDougal. MacDougal had been a partner at McKinsey, CEO of a large profitable company, and a director of UPS. He had been chairman of the board at the Russell Sage Foundation and a trustee of the Casey Foundation, and like many successful people at the top of their pyramid, he wanted to devote time and energy to public policy. When Atwater called him in for a talk, MacDougal had been assisting Teeter with position papers.

Atwater had seen enough of MacDougal to judge that he—unlike most of the Bushes' friends—had enough real feel for politics and campaigns to be trusted. There were always plenty of policy analysts and position papers. What the campaign desperately needed were procedures for developing and executing strategy. Atwater made a blunt pitch to the only person around with political sense, managerial competence, and credibility:

> Most CEOs are assholes, but you're different. You've been getting along with people around here and people like what you do, and you've been helpful. I don't know anything about management. I know politics. Politics is my thing, besides I don't have time for anything else. I'd like you to be the manager…I'll work on politics and anything to do with management, you take care of that.[49]

Bush had seen how bad things were and readily consented to giving MacDougal a shot at building a workable campaign organization. MacDougal identified and eliminated bottlenecks and sped up decision-making within the campaign. As a very successful businessman and investor—and a player in the Illinois Republican Party—he had standing that ordinary hired hands would never have. Instead of leaving him alone in a corner, MacDougal managed to get Ailes directly involved in the campaign's decision-making so that the campaign and media message were in sync.[50] MacDougal could lay out the organization and help Atwater and Ailes manage the campaign without getting bogged down. But no one in the campaign could enforce decisions on the White House staff or defend decisions when Bush's close friends second-guessed them.

Stu Spencer compared the first meeting between staffs to a summit conference: "They were lined up on opposite sides of the table.... They looked like the Russians and the Americans."[51] Spencer could start the ball rolling but only someone who had clout inside the White House and credibility with Bush's powerful friends and family could achieve closure. The obvious person—perhaps the only one who could do it for Bush—was his close friend James Baker, who had managed presidential campaigns and been Reagan's first chief of staff.

Now Bush was ready to cash in the careful credit he had accumulated with Reagan from his loyalty and constant supply of jokes. Initially reluctant to give up his treasury secretary, Reagan finally agreed.[52]

Later, Atwater was asked if he resented Baker's power. He laughed. He was thrilled to finally have someone in charge "with the right kind of cologne." The right cologne meant efficiency and closure. Now Atwater didn't have to "sit around and beat back the Nick Bradys." Once Baker was there, Atwater only had to get Baker's approval. Any friend who came to the vice president with an objection, suggestion, or complaint about the campaign was referred back to Baker.[53]

THE RIGHT ENEMY

When they met with Bush in June, his strategists had already laid out their goals for the summer: Establish Bush as his own man, take control of the agenda, show a clear contrast with Dukakis, and raise his opponent's negatives.[54] Gary Hart had been forced to drop out of the campaign over the revelation of womanizing when pictures were published of him and a young blonde on a yacht named *Monkey Business*. Massachusetts's governor Michael Dukakis won the primaries emphasizing competence and the booming economy of the "Massachusetts Miracle."

Voters considered Dukakis the kind of moderate centrist Atwater had feared all along. He was ahead of Bush in Teeter's campaign polls by eighteen points in June, and the public mood favored a change in parties. Stu Spencer, the experienced campaigner, sensed that the voters were in the mood to "let the little technocrat from Massachusetts come in and fine-tune what Reagan had wrought."[55]

They started the campaign concerned about how to defend Bush against the obvious negative attacks on his character and policies, and how to attack Dukakis's personal and political character. If Dukakis was seen as someone to fine-tune the current situation, they were in trouble. He was fresh, smart, and someone whose family had worked their way up from nothing. He was credible and authentic, and Bush was in trouble on both counts.

Bush was under a cloud from the Iran Contra scandal, and the campaign expected a barrage of attacks on his judgment and competence for selling arms to the ayatollahs in Iran. Ailes feared that everything they had on Dukakis was "penny-ante stuff compared to arms to the ayatollah.... These guys are gonna come in and nuke us someday."[56]

Teeter stressed that "Just tagging him as a liberal alone wouldn't work. You had to define him outside the mainstream of American values." Atwater had already been searching for the telling anecdotes and stories to bring the point to life.[57] They didn't have to look far, because one of the prime examples was so controversial in Massachusetts that there had been near-mutinies among Democrats, and the issue already had been raised during the primaries.

On April 12, during a debate in New York, Senator Al Gore asked Dukakis about a controversial prison reform program that allowed prisoners out of jail on weekend passes. Gore challenged Dukakis for extending the program to first-degree murderers, two of whom had committed other murders while on their passes. Dukakis gave an evasive answer, meaning the issue was never put to rest, and Dukakis was still vulnerable on the issue.

The *Lawrence Eagle-Tribune* had just been awarded a Pulitzer Prize for their reporting about the controversy. One of the furloughed murderers, Willie Horton, had gone to Maryland, where he pistol-whipped, beat, and stabbed a man, tied him up, and raped and assaulted his wife for hours. The couple managed to escape, and police captured Horton. Crime victims' families forced the state government to open records of the furlough program. Then, when Dukakis vetoed a bill to end furloughs for murderers, the families started a statewide petition drive for a referendum to change the program and forced Dukakis to sign the bill.

What Gore had not mentioned was that Willie Horton was black and the victims were white. The Bush campaign, however, did not have to tiptoe around Democratic Party elites who wanted to avoid the explosive combination of race and violence—support for the death penalty was at an all-time high. Bush started talking about Dukakis and furloughs for murderers in June. The July issue of *Reader's Digest* featured "Getting Away with Murder," Robert Bidinotto's graphic account of Horton's crime spree and the outrage and uproar in Massachusetts over Dukakis's dogmatic, dispassionate defense of the program. The *Digest* at the time had a circulation in the United States of over 16 million, higher than any other magazine in the country.[58]

The Dukakis campaign had been warned to expect this kind of attack in advance. Months before Bush raised this obvious issue, Pug Ravenel came to talk to Dukakis about Lee Atwater and tell him how to prepare. Ravenel had been a star quarterback at Harvard and was a Democratic activist in South Carolina. A descendant of an old, Democratic family, he had made a fortune after graduation and was dedicated to restoring the Democratic Party in South Carolina. He ran for governor and was savaged by Atwater in the campaign. He warned Dukakis that the only way to survive Atwater was with fast response to his attacks. Dukakis brushed it off, saying he had been in a tough negative primary and won. Ravenal was so worried about that reaction that he wrote a letter to the Dukakis staff after the visit:

> Atwater is the Babe Ruth of negative politics....I have the deep suspicion that Atwater will begin hitting at Dukakis very early, perhaps even before the convention....If Mike does not respond right away, he could risk having the negatives well set in the minds of Americans before he could begin to change them. The Bush campaign has all the money in the world and can afford to do this on a massive scale and do it early. If you are weeks or even a month behind in terms of preparing countering ads and buying time, it may be too late. It would be fighting an uphill battle for the rest of the campaign. I strongly urge that a full-scale defensive effort be made ready right away.[59]

Dukakis ignored Ravenal's warnings and planned a positive convention. He prepared no defense against the attacks already beginning on his crime policies and no attacks on Bush over his role in selling arms to Iran and funneling money to contras. Instead, he talked about his upbringing as the son of a self-made immigrant while the keynote speaker, Governor Ann Richards of Texas, reminded everyone Bush "was born with a silver foot in his mouth."[60] Both speeches were successful—before his opponent replied.

By contrast, the Republican convention was an all-out attack on Dukakis's liberalism with respect to national defense, crime, and taxes. Governor Thomas Kean of New Jersey keynoted the convention and said, "The Dukakis Democrats will try to talk tough. But don't be fooled. They may try to talk like Dirty Harry. But they will still act like Pee Wee Herman."[61]

Bush's acceptance speech detailed his personal background, and a film told of his heroism in World War II. In his acceptance speech, he made his famous "Read My Lips" pledge against new taxes and attacked Democrats for a history of tax and spend. Just as critical to his campaign and strategy was another theme:

> My friends, these days the world moves even more quickly, and now, after two great terms, a switch will be made. But when you have to change horses in midstream, doesn't it make sense to switch to the one who's going the same way?[62]

With that one line—Reagan's favorite line of the convention—Bush completed his four-year plan to separate and become his own man gracefully. Reagan gave his farewell speech and then left New Orleans. Ron Kaufman, a Bush advisor, said that the key moment of the convention, indeed of the entire campaign, was when "Air Force One took off...in the back of that plane was the yoke of the vice presidency."[63]

From the convention on, Bush never trailed in the polls. He challenged Dukakis on values and policies, not personal biography. When he was asked about the fact that he was born to wealth, he simply said, "I couldn't help where I was born, I just wanted to be near my mother at the time."[64]

DEER IN THE HEADLIGHTS

Dukakis made no verbal gaffes, and no one ever doubted his intelligence. But he was like a deer in the headlights when he tried to react to Bush. His paralysis allowed Bush to build a coalition of people who disliked one or more parts of old-fashioned liberalism. For months Dukakis denied that he was a liberal without ever explaining what he *was*. Then he decided near the end of the campaign to defend liberalism, but his defense said nothing about taxes, crime, or national defense to counter Bush's attacks.

Dukakis was paralyzed because his campaign was out of touch with voters and dominated by the "Harvard Yard mentality" of the issues staff. When reporters asked Dukakis's campaign strategist about the attacks, their answer was "George Bush still hasn't convinced people to love him."[65] That was as true as it was irrelevant. Bush was not trying to make himself lovable; he was trying to emphasize how different Dukakis was from mainstream values.

In Colorado and Montana, Dukakis had been ahead by over thirty points before the negative attacks on his record on gun control and crime. Dukakis's issues staff didn't think it was necessary to respond to such hyperbolic claims: "They just couldn't believe that attacks on these flimsy issues would have any effect," said a Democratic strategist. "They also thought people wouldn't believe lies. But people do believe lies if you don't tell them the truth."[66] At the end of the campaign, Dukakis appeared on *Nightline*, where Koppel repeatedly gave him openings to go on the offensive against Bush. Wondering why there was no passion and fire in response to the relentless attack, Koppel finally asked Dukakis: "Governor, you just don't get it, do you?"[67]

Both candidates talked about Truman and referred to the "give 'em hell" spirit of 1948. As in 1948, it wasn't the winner's oratory that carried the day but his ability to unite a diverse coalition against the other side. Bush could not revive Reaganomics or unite the party behind a new and exciting program, but he didn't have to. He united the party and moderate voters behind his version of Dukakis's record. This was an abiding insight of the academic research on the 1948 campaign; when a party's consensus has frayed and their agenda has faded, party unity could still endure:

> Party members need not agree on specific issues; their unity is at a different level. Their unity lies in the fact that on something important to each, they share a common position of disagreement with the opposition… they have, for one reason or another, the same opposition.[68]

THE SUCCESSOR WITH PEACE
AND PROSPERITY: AL GORE
IN 2000

Al Gore started his presidential campaign in a far better situation than those of other sitting vice presidents since World War II, such as Richard Nixon in 1960, Hubert Humphrey in 1968, or George H. W. Bush in 1988. Gore was serving under a president who wanted him to win (unlike Nixon), his party was not divided over an unpopular war (unlike Humphrey), and he faced no strong competitors from his own party (unlike Bush).

The most formidable potential opponent—Senator John Kerry—had backed off. Kerry was a hero in Vietnam, a moderate reformer, and a rousing orator whose fabulously wealthy wife could help finance his campaign. Still, taking on Gore meant, by extension, taking on the Clinton presidency and dividing the party.

The only person willing to take that risk was the former New Jersey senator Bill Bradley. Bradley was a nondescript campaigner whose résumé, once you removed his college, Olympic, and professional basketball accomplishments, was thin. Dana Milbank summed up Bradley in one sentence: "earnestly bookish, squeaky clean....And boring."[1] Bradley's campaign slogan was "It can happen," a tagline Democratic consultant and commentator

David Axelrod said "may be the most passive tagline in the history of American politics."[2] The only state where Bradley polled anywhere near Gore was New Hampshire, where Bradley had been well covered during his Ivy League and NBA career playing college ball locally against Dartmouth and nearby Harvard, and then battling the nearby Celtics in the NBA.

Like every other vice president at that stage, however, Gore trailed in the polls, languishing far behind his most likely Republican opponent, Governor George W. Bush of Texas.

Gore's closest campaign advisors—Bob Squier, the media expert who had worked with Gore for most of his career; Squier's partner, Bill Knapp; and Mark Penn, his pollster—thought he was in good shape for a vice president who hadn't yet won any primaries or projected his own vision for the next four years.

Gore's family disagreed with the professionals. They did not view his problems as the typical problems of a vice president; they believed the Clintons were patronizing Gore, and that the president wasn't willing to yield the spotlight. Above all, they believed that the bad poll numbers were the residual taint of the Lewinsky scandal.[3] The headlines in the *Washington Post* and the *New York Times* said as much: "Clinton fatigue." This was a term introduced in early 1999 by Andrew Kohut (the most trusted nonpartisan pollster in Washington), and it became a ubiquitous platitude in scores of editorials that diagnosed Gore's predicament as the result of his defense of the president during the long ordeal of lawsuits and hearings related to his sexual relations with former White House intern Monica Lewinsky.[4]

Gore's policy staff also read the *Times* and the *Post*, and knew about all the public polls. But where his family and staff saw a reason to panic, Penn saw a Beltway atmosphere too obsessed with pundit culture. Everyone had "rabbit ears": in the Washington echo chamber, every pundit proclamation was taken seriously. The pollsters who knew the difference between idle pundit chatter and meaningful opinions were constantly at odds with Gore's policy staff and—in particular—his family. Every time there was a bad story in the *Post*, Gore's staff wanted to change strategy that same morning.[5]

In the midst of managing Gore's campaign, former congressman Tony Coelho realized that, for Gore, love trumped all. While his advisors had more experience, they did not have the total loyalty and devotion to him that his family had. First, as with any hired gun, their own interests and agendas would always come first. Second, they had all worked for Clinton and might be pulling their punches to avoid alienating the president. Only Gore's family was unequivocally in his corner.[6]

His daughter Karenna introduced Gore to her friend Naomi Wolf, a former Rhodes Scholar and widely publicized feminist writer who had done some consulting on women's issues for Dick Morris and the 1996 Clinton campaign.

Wolf encouraged Gore's "self-pitying anger," agreeing that the president's personal scandals were the cause of his political problems. She encouraged him to distrust his political advisors for believing his problem was one common to other vice presidents. Her advice resonated, a Gore insider said, with the VP's sense that "for six years he's been the guy cleaning up after Clinton."[7] Marla Romash, Gore's former press secretary, said that Gore saw Lewinsky as the ultimate betrayal:

> The deal was: I will do everything I can to make your presidency successful, and you'll try to help me get elected....He stood by every decision, even the ones he didn't agree with. Bless him. He carried Clinton's water politically, substantively, every way. And Clinton broke the deal in the one way that could undermine everything Gore had worked for.[8]

Gore's wife, Tipper, and his daughters—the same age group as Monica Lewinsky—were personally outraged. Tipper believed that Clinton wouldn't even have won in 1992 without the family values the Gore family exemplified. Besides, fallout from Clinton's scandals was a way for a loyal, loving family to explain Gore's campaign troubles while providing emotional support to their distressed husband and father.[9]

Gore took the advice of Wolf—"the Lady Macbeth of this drama,"[10] a source close to Gore called her—to heart, and decided to break decisively and immediately with Clinton. For Gore, that meant repudiating the president's actions on the very same day he announced his candidacy to succeed him—on a nationally televised interview. That decision had far-reaching consequences, and Gore had not worked through any of them with his strategists.

Instead of distancing himself from the scandals, Gore's decision to denounce on the day he announced only strengthened the link. As Marjorie Williams wrote, "Al Gore, lately intent on distancing himself as much as possible from the president, appears to be the number-one believer in the existence of what pollsters call 'Clinton fatigue.'"[11]

His choice of interviewer went contrary to the advice of his media advisors. Squier urged Gore to give Barbara Walters the interview; he was certain that Gore would be more relaxed and given better camera angles. Diane Sawyer liked to ask more surprising questions, and had once been romantically involved with Bill Bradley. Walters, however, had recently done a much-discussed exclusive with Lewinsky, and that spooked Gore. He decided to go with Sawyer, whose interview turned into everything Squier feared.

First, Sawyer threw a pop quiz at Gore, asking him farming questions designed to challenge Gore's bona fides: How can you tell which farmer owns a fence? What is brucellosis? What is the current price for cattle? Gore didn't ace the test, but he passed. Then Sawyer turned prosecutor and cross-examined him about Clinton. She pushed him about whether Clinton had compromised the dignity of the White House; why Gore had said he was disappointed instead of horrified; whether he knew the president was lying. Over and over Gore said that Clinton's actions were "inexcusable."[12]

This clear declaration of separation changed the entire nature of "Gore World," as his White House staff was known. In the past, working well with Clinton's staff was the way to get ahead. Now staffers learned that anti-Clintonism was "the fastest path to the candidate's heart." For the rest of the campaign there was increasing distrust between the staffs— and increasing trouble for Gore in coordinating his White House Staff, the president's staff, and his campaign staff.[13]

Whether or not Clinton was an albatross, it was obvious to his staffers that the best way to separate was not to openly renounce Clinton on the same day as the official declaration of candidacy. The decision, however, was Gore's alone, based on his judgment that advice from his totally loyal family was better than counsel from self-interested political strategists.

GORE AS CHIEF OF STAFF AND CANDIDATE

Gore's solution to his concerns about the motives of his political advisors was to micromanage his strategists and communications team, and be the interface between family, policy staff, and campaign staff. That meant, whether he realized it or not, that he was trying to be his own campaign manager. That in turn made it hard for him to delegate. "He's not someone who you can give a check-off memo to and say, 'yes or no,'" Greg Simon, his chief advisor on telecommunications deregulation, said. "You can give him information or suggestions and he will always add to it."[14]

The drive to absorb details resulted in perfectionism and near-paralysis when there was no pressure for immediate action. When Gore was in Congress, he seldom used the congressional privilege that granted him six free newsletters to his constituents each year. He believed he could always improve upon any letter written for him—and as a result, Roy Neel, his chief of staff, could recall only one letter Gore had ever sent out in fourteen years as a congressman and senator.[15]

Gore's management style, hunger for details, and distrust of his strategists gave none of his campaign staff enough authority to move the organization in a timely fashion or prepare analyses of the implications of his decisions. Family members saw how Clinton's escapades had strained his psyche. Like all political families, the Gores had an exalted view of the candidate and were suspicious of any strategists who dared to offer criticism. But they did not have the experience with media to consider how his expression of moral disdain for Clinton's immoral and demeaning behavior made him look worse. "It's one of the stranger truths of our blame-shifting species," Marjorie Williams wrote, "that while Americans may be willing to forgive a sinner like Bill Clinton, no one has much pity for a cuckold."[16]

There was also constant turnover among his political advisors because, as one senior aide looked back, "His view is that you can always find more political hacks."[17] As a result, no one in the White House or the campaign ever knew what was entering into Gore's decisions.

GORE'S "BLUE PERIOD"

Gore's White House staff was accustomed to the pomp and circumstance that accompanied the VP's appearances. The campaign staff called this "Blue Goose" campaigning, after the bullet-proof podium with the goose-necked microphone into which Gore delivered his policy speeches.[18]

The continuous shuffle of campaign communications staffers inside the White House continued through 1999. Gore intended to manage his own campaign; his first campaign manager, Craig Smith, was little more than a figurehead. Smith was quickly replaced by Coelho, which neither improved coordination between Clinton's and Gore's White House staffs nor relations with the press. Worse, Coelho had left Congress under suspicion of fund-raising improprieties, so his presence in the campaign revived stories about Gore's own fund-raising practices in 1996.[19]

The crumbling relations between the Clinton and Gore staffs had intensified since the departure of Ron Klain, Gore's savvy chief of staff. Klain had good relations with the Clinton staff, but Klain had committed—in Gore's eyes—the cardinal sin of interfering in a reporter's story about Gore's lagging campaign. Klain suggested the writer contact Clinton for the story, which resulted in what Gore thought was a patronizing comment from the president.[20]

Gore's focus on separation minimized his advantage over Bradley. Karenna, for example, went out of her way to emphasize to reporters that Gore's White House years were "not what matters so much in this election...my dad's experience goes pretty far back. It goes back to 1976, not 1992."[21] Gore and his family, in other words, were so angry with Clinton—and concerned about separation—that they deemphasized the value of being part of decision-making on the economy, national defense, and foreign policy.

With his campaign in total disarray and the bad press upsetting Gore and his family, he reached back to an old acquaintance: Carter Eskew, one of the most talented media people in the party. They had been reporters together in Tennessee, and Eskew had the kind of credentials (e.g., a Yale education) that Gore respected. Inadvertently or not, when Gore hired Eskew, he ended up alienating Squier, his longest-serving consultant. Eskew had started out in media working for Squier, and they had split in a bitter fight over money (with overtones of generational conflict).

The first personnel move Eskew made was to bring in Robert Shrum for help with speeches and media. Shrum, a former national debate champion, was the Democratic consultant most capable of producing great oratory at the drop of a hat. He was best known for his work for Senator Edward Kennedy in 1980—speeches that stirred the passions of old-fashioned liberals, union members, and minorities. When Shrum saw how listless, unmotivated, and directionless the campaign was, he wrote a typically fiery memo to Gore: "You're not in a *fight* for the general election," he warned Gore. "You're now in a *fight* for the nomination."[22]

Bill Knapp called fall 1999 the "Blue Period" of the campaign; everyone had the blues and no decisions were being made.[23] Even Shrum's alarmist memo did nothing to rouse Gore into reorganizing the campaign or facing the contradictions in his strategy.

Eskew asked David Axelrod, then a Chicago-based strategist, to look over the campaign. Axelrod pointed to the same contradictions: First, it was to be expected that any VP would look weak at this stage of a campaign: "When Johnny Carson quit, nobody suggested Ed McMahon for the job." Second, "it's not just about the good ideas Clinton and Gore passed. It's also about the bad ideas they've stopped.... Gore does best—and looks strongest—when he's forcefully railing against entrenched interests."[24]

Gore's wake-up call finally arrived in the form of a *Boston Globe* poll that reported a near tie in New Hampshire. He assembled the strategists to decide how to respond, even though he already took it for granted that Clinton was *the* reason he was in danger.

Coelho had been trying to persuade Gore that distancing himself from Clinton made his relations with Clinton more problematic: "The more you try to downplay [relations], the more your opponents play it up and you look like a fool."[25] At a meeting at the VP's residence, the normally low-key Penn was, Shrum saw, "uncharacteristically exuberant," pumping his arms while defending Clinton: "Clinton fatigue, Clinton fatigue—there is no Clinton fatigue." Penn cited findings at odds with the public polls and dismissed Gore's concerns "out of hand."[26]

That was the last straw. After the meeting Gore told Eskew to drop Penn and get a new pollster. Shrum contacted Stan Greenberg, who had been dismissed by Clinton after the 1994 midterm debacle, but Greenberg declined. Shrum then asked Harrison Hickman. While Hickman was an acerbic, sarcastic loner, Shrum was comfortable with him and trusted his numbers. Besides, Shrum said, "it was an asset and not a liability that Hickman, the pollster who'd been caught faxing the press derogatory information about Clinton's draft status in 1992, was hardly a White House favorite." "At least," Gore told Shrum, "he won't tell me there's no such thing as Clinton fatigue."[27]

That was just the beginning of the shake-up. He promoted his field director, Donna Brazile, to campaign manager, leaving Coelho as chairman in name only. And to emphasize his intent to separate from the White House, he ordered Brazile to move the entire campaign organization to Nashville, Tennessee. Brazile saw at once that Gore was spending too much of his time indiscriminately soaking up a deluge of policy papers. She urged him to *fight* for the nomination. "What are we running for," she asked, "college professor?"[28]

STAY AND FIGHT

Gore couldn't become an outsider after eight years in the White House, but he could be a fighter. He liked direct confrontations but wasn't good at subtlety. In October, he went after Bradley at the Iowa Jefferson-Jackson dinner, challenging Bradley to a series of weekly debates: "How about it, Bill? If the answer is yes, stand up and wave your hand." Bradley sat immobile.

When Bradley did go after Gore, Gore was ready. Bradley was particularly incensed with racial profiling and the frequency with which "driving while black" seemed to be the only reason (proportionally) more African American drivers were stopped by state troopers. He challenged Gore: "Al, I know you would issue an order to end racial profiling if you were president of the United States...but we have a president now. You serve him. I want you to walk down that hallway, walk into his office and say to him, 'Sign this executive order today.'" Gore countered that the president does not need "a lecture from Bill Bradley about how to stand up and fight for African Americans and Latinos. It's one thing to talk the talk, it's another thing to walk the walk."[29]

Gore then put to good use his years of using the VP's office to make friends and connections with elected officials around the country. Sharpe James, the mayor of Newark, New Jersey, criticized Bradley for ignoring his pleas to help on the issue of racial profiling when he was a senator; Bradley had insisted, James said, that it was "a local issue."[30] The coup de grâce came in New Hampshire: while Bradley was campaigning for universal health care—an issue Senator Edward Kennedy had fought his entire career for—Kennedy endorsed Gore. Bradley, Kennedy said, was running on an issue he had ignored while he was in the Senate.[31]

The moment Gore stepped out from behind his "Blue Goose" and started acting like a candidate working for a nomination instead of the heir apparent, the Bradley challenge was over after two primaries. Still, he had a basic problem: the sense of inevitability that comes with being a successor doesn't mobilize or energize voters.

ANOTHER BLUE PERIOD

After the primaries, Gore still lagged behind Bush in the polls. The campaign fell into another period of worries. Shrum and Eskew wanted Gore to concentrate on creating an effective contrast with Bush. Instead, Gore—anguished by a fresh round of ridiculing newspaper stories—decided to improve his coverage.

In November, reporters found out that he was secretly paying Naomi Wolf to advise him. Her fee of $15,000 per month was exorbitant, more than a vice president earned. Among the revelations: Wolf had advised him to wear "earth tones" to look more masculine, and warned him "not to be a 'beta male' to Clinton's 'alpha male.'"[32]

Wolf's advice became a self-fulfilling prophecy. Gore's own campaign staff considered her a female Rasputin, who mesmerized him with answers that encouraged him to blame Clinton for his predicament. The *New York Times* reporter Melinda Henneberger saw Gore turn into a "laughline" among *NYT* reporters.[33] Most of his critics considered hiring Wolf a character flaw; even his defenders—like Gary Wills—were critical:

> Mr. Gore's status as the beta male [is] less a matter of character than of temporary duty, [a] structural problem all vice presidents experience when they try to move up. That he would do so with the help of a person bequeathed him by his boss's evil genius, Dick Morris, and that he would try to hide his use of Naomi Wolf is not a flaw in character but a stunning lapse in intelligence.[34]

Roy Neel, who had been with Gore for thirty years, saw how "It stung to have the political media, the elite political media, buy into this crap."[35] In his senior year at Harvard, Gore had done an honors thesis on the role of television in presidential leadership. Decades later, in the age of the Internet and cable television, he was still concerned about the same elite reporters and shows that he had studied in an earlier age.[36] The keys to the 1992 and 1996 elections had been sidestepping the top reporters in favor of other channels; in 2000 he was somehow still convinced that cleansing his image with the *Times* and *Post* was the way to proceed after the primaries.

The day after he swept all the primaries on Super Tuesday and Bradley conceded, Gore stunned his strategists by telling them he was going to spend the time ahead on campaign finance reform. When Gore, who had been dubbed "solicitor in chief" for his role in fund-raising during the '96 campaign, told them he intended to "get his reputation back," Shrum realized that Bradley had "lost the nomination but captured Gore's head." Gore cared so much about standing up—and clearing his name—that he refused to take time to consider the unanimous objections of his advisors. Instead, he immediately gave the *New York Times* an interview and announced "he would make overhauling the campaign finance system a central theme of his presidential bid."[37]

Campaign finance reform is one of those issues that people will consistently say they are for, like energy independence or protecting the environment. The principle makes great fodder for editorials and speeches but moves few voters in the voting booth. There are inter- and intraparty divides on which interests are special, and it is hard to persuade many voters that a specific reform will actually change politics.

Gore didn't care that his polls showed the limited importance of the issue; it became the driving force of his campaign, to the detriment of other crucial issues—much to the increasing frustration of his strategists. A contrast with Bush was there for the taking, especially on Social Security. Bush's plan was popular on first sight but deceptively destructive over time.[38]

All the time Gore spent on campaign finance in March didn't boost his polls or change the tone of his press coverage. If his strategists couldn't persuade him to abandon the issue, at least they eventually convinced him to target other issues as well, something big that could move the polls.[39] The issue into which Gore decided to wade, unfortunately, was the highly contentious battle over the status of a six-year-old Cuban boy, Elian Gonzalez.

Gonzalez was one of three survivors of a failed attempt to flee Cuba; his mother, her boyfriend, and ten others drowned at sea. Having been rescued by fishermen, Gonzalez had been living in Florida, but his Cuban father wanted the boy returned to him. The battle over where (and with whom) Gonzalez should live became *the* national watercooler issue. What was the "right thing" for a motherless six-year-old boy: life with an uncle in freedom, or living with a father and two grandmothers under communism?

For the large, vocally anti-communist Florida community of Cuban exiles—and their Republican allies, including Bush—the issue was a no-brainer: honor the mother who died to give him life in America.

For the White House and Department of Justice, the answer was also clear. Federal courts upheld the father's right to bring his son home. Any other decision would violate laws, create worldwide problems, and give special rights to Cubans. (The administration earlier had turned away armadas with thousands of desperate Haitians trying to reach Florida.)

Cuban leaders in Florida persuaded Coelho that Gore would win some of the normally Republican Cuban voters if he helped Elian stay in the United States; Coelho, in turn, urged Gore to support the exile community. Hours after Attorney General Janet Reno said Gonzalez should be returned to his father, Gore stated that Congress should grant both father and son citizenship so that they could be together in the United States.[40]

As soon as Gore made the statement, Bush saw an opening to raise the ante. "I'm glad the vice president now supports legal residency for Elian Gonzalez....I hope he'll use his influence to encourage the president and the attorney general to follow suit."[41] Weeks later, amid threats of armed resistance from the exile community, Gonzalez was taken from his uncle in a raid and returned to his father.

Whatever Gore intended, his actions smacked of pandering, and it suggested—as Bush knew it would—that Gore had little power in the White House. He also infuriated many African American supporters in Congress, like Congresswoman Maxine Waters, who angrily told reporters "If this were a Haitian boy, why, he'd be sent back."[42]

To top it all off, Gore's move probably cost him more votes in Florida than if he had denounced Cuban Americans for trying to overturn the law and turn a child into a pawn just to vent at Castro. Nationally, more than 60 percent of the country thought Gonzalez belonged with his father. In South Florida, support for the Cuban community was far lower: 76 percent of non-Hispanic whites and 92 percent of non-Hispanic blacks thought he belonged with his father.[43]

REORGANIZATION AGAIN

Eskew immediately realized that "the campaign failed the candidate." No one had gamed out the moves; no one checked with Brazile; no one looked at how Bush would respond; no one briefed columnists; and no one thought about what Gore would say after Gregg Craig, the well-known Democratic attorney for Elian's father, won an easy decision in federal court.[44] The communications team was filled with experienced, well-regarded people, but there was still no communications strategy.

Coelho was shunted aside. Eskew took over day-to-day decision-making in Tennessee, and Gore brought in more people at the top. Tad Devine, a longtime associate of Shrum's, moved to Nashville to run the campaign staff and free up Eskew for message and media.[45] Penn was secretly brought back to do a poll. Stan Greenberg came in to begin developing a message.[46]

Naomi Wolf was still there as well. With everyone so focused on the little troubles Gore was having with the *Times* and the *Post*, Eskew defended her presence to staffers on the grounds that "We've got a lot of political experts, but no one else is out there reading *People* magazine."[47]

"W"

In an age when his opponent for the presidency had written about the increasing importance of the candidate, George W. Bush was that rare—possibly unique—presidential contender who never ran a basic biographical ad. He didn't need one: everyone knew who his parents were and how reckless he had been.

Bush made no bones about his wild misspent youth. "When I was young and irresponsible," he told people, "I was young and irresponsible." He even parlayed his refusal to focus on his biography into a sign of virtue, turning the questions about his sinful past into a discussion of his newfound piety: "Once you put your hand on the Bible and swear in [to public office], you must set a high standard and be responsible for your own actions."[48]

W had worked with Lee Atwater in the successful 1988 campaign, and then watched in distress as his father's reelection campaign fell apart. When he saw the rats leaving the sinking ship, he learned to be wary of opportunistic consultants who acted like "big game hunters looking to bag him, looking for a trophy, and a rack to hang on the wall."[49]

His solution was to demand loyalty and make sure that there were no power grabs. W learned the strategic value of face time in 1988. He arrived early for campaign meetings so others would see him talking in private with his father: "We were probably talking about the pennant race or, you know, a brother or sister," Bush later said. "They didn't know that. They knew that I had access to him, that it was just me and him alone. It was a very interesting lesson. I watched my stature grow the more that I had access to him."[50] W had seen what a disaster John Sununu was as his father's chief of staff and how Sununu had used his face time and gatekeeping power to further his own agenda. To prevent any single staffer from using their access to do that to him, he made sure that there was always a small group with open, direct access to him.[51]

When W became a co-owner of the Texas Rangers baseball team, the staff and manager were all suspicious of the callow kid whose name had earned him the job. At first he made a lot of mistakes and alienated people, but eventually he won the staff over, made some money, and accomplished his main goal: a public reputation in Texas that paved the way for political ambitions.[52]

W's opponent, Texas governor Ann Richards, had devastating wit and storytelling ability worthy of Mark Twain. Richards managed simultaneously to be a liberal, a feminist, and a "good ol' gal" who talked of riding a Harley on her sixtieth birthday and joked about how hard it was to decide what kind of camouflage to wear for a turkey shoot.

Richards had been very good at counterpunching after over-the-top attacks on her as a woman or liberal. But Bush had good instincts; he told Karl Rove, already his campaign manager, "We're never going to attack her because she would be a fabulous victim....We're going to treat her with respect and dignity. This is how we're going to win."[53] Richards kept trying to provoke Bush and lost control of the campaign. When it was over, she recounted a debate to Larry King: "I say this with real respect—is that rather than tell you the intricacies of what he knows or what he intends to do, he is very good at saying things that are rather all-encompassing. You know, if you said to George, 'What time is it?' he would say, 'We must teach our children to read.'"[54]

Even before he captured the 2000 Republican nomination, Bush knew who his opponent would be, and he planned from day one to use the primary campaign as part of the general election campaign. They had to "face reality"; this meant, Stuart Stevens wrote, accepting that Republican "antics like shutting down the government" had allowed Democrats to paint the party as "a natural home for right-wing lunatics and nutballs."[55]

Rove's formulation, "compassionate conservatism," fit Bush's instincts and differentiated him from the congressional overreach on the budget and the attempted impeachment of Clinton. While governor, W developed a popular moderate program on education and took an inclusionary approach to immigration reform. He condemned the welfare system without looking down on recipients; "[It] saps the soul and drains the spirit."[56]

He was always careful to avoid the inflammatory language of evangelicals or the Republican congressmen who had swept into power in 1994. One evangelical activist secretly taped his meetings with Bush in 1998. He had been told W would pledge never to hire gays, but Bush quickly corrected him: "No, what I said was, I wouldn't *fire* gays." When another conservative religious leader was angry that he wouldn't criticize gays, Bush responded, "I'm not going to kick gays, because I'm a sinner. How can I differentiate sin?"[57]

W and Rove assumed their major primary threat would come from flat-tax zealot Steve Forbes, an awkward, unappealing person willing to spend immense sums of his inherited fortune. Forbes had devastated Bob Dole with his all-out attacks against taxes in 1996, so Bush had prepared his own tax-cut platform. Forbes surprised them by dropping his scorched-earth tax rhetoric and fading away without doing any damage.

Senator John McCain had skipped Iowa, camped out in New Hampshire, and run hard as a maverick reformer willing to give everyone "straight talk." McCain attracted most of the independent and moderate primary voters and blew Bush out of the water in New Hampshire, 49 percent to 30 percent. The defeat was so bad that Matthew Dowd, Bush's pollster, read only the obituaries the next day; he couldn't even read the sports page for fear of seeing a headline comparing a lopsided win to McCain's thumping of Bush.

The next primary was South Carolina, a state with few Independents or moderates. Bush ran as a "Reformer with Results," and crushed the maverick in a bitter primary from which McCain never really recovered.[58]

PROSPERITY AND PURPOSE

By March, the Bush team began to reposition themselves for Gore. McCain's appeal was to moderate and Independent voters, so Bush had ended up using the primary to consolidate the Republican base. Now, W traveled the country spreading his vision of the next four years to moderates and Independents. To their amazement, instead of trading fire with Gore, they had the field to themselves.[59]

The Gore campaign, Knapp realized, was being "yanked around" by the Washington echo chamber that kept asking, "Why are you being so negative?" Gore had stopped giving press conferences during his fruitless month on campaign finance, then lost another month on the Elian Gonzalez minefield.[60]

Gore's miscalculation on Elian Gonzalez "reinforced the perception that Gore would do things for political reasons, not for the right reason." This played directly into Bush's chosen contrast with Gore and opened the door for his policy initiatives.[61]

The Clinton White House was consumed with message polling, and Gore was often portrayed as an exaggerator. W, in contrast, had a well-crafted set of lines to make the difference between them easy to remember:[62]

> You know, the great thing about coming from Texas? If anybody doubts my leadership skills, all I got to say is, Go ask my fellow citizens. Ask my fellow Texans whether or not I know how to set a clear agenda. Ask my Texans whether I stand on principle or on polls and focus groups.... If you are sick and tired of the politics of division and cynicism, of polls and focus groups in Washington, D.C., if you're sick of that kind of politics, you come and join this campaign.... I don't even care what the polls say, it's what I believe.

Bush was a popular governor of a big state, and that meant an assumption of executive ability along with his emphasis on authenticity over calculation. Both Rove and Bush's longtime aide Karen Hughes believed that the critical contrast with Gore somehow had to emphasize Bush's strong leadership,[63] and the polls showed that it was working.

The campaign wanted a way to demonstrate what strong leadership by Bush would accomplish. Gutsy or weak, authentic or calculating, his campaign had to deal with the fact that the economy was in great shape, and there was even going to be a budget surplus after years of deficits. Jim Ferguson, head of the prestigious ad agency Young and Rubicam and a Texan, started from the basic premise that "We can't make the case that the governor is going to improve the economy. We can't fix what ain't broke."[64]

It didn't get any easier when they tried to decide what theme would present a winning contrast to Gore. The depressing part for Stevens was the missing issues: typical Republican red meat like welfare reform, national defense, and taxes "weren't even on the radar." All the top concerns were Democratic issues: education, Social Security, and health care. Whether or not they could "win" on those issues, they had to at least minimize the Democrats' advantage or W's leadership credentials would be meaningless.[65]

Bush could use his record as governor to make inroads on education, but he needed something bolder. He wanted to take on the "third rail" of American politics: Social Security reform.[66] He would push a plan that was very attractive for younger voters—investing their Social Security funds in the stock market. The market was booming, younger voters didn't believe the government would ever be able to pay them their Social Security benefits otherwise, and they believed they could invest their funds better than the government could.[67]

By August 1999, Bush's pollsters had already seen how the political terrain had shifted during the Clinton administration. Demographic shifts—increasing numbers of minority voters—meant Democrats had a shot at Florida. On the other hand, Clinton's progressive social policies had alienated large numbers of people in West Virginia and Tennessee, and gave Republicans a good chance. Rove's assessment was blunt: "West Virginia was socially conservative (faith, guns, abortion) and dependent on coal for jobs and prosperity. Bush was right and Gore was wrong on all four."[68]

GORE'S MESSAGE BOX

Throughout the spring and early summer, Bush led Gore by four to six points in the national polls.[69] Post-Elian, four months after the primaries effectively ended, Gore was still going back and forth over staffing and his campaign, "ricocheting from gimmick to gimmick" while the campaign battled over whether Gore should be non-ideological (like the 1996 campaign) or add a populist edge to the message.[70] By June, Carter Eskew was in despair; the campaign was "a collection of issues"[71] without any thematic framework to portray Gore's vision and approach to government. ~~If Gore was going to be his own person, he needed a coherent summary~~ of *who he was*, and not just who he wasn't.

Out of frustration, Mark Fabiani and Chris Lehane, the communications director and press secretary, took action on their own and proposed a question to use as an umbrella over all the contrasts between Gore and Bush: "Does He Have What It Takes?"[72]

"Does he have what it takes?" they suggested, was a better contrast than "Who is more likable?" Bush was personally appealing and obviously inexperienced; Gore was clearly experienced and less likable. R. W. Apple summarized the difference as "Mr. Bush needed to show some gravitas, while Mr. Gore needed to show some levitas"—or in other words, "One needed to show he was not a lightweight, the other to lighten up."[73]

Bush surprised most strategists in both parties by choosing Dick Cheney, the chair of his VP selection committee, as his running mate. After his performance as secretary of defense during Desert Storm, and his experience as chief of staff for President Ford, there were no worries about a running mate with Quayle-like inexperience. And though Cheney was extremely conservative in his congressional days, he had a low-key demeanor that did not signal Gingrich-like hostility or unreasonableness.[74] Like him or not, no one could say he didn't have what it takes.

Shrum and Eskew were also frustrated by the lack of story line or overarching rationale for the campaign, and had drafted Greenberg to develop a message that would move them beyond voting blocs to a road map. By the end of July, Greenberg completed his message box just as the Republicans were holding their convention.[75]

W's overall tone was inclusive and tolerant, unlike his father's disastrous 1992 convention. Bush's acceptance speech mocked Gore for the obsessive use of canned mantras and focus-grouped messages for eight years of what W called "coasting":

> Every one of the proposals I've talked about tonight, he has called a "risky scheme," over and over again. It is the sum of his message—the politics of the roadblock, the philosophy of the stop sign....If my opponent had been there at the moon launch, it would have been a "risky rocket scheme"...If he'd been there when Edison was testing the light bulb, it would have been a "risky anti-candle scheme"...And if he'd

been there when the Internet was invented, well...I understand he actually was there for that.[76]

Gore had to find a way to deflate Bush's claims and deal with Bush's blurring of the differences between the parties on education and health care; W had effectively taken the sting out of those contrasts. Gore also had to convince people that good times were no time to try a big change. Gore tried a "Progress and Prosperity tour," but when Gore talked up continuing the good times, voters thought he was taking credit for the president's achievements.[77]

Before Gore could sell policies, however, he had to persuade people he was credible and that he personally had what it takes to be a leader. Greenberg saw at once that the campaign was operating as if people knew Gore's background while little was known other than that he was Clinton's vice president. People didn't know his father had been a distinguished senator, that he had volunteered for service in Vietnam, that he had been an investigative reporter. Volunteering for Vietnam was particularly important: it showed he hadn't pulled strings to take the easy way out like many of his Ivy League cohort and let someone else go in his place. Even having a father in politics was an asset, for it rooted his ambition in an admirable family tradition of public service.[78]

While the message box gave the campaign a direction everyone could agree on, it never acknowledged the eight-hundred-pounder in the room: Bill Clinton. If Gore couldn't get credit for peace and prosperity, and if Clinton was an albatross, what could Gore say about the last eight years that made him the right change instead of Bush? Gore had to do what Bush had done at his convention: convince people that if you had to change horses in the middle of the stream, he was the one going in the same direction. And that meant explaining what the direction was and why he was the better change.

Gore also had to select his running mate for the campaign. The long, extensive screening process boiled down to three serious candidates: Senators John Kerry, John Edwards, and Joe Lieberman, from which Edwards and Lieberman emerged as the top two.

The strategists (particularly Shrum and Hickman) knew that part of the inherent value of a VP pick is his or her ability to defend the candidate and attack the opponent—something Edwards, skilled as he was at

The Gore Campaign Message Box

GORE ON GORE	GORE ON BUSH
Biography—Tell the Gore Story • Family (4 generations) • Vietnam, returned to nonpolitical life • Record—toxic waste, Persian Gulf (broke with party), welfare reform	**The Image—Defining Bush/Cheney** • Old guard, backward-looking, same old GOP • All-oil ticket • Bush and the Cheney record
Reassurances—Overcoming Partisan Stereotypes • Welfare reform • Targeted tax cuts • Crime—enforcement, victims' rights	**The Tax Record—Undermining the Foundation** • Environment—two steps • Health care • Education
Issues—Look Forward • Goal is helping working families build a better future for themselves • Education • Medicare—lockbox and drug benefit • Surplus—responsible, priorities • Health care	**The Issues—Defining the Differences** • Tax cut—all roads lead back to the tax cut • Surplus—populist approach works best • Health care—sides with HMOs and insurance companies • Education
BUSH ON BUSH	**BUSH ON GORE**
A Different Kind of Republican • Hopeful, optimistic, focus on positive • Reaching out to new constituencies	**Old-Style Politics** • Negative, pessimistic • Scare tactics
Compassionate Conservative • Tax record is the blueprint • For education and (legal) immigration • Faith-based organizations	**Who Is Al Gore?** • Flip-flops • Campaign finance reform • Social Security—partial privatization • Negative campaigning—soft money ads • Say or do anything to get elected
Real Change • Restore honor and dignity to WH • Bring people from both parties together • Return power to states	**Higher Taxes and Bigger Government** • Keep surplus in Washington • Throw money at problems rather than reform them—Social Security, failing schools • Government programs over private solutions • Higher taxes on gasoline
Lower Taxes and Smaller Government • Marriage penalty • Estate tax—family farms and small business • Money out of Washington before they spend it • Tollbooth to the middle-class	
The Issues • Education—invest, but with accountability • Social Security—lockbox and private accounts • Defense—full missile defense system	

winning over North Carolina juries, could do in his sleep. Lieberman, on the other hand, was idiosyncratic, thoughtful and nonconfrontational. He also had another quality that made him attractive to Gore: he had made headlines with a Senate speech decrying the shameful nature of Clinton's scandals. Warren Christopher argued that Lieberman's gravitas was good for the ticket while Edwards was untested.[79]

Ed Rendell, the head of the DNC and a Jew, advocated against Lieberman, arguing that the country was not ready for a Jewish president. Gore got "incandescently angry"—the vice president wanted to make history, and he always was drawn to the bold choice.[80] But while the bold choice may generate headlines in the days after the pick, the campaign was wary of a choice that may not help them when it counted. Tad Devine summarized it best: "Mr. Vice President, you need Mr. October, not Mr. August."[81]

THE JEW AND THE KISS

Karl Rove's assessment of Al Gore's comeback was frank and concise: "I was surprised at how he did it: by picking a Jew and kissing his wife." Like most observers, Rove dismissed the kiss as "corny and contrived," though he admitted "it undercut the public perception of Gore as a stiff and unlikable know-it-all."[82] Picking Lieberman, a Clinton critic, and showing some humanity had prompted a reassessment of Gore as a leader in his own right and had given Gore the lead in all the polls.

When Gore walked out at the Democratic Convention to give his speech, he eschewed the traditional hug of the spouse and gave Tipper a passionate kiss. That unscripted moment (which apparently surprised Tipper and definitely unnerved aides worried about another gaffe) set the stage for Gore's coming-out party.

He talked about the surplus and argued that his tax cut was responsible; while Bush's gave about a "Diet Coke" a day to the average family, it gave ten dollars to the top 1 percent for every dime that went to middle-class families. He also managed to talk about the economy in a manner that made a valuable contrast with Bush: "A few years ago...your hard work was undone by a government that didn't work, didn't put people first, and wasn't on your side....Together we [unleashed] the private sector." And he identified himself with the government without taking any credit: "This election is not an award for past performance....I'm not asking you to vote for me on the basis of the economy we have.... Tonight, I ask for your support [for a] more prosperous America we can build together."[83]

Despite the Sturm und Drang of a campaign that shifted personnel constantly, and Gore's constant dyspepsia and fretting over Clinton, he was suddenly in the exact same position as "Poppa" Bush after his dramatic success at the 1988 Republican convention. Averaging all the national polls, W was 16.4 points behind and Gore was 15.2 points behind after the out-party's convention; after the in-party's convention W was ahead by 5.3 the last week of August, and Gore was ahead by 5.7 points; in the first week after Labor Day, W was ahead by 4.1 points and Gore by 5.2.[84]

Matthew Dowd saw no good news for W in the polls. The numbers on whether the country was on the right track or wrong track had jumped twenty points, so why would the public vote for a change? "Basically, if they like us and they like him, then he wins," Dowd told the others.[85] Stuart Stevens had worried about this all along: "All Gore needed to do was to find a way to articulate why it was silly to think about taking a chance on an unknown when things were going along just fine," and Bush would be "toast."[86]

DEBATES

The Bush team had dreaded the now-obligatory trio of ninety-minute presidential debates. Debates were W's Achilles' heel, a place where, once you got past his pithy generalities, he looked most inarticulate and least knowledgeable. Now, though, Bush needed the debates to shake up the race and give people a reason to look at him again.[87] When, after weeks of stalling, W announced that he would agree to participate in debates, he wanted two of the debates to be only sixty minutes long, and asked for them to be with *Larry King Live* and *Meet the Press*. That gambit not only failed, it added to the perception that he was both behind and uninformed.[88]

In the run-up to the debate, Gore started to revert to form with the kinds of unnecessary exaggerations that got him in trouble and made him look unreliable. He claimed his mother used to sing him a union song when young, but that song hadn't yet been written. Then he said his mother-in-law paid more for her medicine than his dog did for the same prescription; that, too, proved false.[89] These minor exaggerations were followed by a major miscalculation. Heating oil prices were rising rapidly in the Northeast and appeared likely to double by winter. Gore called for the president to release oil from the strategic petroleum reserve—something that had never been done in peacetime...and which Gore himself had argued against a year ago. This revived the charge that he would do anything to get elected and did more damage than any Republican ads; Gore's honesty and character ratings took a dive.[90]

Despite Gore's missteps, he maintained a slim lead in the polls. Rove thought the debates were their best chance to contrast Bush's amiable personality with Gore's bullying.[91] There was real risk, because Gore knew the material far better than W, who frequently stumbled on content and pronunciation. The campaign intensively studied all of Gore's debates throughout his entire career. They knew his bag of debate tricks and "well-rehearsed themes," and Stevens worked on countermeasures.[92]

Gore liked to put opponents on the defensive with aggressive ploys. He might pull a pledge out of his pocket and ask the opponent to sign it right on the spot. He might intrude into an opponent's space when talking to them or even when they were talking. One of his craftiest ploys was ending his answer with a question for the opponent, then baiting the opponent with "Why don't you have an answer?"

Bush worked with his campaign to develop effective responses to Gore. If he answered Gore's question, ignored Gore's baiting, or asked the moderator to make him behave, Gore had in effect commandeered the discussion. Bush saw that the single most effective response was to continue answering the moderator, but look at Gore while raising his voice enough to make it clear he was talking over Gore and turn back to the moderator.[93]

Gore went about debate preparation the way a boxer might train for a title bout, with a large retinue to cheer him on. Unlike Mike Tyson, Gore concentrated on tactics and downplayed strategy. Until his death in January, Bob Squier had worked with Gore on debates for years and had given up trying to develop strategy for him. His standard advice for newcomers to Gore Land was never to bother with strategy memos. Just give him killer lines, killer facts, killer statistics. The campaign studied all of the moderator Jim Lehrer's prior debates to see what kind of questions he would ask, but they did not study Gore and predict what kind of counterattacks a good campaign might prepare for Gore's ploys.[94]

Before the first debate with W, Gore followed a "formula for hyperaggression"; he "gulped down four or five diet colas and bolted down several protein bars." Instead of coming across with strength, he became what debate coaches call an "inappropriate aggressor," which is a fancy term for what schoolchildren call a bully.[95] People in the hall for the first presidential debate thought Gore won on content. Two days later, the Bush campaign got their best news since the Democratic convention: polls and focus groups showed that while content was a draw, Gore's mannerisms and sighs were off-putting and unctuous. Gore was hurting himself badly.[96]

The vice presidential debate was next, and the Democrats needed Lieberman to bring issues back to the fore instead of Gore's likability. As Tad Devine had predicted, Lieberman was no clutch hitter; he came off as bland, ineffective, and meek.

After two presidential debates and a VP debate, Bush now led Gore by one to two points. There were still doubts about both candidates. Suddenly, Cheney was the most popular person on either ticket,[97] which indicated just how much unease there was about Bush and dislike of Gore.

His last chance to confront Bush directly came at the third debate, a so-called town hall meeting with questions from the audience. Gore went after Bush on clear issue contrasts. He stated clearly that most of the Bush tax cut went to the very wealthy, and he poked a hole in Bush's plan to put new Social Security taxes into individual accounts: many retirees thought the money they were receiving was the money they had paid over their working lifetimes, and which was waiting for them.

Once again, Gore scored on the issues and lost on character. Despite advice from his staff to stay on his side of the stage, he got off his stool and—looking like "the robot in *The Day the Earth Stood Still*"—slowly advanced on W while answering a question. Bush was ready; with a "pointed glance...followed by a quick, dismissive nod of the head," Bush exposed Gore's "hokey stagecraft." That exchange, which prompted the audience to laugh at Gore, was one of the most replayed excerpts from the debate.[98]

Gore had violated one of the cardinal rules of debate: People don't mind attacks, the debate scholar Diana Carlin has found, but instead of attacking each other, "they want people to attack ideas."[99] Fortunately, for Gore, at least one attack managed to hit home. Bill Knapp had created a clear, straightforward, and very effective ad that critiqued Bush's plan for Social Security. Bush had promised to put a trillion dollars into the stock market and also to pay the trillion dollars to retirees: "Which promise," the ad asked, "would he break?"

By the time the Bush campaign realized the attack would be sustained, they were "already bleeding."[100]

The campaigns were all maneuvering to see which states were still in play. The focus now was on the "venison belt" and the "Bible Belt." Rove had seen a year ago that West Virginia was ripe for the picking. With all the turnover and churning and focus on a national message, it wasn't until August that Gore's campaign saw that West Virginia, Tennessee, and Arkansas were all trouble spots. The campaign had debated for months about how to deal with peace and prosperity, and whether Gore should fight for working families or middle-class families. Amid all the concern with refining the message in class divisions, the growing urban rural gap on cultural issues was given short shrift.

Abortion, gay rights, and gun control were divisive within the Democratic Party compared to clean air and clean water. New England states like New Hampshire were now more receptive to Democrats on cultural and religious grounds than were states like Tennessee and Arkansas, to say nothing of coal mining West Virginia. The Gore campaign, however, was slow to react to either shift.

CONCLUSION

When he was an undergraduate at Harvard, Al Gore placed a picture of Daniel in the lion's den on his wall. In the Bible, Daniel had been thrown into the den because of his refusal to compromise his religious principles. He survived because an angel had protected him. For Gore in the 2000 campaign, facing the lions was misguided hubris. Daniel didn't enter the den voluntarily to trumpet his virtue, but Gore *chose* to face the lions of the press to restore his virtue. When Gore looked for the big issue or the big battle, he chose to promote his own righteousness and power over the concerns of the people he wanted to lead.[101]

After the campaign, bewildered Democrats wondered why he didn't run on "Peace and Prosperity," how he could have lost his and Bill Clinton's native states, and why he didn't use Clinton more. The first two questions are the wrong questions, and the third question is far less simple than it appears.

Gore always had three plans and three message boxes colliding with each other: one from his family, one from his White House staff, and one from his campaign. In the mob-like setting of his campaign, listening to everyone meant deciding nothing, and Gore ended up making snap decisions on his own without informing anyone. The result was pervasive, utter confusion; one senior aide said, "I never felt that I was operating with more than 50 percent of the information that he was operating with."[102]

Gore emphasized that he was fighting for "the people against the powerful," but never explained why a governor like Bush, someone outside the corrosive environment of Washington, was on the other side. The columnist Michael Kinsley paraphrased Gore's message as "You've never had it so good, and I'm mad as hell about it. Keep the team that brought you this situation, and I'll fight to take back power from the evil forces that have imposed it on you." Trying to brag about the economy while attacking economic royalism was not impossible, Kinsley added, "But why juggle three tennis balls and keep a saucer spinning on a stick at the same time if you don't have to?"[103]

If ever there was a campaign that showed the importance of organization, it was this one. Gore didn't lose because Bill Clinton was immoral and tried for impeachment; he lost because he could not build an organization that could develop a strategy and adapt to the changes in political terrain resulting from the budget surplus, a booming stock market, and the shifting cultural landscape. Ralph Nader and the confusing Florida butterfly ballots would never have been discussed if he had been able to build a campaign organization to sustain him, prepare for contingencies, and prevent short-term tactical miscalculations from derailing his campaign.

Gore had been in three previous presidential campaigns, while Bush had been closely involved in only one of his father's campaigns. But Bush had learned more about clear communication and coordinating family and friends with the campaign, and after the dust settled from the Supreme Court's historic ruling on Bush v. Gore, Gore was left introducing himself to crowds as the man who "used to be the next President of the United States."

TEAMS THAT WORK

There is an epic quality to the men and women who decide to run for president, but a candidate's psychological makeup is but one essential ingredient of a good campaign. I know of no scale or test by which to determine whether Barack Obama, Bill Clinton, and George W. Bush all had more specific inner resources than Hillary Clinton, Robert Dole, or Al Gore. Winners and losers alike had obvious flaws and displayed lapses of judgment; every single one of them made miscalculations and stumbled badly during his or her campaign.

As I said at the beginning of the book, even sophisticated politicos make the common mistake of falling for the person who seems to have all the inherent God-given leadership traits, including a powerful presence. Time and again we are wrong about which qualities that a candidate must ultimately have are present from birth and which can be learned.[1]

I have concentrated not on individual character but on the one thing that is essential to *any* successful campaign: a team that works. Anyone audacious enough to run must also be agile and resilient, and it is the candidate's assembled team that determines the level of the candidate's agility and resilience. Candidates are made, not born, and they are made by the team that they—and only they—can build.

A candidate for president is like a captain preparing to take a perilous voyage through uncharted waters. A heroic image will help the captain find patrons and raise money, but in the end, the captains who go the farthest are the ones who prepare carefully, attract good sailors, and turn them into a strong crew. Candidates only get as far as their team can take them, and the strongest-looking candidates do not necessarily develop the strongest teams.

AGILITY

Candidates have to be agile to balance conflicting demands, reconcile seemingly incompatible pledges, adjust to changing conditions, and show how an (inevitable) change of an old position is compatible with strong, consistent values. They have to know when to sound strong while being vague and when to sound vague while being strong.

Candidates can build coalitions and make credible commitments only if they know how far they can go without contradicting other commitments or compromising their values. This is harder than it sounds: so many people make so many demands about so many issues. Businessmen, union leaders, and the heads of dozens of religious, ethnic, racial, environmental, and social groups make incompatible demands and push for detailed commitments. A candidate must reconcile promises for smaller government with promises for increased defense spending, promises to cut energy consumption with promises to save jobs in manufacturing—all the while establishing her reliability and sincerity.

When a candidate can establish trust with one group without making specific promises that will alienate others, the job of juggling and balancing the coalition is easier. Each candidate will attempt to perform triangulation. Unless the candidacy has good balance, all the cleverness amounts to spitting into the wind.

A large part of establishing and maintaining trust requires the candidate to have clear core values. After working with five Republican presidents, Stu Spencer concluded it was inconceivable that anyone could be president who didn't know what he stood for well enough to know when he was about to compromise himself. He worked with potential candidates to see whether they knew where they stood:

You test them. You take an issue and you ask them, "Where do you stand on this issue?" Once they tell you, you start playing devil's advocate. You start working them over, coming at them.... If you can move them...you know that they don't have a very hard-core value system.... [You know they have values if] at the end of the day they still smile and say, "All well and good, but this is where I stand."[2]

A candidate's stand is the political equivalent of a dancer's spot. To avoid losing their bearings, dancers focus on a single spot and return to it as they dance and spin. If candidates know their stand well enough to keep it in focus, they can dance around their positions, adjusting their rhetoric to the audience and occasion without losing their balance.

RESILIENCE

At some point along the trail, every candidate suffers major setbacks. They all have strategies before they got knocked down, but they cannot pass the Mike Tyson test—having a strategy after they get hit—without a team. Endurance will not get a candidate back on track without a team that is prepared to handle the setback. Increased effort will not suffice, because without an appropriate strategy "they'll just do the wrong thing with more gusto."[3]

In each of this book's three case studies, the candidate was wrong about his or her major opponent or the political terrain on which the battles were fought. Barack Obama thought Democrats would consider Hillary Clinton too polarizing to win and that she would be unable to explain away her vote to authorize the use of force in Iraq. George H. W. Bush believed he would get credit for his foreign policy successes in 1992 and that he would be able to raise tax rates without a furor. Al Gore thought he needed to separate immediately from President Clinton to become an effective candidate and that it was more important to make an immediate splash when he selected his running mate than to have someone who would defend him in debates.

The winners didn't make fewer miscalculations than the losers, but they adjusted faster to the changes in terrain, media, and competition. In some cases, they took less of a pounding than their opponents because their team had what it takes to give them both certainty and contingency plans.

Like athletes, candidates have to be forward-thrusting, concentrating on the next play, not brooding on past mistakes. That means they cannot go full speed ahead in front of a crowd of thousands (or in a crucial meeting of two) if they're worrying about making the right move. While the candidate concentrates on the next pitch, a good team looks several pitches ahead and prepares defenses and attacks.

All candidates feel the urge to let out their road rage and swing at their opponent, but only the ones who have strong teams can remain centered. As David Plouffe said afterward, even the "No drama Obama" campaign had to deal with the desire to attack: "You wake up every day trying to really do damage to them."[4] When the candidate piles it on instead of carefully trying to separate an opponent from his supporters, it is a team failure, not a personality problem. Lashing out is often a mistake of timing, a failure of the team to help the candidate wait for the appropriate time and manner to attack. Karl Rove believed a candidate should "Try to figure out how to get your opponent to attack you, because you are always stronger on the counterattack."[5] Neither Hillary Clinton nor Al Gore ever figured that out.

Teamwork is necessary for candidates to keep their composure and avoid acting like a bully. The team can delegate the appropriate attacks to compatriots, so they don't lose style points or act like the inappropriate aggressor. "To include the rank and file of the opposition in a rebuke is to drive them to be defensive or pugnacious," counseled James Farley, FDR's campaign manager in 1932 and 1936. "Always talk to them as if they had been betrayed by the political machine of the opposition."[6]

No Silver Bullets

All candidates are overloaded. While the adrenaline of a presidential campaign keeps them pumped up, they face more decisions and issues than ever before. Every step, from the primary to the general to reelection, gets more complicated. At each successive level, the candidates have more natural reluctance to do new, unfamiliar tasks they are not good at.

Overloaded candidates, particularly when they are behind or in unfamiliar circumstances, are particularly vulnerable to someone who claims to have a "silver bullet"—a can't-fail ploy, tactic, issue, or move that will win the battle or even the war. The myth of an ultimate winning weapon is what Herb York, the late nuclear physicist and arms control negotiator, called the "fallacy of the last move."[7] Simply put, there are no silver bullets; there is no attack so devastating that the opponent cannot recover to fight and win another day.

Every candidate should take it as a given that whatever new media, message, issue, or weapon is credited with providing a unique advantage in the last campaign was overrated then and is widely available now. As baseball analyst Bill James points out, "knowledge is a very dynamic universe—and what is most valuable is not the body of knowledge, but the leading edge of it."[8] That doesn't keep strategists from selling the last campaign's sizzle as this year's steak, nor does it prevent overloaded candidates from looking for an excuse to stay in their comfort zone.

Gurus and sycophants are made, not born. When candidates fall under the spell of one person—as Hillary Clinton did with Mark Penn, and Al Gore did with Naomi Wolf—they enable their gurus by giving them the opportunity to block out all other advisors. Gurus always offer a clean, straightforward reason for a complicated choice that makes everything seem clearer and easier.[9] Invariably, they bolster candidates at their moment of greatest insecurity, giving them the words to use or the theme or tactic that will sell—for the moment.

Snake-oil salesmen undermine the candidate's staff and other team members by keeping everyone in the dark about strategy and tactics. They keep their advice to the candidate as confidential as possible to prevent thorough examination from others that might throw doubts on their position. To keep the candidate from double checking, they will avoid giving bad news or pushing the candidate to do undesirable tasks. Spreaders of false confidence inevitably downplay the candidate's vulnerabilities and their opponent's strengths. Selling their own strengths and attacking their opponents' weaknesses is the easy half of the campaign.

Candidates all know the dangers of gurus, and yet it is tragically hard to avoid the lure of an easy solution to the immediate crisis, no matter its impact on strategy. Such dependence can enmesh the candidate in a sycophantic web. Who wouldn't like to be the person whose advice is valued above all others by a candidate? Who wouldn't like to be the wise master consulted before fateful decisions?

Robert Shrum is one of the most famous and controversial speechwriters in the Democratic Party. If there were an Olympic event for sound bites, Shrum would take the gold. It appears to take him only thirty seconds to write a better thirty-second statement or ad than most people could create in a day. His speeches for Senator Edward Kennedy and others consistently produced unforgettable lines and received brilliant ovations.

His words aroused true believers and captured the essence of what candidates want to be at that moment. Shrum served as a speechwriter for eight Democratic presidential candidates—all of whom lost. Many of his eloquent, passionate speeches were bridges to nowhere, espousing policies that were never enacted…but they always sounded great.

Joe Klein pinned the blame for the defeats on Shrum—the poster boy, as Klein sees it, for overpaid consultants who rob contemporary politics of the last shreds of authenticity while milking candidates for ever-bigger payrolls.[10] But Shrum is a symptom of a deeper problem: a candidate too willing to embrace a sugarcoated quick fix.

There are people like Shrum in both political parties—those who can devise a brilliant statement on the spot or offer an ingenious, allegedly "poll-tested" statement. Frank Luntz convinced Newt Gingrich to enact a "Contract with America," which played well up until the moment the Republican Congress tried to enact the internally contradictory, unpopular, or expensive pledges in the contract. It gave Gingrich a big short-term gain and then painted him into a corner, even before anyone realized that Luntz's research did not support the claims he urged Gingrich to make.[11]

Candidates habitually develop special closeness to their gurus. Carter Eskew explained why:

> Candidates at Shrummy's level are all type-A achievers who, for the first time in their lives, aren't sure they're going to make it. One of the things Shrum offers them is a sense of security, that there is a knowable path and answer and that there are things that can be done to affect the outcome.[12]

Because of that tight-knit relationship with the guru, no candidate will ever be able to identify the sycophant herself; only when someone else is vetting the advice can that person determine if the candidate is going down a dead-end path with obvious pitfalls. And that depends upon teamwork.

TEAMS THAT WORK

There is no magic formula for an ideal team. Teams that work help the candidate in the same ways, but they have different kinds of skills because the mix that works depends upon the candidate, her family and friends, the terrain, the media, and the opponent. Every team that works well completes the candidate and includes: a chief of staff who is a near equal; a peer; an objective navigator; a "body man" or sidekick; a mediator between professionals and family and friends; and a protector of the candidate's brand name. A team completes the candidate by providing complementary expertise on the roles and subjects where candidates are in over their head (as every candidate is at some point).

No candidate can possibly be knowledgeable on all the issues, interest groups, and tactics. Ronald Reagan didn't need anyone to tell him how to stand or speak; George H. W. Bush did. George H. W. Bush didn't need anyone to tell him about foreign policy; Ronald Reagan did. Barack Obama didn't need anyone to tell him how to talk about law or the constitution; John McCain did. John McCain didn't need anyone to tell him how to talk about military service; Barack Obama did.

None of them have all the necessary virtues and personal and interpersonal skills, either. Richard Nixon didn't need anyone watching out for women with a gleam in their eye; Bill Clinton did. Jimmy Carter didn't need a staffer to go through his suit pocket and find all the coasters and napkins on which he wrote down the promises he made drinking with his pals; Gerald Ford did. Barack Obama didn't need anyone to keep him from overeating on the campaign trail; Al Gore did. George W. Bush didn't need anyone to keep him away from craps tables and make sure photographers didn't catch him shooting dice with a friendly blonde standing next to him "for good luck"; John McCain did.

Strong Chief of Staff

The single most important part of a successful team is a chief of staff strong enough to be an honest broker. Weak chiefs of staff are the biggest reason campaigns flounder. A chief of staff is weak not because of her personality or character but because the candidate sets her up to be weak: Some candidates want to be their own chief and put someone in the job who is more of a personal assistant than a chief; more commonly, the candidate never gives the chief enough authority to mediate and coordinate, let alone level with the candidate.

Candidates consistently underestimate how much they can do themselves in a presidential campaign, and how much more they need to rely on someone else to mediate disputes and problems with strategy and tactics. When seemingly well-prepared campaigns get bogged down as the pace picks up, the root of the problem is most often candidates who cannot let go, who believe they can be the CEO, the start-up visionary, and the royal family simultaneously. A strong chief can coordinate all the skills and staffing involved in all three jobs, but only if the candidate is willing to delegate.

Hillary Clinton, Michael Dukakis, Bob Dole, and Al Gore all tried to make more decisions than they had time for during their campaign. Their over-reaching led to slow responses, rigidity, and decisions based on inaccurate or undigested information. The toughest decision for powerful candidates is finding a way to delegate more of their "life" to someone else and finding a chief of staff they can trust with new powers over their routines. They are all aware of the dangers of letting someone else manage their life, but they do not comprehend the dangers of thinking they know more than they do about what actually is going on or how they are being viewed by voters.

Hillary Clinton seemed to understand the problems of delegating authority without proper oversight: "you cede too much authority...water will flow downstream, and often pool in great reservoirs of power that will then be taken advantage of by those who have been smart enough to figure out how to pull the levers."[13] In her campaign, however, she did the exact opposite, appointing a chief of staff who was more like a daughter than a peer.

Any time the candidate gives direct orders to people who don't understand the candidate's manner, "captainitis" is likely. Captainitis was a term coined for situations when alerting a superior would embarrass him by questioning his leadership in front of others. Investigators learned that some airline tragedies occurred because crew members noticed a serious problem and didn't say anything to the captain, rationalizing that the captain probably knew anyway. Other researchers found that nurses seldom reminded a doctor when the doctor failed to order a new intravenous line after two days—a sure guarantee of infection—because they were reluctant to say anything in front of residents.[14]

The only solution to captainitis is more delegation of authority, so that the chief of staff has the necessary stature and legitimacy to handle the responsibility and handle the tough calls. A strong chief doesn't necessarily enter the campaign with personal stature but is someone whom the candidate respects enough to make her a strong chief.

Only when the chief is the candidate's near-equal in authority can she keep the campaign focused on the game plan. There are always more people who want to talk to the candidate about an idea, problem, or crisis than there are minutes in the day. If someone else doesn't monitor the environment and decide who gets a hearing and when, indecision reigns.

The authority given the chief determines whether there will be reciprocity and coordination, or a group of backstabbing specialists out for themselves. Mutual accountability is possible only when the specialists commit to victory over personal goals. That cannot happen without a chief to balance, mediate, and referee among the principals; candidates cannot do it themselves.[15]

If Barack Obama had not given David Plouffe adequate authority and kept him in the loop at all times, Plouffe would not have been able to create the teamwork and coordination that provided him the edge over Hillary Clinton (whose campaign manager was scapegoated for failing at the impossible task of running a contentious campaign with neither adequate authority nor feedback from her candidate). Even with adequate authority, teamwork breaks down when the chief has a personal agenda. President George H. W. Bush realized this too late with John Sununu to save his campaign.

The Peer

There are times in most campaigns when the candidate digs in her heels and just simply refuses to admit error, revise a position, fire an employee, change her schedule, or face some sort of music she is avoiding. Often a close friend—not someone who has been mentored by the candidate, or an employee or a befriended staffer—is the only one who can cajole the candidate into taking a deep breath and rethinking some knee-jerk position. When George W. Bush decided to run for president, *Newsweek's* campaign team learned that his father's only advice was to "have someone on his campaign staff [who could say] 'George, what the hell are you thinking?'"[16]

A team cannot function without a peer: someone who is close to the candidate and knows her well enough to deliver painful (but necessary) truths. In a group meeting, people who need face time with the candidate will not dare to say something unpleasant. Some of these uncomfortable truths will be too personally upsetting or disturbing to hear in front of the group. When there are rivalries among the group, no one is likely to tell the candidate anything that will get him denounced; someone can always score points by disparaging the criticism or denying the need for any painful changes. (That is why, for example, it is always someone who doesn't need face time with the president who plays the opponent in mock debates.)

It is not always the chief who delivers these painful truths, because chiefs usually are not with the candidate and often don't have the chemistry to make them go down smoothly. Instead, there might be one professional that is trusted by the others to smash through the fatigue, defensiveness, and pride; or different people for different kinds of heart-to-heart talks; or a very small group that always does the talk with the candidate; or a close friend. It will always be a small group, though, and it will be the only way for a candidate to hear things that will never be said to him directly in larger groups.

Whether or not it's the chief delivering the bad news, the unpalatable information emerges only with a strong chief. Without a chief to thrash out tough calls for an overloaded candidate, there will always be someone who can curry favor by subverting the consensus for his own good.

In 1988, before his old friend James Baker came on board, Roger Ailes was the person who could talk turkey with Vice President George H. W. Bush. When the staff wanted to persuade Bush to attack Dole in the primaries or focus more on a speech, Gary MacDougal and Lee Atwater scheduled private time for Ailes and Bush. Ailes had the stature and personality, as well, to turn criticism into friendly jousting. Trying to persuade Bush to look less old-fashioned and dull, Ailes roared at him, "Don't *ever* wear that shirt again!...You looked like a fucking CLERK!"[17]

When a campaign is consumed with attacking the opponent, it is generally a result of an organization where the candidate kept too much responsibility; the chief could not develop a plan to play the whole message box, and there was no one to get the candidate out of his comfort zone. In response to books attributing the wild attacks on Obama to Hillary Clinton's personal character and personality, Peter Daou's spirited defense of her personal warmth, humor, and decency was also an indictment of a campaign organization with a weak chief and no one to speak unpleasant truths on behalf of the campaign. The unraveling of her lead, Daou wrote, was not a "character narrative" but a "convoluted and harrowing tale [including] internal campaign struggles, dysfunctionality, careless mistakes, leaks, 'surrogates gone wild.'"[18]

In other words, it was the campaign she organized: one in which she tried to do too much and ended up controlling too little.

Objective Navigator

A good team must have confidence in the plan, and that is possible only when they trust the navigator providing the information upon which it is based. Teamwork does not develop unless the navigator shares reliable information within the team *before* the options are debated. In the past, navigators were the party leaders who kept track of the local machines; today they generally are pollsters who evaluate how people respond to the campaign. (Tomorrow it might be people who monitor Facebook or Google searches, or employ hitherto unutilized methods and theories.) As long as key personnel know the basis for decisions and no one hides critical information, reciprocity and teamwork are possible.

However, the effective navigator has to maintain at least some distance from the campaign's principals. Ann Lewis, who was a major spokesperson in presidential campaigns in every decade since the 1970s, concluded that one of the major dangers in any campaign was a pollster who attended too many policy meetings. Inevitably, that pollster would become enmeshed in staff disputes and lose his objectivity when evaluating how voters were responding to certain policies.[19]

When Hillary Clinton made Mark Penn both her strategist and her pollster, she destroyed the basis of teamwork by ensuring that her pollster would defend her strategist instead of evaluating the strategy and building mutual trust. Indeed, Penn was a classic example of Galbraith's Law: Faced with the choice between changing one's mind and proving that there is no need to do so, almost everyone gets busy on the proof. In a campaign where he was both pollster and strategist, he was free from review by any other pollster and could wield his data against challenges to his status or to his ideas. And since the most sensitive data was shown only to her, like CIA directors, he could always tell dissenters, "If you only knew what we know."[20]

Body Man

One person almost always stays within close proximity to the candidate, reporting on moods, doing errands, or simply hanging out. Whether he's

called the body man, the sidekick, or the personal assistant, he tends to
~~the candidate's routine.~~

This person—part valet, part sounding board, and part sentry—caters
to the candidate's moods. There are good times and bad times to brief
candidates, tell them bad news, or put through a phone call they need yet
don't want to take. There are good and bad ways to keep them going, help
them blow off steam, stick to their diet, or play "Jiminy Cricket" and steer
them away from trouble of many sorts.

When the future secretary of state Warren Christopher saw Bill Clinton
take hit after hit from the press, he praised Clinton's amazing resilience and
the fact that "he doesn't whine about the hits." Once he was in the administration, he learned that Clinton never whined in public because there was
always someone around to whom he could whine in private...and that
whining was actually "a very important part of his makeup."[21]

That someone was Steven Goodin, Bill Clinton's personal aide in the
White House for three years, a job that included "tak[ing] the brunt of
Clinton's frequent outbursts of anger." "Ninety-nine percent of the time,"
one of Goodin's friends said, "it's because of something someone else has
done." George Stephanopoulos learned that he had to handle outbursts
too: "The trick was to have a kind of thin skin—to understand that Clinton
didn't really yell at you; he yelled through you, as the rage passed through
him. My job was to absorb the anger and address its cause."[22]

Mediator between Professionals and Family

As much trouble as inexperienced friends and family members can cause
professionals, they are essential to the candidate, both as part of the royal
family and as watchdogs against campaign professionals putting their own
interests ahead of those of the candidate.

Consultants, however, want total control of the campaign and usually
resent the disruptions friends and family cause, wandering around and pok-
ing their heads into meetings and second-guessing the experts. To campaign
professionals, family and friends should be compliant window dressing, to
be trotted out as props when needed and otherwise kept off stage.

The mediator keeps friends and family in the loop with the campaign.
This role ensures that well-meaning, last-minute advice is vetted by the
campaign. Since Gore's campaign staff seldom knew what the family and

friends were telling him, and the principals seldom knew what kinds of suggestions they were making on an ad hoc basis, Gore ended up making several poorly planned, impromptu decisions that plagued him throughout the campaign.

In 1992 James Carville learned that the Clintons never did anything without first talking—often ad nauseam—to their powerful, sometimes brilliant, always opinionated friends. So Carville kept the campaign moving by determining which friend to "wire up" in advance: "If it was a Democratic Leadership Council issue like reinventing government, you'd call Al From. If it had to do with worker retraining, you'd call Bob Reich. If it had to do with a black event, call John Lewis or Mike Espy. And when in doubt, call Hillary."[23]

A mediator also makes sure that friends and family understand the strategy, and assuages unfounded fears that the strategists are out for themselves. Valerie Jarrett could reassure Michelle Obama and black leaders that the three white men running Obama's campaign understood their concerns. The kind of teamwork and integration between Jarrett and the others is seldom achieved, however, as those who dealt with Nick Brady in the Bush 41 administration or Nancy Reagan will testify.

It wasn't that easy in the 1992 Clinton War Room either. Susan Thomases, an administrative partner at a top New York law firm, was Hillary's watchdog and consigliore, a primal force of nature in the campaign. Even in what Peggy Noonan had called the testosterone-poisoned atmosphere of presidential politics, Thomases held her own with everyone. Known as the King Kong Kibitzer, she was supremely self-confident—and so combative that the journalist Hunter S. Thompson believed that her spleen could be sold for enough money to pay the medical premiums for half the people in Maryland.[24] When Thomases tried to cancel a poll written by Stan Greenberg—on the grounds that he didn't know what he was doing, Greenberg, George Stephanopoulos, and three of the other principals turned in resignations on the spot.[25] After a showdown meeting, Thomases was removed from the strategy loop and put in charge of scheduling, a post where her competence mattered more and her strategy interests less.

To try and get decisions made on a timely basis despite the number of second-guessers, the major principals—Greenberg, Stephanopoulos, James Carville, Grunwald, and Begala—made a pact that once they reached a

consensus, no one would undermine the group by reopening the issue
with the Clintons.

In 1976 Jimmy Carter delivered a speech in which he talked about the
integration of old ethnic neighborhoods in Pittsburgh. The speech was
largely diplomatically worded, peppered with lines like "I would not force
a racial integration of a neighborhood by government action. But I would
not permit discrimination against a family moving into the neighborhood."
But it also contained a lightning rod of a line: "I see nothing wrong with
ethnic purity being maintained." His campaign staff tried to persuade him
to apologize, but only his old friend Charlie Kirbo, who was mediating
between family, friends, and staff, was able to talk with him. Kirbo told
him that he was embarrassing black friends like Andrew Young and Coretta
Scott King, at which point Carter finally asked for forgiveness.[26]

Alter Ego/Guardian of the Brand Name

In the course of any campaign, staffers might employ tactics that advance
the current campaign (or their own agenda) while having deleterious
effects on the long-term career of the candidate. Guardians keep their
eyes open for misuse, overwork, or tactics that might damage the candidate's reputation or future viability. George W. Bush, calling himself
the "loyalty enforcer,"[27] filled that role in his father's 1988 campaign.
Sometimes this role is filled by the candidate's spouse, as with Nancy
Reagan. She was constantly on the lookout for people who might be pushing their own agendas instead of her husband's, or who were overloading
him. Despite her reputation, Nancy Reagan did such an effective job that
the late Richard Neustadt, who advised presidents from Truman though
Clinton on White House organization and presidential power, advised
scholars studying future presidents to find out who fulfilled "the Nancy
function."[28]

In the Kennedy administration, Theodore Sorensen knew every speech,
every vote, and every position of John F. Kennedy, and no one dared
make a statement or commitment on JFK's behalf without checking with
Sorensen first. (The guardian need not be close to the candidate; Sorensen,
in all his years with Kennedy, was never part of the Kennedy social circle.
The "cool crowd" didn't even bother to conceal their "thinly veiled patronizing" for a serious intellectual who didn't drink.[29])

In the 1992 Clinton campaign, Betsey Wright, a longtime aide who had run three of Clinton's Arkansas campaigns and served as his chief of staff, was the "secretary of defense"—meaning she was part of the defense against any and all personal charges involving the draft, corruption, or adultery, which she termed the "bimbo eruptions." Mark Salter was the keeper of the John McCain legend and protector of the brand name. Staffers even called Salter "McCain's wife," and were frank with *Newsweek* about the natural tensions between the guardian and the consultants: "Our job is for Candidate X to win. The candidate's wife's job is always to protect the candidate. Those two goals are often in conflict."[30]

CHEMISTRY AND DISCRETION

Every candidate *wants* a team greater than the sum of its parts, a team where the principal decision-makers care more about victory than about their personal profits, status, glory, or policy choices. But dedication and loyalty to the candidate are neither necessary nor sufficient to assure mutual accountability, reciprocity, or efficiency. People who put victory first may not have adequate chemistry to work well with the candidate or with each other. People entirely loyal to the candidate may not understand imperatives of the terrain or media or new role the candidate is assuming.

On paper, it sounds simple and straightforward to customize a team for the next campaign. But developing chemistry and real teamwork is never simple, and upgrading the old staff for the new campaign is treacherous. Candidates have a difficult time separating their stakes in any proposed change from the personal stakes for their principal staffers. They continually must balance chemistry and competence: Do they keep the adequate staffer whom they know well and with whom they are comfortable, or do they bring in a more competent person with whom they have little familiarity?

Candidates always have to decide what the right choice is *this* time while surrounded by people who typically find reasons to favor the tactics or strategies that are good for their careers, bank accounts, or causes. At every step up the ladder, it gets harder and harder for candidates to become comfortable enough to trust staffers, because there are more opportunities for staffers to try to advance themselves at the expense of the candidate. And this makes it harder for candidates to ever move out of their comfort zone.

When Howard Dean stayed with his Vermont chief of staff to run his presidential campaign, he chose total loyalty over competence and never knew what he needed to know when he needed to know it. When Hillary Clinton put Patti Solis Doyle in charge of her campaign and let her pollster also be her strategist, she got neither chemistry nor efficiency in her campaign.

It takes a long time to develop chemistry and integrate individuals into a team. In the National Football League, quarterbacks communicate with a coach for fifteen seconds before each play. There is no time for explanations, discussions, or arguments among the coaches or with the players. The brief communication is successful only if the team members have developed a shorthand language and a structure for decision-making. Someone has to decide what option to use; not every player can be the star at the end of the game.

As much as candidates need big talents and must learn how to handle their egos, they never need people who will make them look bad. It is one thing to be a game-saver who can use his bureaucratic black belt to help a president look better. It is quite another to be an expert who embarrasses the president to enhance his reputation.

Competence without discretion is as dangerous for a candidate as discretion without competence. The ideal, of course, is both at once. Myer Feldman, an aide to President Kennedy, was once profiled as "the White House's Anonymous Man." Helping with debate preparation in 1960, Feldman was resourceful enough to find Irish-sounding names among the Texans who died at the Alamo; these names came in handy when Kennedy gave a speech defending his Catholicism before religious leaders in Houston. Feldman was also an unheard, unnoticed liaison between the White House and business leaders, with enough connections to have obtained the lowest District of Columbia license plate number, a prestige symbol akin to playing touch football with the Kennedys or visiting Camp David. "If Mike ever turned dishonest," Kennedy told Sorensen, "we could all go to jail."[31]

WHAT DID REAGAN HAVE?

The Best Man was one of the triumphs of the 1960 Broadway season. Gore Vidal's play about a battle for the presidential nomination raised eternal, Shakespearean questions about noble ends and shady means. One protagonist was an unethical monstrosity, a glib ruffian with an attractive public image as a virtuous family man who understands ordinary people; the other was an intellectual, so dedicated to his principles that he was indecisive and unable to act swiftly. Top Hollywood actors fought for a chance to portray a presidential contender on Broadway, and even more went after the roles in the "razzle-dazzle" 1964 movie version.[32]

Ronald Reagan wanted to play a politician; he had been politically active since the 1940s and dreamed about getting into politics himself. His Hollywood agent flew to New York to make the case for Reagan. Vidal and the producers all laughed. They could not see any audience finding him a convincing presidential candidate.[33]

So much for the idea of "Reagan the Natural." And so much for the idea that as an actor he could just *play* the part of president.

Throughout his political career, his opponents—and even some of his closest associates—underestimated him, scoffing at the idea that someone who was "just an actor" could persuade people to vote for him.[34] When Reagan ran in California's Republican gubernatorial primary in 1966, Democratic governor Edmund G. "Pat" Brown and his strategists took it as gospel that Reagan would be easier to beat than his primary opponent, San Francisco mayor George Christopher, so they leaked old, misleading stories about Christopher to help Reagan win the primary.[35] When Governor Reagan ran for reelection in 1970, Jess Unruh, a popular Democratic legislative leader, thought he could beat Reagan because people had seen him in action. In the 1976 presidential primary, Stu Spencer, who had been instrumental in making Reagan governor and had been pushed out in a palace coup, tried to alert Donald Rumsfeld and Dick Cheney to the threat Reagan posed to President Ford's election, but he was brushed off as an alarmist. In 1980 when Reagan won the Republican nomination, a chastened Unruh traveled to Washington to warn Jimmy Carter and his staff that Reagan was more than just an actor. "Do you believe they don't think Reagan is tough?" Unruh vented afterwards, "I told them, I told them five different ways. Don't underestimate this guy."[36]

Even in the White House, Reagan was often underestimated. Donald Regan, his second-term chief of staff, patronized Reagan as an unthinking person who just "listened, acquiesced, played his role."[37] He later acknowledged to Richard Reeves just how badly he had misjudged Reagan:

REEVES: "What was the biggest problem in the White House when you were there?"

REGAN: "Everyone there thought he was smarter than the President."

REEVES: "Including you?"

REGAN: "Especially me."[38]

How was this man so thoroughly underestimated by everyone he met—and defeated—on the way to the presidency? For one thing, he was not a commanding presence in person, and was often so shy that he could only tell canned jokes. Reagan could be weak, too; during his entire career, he never once fired anyone himself, explaining, "You never shoot your own horse. Your neighbor does it for you."[39]

But there was much more to Reagan, and his Hollywood career gave him advantages in team building that are as important as any of his policies or oratorical abilities. After laughing at the idea of him in a presidential role on Broadway, Gore Vidal saw Reagan at the 1964 Republican National Convention. When Eisenhower spoke, Reagan was "totally concentrated" on the former president, studying him the way "the understudy examines the star's performance, and tries to figure how it is done."

Anyone who has spent time with politicians knows how unusual Reagan's examination of Eisenhower was. When someone outranking them speaks, most politicians try to look interested for the cameras while muttering to themselves or aides that they could do better; Reagan the actor-turned-governor actually did the hard, unglamorous drudgery.

Four years later, Vidal saw Reagan again at the next Republican Convention, expertly handling the national press. When the reporters tried to trap Reagan, he knew how to sidestep their bait and speak over their heads—and directly to the viewers—in a "warm, and folksy manner."[40]

He recognized his personal weaknesses and built an inner circle that compensated for them. He did his homework too. Before running for office, he had written hundreds of radio columns about conservatism, but he had never learned anything about actual government. He didn't understand legislatures, how ideas became bills, or how budgets operated. So, two years before his 1966 campaign for governor, Reagan started learning the California budget process. His first advisors were social science researchers hired to educate him about issues, but Reagan could not understand their briefings and memos. Instead, Reagan found an old (Republican) actor in the legislature, Charlie Conrad, and worked with him for two years until he was comfortable with the legislative process:

> It was so great because both actors could talk at the same level about things.... The rapport was there between them. Charlie would say, "Okay Ron, we have a bill here, Bill 1A. We want to get that bill through the process," and he'd say, "This is how we get it through the process. We go to this committee and we get an author here and we get a co-author here. We go through that committee, and then we go to a committee as a whole, then we go to the legislature."[41]

Reagan continued to study after arriving in Sacramento. In 1970, five years before he first ran for president, Reagan began to learn the federal budget process. When George Shultz, who served multiple roles in Nixon's cabinet, returned to California, Reagan invited him for lunch. Reagan impressed Shultz with what he already knew and how much he wanted to learn:

> It turned out to be a grilling of me by him on how the federal government worked and particularly how the budget worked....I remember coming away from that feeling, *well, this man obviously wants to be president, but he clearly wants to be president because he wants to do the job. Otherwise he wouldn't be interested in all this stuff, because this is down in the dirt.*[42]

Shultz was stunned by the contrast with President Nixon, for whom "the budget was something you had to do. But with Ronald Reagan it was something he liked and he could see how central it was."[43]

"Just" an Actor?

Politicians use "just" as an adverb when they are trying to limit a discussion with an implicit comparison. "*Just* an actor" means Reagan is *only* an actor, whereas the politician saying it is *more* than an actor.

Every politician knows he is acting much of the time. Politicians can talk passionately about bills they have never read, with opinions derived from talking points from staff, party leaders, pollsters, or prominent supporters. They have to act like they are mulling a decision in front of constituents when they have already made up their minds. And they are all afraid of being exposed as insincere, inauthentic, and phony—as "just" actors.

Stu Spencer thought Reagan was one of two actors he ever met in Hollywood with strong core values and the political knowledge needed to apply those values. (Warren Beatty was the other.) That meant Reagan couldn't be pushed around too easily by supporters.

Instead of studying the lines that worked for Reagan, politicians would be better off studying what else Reagan learned in Hollywood. What Reagan got from movies was not great oratorical ability as much as a deep understanding of the unusual teamwork and fluidity necessary to be president. Reagan was easier to work with than other politicians because he understood how to work with teams of high-powered, hard-charging men and women where everyone's work is closely related and roles are constantly shifting. He was used to leaving the technical issues to others and working with a director and producer.[44]

Reagan's Hollywood experience helped him understand when political consultants were trying to manipulate him for their own interests. Actors hear pitches every day of the year from agents and directors trying to get them to shortchange their career for the sake of someone else's fast buck. They instinctively understand upstaging and credit-claiming, and the good ones—including those who never got the girl and had to co-star with chimps—know that their lines depend upon other actors as well as themselves. "The professionals don't really have a high regard for candidates," Reagan said with a laugh. "They kind of think of them as a horse in the stall, and they'll take them out and run 'em when they think they should be run."[45]

As an actor, Reagan also learned how to control himself against both the adulation and personal demands others always put on candidates. Edmund Morris studied enough presidents and statesmen to see that leaders have to hold back if they are to function: "[Reagan's] detachment was a necessary armor against the emotional demands that responsibility attaches to power."[46]

Reagan's pollsters and media men never overrode his judgments about what to say and how to say it. Actors understand team chemistry and the difference between an all-Oscar–winning crew and an Oscar-winning movie.

Reagan knew how to upstage his rivals without looking like he was trying to dominate them; his most famous lines, like "There you go again" and "Mr. Gorbachev, tear down this wall," called upon other leaders to do better without self-promotion or strutting. Nor was he indignant about sharing the limelight. When he was asked if he minded that Soviet premier Gorbachev was more popular and getting more credit for their negotiations, he told the audience, "I don't resent his popularity or anything else. Good Lord, I costarred with Errol Flynn once."[47]

Reagan's competitor for the 1980 Republican nomination, John Connally, was the exact opposite. Whereas Reagan bested his competitors with grace, Connally relished the battle. "You will be measured in this town by the enemies you destroy," he told Henry Kissinger. "The bigger they are, the bigger you will be." For Connally, a victory was meaningless unless his opponents knew they had been defeated[48]—and that made him less attractive to ordinary people. "John Connally understands power," wrote Nixon's speechwriter Aram Bakshian, "but who will trust him with it?"[49] Reagan could look like he was in charge without others even realizing they had been trumped, and he never looked like he wanted power for personal advancement.[50]

What else did Reagan have? A large part of the answer is Nancy Reagan. She was as contentious, meddlesome, and irritating as any presidential spouse—including Hillary Clinton or Barbara Bush—and some of her friends caused as much pure trouble as George H. W. Bush's and Hillary's talented, powerful, and intrusive friends. Yet for all the tirades thrown at her by staffers wise or petty, she did more good for her husband and had less policy power on her own than her detractors claim.

During her husband's presidency, Nancy was vilified by the Left for her lack of concern with poverty, and by the Right for, they believed, naively encouraging her husband that he could work with Mikhail Gorbachev when he became the Soviet premier. In the Bush White House, however, when the president waited over a year to remove John Sununu, senior staffers asked, "Where is Nancy when we need her?"[51]

Nancy was "a screen between him and the predatory outside."[52] Reagan's "kitchen cabinet" of old Los Angeles cronies always considered Nancy the person without whom Reagan would have gotten nowhere:

> We are convinced that with all of the abilities of Ronald Reagan, he never could have made the Presidency without Nancy—her encouragement,

her sensors for helping him avoid the kinds of areas that might be entrapment as far as career advancement and that kind of thing. I guess I never thought about it this way, but somebody might say, "What do you mean, he couldn't have made it without Nancy? The guy's supposed to have all these abilities." Yes. It reminds me of Nancy being the rocket launcher, and once he gets into orbit, man, he covers the world and sends back imagery of everything that's happening.[53]

She could reduce tough guys like heavyweight operative Ed Rollins to a cold sweat; the speechwriter Peggy Noonan would hide behind a pillar if she heard the tap of Nancy's high heels in the corridor. But for all the legendary trouble Nancy caused staffers, neither she nor the president's friends ever went around the staff. When James Baker was chief of staff, he made sure his staff always listened to what she and her friends wanted or thought should be done. That meant there was always opportunity for the senior staff to argue, cajole, or plead when they thought she was wrong.[54]

When she suspected someone was pursuing his own agenda and ignoring her husband's interests, she hounded her husband's staff to investigate. If people she trusted agreed and could assemble a case, she would browbeat her husband into hearing the case. If he disagreed, he would do so loudly, but if he realized they were right, he would look away while the deed was done by others.[55]

A self-made Harvard man, Marine veteran, secretary of the treasury, and successful former CEO of Merrill Lynch, Donald Regan was determined to be a White House chief of staff with all the powers of a corporate COO working under an aging CEO. He claimed the entitlement to call the shots for the president on his own. He thought the president's wife had no right to interfere in the work of the government. "When you have a president who likes to delegate, assisted by a White House chief of staff who likes to amass power," Speaker of the House Tip O'Neill wrote later, "it's a formula for disaster."[56]

Regan believed the president needed protection from his wife and the staffers who had been with them since California. Mrs. Reagan particularly galled him by acting as if she—not the chief of staff—was the president's alter ego.[57] Regan became so offended by Nancy's incessant, time-wasting telephone calls and visits that he tried to bar her from the West Wing.

Nancy called upon Stu Spencer, whom Regan despised as a hack, to investigate her charges. When Spencer decided she was right, she had him present the case against Regan to her husband. Soon, Donald Regan was toast.

Regan's mismanagement and attempt to make decisions himself contributed to the Iran Contra scandal. When David Abshire was called into the White House as special counsel for the investigation, he realized that "Nancy Reagan's instincts on political issues were superior to Don's," and he also saw that all First Ladies are a critical part of White House decision-making:

> It does not seem so strange to conclude that one requirement of the White House chief of staff is to be able to get along with the First Lady. It is hard to imagine a chief of staff who could not get along with Hillary Clinton or Barbara Bush or Betty Ford or Rosalynn Carter but still tried to stay in that position.[58]

James A. Baker, Don Regan's predecessor, understood that the chief of staff was "hired help," and made sure there was always someone on his staff whom Nancy trusted. Reagan made Baker his first chief despite the fact that Baker was George Bush's dear friend and campaign manager, because Reagan's loyal aide Ed Meese couldn't manage his briefcase, let alone an administration. Reagan brought in rivals and enemies to be sure he could govern. He let Meese be a watchdog but chose competence over loyalty to begin his presidency.

Reagan's Hollywood career gave him talents useful in a candidate and in a president. Keeping a few simple ideas alive and prominent in politics is only possible with a candidate who has built an organization that keeps him agile and resilient. It is not easy to stay focused on simple themes in a presidential role.

CONCLUSION

Ronald Reagan learned what all actors know: there are always at least two audiences—the one inside the theater, and the one who will read about the performance or see it elsewhere. But Reagan also knew that those performances required a hardworking, organized team working behind the scenes.

If teamwork didn't matter, former senator Fred Thompson might have been the Republican presidential nominee in 2008. Many conservatives believed he was the only candidate who could maintain the Reagan alliance of fiscal and social conservatives. He attracted some of the top operatives in the Republican Party from both Reagan's and Bush's campaigns. In summer 2007, John McCain was floundering so badly that a number of his top staffers even defected to Thompson. In late 2007, in fact, he moved ahead of John McCain and was second only to Rudy Giuliani.

Like Reagan, Thompson was a former actor with an ability to communicate effectively. He "talked like an American" and electrified conservatives with an Internet video mocking Michael Moore's praise of the Cuban health care system—"A mental institution, Michael. Might be something you ought to think about." Unlike Giuliani, the Tennessean knew the conservative gospel and toed the line.

Thompson could not build a team; he went through three campaign managers, two press secretaries, and two communications directors in six months. He assured Floridians that he supported offshore oil drilling and made sure Iowans knew he would have vetoed the recent prescription drug benefit added to Medicare. He didn't know that Florida Republicans supported oil drilling *except* in Florida. When he attacked President George W. Bush's prescription drug addition to Medicare, he didn't know that Iowa's popular Republican Senator Chuck Grassley, whom he was courting, had written the bill. Without a good script that begins with a unified vision and ends with team organization, no actor—or politician—will win the reviews that lead to the White House.[59]

IS THIS ANY WAY TO PICK
A PRESIDENT?

After his devastating defeat by Ronald Reagan in 1984, Walter Mondale ran into George McGovern and asked him how long it took to get over his 1972 pasting by Richard Nixon. "I'll let you know when I get there," McGovern said. Twenty years later, Mondale still had not gotten over losing: "There's no school of medicine that deals with that kind of [disappointment]. . . . You move on. But you carry what you did, that history, for the rest of your life."[1]

On the night he withdrew from the presidential race in 1988, Bob Dole told the press he slept like a baby: "Every two hours I woke up and cried."[2]

Al Gore could barely talk about his feelings years after his unusual loss in the 2000 election, save to acknowledge that it was a "crushing disappointment" to come so close and not to get it. "They let other cars on the road with me now!" he told audiences in a plaintive attempt at humor.[3]

Anyone willing to run for president puts his neck on the line. No one should think it is all smoke and mirrors, or that it doesn't take brains and courage to do well. It is the toughest, fastest political competition there is. The winner of a presidential election is the most powerful person in the world; the runner-up is the biggest loser in the world.

But is this any way to pick a president? Does the protracted, expensive, long march that begins with state primaries and ends with the general election produce better or worse presidents than we got in the age when party leaders picked their party's nominee?

Does having what it takes to get to the White House and stay there bear any relation to what it takes to be a great president? Are today's presidents better prepared than in the old days of smoke-filled rooms? My answer to both is a qualified yes. An individual who can put together an effective campaign team is a better bet than the candidate picked by party leaders.

The recurring talk of a dysfunctional political system in decline is as overwrought as the millenarian hope of a brave new world.

Whenever there is "regime change" in Washington, there is utopian talk from the victors that new media or technology have unleashed social forces and restored virtue. In 2008 Arianna Huffington celebrated the death of Karl Rove's style of "fear-based and smear-based" attacks. Eric Schmidt, then Google's CEO, credited the Internet and the easy access to information for neutralizing the kind of misinformation campaigns he credited Rove for masterminding.[4]

The "free at last" cheers of Democrats in 1960, 1992, and 2008 (or Republicans in 1980 and 2000) were proclaimed as evidence that we are living in what Adam Gopnik calls a "never-better" age—"the brink of a new utopia."[5]

The other side of the permanent debate is the cry from the newly exiled party or the outmoded political style, that this is now the era Gopnik calls "better-never"; that "the world that is coming to an end is superior to the one that is taking its place."[6]

The clearest statement of the decline and degradation case was presented by an eminent scholar of political parties, the late Austin Ranney, professor of political science at UC Berkeley. He believed the unending primary process killed political parties and did not separate the wheat from the chaff:

> There is absolutely nothing in the process, in terms of organization, in terms of what the candidates do, in terms of how the voters vote, that really raises the question of the candidates' qualifications to be a good President. We have, in my view, completely separated the Presidential nominating process from the governing process.[7]

When Bill Moyers argued that candidates used to be more capable in the days when they had smaller staffs and did most of the campaigning on their own, he was echoing a similar belief that today's campaigning is a less stringent test of presidential capability. In other words, it is easier to get farther with less today than in the days of smoke-filled rooms, the days before Oprah, YouTube, and Facebook, when only reporters grilled candidates and put them through their paces.

Each side of the enduring argument overstates its case and evades the tough questions. First of all, no media change has ever been a permanent fix for any political problem. When Obama's victory was declared the end of Rovian politics, Rove was quick to point out the naïveté of the dream of salvation through technology: "Google has helped many campaigns launch a smart bomb at an opponent by providing ready access to embarrassing, but often highly relevant, quotes or images."[8]

Nor is the Internet the end of vilification. When one of the best ways to persuade progressives to open their checkbooks is to blame one person in the other party as the mastermind of dark forces in American politics, it hardly is the end of fear- or smear-based politics.[9] Demonization is demonization.

Demonization and canonization are misleading simplifications. Characterizing the Carvilles, Roves, and Shrums as saviors or demons is satisfying in the same way that a sermon about sin makes listeners feel virtuous and does nothing to improve the world. Blaming them for dark forces or silly themes is always premised on the belief that without these campaign advisors, voters wouldn't have the opinions and beliefs we find abhorrent or absurd.

Whatever side of the political spectrum you lean toward, it's an easy mistake to assume that the other side's strategist—be it Rove or Carville—is more ruthless or immoral than your side, or than strategists in days past. It is simply that the voters courted by a Rove generally respond to different arguments than the voters courted by a Carville.

The complaints with the current system begin with the assumption that when party leaders picked candidates, they had the experience and judgment to know who would make a good president, and they chose that person. Not so!

James Bryce traveled for years in America and was later Great Britain's ambassador to the United States. Conservatives who read Adam Smith and liberals who read Tocqueville should all read Bryce; no one before 1900 better understood American political institutions and the nature of public opinion and elections. Bryce noted that the reason "Why Great Men Are Not Chosen Presidents" was that there were so many opportunities to earn distinction in business that fewer men of great talent were drawn to politics. In politics, the deeds that men of great talent have to accomplish to achieve political eminence—overturn a law, say, or oust an entrenched politician—tends to make them important enemies...and a candidate with enemies scared off the party bosses.[10]

Bosses were frank with Bryce about their priorities: a great candidate was always preferable to a great president. A bad president was "a misfortune to the party, as well as to the country," but "it is a greater misfortune to the party that it should be beaten in the impending election." Besides, the bosses reasoned, "the previous career of the possible candidates has generally made it easier to say who will succeed as a candidate than who will succeed as a president."[11]

Twentieth-century political elites continued to think more about victory than qualifications to be a good president. When John Kennedy was working to get the nomination as vice president in 1956, his speechwriter, Ted Sorensen, wrote a memo for Boss Bailey of Connecticut to circulate, which was entirely about the electoral advantage of a Catholic on the ticket.[12] The memo said nothing about Kennedy's accomplishments or why he would be a good president. All that mattered was that he would help the party gain office.

Political elites still think about victory more than about qualifications to be a good president. It was no different when George W. Bush spent an afternoon at the Hoover Institution and wowed Ronald Reagan's old think tank with his electability. Although he thought Bush "still has some growing to do," Michael Boskin declared him "the most impressive presidential or potential presidential candidate that I've seen in decades."[13]

John McCain's roll of the dice with Sarah Palin as his vice presidential candidate might never have happened if Palin hadn't electrified some of the top conservative minds in the country over lunches in her statehouse in Alaska. Michael Gerson, then editor of the *Weekly Standard* and formerly George W. Bush's chief speechwriter, called her a mix of "Annie Oakley and Joan of Arc" and Fred Barnes, executive editor of the *Weekly Standard*, dubbed her America's "most popular governor." William Kristol, called her "my heartthrob," on Fox and urged John McCain to "Go for the gold here with Sarah Palin."[14]

Magical thinking about the future is part of human nature. Highly educated, sophisticated elites are no better than ordinary people at untangling electability from leadership—and just as likely to let the allure of victory eclipse concerns with performance.

While the initial judgments of many sophisticated and knowledgeable political leaders are no better today than in the past, the candidates who make it through the system are, on average, better prepared now. The process is long enough and complicated enough to force candidates to show more of their capabilities. And everyone has better opportunities to learn more about them as they are subjected to media scrutiny and competition.

It is harder today for presidential candidates to triumph solely on the basis of a good first impression. Rick Perry, Howard Dean, Rudy Giuliani, Bill Bradley, Gary Hart, and Ross Perot all made first impressions that might have carried them to the White House in an earlier era. They all faded because they were not able to survive a longer process with more tests and more opportunities for their rivals to challenge them.

Everyone complains about the length of the campaign for the presidency and the money spent in Iowa and New Hampshire, two states far from the social or economic centers of gravity for the country. Yet the retail politics required of candidates in these states is a good test of their adaptability to new terrain. And no matter which states come first, there is no way to shorten the process without removing some of its screening value.

In the nineteenth century the great English historian Walter Bagehot argued that the monarchy needed privacy and freedom from scrutiny. "When you let daylight in upon the magic," he wrote, then "you cannot reverence it."[15] There is still a monarchy today in England and political elites in every country. But the increased exposure—daylight—means less magic in the American presidency, and that is a positive development resulting from the peculiar mélange of elite and populist.

The history of presidential campaigning is a history of vulgarization and pandering, of permanent democratization. Every time the rules or media are changed, more daylight is let in, and the old elites complain about a lowering of standards and the loss of reverence. Democracy inevitably constrains reverence, and that is all to the good, because scrutiny by citizens is a better test of candidates than selection by political elites.

I am not basing my arguments for lengthy, public screening on any belief that the average voter knows more—or better—than political elites. Voters get it wrong frequently. In every political campaign both sides complain about (different) facts of which voters are unaware. The length of the process adds screening value to the primaries by encouraging an open, active civil society. There has always been a permanent campaign, but now it goes public sooner and longer.

More Content

When John Kennedy won the 1960 election he had never met Dean Rusk and Robert McNamara, his future secretaries of state and defense. He read and liked a *Time* magazine article about McNamara and offered him his choice: secretary of defense or secretary of treasury. Rusk himself was so unfamiliar with Kennedy and his well-publicized family that when JFK's brother-in-law, Sargent Shriver, called to ask whether he wanted to be secretary of state, Rusk was befuddled. He didn't know that Sargent was the first name of an important family member. Why, he asked friends, did such a significant call come from a military man—and an enlisted man, no less? Kennedy's final cabinet was described as "nine strangers and a brother," and it was in fact literally true that the only person he knew well was his attorney general, Robert Kennedy.[16]

Kennedy didn't need a large staff because there were fewer topics he had to discuss in his six years of campaigning. Today, candidates face more public scrutiny on more issues, so they need more specialists on policy and more liaisons to interest groups. Larger staffs raise the demands on the candidate. Each expert wants the last word; the candidate must decide which competing advice to heed and whether the advice is consistent with her beliefs and goals.

It takes a lot of work to give credible presidential statements, be they speeches or sound bites. Today, candidates spend months working with former officials and specialists in every area they expect to discuss during the campaign. George W. Bush started working with Condoleezza Rice, a former member of the National Security Council, two years before he ran for president. Rice resigned as provost at Stanford University and moved to Texas, giving Bush daily NSC-style briefings to prepare him for the daily barrage of questions from reporters. Bush also met regularly with members of his future economic team.[17]

Candidates once needed little more knowledge of issues than they already had as senators or governors. Today they must be prepared to answer questions on a wide variety of issues and to defend their answers.

SCREENING OUT AUTOCRATS

The presidency is three jobs in one. What makes an admirable First Family or a compelling visionary or an effective CEO is dependent upon external circumstances. The president who is well matched with an economic crisis might be a poor choice to deal with a terrorist attack or regional war. A president with a great vision of educational reform might be inept at adapting to an energy crisis. A president who knows how to reorganize the military might be inept at managing trade negotiations. Therefore, no process can guarantee a great president is chosen. The best a process can do is screen candidates for all three jobs.

A democratic process is not necessarily a good process simply because citizens are treated democratically. At the minimum, the process must reveal enough about the candidates for their character to be assessed so that citizens know whether the candidate they choose is committed to democratic principles.[18] In other words, we care not just how good the winners are, but also how well the dangers are eliminated (or at least revealed). No system can prevent citizens from choosing a president who runs roughshod over democratic principles, but at least voters should know in advance whether they are supporting a person ready to stomp on the Constitution. The primary process has a good record on this score.

Before 1900, a victorious (but otherwise unknown) general made a great presidential candidate to pull in additional voters for a party.[19] Since World War II, commanding generals have had to demonstrate they could get off their pedestal to win primaries. General Douglas MacArthur was rightly called an "American Caesar." He was a legendary military commander possessing an extraordinary intellect; he was also a towering ego prone to paranoia, with little use for civilian oversight of the military or democratic principles.[20] In 1948 he let his supporters put him on the ballot in the primaries. He had higher initial support than Dewey or Taft in his native state of Wisconsin and support of the most powerful paper in the entire Midwest, the *Chicago Tribune*. He stayed aloof, did not talk about his vision for the country, and quickly faded from the race. In 1952 he campaigned again, enjoying "evangelical fervor" from his supporters. Nevertheless, in New Hampshire, MacArthur got only 4 percent of the vote, to Eisenhower's 50 percent and Taft's 39 percent.[21] Eisenhower also worried voters before the primaries. Unlike MacArthur, though, he let voters see enough of him to assess whether he was in touch with ordinary people and their lives. He found television advertising and campaigning humiliating, but he did a "groundbreaking" set of television ads in which ordinary people asked him questions. He was also helped—to the surprise of most media researchers—by television. The new medium was supposed to advantage articulate, handsome candidates, but bald, plain Eisenhower did better there than on radio because voters who saw his unthreatening, plain manner were more favorable to him.[22]

REELECTIONS

The Nobel Laureate Amartya Sen has noted how significant it is that there are no famines in democracies.[23] There are also no great leaps forward, no permanent revolutions, and no bloody purges.

It is not because the leaders chosen at the polls are more enlightened, or less prone to grandiosity. Like everyone else, they are prone to holding on to a policy rather than give it up at a loss, the way people hold on to investments rather than sell them at a loss. What George Reedy observed of Lyndon Johnson is true of most, if not all, presidents: Johnson "never told a deliberate lie," but he willed "what was in his mind to be reality."[24]

Johnson could not bear to reconsider his Vietnam war decisions. "He had committed everything he had to Vietnam," Doris Kearns Goodwin wrote. "Regardless of all evidence, he simply had to be right."[25] Matthew Dowd saw the same aversion in George W. Bush about Iraq: "You've spent 75 or 80 percent of your money and you realize you've put the building in the wrong place. So you end up putting 20 percent more into a failure because you're afraid to say you misspent the 80 percent."[26]

Just as we cannot guarantee that the president elected will be a president for all seasons, we cannot expect presidents to acknowledge his mistakes if doing so means losing power or legitimacy. As Governor Arnold Schwarzenegger noted, "Political courage is not political suicide."[27]

But the requirement to campaign for reelection after four years protects against leaders who throw good money and lives after bad policies or pursue witch hunts against political enemies. I know of no objective standard to compare democracies. I do believe, however, that the US is doing somewhat better since World War II at limiting the ability of presidents to equate disloyalty with treason when defending their military and defense policies.[28]

Running for reelection is fundamentally different from running for election, and that is all to the good. When an incumbent offers "more of the same," it exposes him to public censure if he cannot justify staying the course. That means incumbents are more, not less, constrained by the powers of the presidency in winning four more years.

THE VALUE OF HUMILITY

The kinds of old-fashioned, outside-of-Washington politics that appear to have nothing to do with governance are exactly the kinds of activities that help to screen out some of the most undemocratic, autocratic candidates. Perot and MacArthur couldn't get down from their pedestals and expose themselves to the grilling of activists and press, and Rudy Giuliani was too comfortable being "America's mayor" to get real.

The strange chicanery and rituals of the primaries are valuable for people who do not take it as given that any particular elite can be trusted to tell them what they should know about the character and programs of the candidates.

Ben Franklin considered humility an important virtue but confessed he could not "boast of much success in acquiring the reality of this virtue; but I had a good deal with regard to the appearance of it." He learned to avoid acting as if his mind were made up by avoiding words like "certainly," "undoubtedly," and "positively," and instead used words that suggested he was interested in hearing what the other person had to say, like "it appears to me," or "if I am not mistaken," or "I imagine."[29]

It is foolish to imagine that anyone audacious enough to think he should be president could actually be humble. Yet even learning enough about ordinary people to look authentic or act humble is valuable: first of all, it screens out the people too self-important and imperious to stoop to learning enough about ordinary people to connect with them; second, you cannot act humble or look authentic without learning enough about the people you are interacting with to show empathy.

Taking a Hit

Primaries force candidates to demonstrate they can go face-to-face with their rivals. This public competition gives other candidates a chance to test whether challengers who run as the candidate of hope and change have grounding in reality. This process also lets voters see whether candidates can take a hit and know how and when to hit back. When Roger Ailes advised Vice President Bush, he was emphatic that if the VP wanted to assure voters he was strong enough to be president, he had to show "You can take a punch, and you can throw a punch." James Carville emphasized the same point as one of the values of a campaign. Campaigning is good training for governing, he said, because it prepares candidates to "get hit, stand strong, and, if necessary, hit back."[30]

The "if necessary" qualifier, Ailes would agree, is particularly important because voters are sensitive to the critical difference between a person willing to fight whenever necessary and a person eager to fight whenever possible.

Knowing when and how to fight is good training for governing, because some advisors will urge the president to be aggressive and others will counsel patience. In an inadvertently taped discussion about foreign policy, President Kennedy discussed his frustration with Foreign Service "softies" who "don't seem to have cojones," while Defense Department officials were all men of action who "haven't any brains."[31] Learning the difference— and surrounding yourself with people who can acknowledge when their preferred approach won't work this time—is essential to campaigning and governing.

Coalition Building

Finally, campaigns test whether candidates can be credible enough panderers to build a governing coalition. Dealing with so many groups and their inconsistent demands is a great leveler. Sixty years ago, Richard Rovere saw that any candidate who campaigns actively is "sooner or later forced to abandon themselves to the ancient practices of audience-flattering, enemy-vilifying, name-remembering, moon-promising, and the like."[32]

Pandering is an essential part of building a coalition, and campaigns test whether a candidate is capable of responsible, principled pandering. People know that politicians will make promises on which they cannot deliver. A critical part of pandering is justifying it to people beyond those who benefit from the program with principles that can evoke broad public support. To paraphrase Aristotle, expressing the interests of the audience as universal truths brings moral justification to a policy. Wheat farmers readily accept that the government should pay them for surplus grain in order to feed hungry people around the globe, and corn farmers just as easily accept that government should require the use of ethanol fuel made from corn. For nonfarmers, however, it took "Food for Peace" and "Energy Independence" to justify the programs as more than pork barrel boondoggles.

Irresponsible, unsustainable pandering exposes many politicians as insincere because they didn't understand the limits of the promises they can make without destroying their coalition. Governor Bush was not willing to give evangelicals all the commitments they wanted, but Governor Rick Perry went so far that it alienated as many voters as it attracted.[33] Because he was from Hollywood, had gay friends, and had been divorced, evangelicals distrusted Ronald Reagan. Before his 1980 presidential run, he was asked whether the Bible was the literal word of God. His answer was eloquent, passionate, positive... and noncommittal:

> I have never had any doubt about it being of divine origin. And to those who... doubt it, I would like to have them point out to me any similar collection of writings that have lasted for as many thousands of years and is still the best seller worldwide. It had to be of divine origin.[34]

There is no other way to govern and make policy in a country as diverse as America but to know how to pander within reasonable limits.

Examining all the imperfect people who run for president, I believe more strongly than when I began this research that the most dangerous loophole in the process is the recurring belief—the fantasy—of the anti-politician. Over a century ago, Henry Jones Ford, a Renaissance man whose résumé included editing newspapers, a professorship at Johns Hopkins University, and government service, said, "politicians there will always be so long as there is politics. The only thing that is open to control is what sort of politicians we shall have."[35]

Every step of the way, from challenger to incumbent to successor, it is harder to be successful on changing terrain with new media and new competition. All we can do is screen out bad choices and hope that the odds improve. So far, there is no screening process that can accurately predict the future, so we cannot be sure we are packing for the right trip. This screening process, at least, is better than the last one in smoke-filled rooms of party leaders.

When I studied elections from the point of view of voters and how they made sense of candidates, my most important rule was that candidates "should never tell voters they are selfish, and never assume they are not." As long as voters have irreconcilable expectations, candidates will overpromise, act as if the goals of the voters they court are feasible, and pretend they have more influence over policies than they do. Given all this, looking at the three kinds of campaigns, I believe that the most important quality we should look for in candidates is whether they understand the distinction between what sells and what works. Both are necessary; knowing the difference is critical.

ACKNOWLEDGMENTS

I chose to put these acknowledgments at the end because I hope that reading the book will help people realize how much I benefited from those thanked here. I didn't know that writing this book would be so arduous. I'm fortunate to have had support and encouragement from so many campaigners, scholars, and writers who helped me move beyond my preconceptions, escape from blind alleys, notice the dogs that didn't bark, and stay on track.

There isn't much I could have done without my wife, Susan Shirk, so adding this book to the list does not begin to show my appreciation for our life together, our family, and the wonderful extended family of friends we have around the globe. I've often said that I have the easy job—help a candidate get elected—while she has the more difficult task: help them accomplish something. Now I say it without any false modesty. Our children, Lucy and David, and our son-in-law Seth Demain, were always supportive and understanding, and confident that there would be a book at the end of my tunneling.

By granting me a fellowship in 2004–2005, the Center for Advanced Study in the Behavioral Sciences at Stanford University provided an opportunity to rethink my understanding of news and news media as I began this book. I am particularly grateful to their librarian, Tricia Soto, for her help with obscure sources and to my wife—again!—for organizing a lunch group for fellows writing books for broader audiences.

The Russell Sage Foundation in New York named me a Fellow in 2008–2009, gifting me the time to organize my research and begin writing. I am particularly grateful to my co-Fellow, Phillip Atiba Goff, for his insights about presentation, in addition to the serendipitous benefits for me of his research on manhood and race. Without that fellowship, I would not have met Phil

Blumberg and Peter Goldman. I doubt anyone who had not been a movie studio executive, Yale Drama School graduate, social psychology PhD, and a psychoanalyst would have noticed, as Phil did, two critical points hiding in plain sight in my drafts. Peter was encouraging at a crucial time and never failed to remind me to show the signs pointing to the toy store.

The late John Chancellor came to UC San Diego three times for PBS shows based on conferences with White House chiefs of staff, press secretaries, and campaigners. These symposia were a master class with Chancellor and gave me an opportunity to meet and talk at length with those on the other side of campaigns from me: Donald Rumsfeld, Richard Cheney, Stu Spencer, Mike Deaver, and Ed Rollins in particular.

I owe Richard Norton Smith, Gary MacDougal, and Dan Balz a special debt of gratitude for being kind enough to share documents and insights with me from their own exhaustive research. James T. (Jay) Hamilton, shared his insights and analyses of media as I rethought my perspective.

My agent, Jill Marsal, helped me find a pattern for the book I wanted to write. I am grateful to her for appreciating the possibilities of a different manner of campaign book. At Oxford, my editor, David McBride, was willing to take a chance on a book like this and get it out months ahead of other presses. How he persuaded me to cut over twenty thousand words from the Clinton-Obama analysis I'll never know.

During the two years of writing, rewriting, and reorganizing the material, my working relationship with Gabriel Greene, literary director at La Jolla Playhouse, has been my game changer. Gabe's understanding of flow and structure helped me stick to my own argument, only use the examples that were necessary to develop the line of reasoning, and keep the themes clear.

My son David Popkin made sure that there were clear and coherent takeaways from every chapter and case study. Steven Clermont and Gary Jacobson read the entire manuscript and offered important corrections and clarifications. My daughter, Lucy Popkin, helped me refine many chapters. Paula Jacobson helped me clarify and verify my case studies.

Matt Childers's exhaustive data analysis has been essential to my understanding of voter engagement. His PhD thesis was an eye-opening supplement to my prior research. Lynn Vavreck and David Redlawsk generously shared their data and analyses.

Several colleagues, writers, friends and campaigners helped me more than footnotes and citations can convey. I think of them as my "osmosis acknowledgments," people whose questions and conversation shaped this book beyond any specific cite or fact: Jay Hamilton, Arthur Lupia, Alan Gerber, Brandice Canes-Wrone, Roger Noll, Daniel Kahneman, Norbert Schwarz, Richard Thaler, Craig Fox, Strobe Talbott, Simon Lazarus, Doug Baily, Stuart Eizenstat, Matt McCubbins, Sam Kernell, Jon Krosnick, Daron Shaw, Dotty Lynch, Robert Kaiser, Ann Lewis, Peter Hart, Andy Kohut, Doug Rivers, Geoff Garin, Stan Greenberg, James Carville, Paul Begala, Nick Gourevitch, Bill Knapp, Barbara Lewis, Robert Solow, and Malcolm and Carolyn Wiener.

I wish that Johnny Apple, Richard Holbrooke, Robert Ellsworth, Paul Tully, Warren Mitofsky, Diane Blair, Robert Teeter, and John Gorman were still here to be thanked in person for their support and friendship.

Electronic editing and file sharing enhance research and also create new ways to inject errors into manuscripts. I am grateful to Isaac Cowhey and Katie Montgomery Lewis for going through the sources to reconcile text and footnotes. Katie also shepherded the page proofs and bibliography through the final production stages. And I join a long line of Oxford University Press authors indebted to Mary Sutherland for a copy editing worthy of any book in any time period.

I hope someday to meet the wonderful British dramatist Michael Frayn and tell him that his play about Willy Brandt, *Democracy*, was an epiphany for me in its portrayal of the clashes between the workhorses and show horses of politics.

NOTES

PROLOGUE

1. MSNBC "Tucker" 2007; Robinson 2000. Peter Robinson, the editor of the conservative *Hoover Institution Digest*, even equated his elation over seeing a squeegee-free New York with watching the Berlin Wall fall.
2. Giuliani and Kurson 2002.
3. *Hotline* 2007g.
4. Vitello 2008.
5. Kahneman and Tversky 1972; Lewis 2004.
6. Kaufmann 2009.
7. Halberstam 1979, 472.
8. Tuchman 1981, 22.
9. Kinsley 2000.
10. This quote is widely cited by military historians and strategists, yet I can find no evidence that she used this phrase. It does, however, capture her writing perfectly.
11. Kaiser and Harris 1998.

CHAPTER 1

1. Balz and Johnson 2009, 34.
2. Anderson 1994, 133.
3. Ibid., 117.
4. Wooten 1976.
5. Dembart 1976.
6. Gwertzman 1976.
7. Cannon 1976; Morgan 1976.
8. Lelyveld 1976; AP 1976; Burros 1976; King 1976.
9. Quinn 1976.
10. Apple Jr. 1976b.
11. Mohr 1976.
12. Apple Jr. 1976a.
13. Anderson 1994, 102.
14. *Post-Gazette* Staff 1976; Byman 2005, 23–24.
15. *Saturday Night Live* 1991.

16. Germond and Witcover 1993, 143.
17. Roll Call 1991.
18. Germond 1993, 139.
19. Ibid., 139–40, 246.
20. *Hotline* 1991d.
21. *Hotline* 1991c.
22. Goldman 1994, 621; Yang and Devroy 1991.
23. Radcliffe 1991a; AP 1991; *Washington Post* staff 1991.
24. Royer 1994, 18.
25. Yang 1991.
26. Barker 1991; Radcliffe 1991b.
27. Chipello 1991.
28. Wines 1991a.
29. *New York Times* staff 1991; Toner 1991b.
30. Wines 1991b.
31. Connolly 1999.
32. *Hotline* 1999d.
33. Branch 2009, 553–54.
34. *Hotline* 1999e.
35. Dunne 1986.
36. *Good Morning America* 1999.
37. Gellman 2000.
38. *Good Morning America* 1999.
39. *Hotline* 1999f; *Hotline* 1999a.
40. Kennedy 1960.
41. Heale 1973, 417.
42. Greenstein 1990, 8.
43. British Monarchy 2011; Caldwell 2002.
44. Morris 2001, 55; *New York Times* staff 1901.
45. White 1961.
46. Simon 1967, 98. Simon made the comparisons with head chef when he presented the paper at the 1966 Annual Meeting of the American Political Science Association. It is not in the published paper.
47. Williams 1990b.
48. Beverland 2006; Beverland, et al. 2008.
49. Langlois 1992.
50. Kantor 2011.
51. Hallin 1991, 85–86; Moore and Slater 2003; Auletta 2004; Klein 2002; Klein 2008.
52. Brubach 2011.
53. McManus 2005.
54. Roberts 2004.

CHAPTER 2

1. Strother 2003, 2; Cramer 1992, viii.
2. Cramer 1992, 254–55.

3. Rove 2010, 9.
4. Canes-Wrone 2006; Schattschneider 1983.
5. Lizza 2004.
6. Popkin 1994, 97; Fenno 1978, 56; Fiske, et al. 2007, 79; Shogan 2006, 10.
7. Fenno 1978, 78.
8. Cooperman 2004.
9. Morris 2001, 354.
10. Goldman 1994, 107.
11. Catledge 1940.
12. Koplinski 2000, 227.
13. Horrigan 2007.
14. Abelson 1986; Nyhan and Reifler 2010, 323; Chong and Druckman 2010, 663.
15. Baker 2003. See also Pitney 2000 for an analysis of the use of military terminology in politics.
16. Broder, David S., and John F. Kennedy School of Government, Institute of Politics 2006, 35.
17. Apple Jr. 1976b.
18. London *Times* Staff 1976; *Irish Times* Staff 1976; Farrelly and Kelly 1976; London *Times* editorial staff 1976.
19. Oberdorfer, et al. 1992.
20. Weisman 1991.
21. Gigot 1991; Auerbach 1991; Blustein 1991.
22. Abramson and Chipello 1991; Chipello and Chandler 1992; *Wall Street Journal* editorial staff 1992.
23. Gellman 2000.
24. *Hotline* 1999b.
25. Sawyer was serious enough about Bradley to bring her parents to spend Christmas with his parents in 1966 when she was a Wellesley college student. She was so beautiful that Marty Glickman, then a sportscaster and later Bradley's business agent, called her the most beautiful girl he had ever met when Bradley introduced them. Gellman and Russakoff 1999.
26. Williams 2001, 135; *Newsweek* 2000b; *Hotline* 1999c.
27. Jamieson and Waldman 2001, 73; Seelye 1999.
28. Monmonier 1991, 1.
29. Hollitz 1982, 31.
30. Viguerie and Franke 2004, 148–50, 213–17.
31. Grove 1989.
32. Stelter 2008b.
33. Gabriel 2011.
34. Russell 2003; Smith 1976; Reeves 1972b, 26.
35. Hartmann 1971, 189–90.
36. Matalin and Carville 1994, 321.
37. Milbank 2006.
38. Fisher 2006.
39. Goldman 1994, 273.
40. Stephanopoulos 1999, 86.

41. Draper 2011.
42. Heilemann and Halperin 2010, 53.
43. Maslin 2004.
44. Milgrom and Roberts 1988, 177; Sprey 2011, 102.
45. Walt 1987, 147.
46. Kantor 2009.
47. I knew the details of this minicrisis as part of the Carter campaign. I verified the details later with participants involved in the cabinet debates in Ireland. Robert Teeter also confirmed to me that the Ford campaign had not learned of the crisis before the election.
48. Will 2006.
49. Halberstam 2001, 172.
50. Goldsmith and Reiter 2007.
51. Matalin and Carville 1994, 162.

CHAPTER 3

1. Weiner 1980.
2. Yoda was designed with Einstein-like features to emphasize his supreme knowledge. BBC 2005.
3. Gay 1984, 66.
4. Reeves 1972a.
5. Galbraith 1993, 13.
6. Caddell 1988.
7. Brady 1997, 146–47.
8. Ibid., 142–43.
9. Hoagland 1999.
10. Shapiro 1984, 21.
11. Hetherington 1998; Hetherington 1999.
12. Liberman and Trope 1998; Trope 1986; Trope and Liberman 2003; Trope, et al. 2007.
13. Balz 2011b.
14. Kinder, et al. 1980; Boskin 2001, 6.
15. This paraphrases the late Paul Tully's analysis of George H. W. Bush in 1992. To placate alienated social conservatives he featured a number of "culture warriors" at the Republican National Convention." Tully correctly noted that "The closer Bush gets to 40%, the farther he gets from 50%."
16. Stone 2006.
17. Kahneman 2002; Hsee et al. 1999.
18. Levinson 2008.
19. Converse et al. 1961.
20. Massa 1997, 298.
21. Ibid., 299.
22. Ibid., 297.
23. Sorensen 2008, 147–54.
24. Massa 1997, 304–5.
25. *The American Experience* 2000.

26. Rovere 1962.
27. Matthews 1982, 508–9.
28. Rovere 1962.
29. Goldman 1956, 29.
30. Green 2002.
31. Ibid.
32. Edelstein 2002.
33. Edsall 1992.
34. Ambinder 2007.
35. Remnick 2008.
36. Clymer 1999, 284.
37. O'Neill and Novak 1987, 326.
38. Burke 1992, 216; Clymer 1999, 278.
39. Anonymous interview 2005.
40. Shrum 2007, 82.
41. Discussed in chap. 5.
42. Strother 2003, 217.
43. Ifill 1992; Kornheiser 1992.
44. Farhi 2003.
45. Kurtz 2004.
46. Wilgoren and Rutenberg 2004.
47. Wolf 2003.
48. Ibid.
49. Broder and John F. Kennedy School of Government, Institute of Politics 2006, 57.
50. *Hotline* 2004.
51. Bauder 2004; Wolf 2003. Wolf noted months earlier that the endings of his speeches could come "perilously close to a screech."
52. Maslin 2004.
53. Kinder and McConnaughy 2006, 145.
54. Podhoretz 2006a; Podhoretz 2006b.
55. Bai 2007a; Boyer 2007; Giuliani 2007.
56. Boyer 2007.
57. Boyer 2007; Giuliani 2007.
58. Giuliani and Kurson 2002.
59. Boyer 2007.
60. Podhoretz 2007; Boyer 2007.
61. Kolbert 2008.
62. Boyer 2007.
63. Shogan 2007, 297.

CHAPTER 4

1. Wolffe 2007.
2. Penn 2006.
3. Penn and Zalesne 2007, 136–38. Penn emphasized that there were far fewer young voters, proportionately, in the 2006 congressional elections than in the 2004 presidential election.

4. Balz and Johnson 2009, 34.
5. Wallace-Wells 2007.
6. Balz and Johnson 2009, 179.
7. Ibid., 182–83.
8. Simon 2008.
9. Hart 2007.
10. Penn 2006.
11. Penn 2007b.
12. Penn 2006.
13. Penn 2007a; Penn 2007b; Penn 2006; Milbank 2008.
14. Balz and Johnson 2009, 113; Penn and Zalesne 2007, 13, 167.
15. Todd 2007.
16. Popkin 1991.
17. Marton 2001, 316.
18. Penn 2006; Penn 2007b.
19. Balz and Johnson 2009, 117.
20. Lizza 2008.
21. Balz and Johnson 2009, 105.
22. Balz and Johnson 2009, 30; Popkin 1994.
23. Purdum 2008.
24. Milbank 2008.
25. Bacon Jr. 2007; Cooper 2007.
26. Lizza 2008.
27. Balz and Johnson 2009, 122.
28. Ambinder 2007.
29. Wolffe 2009; Scott 2007.
30. *Hotline* 2007b.
31. Cillizza and Balz 2007.
32. Mosk 2008b.
33. Plouffe 2009, 36.
34. Benderoff 2007; McGirt 2009.
35. Plouffe 2009, 51.
36. Green 2008; Wolffe 2009, 73–74.
37. Advertising buys are measured in points. Each 100 points means that the average person will be exposed once to the ad, so a 1,000-point buy means that, on average, persons will see the ad ten times.
38. Dunn and Wallace 2009, 223.
39. Fisher 2006.
40. Vargas 2008a; Vargas 2008b; Martelle 2008; Bardeeby 2008; Exley 2007b; Exley 2007c.
41. Thomas 2009, 108–9.
42. Broder and John F. Kennedy School of Government, Institute of Politics 2009, 97–98.
43. Plouffe 2009, 86.
44. The Nielsen Company 2007; Vargas 2007.
45. Plouffe 2009, 92; Benderoff 2007.

46. Jamieson 2009, 221–22.
47. Bai 2005; Trippi 2008, 248–49. Trippi goes farther and says Penn claimed the Internet wouldn't have value in 2008. Given Penn's other comments, it is more likely that he was talking about the online political community, not the Internet. "One more place" is from an interview with a campaign principal.
48. Sosnik, et al. 2006, 22, Heilemann and Halperin 2010, 78, 82; Sosnik, Dowd, and Fournier 2006.
49. Benderoff 2007; Harris 2000; Harris and VandeHei 2007.
50. Personal conversation, Popkin and Begala, November 1992.
51. Leibovich 2007.
52. Romano 2007; Healy 2007.
53. Romano 2008.
54. Cottle 2008a; Cottle 2008c.
55. Heilemann and Halperin 2010, 95; Baker and Kornblut 2008.
56. Sheehy 2008.
57. Ibid.
58. Balz and Johnson 2009, 122.
59. Heilemann and Halperin 2010, 32–33.
60. Plouffe 2009, 8.
61. Ibid., 8, 35.
62. Ibid., 35–36.
63. Stelter 2008a.
64. Schatz 2007; McGirt 2009.
65. Milbank 2001, 142.
66. New Hampshire is small enough that activists there expect the same kind of courtship and the right to scrutinize the candidates up close and personal. In addition, New Hampshire has the honor of hosting the "first in the nation" presidential primary, even though there are more registered Independents than Democrats or Republicans in the state.
67. Balz and Johnson 2009, 73.
68. Simon 2008.
69. Heilemann and Halperin 2010, 110.
70. Ibid., 110; Thomas 2009, 10–11.
71. Balz and Johnson 2009, 90.
72. Plouffe 2009, 96–98. If Edwards had won Iowa, there would have been a two-way race, and blacks would have certainly sided with Hillary, who was, in their minds, far preferable to Edwards.
73. Ibid., 98.
74. Draper 2009; Suskind 2008.
75. Heilemann and Halperin 2010, 112–15.
76. Balz and Johnson 2009, 117.
77. Heilemann and Halperin 2010, 78.
78. *Hotline* 2006; Distaso 2006; Tim Russert 2006. James Carville had already been blunt about the need to go local and work for the nomination. Carville told her that a front-runner strategy was a losing strategy, and he said it on *Meet the Press* to emphasize the point.

79. Skiba 2007.
80. Simon 2008.
81. Balz and Johnson 2009, 112–13.
82. Ambinder 2007; Simon 2008.
83. Balz and Johnson 2009, 104. The Obama campaign minimized their total by noting that about $270,000 was for an Iowa firm that handled part of their first announcement tour. Hiring that Iowa firm, however, was clearly related to its place in Iowa and not its national reputation or experience. And even without the money spent on Caudill Associates, their total was still greater than all the other candidates combined.
84. Heilemann and Halperin 2010, 95.
85. Green 2008a.
86. Balz and Johnson 2009, 112; Pickler 2007; Lorentzen 2007.
87. Balz and Johnson 2009, 107; Simon 2008.
88. Ambinder 2007.
89. Finnegan 2004.
90. Ambinder 2007.
91. Rainie 2008; Kohut 2008; Kohut, et al. 2008, 2, 9. Rainie has the overall summary. I am indebted to Robert Bond's dissertation research for the Facebook data about users older than twenty-nine.
92. Cillizza 2007; Pew 2007. Pew titled this report "Modest Interest," but it was, in fact, a record high for that part of the campaign, as the report indicates.
93. Plouffe 2009, 76, 123.
94. Simon 2008, 124; Balz and Johnson 2009; Crowley 2007.
95. Heilemann and Halperin 2010, 104.
96. Ibid.
97. Nagourney 2007a; Heilemann and Halperin 2010, 84.
98. Smith 2007.
99. Penn 2007a. Ickes knew the process better than anyone else but was not around the headquarters unless called upon. Ickes withdrew rather than battle fruitlessly with Penn over the differences between a primary campaign and a general election.
100. Balz and Johnson 2009, 183. Three witnesses told Dan Balz that Mark Penn had assumed that California was winner-take-all. While Penn strenuously denies that he ever said this, his September 29 memo and complete passivity on Florida show he did not understand "delegate strategy 101." While few pollsters do, strategists usually do.
101. Ibid., 182–83. It gets even more complicated because the number of delegates in any district depends upon the past Democratic vote in that district, not just the population of the district. Since districts of the same size might have three, four, five, or six delegates, campaigns that took into account the number of votes needed to gain an additional delegate could be more efficient in deciding where to place staff and volunteers.
102. Simon 2008.
103. Plouffe 2009, 101–3.
104. Gilbert 2007; Simon 2008.

105. Exley 2007c.
106. Balz and Johnson 2009, 113; *Hotline* 2007f; *Hotline* 2007e.
107. Balz and Johnson 2009, 115–16.
108. Ibid., 116.
109. Mellman 2007.
110. Bai 2007b.
111. Malcolm 2007. Clinton denied that she knew the student without ever denying that she knew what the question would be.
112. Plouffe 2009, 109.
113. Heilemann and Halperin 2010, 150.
114. Balz and Johnson 2009, 118.
115. Interview with senior staffer.
116. *Hotline* 2003; Heilemann and Halperin 2010, 19; Kornblut 2003.
117. Simon 2007.
118. Wolffe 2009, 92.
119. Plouffe 2009, 133.
120. Wolffe 2009, 92.
121. Yepsen 2007.
122. Heilemann and Halperin 2010, 152.
123. *Hotline* 2007c.
124. Balz and Johnson 2009, 120–21.
125. Heilemann and Halperin 2010, 155.
126. Balz and Johnson 2009, 121; Green 2008c.
127. *Hotline* 2007d.
128. Sheehy 2008.
129. Heilemann and Halperin 2010, 170; *Hotline* 2007e.
130. Thomas 2009, 26; Balz and Johnson 2009, 123; Beaumont 2008; Plouffe 2009, 126.
131. Balz and Johnson 2009, 123.
132. Heilemann and Halperin 2010, 172.
133. Balz and Johnson 2009, 125.
134. Ibid.
135. Ibid., 111.
136. Heilemann and Halperin 2010, 6, 125–26.
137. Balz and Johnson 2009, 125–26.
138. Ibid., 126.
139. Heilemann and Halperin 2010, 7.
140. Cottle 2008b; Heilemann and Halperin 2010, 178–79; Thomas 2009, 27; Balz and Johnson 2009, 129–30. The depictions of the conference call agree on the tone and nature of the call with slightly different versions of the comments by Hillary Clinton.
141. Balz and Johnson 2009, 126–27.
142. Thomas 2009, 27; Heilemann and Halperin 2010, 179.
143. Balz and Johnson 2009, 130.
144. Ibid., 180.
145. Federal News Service 2008.

146. Balz and Johnson 2009, 135; Plouffe 2009, 145.

147. Thomas 2009, 28; Plouffe 2009; 147, Balz and Johnson 2009, 137.

148. Heilemann and Halperin 2010, 181.

149. Ibid., 182–87; Balz and Johnson 2009, 145.

150. Heilemann and Halperin 2010, 179.

151. Wolffe 2009; Green 2008b; Mosk 2008a; Luo 2008.

152. Balz and Johnson 2009, 132.

153. Plouffe 2009, 131–33, 154–55.

154. Oreskes 2008.

155. Heilemann and Halperin 2010, 194.

156. Exley 2008.

157. Plouffe 2009, 66–67; Cooper, et al. 2008. One local politician liked Obama but walked away when he was offered $5,000 a month to organize; he ended up working for Clinton for about $20,000 a month—more than any single person in the Obama campaign was getting paid.

158. Plouffe 2009, 66.

159. Cooper, et al. 2008.

160. Balz and Johnson 2009, 165; Bones 2008. Carol Fowler, the South Carolina Democratic Party chairwoman, said Obama's organization was "the best I have ever seen."

161. Edsall 2008; Balz and Johnson 2009, 166.

162. Hotline 2008c; Freedland 2008; Balz and Johnson 2009; Hotline 2008a.

163. Simon 2008; Thomas 2009, 55.

164. Baker and Kornblut 2008.

165. Plouffe 2009, 166–67.

166. Ibid., 168.

167. Plouffe 2009, 168–69.

168. Balz and Johnson 2009, 187; Kuraitis 2008.

169. Cecil 2008; Baker and Kornblut 2008.

170. Heilemann and Halperin 2010, 234.

171. Wallace-Wells 2007.

172. Hastings 2008.

173. Kornblut and Cohen 2008.

174. Thomas 2009, 102.

175. Healy 2008.

176. The transcripts were analyzed by Ashley Bullock. I am grateful to Professor Philip Atiba Goff of the UCLA Psychology Department for help with this analysis. There were eight DNC-sanctioned debates before the Iowa caucus and in those eight, while Clinton was self-centered, Obama used unifying we-words slightly more than I-words.

177. Baker and Rutenberg 2008.

178. Kirby, et al. 2008; Redlawsk et al. 2011, 77. In November polls, Clinton was close to Obama among under 30 participants. The Obama campaign contacted one in five of them in person, the Clinton campaign two percent.

179. Depaulo 2008b; Penn 2008; Depaulo 2008a.

180. Balz and Johnson 2009, 221.

CHAPTER 5

1. Ten years later, Barry Sherman (Sherman 1990) revisited the debate and obtained a copy of three of the four practice session tapes from a cameraman who had held on to them for posterity. All quotes are taken from these tapes. Professor Phillip Goff of the UCLA Department of Psychology and Allison Hoffman, a psychologist also trained in coding facial expressions and body language, analyzed the films of President Carter. The coding was done without sound, so that they would not know what Reagan/Popkin was saying when they studied the emotions the president was displaying. All quotes are from these tapes, which were given to me by Sherman.
2. Brydon 1985, 52.
3. Goldsmith and Reiter 2007.
4. Schroeder 2000, 45–46. Schroeder credits Richard Wirthlin, President Reagan's pollster for this insight.
5. Ibid., 74; Spencer 2001, 54; *Newsweek* 1996; Easton, et al. 2004.
6. Berman and Moe 1982, 57.
7. Reedy 1987, 18.
8. Napolitan 1986, 29.
9. Eggen 2008.
10. Kolbert 1996.
11. Woodward 1996, 53.
12. Caro 2002a, 525.
13. Ibid.
14. Ibid., 528.
15. Clift and Brazaitis 1996, 35.
16. Lemann 2003. The only group Governor Bush referred to in his 2000 campaign debates with Al Gore were Arab Americans in Michigan, and the first Arab American ever appointed to the cabinet was former Michigan senator Spencer Abraham, who was also an advocate of immigration reform.
17. Lizza 2012, 45.
18. Williamson, et al. 2011.
19. Westen 2011; Balz 2011a; Chait 2011; Tarloff 2011; Ornstein 2011.
20. Lizza 2012, 47.
21. Stephanopoulos 1999, 89.
22. Rutenberg, et al. 2009.
23. Kaufman 2005.
24. Anderson 2001, 21.
25. Broder and John F. Kennedy School of Government, Institute of Politics 1997, 99.
26. Noonan 1990, 66–67; Broder and John F. Kennedy School of Government, Institute of Politics 1997, 128.
27. Reedy 1987, 18.
28. Weisberg 1993.
29. Kantor 2008; Kantor 2012, 126.
30. Purdum 2007.
31. Fitzwater 1995, 71.

32. Podhoretz 1993, 54–55.
33. Popkin and Kernell 1986, 18–30.
34. Gellman 2008, 86.
35. Noonan 1990, 72.
36. Bakshian 2002, 10; Popkin and Kernell 1986, 10–11, 172.
37. Hallin 1991, 86–87, 50.
38. Noonan 1990, 62; Lance 1982; Marton 2001.
39. Shapiro 2010; Scott 2011.
40. Jamieson 2006, 37; Schroeder 2000, 52.
41. Catledge 1940.
42. Steeper and Teeter 1976.
43. Nixon and Haldeman 1972. Burden and Hillygus 2009. Burden and Hillygus note some of the ways voters are less uncertain about incumbents than about challengers.
44. Stephanopoulos 1999, 406.
45. Lott 2005, 139–40; Broder and John F. Kennedy School of Government, Institute of Politics 1997, 115.
46. Obama 2012.
47. *Frontrunner* 2001; Krugman 2002.
48. Landau, et al. 2004; Glenn 2004.
49. *Advertising Age* 2004.
50. Woodward 2004.
51. Rove 2011.
52. Lee 1966; Karabell 2000, 37.
53. Jenkins 1986, 126–30.
54. Ibid., 87–89.
55. McCullough 1992, 590–92; Rowe 1969.
56. Donaldson 1999, 71; Jenkins 1986, 87; Popkin 2006, 246–48.
57. Strunk 1948b, 557–58.
58. Strunk 1948a, 577; Hitchens 1968, 68; Elsey 1965; Strunk 1948c, 758.
59. Acheson 1971. Taft's view, Acheson said, was "to hell with [foreigners], they didn't vote in Ohio and they were not good, and shiftless. Get a good Army, Navy and Air Force, and to hell with it."
60. Goldman 1956, 30.
61. Pruessen 1982, 357–65.
62. Acheson 1971; Trubowitz and Mellow 2005; Dewey 1965, 17.
63. Hoeber 1966, Appendix A: "Should the President Call Congress Back"; Hartmann 1971, 193.
64. Brownell; Brownell and Burke 1993, 80–83.
65. Rowe 1969; Patterson 1972, 420–21.
66. Lowry 1969.
67. Jenkins 1986, 141; Hartmann 1971, 206; McCullough 1992, 713; Lowry 1969.
68. Wilson 1948.
69. Brownell and Burke 1993, 53, 83; Gullan 1998, 153; Abels 1959, 291; Loeb 1970; Riggs 1972.
70. Alsop and Alsop 1948.

71. Reinhard 1983, 40; Strunk 1948c, 780; Lambert 1956; Abels 1959, 59; Divine 1974, 192; Davis 1944.

72. Batt 1966; Hoeber 1966; Donaldson 1992.

73. Lowry 1969.

74. Anderson 2001.

75. Carney 2001.

76. Brady 1997, 146–47.

77. Bai 2008; Hertzberg 2009b; Hertzberg 2009c; Hertzberg 2009a; Mattson 2009.

78. Bosch 2002; *The American Experience: Jimmy Carter* (Transcript), Adriana Bosch, director, 2002, PBS.

79. Noonan 1990, 122.

80. Spencer 2001.

CHAPTER 6

1. Church 1991.

2. Ibid.

3. Blumenthal 1993, 29–31; Woodward 1992d.

4. Pfiffner 1993, 91; Woodward 1992d.

5. Allen 1981; Kinsley 1986; Greider 1981.

6. Drew 1990a, 98.

7. Bush 1999, 420–21.

8. Frankel 2003, 32.

9. Ibid., 45; Woodward 1992d.

10. Boskin 2001; telephone discussion November 7, 2011.

11. Drew 1990b, 97.

12. Balz and Devroy 1990.

13. Ibid.

14. Fitzwater 1995, 215–16.

15. Ibid.

16. Ibid., 216.

17. Noonan 1990, 298–317; Woodward 1992a.

18. Drew 1992, 80; Woodward 1992b.

19. Dowd 1991; Kolb 1994, 181–82.

20. *Hotline* 1990b; *Hotline* 1990a; Komarow 1990; Mondale 1990.

21. Williams 1990a; Jacobson 1993.

22. Woodward 1992b.

23. Jacobson 1993, 392; *Hotline* 1990c.

24. Kellerman 1990.

25. Hamilton 2009, 221–23.

26. Klein 1989.

27. Ibid.

28. Ibid.; Kurtz 1996, 297. The widely respected (and normally mild-mannered) columnist David Broder erupted: Nader had become a "moralistic blackmailing National Nag."

29. Rapoport and Stone 2005, 52–55.

30. *Hotline* 1991e; *Hotline* 1991b; *Hotline* 1991a; Popkin 1994, 240–42.
31. Podhoretz 1993, 39–40.
32. Ibid., 42.
33. *Hotline* 1991a; *Hotline* 1991b.
34. Fitzwater 1995, 180–81; Woodward 1992c.
35. Pfiffner 1993, 1.
36. Royer 1994, 114.
37. Fitzwater 1995, 180–81; Woodward 1992c; Pfiffner 1993, 92.
38. Pfiffner 1993, 94; Fitzwater 1995, 180–81.
39. Goldman 1994, 303–10.
40. Ibid., 4.
41. Ibid., 304; Woodward 1992c.
42. Woodward 1992c.
43. Steeper 1991a; Steeper 1991b.
44. Kolb 1994, 257–58; Podhoretz 1993, 39–40; Rosenthal 1991.
45. *Hotline* 1992f.
46. Abramson and Chipello 1991; Chipello and Chandler 1992; *Wall Street Journal* editorial staff 1992.
47. Popkin 1994, 243–44.
48. Ibid.
49. *Hotline* 1992a.
50. Ibid.
51. Ibid.
52. Kohut 1991.
53. Rosen 1991.
54. Gelb 1991; *Post* Financial Desk 1991; Sack 1991; Silk 1989.
55. Rosenstiel 1993, 163–97; *Hotline* 1992d.
56. Mughan and Lacy 2002; Wattenberg 1998.
57. Germond and Witcover 1993, 240.
58. Matalin and Carville 1994, 162.
59. Ibid., 165–66.
60. Fitzwater 1995, 335.
61. Ibid., 324.
62. Birnbaum 1992.
63. Goldman 1994, 355–56.
64. Toner 1990; Goldman 1994, 356.
65. Steeper 1992a.
66. Steeper 1992c.
67. Ibid.
68. Ibid.
69. *Hotline* 1992c.
70. *Hotline* 1992e; Steeper 1992c.
71. Royer 1994, 144–45.
72. *Hotline* 1992d; Steeper 1992c.
73. *Hotline* 1992d, 144–45; Royer 1994.

74. Fitzwater 1995, 343.
75. Goldman 1994, 369–72.
76. *Hotline* 1992g.
77. Goldman 1994, 371.
78. Lyons 2000.
79. Bremner 1988.
80. Royer 1994, 264.
81. Fallows 1994.
82. Goldman 1994, 247. After a focus group respondent said she thought his favorite color was plaid, "Gone plaid" became campaign shorthand whenever Clinton gave meandering answers.
83. As a member of the group, some of this analysis is based upon personal participation.
84. Lipset 1993, 13.
85. Goldman 1994, 260.
86. Rosenstiel 1993, 183; Popkin 1994, 254–55; Frey 2004.
87. Clinton 1991.
88. Bremner 1988.
89. Pinkerton 2001, 90.
90. Sullivan 2008, 92–93. The original line—abortion should be legal, safe, and rare—was developed by Samuel Popkin when a San Diego legislator, Lucy Killea, was threatened with excommunication for voting for funding clinics where abortions were performed. Clinton refined the formulation in 1991.
91. Goldman 1994, 187–89; Greenberg 2009, 49–50.
92. Royer 1994, 285; Wills 1992.
93. Royer 1994, 285.
94. Germond and Witcover 1993, 411–13.
95. Goldman 1994, 399–409.
96. Ibid., 494.
97. Ibid., 404.
98. Steeper 1992a.
99. Goldman 1994, 508–10.
100. Germond and Witcover 1993, 425, 513.
101. Podhoretz 1993.
102. Teague 2011.
103. Devroy 1992.
104. The three-line "campaign haiku," as Stephanopoulos called it, was "Change vs. More of the Same; The economy, stupid; Don't forget health care." Many recollections and references erroneously add "it's" before "the economy," which was used only in statements to the press and interviews. Stephanopoulos 1999, 88.
105. Toner 1991a.
106. Toner 1990.
107. Fitzwater 1995, 327.
108. Goldman 1994, 410; McCullough 1992, 653.

109. Brady 1997, 116–17. Atwater attributed the strategy to Clark Clifford as, it was not yet known that James Rowe wrote the memos. The text refers to aspects of both memos but mentions only the second.
110. *New York Times* 1992.

CHAPTER 7

1. Woolf 1937; Whitman 1967.
2. Cox 2008. Cox writes that Garner may never have made that statement. However, he did say "Our firm has two members. The senior member does all the talking and I do all the work."
3. Lott 2007.
4. Von Drehle 2000.
5. In order listed the vice presidents accompanying the revelations are Richard Nixon, 1952; Spiro Agnew, 1968; Senator Thomas Eagleton, 1972; Geraldine Ferraro, 1984; Senator James Danforth Quayle, 1988; former Secretary of Defense Richard Cheney, 2000; and Governor Sarah Palin, 2008. The payoffs to Agnew were revealed after the campaign, and he resigned from office later.
6. Gellman 2008, 22.
7. Ibid., 24.
8. Von Drehle 2000; Gellman 2008, 19.
9. Cramer 1992, 13; Reeves 1993, 17; Caro 2002a, 1035–40; Kengor 2000, 175; *Time* 1969.
10. Cramer 1992, 13.
11. Popkin and Kernell 1986, 219.
12. Boyd 1987.
13. Will 1986.
14. Janos 1969.
15. Safire 2009.
16. Kinder, et al. 1980.
17. Wallison 2003, 70; Weisman 1981.
18. Clymer 1993.
19. Personal communication Prof. Larry Bartels, November 4, 2011.
20. Caro 2002b.
21. Ibid., 46.
22. Janos 1969.
23. Latimer 2009, 273.
24. Wolffe 2009, 275; Paulson 2010; Toobin 2009.
25. Kilpatrick 1982.
26. Hallin 1991, 92.
27. Waterman 1996, 343.
28. Marton 2001, 264. Nancy Reagan asserted her determination to minimize Barbara Bush's role, even if it meant a "blatant breach of protocol," by dropping the Bushes from a state dinner for Prince Charles and Princess Diana.
29. Hoffman and Devroy 1988.
30. Pinkerton 2001, 7.

31. Ibid., 13.
32. Boaz 1986, 32–58.
33. Germond and Witcover 1989, 70.
34. Cramer 1992, 12.
35. Borger and Finch 1999; Kaplan 1993.
36. Cramer 1992, 569; Brady 1997, 141.
37. Didion 1992, 87–88; Hoffman and Devroy 1988.
38. Cramer 1992, 70–73.
39. Sussman 1986.
40. Hoffman 1986.
41. Shenon 1987; Brinkley 1987; Dionne Jr. 1987.
42. Edsall 1987.
43. Ibid.
44. Cramer 1992, 17; Romano and Lardner Jr. 1999; Pinkerton 2001, 7.
45. Brady 1997, 138–39.
46. Goldman and Mathews 1989, 309.
47. Brady 1997, 187.
48. MacDougal 1988.
49. MacDougal 1990.
50. MacDougal 1988.
51. Romano 1988b.
52. Baker 2000, 4; Baker and Fiffer 2006, 239, 41.
53. Brady 1997, 187.
54. Germond and Witcover 1989, 400–401.
55. Goldman and Mathews 1989, 298.
56. Germond and Witcover 1989, 159.
57. Blumenthal 1988; Brady 1997, 173.
58. Pinkerton 2001, 23; Popkin 2007; Bidinotto 1988.
59. Brady 1997, 177.
60. Fallows 2004.
61. *New York Times* Staff 1988.
62. Noonan 1990, 308.
63. Ibid., Hoffman 1988.
64. Noonan 1990, 56–57.
65. Margolis 1988.
66. Ibid.
67. Romano 1988a.
68. Berelson, et al. 1954, 206.

CHAPTER 8

1. Milbank 2001, 6.
2. Teinowitz 2000.
3. Williams 2001, 133.
4. Kohut 1999.
5. *Newsweek* 2000b.

6. *Newsweek* 2000b.

7. Williams 2001, 133.

8. Ibid., 137.

9. Shrum 2007, 305; *Newsweek* 2000b; Williams 2001.

10. Williams 2001, 135.

11. Williams 1999.

12. *20/20* 1999.

13. Williams 2001, 135.

14. Harris 2000.

15. Ibid.; *Newsweek* 2000b.

16. Williams 1999.

17. Harris 2000.

18. *Newsweek* 2000b; Berke and Seelye 1999.

19. *Newsweek* 2000b; Bennet 2000.

20. See chap. 2.

21. Bennet 2000.

22. *Newsweek* 2000b.

23. Ibid.

24. Axelrod 2000.

25. *Newsweek* 2000b; Romano 2002.

26. Shrum 2007, 309.

27. Harris and Balz 1999; Special to the *New York Times* 1992; Shrum 2007, 310.

28. Bennet 2000; Henneberger 1999.

29. *Hotline* 2000d.

30. Ibid.

31. Shrum 2007, 318.

32. *Newsweek* 2000b.

33. Peretz 2007; *Newsweek* 2000b.

34. Wills 1999.

35. Peretz 2007.

36. Ambinder 1999.

37. Shrum 2007, 328.

38. Ibid.

39. Ibid., 329.

40. *Hotline* 2000c; Pressley and Harris 2000.

41. Ibid.

42. *Hotline* 2000b.

43. Steinback 2000.

44. Jamieson and Waldman 2001, 78; *Newsweek* 2000e.

45. *Newsweek* 2000e.

46. Harris 2000; Shrum 2007, 340.

47. *Newsweek* 2000e.

48. Kirkpatrick 2005.

49. Romano 1999.

50. Woodward 2002.

51. Ibid. While Bush was talking specifically of open access in the Oval Office, he applied that principle in his campaign and with the Texas Rangers baseball team too.
52. Romano and Lardner Jr. 1999.
53. Ibid.
54. Ibid.
55. Stevens 2001, 25.
56. Kirkpatrick 2005; Rove 2010b, 83–84.
57. Kirkpatrick 2005.
58. Rove 2010b, 142; Dowd and Steeper 2001, 20.
59. *Newsweek* 2000e.
60. Jamieson and Waldman 2001, 179.
61. Dowd and Steeper 2001, 20.
62. Green 2002.
63. Stevens 2001, 152.
64. Ibid., 151–52.
65. Ibid.
66. *Newsweek* 2000c.
67. Dowd and Steeper 2001, 25–40.
68. Ibid., 15; Rove 2010b, 164.
69. Based on an average by month of all the large national media polls from the major networks and newspapers.
70. Shrum 2007, 332–33.
71. Ibid., 333.
72. Fabiani and Lehane 2000.
73. Apple Jr. 2000. Apple was quoting Popkin, who was consulting on polling and targeting in the campaign.
74. Stevens 2001, 191.
75. *Newsweek* 2000d.
76. *World News Digest* 2000b.
77. Shrum 2007, 335.
78. *Newsweek* 2000d.
79. Shrum 2007, 345.
80. Ibid., 344.
81. Ibid.
82. Rove 2010b, 177–78.
83. *World News Digest* 2000a.
84. These averages are computed using all available national polls from ABC, CBS, NBC, Fox, and CNN; *LA Times, New York Times, Wall Street Journal*; Gallup, and Pew.
85. *Newsweek* 2000d.
86. Stevens 2001, 220.
87. *Newsweek* 2000d.
88. Schroeder 2008, 23–24.
89. Stevens 2001, 220.
90. Johnston, et al. 2004, 142; *Hotline* 2000a.

91. *Newsweek* 2000d.
92. Stevens 2001, 156–61.
93. Ibid.
94. *Newsweek* 2000a. Before his death from cancer in January 2000, Squier also gave this advice to the author in 1999.
95. Shrum 2007, 355; Schroeder 2008, 64.
96. *Newsweek* 2000a.
97. Shrum 2007, 356–57.
98. Schroeder 2008, 64.
99. Ibid., 62, 64.
100. Dowd and Steeper 2001, 14.
101. Williams 2001; Ambinder 1999.
102. Harris 2000.
103. Kinsley 2000.

CHAPTER 9

1. Kahneman and Tversky 1972; Lewis 2004.
2. Spencer 2001, 12–13. Spencer called candidates who couldn't be pushed stubborn. I think a more apt word—still consistent with Spencer—is dogged or firm. "A lot of people in my business would say that kind of candidate is stubborn. Most candidates are stubborn in public life. Every president with whom I've been close has been very stubborn. I don't like the word stubborn, but it's a quality that bodes well in the job that they have."
3. Schwarz, et al. 2007, 2.
4. Grove 2008.
5. *Hotline* 2008a, March 4.
6. Catledge 1940.
7. York 1970, 211.
8. Ackman 2007.
9. Shafir, et al. 1993, 15.
10. Klein 2006.
11. Morin 2000.
12. Wolff 2004. Wolff adds that, for Shrum, all political strategy is media strategy.
13. Packer 2008, 29.
14. Cialdini 2009, 181; Gawande 2010.
15. Katzenbach and Smith 1993, 112.
16. *Newsweek* 2000e.
17. Cramer 1992, 566.
18. Daou 2010.
19. Interviews with Ann Lewis in 2005, 2006.
20. Cottle 2008c; Nelson 1999.
21. Halberstam 2001, 170.
22. Grove 1998; Stephanopoulos 1999; Kindle Locations 1622–1626.
23. Matalin and Carville 1994, 435.
24. Streitfeld 1994; Grove 1993.
25. Evans and Novak 1992; Greenberg 2009, 52–53.

26. Schram 1977, 122–24.
27. Lardner Jr. and Romano 1999.
28. Anderson 2001, 45; Bakshian 2002, 24; Weinberger 2002, 33.
29. Sorensen 2008, 114–15.
30. Thomas 2009, 150–51.
31. Martin 2007.
32. Atkinson 1960; Crowther 1964.
33. Atkinson 1960; Crowther 1964; Vidal 1983.
34. Spencer 2001, 36, 42.
35. McDowell 1983, 8–9; DeGroot 1997, 433.
36. Spencer 2001, 42.
37. Regan 1988, 248.
38. Reeves 2005.
39. Ibid.
40. Vidal 1968; Vidal 1983.
41. Spencer 2001, 19.
42. Shultz 2002, 6. Italics in original.
43. Ibid.
44. Spencer 1980, 32.
45. Reagan 1979, 21.
46. Morris 2004, 48.
47. Cannon 1987.
48. Kissinger 1979, 952; Kissinger 1982, 386.
49. Bakshian Jr. 1980.
50. As George Christopher witnessed in 1966, "Reagan could look like he was in charge without others even realizing they had been trumped and he never looked like he wanted power for personal advancement. Every time we'd meet in Los Angeles at a joint meeting and there were other candidates present, and they would put us in a line for a photograph, the same thing happened. As soon as the photographer was ready to snap the picture, Reagan would put up his hand…and make it appear that all of us were deferring to him and looking to him for advice." DeGroot 1997, 434.
51. Sidey 1991.
52. Clift 1995.
53. Wick 2003, 64. Charles Wick, an old friend who served as USIA director, made this observation.
54. Noonan 1990, 62.
55. Spencer 2001, 12.
56. O'Neill and Novak 1987, 372.
57. Regan 1988, 248.
58. Abshire and Neustadt 2005, 142–43.
59. Shear 2007; Shear, et al. 2007; Hotline 2007f; Nagourney 2007b.

CHAPTER 10

1. Leahy 2005.
2. Schwartz 1989.

3. Mundy 2002.

4. Huffington 2008.

5. Gopnik 2011, 124.

6. Ibid.

7. *New York Times* staff 1979; *New York Times* staff 1980. Norrander 2010, 70–104. Barbara Norrander provides a detailed discussion of the ongoing debates over specific features of the rules governing primaries: primaries versus caucuses; front loading; delegate allocation; etc.

8. Rove 2010b, 75.

9. Wolff 2005.

10. Bryce 1888/1941, 54.

11. Ibid., 55.

12. Sorensen 2008, 157–59.

13. *Newsweek* 2000c; Anderson 2001, 108; Berke and Lyman 1999.

14. Mayer 2008, Purdum 2009.

15. Smith 2001, 49–50.

16. Rusk, et al. 1990, 201; Reeves 1993, 25–29.

17. Schmitt 1999.

18. Thompson 2010, 209–10.

19. Kinder and McConnaughy 2006.

20. Manchester 1978.

21. Reedy 1987, 52–53.

22. Pool 1959; Kurson 2011; Dishman 1953; Reinhard 1983.

23. Sen 1999.

24. Reedy 1982, 3.

25. Purdum 2007.

26. Ibid.

27. Orlov 2005.

28. I am not arguing that presidents don't try to skirt the constitution and abridge civil liberties in wartime. I am arguing they don't get as far for as long. VP Cheney and President Bush were thwarted within their own administration and their efforts to strengthen executive authority "reined in presidential power." Goldsmith 2011.

29. McCloskey 2006, 149; Franklin 1909, 87.

30. Cramer 1992, 997; Greenberg 2008.

31. Rutenberg 2006.

32. Rovere 1948, 82–83.

33. Kirkpatrick 2005; Oppel 2011.

34. von Hoffman 1981.

35. Thompson 2010, 208.

BIBLIOGRAPHY

20/20, ABC. 1999. "Speaking for Himself." Diane Sawyer with Al and Tipper Gore, June 16.

Abels, Jules. 1959. *Out of the Jaws of Victory*. New York: Holt.

Abelson, R. P. 1986. "Beliefs Are Like Possessions." *Journal for the Theory of Social Behaviour* 16 (3): 223–50.

Abramson, Jill, and Christopher Chipello. 1991. "High Pay of CEOs Traveling with Bush Touches a Nerve in Asia." *Wall Street Journal*, December 30, A1.

Abshire, David M., and Richard E. Neustadt. 2005. *Saving the Reagan Presidency: Trust Is the Coin of the Realm*. College Station: Texas A&M University Press.

Acheson, Dean. 1971. Oral History Interview. Harry S. Truman Library Oral History Interviews, June 30.

Ackman, Dan. 2007. "The Boston Red Sox's Sultan of Statistical Analysis." *Wall Street Journal*, June 20.

Advertising Age. 2004. "10 Who Made a Mark on Marketing." *Advertising Age*, December 20, 6.

Allen, Jodie T. 1981. "What Stockman Really Said." *Washington Post*, November 15, C8.

Alsop, Joseph, and Stewart Alsop. 1948. "Who Won the Election, President or the Party?" *Los Angeles Times*, November 25.

Ambinder, Marc. 1999. "At Harvard, Gore Was a Different Man Than His Current Public Image." *Harvard Crimson*, November 17.

———. 2007. "Teacher and Apprentice: Hillary Clinton Tried to Teach Barack Obama About Power, but Then He Got Ideas of His Own. A Story of Nasty Surprises, Dueling War Rooms, and the Drudge Report." *Atlantic Monthly*, December.

Anderson, Martin. 1990. *Revolution: The Reagan Legacy*. Stanford: Hoover Institution Press, Stanford University.

———. 2001. Interview. Miller Center, University of Virginia, Ronald Reagan Presidential Oral History Project, December 11–12.

Anderson, Patrick. 1994. *Electing Jimmy Carter: The Campaign of 1976*. Baton Rouge: Louisiana State University Press.

AP. 1976. "Halloween Magic." *New York Times*, October 31, 35.

———. 1991. "Mrs. Bush Pays Filing Fee." *New York Times*, December 19, B19.

Apple, R. W. 1976a. "Carter Emphasizing Mondale as an Asset." *New York Times*, October 29, 18.

———. 1976b. "Pennsylvania Race Is Viewed as Close." *New York Times*, October 30, 53.

———. 2000. "Democrats: The Overview; Gore, in Debut as a Presidential Nominee, Says 'I Stand Here Tonight as My Own Man.'" *New York Times*, August 18, 1.

Atkinson, Brooks. 1960. "'The Best Man': Gore Vidal's Cartoon of American Politics." *New York Times*, April 10.

Auerbach, Stuart. 1991. "A Presidentially Led Trade Mission; Bush to Take U.S. Business Executives on New Year Trip to Asia." *Washington Post*, December 20.

Auletta, Ken. 2004. "Kerry's Brain; Bob Shrum Is One of the Biggest Names in the Campaign Business—but Is He Prepared to Take on Bush?" *New Yorker*, September 20.

Axelrod, David. 2000. "Thoughts." Gore Campaign, July 5.

Bacon, Perry, Jr. 2007. "The Outsider's Insider: After Three Decades in Washington, Pete Rouse Is a Voice of Experience for Sen. Barack Obama." *Washington Post*, August 27.

Bai, Matt. 2005. "Mrs. Triangulation." *New York Times*, October 2.

———. 2007a. "America's Mayor Goes to America." *New York Times*, September 9.

———. 2007b. "The Clinton Referendum." *New York Times*, December 23.

———. 2008. "No We Can't." *New York Times*, August 2.

Baker, James A. 2000. Interview. Miller Center, University of Virginia, George H. W. Bush Oral History Project, January 29.

Baker, James Addison, and Steve Fiffer. 2006. *Work Hard, Study—and Keep Out of Politics!: Adventures and Lessons from an Unexpected Public Life.* New York: G. P. Putnam's Sons.

Baker, Peter. 2003. "'The Plan Is Nothing; the Planning Is Everything'; Military Planners Must Adjust, Deal with the Unexpected." *Washington Post*, March 23.

Baker, Peter, and Anne E. Kornblut. 2008. "Clinton Team Is Battling Itself, Even in Victory." *Washington Post*, March 6.

Baker, Peter, and Jim Rutenberg. 2008. "The Long Road to a Clinton Exit." *New York Times*, June 8.

Bakshian, Aram, Jr. 1980. "The Imperial Candidacy: John Connally Understands Power, but Who Will Trust Him with It?" *American Spectator*, March 1.

———. 2002. Interview. Miller Center, University of Virginia, Ronald Reagan Presidential Oral History Project, January 14.

Balz, Daniel. 2011a. "For Obama, Will It Be Truman or Clinton?" *Washington Post*, December 5.

———. 2011b. "In Ohio, Praise and Questions for Herman Cain." *Washington Post*, October 26.

Balz, Daniel, and Ann Devroy. 1990. "The Power of 'Me'; with Words Added by Democrats, Bush Erased His Pledge on Taxes." *Washington Post*, July 1.

Balz, Daniel J., and Haynes Bonner Johnson. 2009. *The Battle for America 2008: The Story of an Extraordinary Election.* Waterville, ME: Thorndike Press.

Bardeeby, Karim. 2008. "Marshall Ganz: Lighting a Fire." *Harvard Crimson*, February 12, 2008.

Barker, Karlyn. 1991. "D.C. Sets Lofty Goals for Schools." *Washington Post*, December 20, C6.

Bauder, David. 2004. "Fallout from Dean's Scream on News Networks: Get Used to It." *Associated Press*, February 8.

Batt, William L., Jr. 1966. Oral History Interview. Harry S. Truman Library Oral History Interviews, July 26–27.

BBC. 2005. "Works Down the Chippy, Swears He's Yoda." *Southern Counties: Strange South.*

Beaumont, Thomas. 2008. "We Slipped Up, Clinton's Iowa Advisers Say." *Des Moines Register*, June 6.

Benderoff, Eric. 2007. "Social Sites Go Political: A Facebook Founder Helps Design Obama's Online Network, and Other Candidates Are Doing What They Can to Add 'Friends.' " *Chicago Tribune*, September 23.

Bennet, James. 2000. "Al Gore Moves Beyond Meta." *New York Times*, January 23.

Berelson, Bernard, Paul Lazarsfeld, and William Mcphee. 1954. *Voting: A Study of Opinion Formation in a Presidential Campaign*. Chicago: University of Chicago Press.

Berke, Richard L., and Katharine Q. Seelye. 1999. "Political Memo; Gore and Bradley Take Steps out of Character." *New York Times*, October 10.

Berke, Richard L., and Rick Lyman. 1999. "Training for a Presidential Race." *New York Times*, March 15.

Berman, Michael, and Richard Moe. 1982. Interview. Miller Center, University of Virginia, Carter Presidency Project, January 15–16.

Beverland, M. 2006. "The 'Real Thing': Branding Authenticity in the Luxury Wine Trade." *Journal of Business Research* 59 (2): 251–58.

Beverland, M. B., A. Lindgreen, and M. W. Vink. 2008. "Projecting Authenticity through Advertising—Consumer Judgments of Advertisers' Claims." *Journal of Advertising* 37 (1): 5–15.

Bidinotto, Robert James. 1988. "Getting Away with Murder." *Reader's Digest*, July, 57–63.

Birnbaum, Jeffrey. 1992. "Clinton Received a Vietnam Draft Deferment for an ROTC Program That He Never Joined." *Wall Street Journal*, February 6.

Blumenthal, Sidney. 1988. "Willie Horton & the Making of an Election Issue; How the Furlough Factor Became a Stratagem of the Bush Forces." *Washington Post*, October 28.

———. 1993. "The Sorcerer's Apprentice." *New Yorker*, July 19, 29–31.

Blustein, Paul. 1991. "Tensions Rise in Tokyo as Bush's Visit Nears; Officials Struggle over Trade Differences." *Washington Post*, December 25.

Boaz, David. 1986. *Left, Right & Babyboom: America's New Politics*. Washington, DC: Cato Institute.

Bones, James. 2008. "Why One Young Briton Is Putting the Accent on Change for Obama." London *Times*, January 30.

Borger, Julian, and Julia Finch. 1999. "Prophet Motive; Why Has the Bank of Scotland Teamed up with Pat Robertson to Launch a New American Bank? Is It Because He Believes He Can Speak in Tongues, Converse with God and Satan and Divert Hurricanes? Or Because He Managed to Sell His TV Channel to Rupert Murdoch for Pounds 200m?" *Guardian*, March 3.

Boskin, Michael. 2001. Interview. Miller Center, University of Virginia, George H. W. Bush Oral History Project, July 30–31.

Boyd, Gerald M. 1987. "Bush Quietly Sets Stage for Drive." *New York Times*, April 19.

Boyer, Peter J. 2007. "Mayberry Man; Is What New York Never Liked About Rudy Giuliani Exactly What the Heartland Loves?" *New Yorker*, August 20.

Brady, John Joseph. 1997. *Bad Boy: The Life and Politics of Lee Atwater*. Reading, MA: Addison-Wesley Pub. Co.

Branch, Taylor. 2009. *The Clinton Tapes: Wrestling History with the President*. New York: Simon and Schuster.

Bremner, Charles. 1988. "Defeated Democrats' Hope of Resurrection Pinned on Phoenix; US Presidential Election." *Times* (London), November 12.

Brinkley, Joel. 1987. "Contra Arms Crews Said to Smuggle Drugs." *New York Times*, January 20.

British Monarchy, Official Website of The. 2011. Queen and Honours, January 24.

Broder, David S., and John F. Kennedy School of Government, Institute of Politics. 1997. *Campaign for President: The Managers Look at '96*. Hollis, NH: Hollis Publishing Co.

———. 2006. *Campaign for President: The Managers Look at 2004*. Lanham, MD: Rowman and Littlefield.

———. 2009. *Campaign for President: The Managers Look at 2008*. Lanham, MD: Rowman and Littlefield.

Brownell, Herbert. 1958. Interview. University of Rochester, Thomas E. Dewey Papers.

Brownell, Herbert, and John P. Burke. 1993. *Advising Ike: The Memoirs of Attorney General Herbert Brownell*. Lawrence: University Press of Kansas.

Brubach, Holly. 2011. "Here's Looking at Him." *New York Times*, February 4.

Bryce, Viscount James. 1888/1941. *The American Commonwealth*. London: Macmillan and Co.

Brydon, S. R. 1985. "The 2 Faces of Jimmy Carter: The Transformation of a Presidential Debater, 1976 and 1980." *Central States Speech Journal* 36 (3): 138–51.

Burden, Barry and D. S. Hillygus. 2009. "Opinion Formation, Polarization, and Presidential Reelection." *Presidential Studies Quarterly* 39 (3): 619–35.

Burke, Richard E. 1992. *The Senator: My Ten Years with Ted Kennedy*. New York: St. Martin's Press.

Burnham, Walter Dean. 1970. *Critical Elections and the Mainsprings of American Politics*. New York: W. W. Norton.

Burros, Marian. 1976. "Rosalynn Carter: On the Road, Off a Healthy Diet." *Washington Post*, October 14, 83.

Bush, George H. W. 1999. *All the Best, George Bush: My Life in Letters and Other Writings*. New York: Scribner.

Byman, Daniel L. 2005. "Confronting Passive Sponsors of Terrorism." Saban Center for Middle East Policy Analysis Papers. no. 4, November 4.

Caddell, Patrick. 1988. "In Search of Mr. Smith: An Essay Inquiring into the Current State of American Politics." Unpublished manuscript, February 7.

Caldwell, Christopher. 2002. "'Star-Spangled Manners': Etiquette for a Pluralistic Society." *New York Times*, December 8.

Canes-Wrone, Brandice. 2006. *Who Leads Whom?: Presidents, Policy, and the Public*. Chicago: University of Chicago Press.

Cannon, Lou. 1976. "Ford Hits Foreign Policy of Carter, Calls It 'Untried.'" *Washington Post*, October 27, A1.

———. 1987. "More Than Teflon and Tinsel." *Washington Post*, December 7.

Carney, James. 2001. "Losing Control of the Spin." *Time* magazine, July 1.

Caro, Robert A. 2002a. *The Years of Lyndon Johnson: Master of the Senate*. New York: Alfred A. Knopf.

———. 2002b. "The Orator of the Dawn." *New Yorker*, March 4, 46–63.

Catledge, Turner. 1940. "The ABCs of Political Campaigning: Classic Rules Govern the Strategic Battle of Rival Presidential Candidates." *New York Times*, September 22.

Cecil, Guy. 2008. "February 5th Primary State Targeting (Revised)." Joshua Green. *Atlantic.com* Collection of HRC Memos, January 21.

Chait, Jonathan. 2011. "What the Left Doesn't Understand About Obama." *New York Times*, September 2.

Chipello, Christopher. 1991. "Baker Says US Is Committed to the Pacific." *Wall Street Journal*, November 12.

Chipello, Christopher, and Clay Chandler. 1992. "U.S. Executives Will Seek Protectionist Measures If the Deficit Isn't Cut." *Wall Street Journal*, January 8.

Chong, Dennis, and James N. Druckman. 2010. "Dynamic Public Opinion: Communication Effects over Time." *American Political Science Review* 104 (4): 663–80.

Church, George J. 1991. "A Tale of Two Bushes." *Time* magazine, January 7.

Cialdini, Robert B. 2009. *Influence: Science and Practice*. Boston: Pearson Education.

Cillizza, Chris. 2007. "Obama Campaign Aims to Turn Online Backers into an Offline Force." *Washington Post*, March 31, A03.

Cillizza, Chris, and Dan Balz. 2007. "On the Electronic Campaign Trail; Politicians Realize the Potential of Web Video." *Washington Post*, January 22, A01.

Clift, Eleanor. 1995. "Nancy with the Centrist Face; Derided as an Elitist, Mrs. Reagan's Impact Was Unequaled." Outlook, *Washington Post*, January 8, C5.

Clift, Eleanor, and Tom Brazaitis. 1996. *War without Bloodshed: The Art of Politics*. New York: Scribner.

Clinton, Bill. 1991. Keynote Address of Gov. Bill Clinton to the DLC's Cleveland Convention. *DLC.org*. May 6.

Clymer, Adam. 1993. "Lawmakers Revolt on Lifting Gay Ban in Military Service." *New York Times*, January 27, A1.

———. 1999. *Edward M. Kennedy: A Biography*. New York: Morrow.

Connolly, Ceci. 1999. "The Gore Machine; in the Sprint for Campaign Cash, He's Got the Best Staff, the Most Experience and a Tested Game Plan. But Al Gore's Greatest Strength Could Also Prove to Be His Greatest Vulnerability." *Washington Post*, April 4, W6.

Converse, Philip E., Angus Campbell, et al. 1961. "Stability and Change in 1960: A Reinstating Election." *American Political Science Review* 55 (2): 269–80.

Cooper, Christopher. 2007. "Obama Stings with Subtle Jabs." *Wall Street Journal*, December 29.

Cooper, Christopher, Valerie Bauerlein, and Corey Dade. 2008. "New Machine: In South, Democrats' Tactics May Change Political Game." *Wall Street Journal*, January 23, A1.

Cooperman, Alan. 2004. "Openly Religious, to a Point: Bush Leaves the Specifics of His Faith to Speculation." *Washington Post*, September 16.

Cottle, Michelle. 2008a. "Poison Penn: The Complicated and Varied Reasons Why the Clintons Held on to Their Chief Strategist for as Long as They Did." *New Republic*, April 8.

———. 2008b. "Putsch in Hillaryland: The Clinton Campaign's Silent Shake-Up." *New Republic*, January 25.

———. 2008c. "Voices in Her Head: Inside Hillaryland's Fatal Psychodrama." *New Republic*, May 7.

Cramer, Richard Ben. 1992. *What It Takes: The Way to the White House*. New York: Random House.

Crowley, Michael. 2007. "Hope Sinks: The Disappointingly Conventional Obama Campaign." *New Republic*, October 8.

Crowther, Bosley. 1964. "The Screen: Gore Vidal's 'Best Man.'" *New York Times*, April 7.

Cox, Patrick. 2008. "Not Worth a Bucket of Warm Spit." History News Network. August 20.

Daou, Peter. 2010. "To Heilemann, Halperin and Politico: I'll Proudly Defend Hillary Clinton, on the Record." *Huffington Post*, January 23.

Daniels, Mitch. 2012. "Daniels Gives GOP Response to State of the Union." (Transcript). *CNN.com*, January 24.

Davis, Forrest. 1944. "Dewey's April Choice." *Saturday Evening Post*, August 12, 9–19.

De Groot, G. J. 1997. "'A Goddamned Electable Person': The 1966 California Gubernatorial Campaign of Ronald Reagan." *History* 82 (267): 429–48.

Dembart, Lee. 1976. "Carter's Comments on Sex Cause Concern." *New York Times*, September 23.

Depaulo, Lisa. 2008a. "Deconstructing Hillary." *GQ*, August, vol. 78, no. 8.

———. 2008b. "Why She Lost: Hillary's Message Man, Mark Penn, Gives Us the Exclusive Postmortem. And Still Wonders Where All the Money Went." *GQ Online*. June 8.

Devroy, Ann. 1992. "The Reluctant Activist; Domestically, Bush Tries to Recast Himself." *Washington Post*, August 17, A1.

Dewey, Thomas E. 1965. Interview. Seeley G. Mudd Manuscript Library, Princeton University, The John Foster Dulles Oral History Project, January 22.

Didion, Joan. 1992. *After Henry*. New York: Simon and Schuster.

Dionne, E. J., Jr. 1987. "Iran-Contra Hearings; North Says Casey Proposed Using Arms Profit for Fund Kept Secret from President; Many Are Found to Believe North." *New York Times*, July 11, A1.

Dishman, Robert B. 1953. "How It All Began: The Eisenhower Pre-Convention Campaign in New Hampshire, 1952." *New England Quarterly* 26 (1): 3–26.

Distaso, John. 2006. "Granite Status: More Than One Dem Eyeing 2008 Senate Primary." *Union Leader,* December 14.

Divine, Robert A. 1974. *Foreign Policy and U.S. Presidential Elections, 1940–1948.* New York: New Viewpoints.

Donaldson, Gary. 1992. "The Wardman Park Group and Campaign Strategy in the Truman Administration, 1946–1948." *Missouri Historical Review,* LXXXVI (3).

———. 1999. *Truman Defeats Dewey.* Lexington: University Press of Kentucky.

Dowd, Matthew, and Fred Steeper. 2001. Untitled Commentary. In *Electing the President, 2000: The Insiders' View,* edited by Kathleen Hall Jamieson and Paul Waldman, 13–48. Philadelphia: University of Pennsylvania Press.

Dowd, Maureen. 1991. "White House Isolation; an Image of Bush as a Captive of Top Aides Who Make Their Own Sweeping Decisions." *New York Times,* November 22, 5.

Draper, Robert. 2009. "The Ultimate Obama Insider." *New York Times Magazine,* July 21.

———. 2011. "Building a Better Mitt Romney-Bot." *New York Times Magazine,* November 30, 37.

Drew, Elizabeth. 1990a. "Letter from Washington." *New Yorker,* February 19, 98–107.

———. 1990b. "Letter from Washington." *New Yorker,* June 4.

———. 1992. "Letter from Washington." *New Yorker,* February 17.

Dunn, Anita, and Nicole Wallace. 2009. "The Campaign and the Press." In *Electing the President, 2008: The Insiders' View,* edited by Kathleen Hall Jamieson, 224. Philadelphia: University of Pennsylvania Press.

Dunne, John Gregory. 1986. "The War That Won't Go Away." *New York Review of Books,* September 26.

Easton, Nina J., Michael Kranish, et al. 2004. "On the Trail of Kerry's Failed Dream." *Boston Globe,* November 14.

Edelstein, David. 2002. "The Happy Hipster of Film." *New York Times,* October 27, 2.1.

Wall Street Journal editorial staff. 1992. "Executive Pay—an Embarrassment to Free Marketers." *Wall Street Journal,* January 10, A8.

Edsall, Thomas B. 1987. "GOP Gathers with a Host of Problems." *Washington Post,* January 21, A1.

———. 1992. "Clinton Stuns Rainbow Coalition; Candidate Criticizes Rap Singer's Message." *Washington Post,* June 14, A1.

———. 2008. "Obama's South Carolina Test: How Many White Votes Will He Get?" *Huffington Post,* January 26.

Eggen, Dan. 2008. "Bush Praises Obama's Campaign." *Washington Post,* November 21, 2008.

Elsey, George M. 1965 Oral History Interview. Harry S. Truman Library Oral History Interviews, March 9.

Espo, David, and Shannon McCaffrey. 2011. "Gingrich Aides Resign, Leave Campaign in Tatters." *USA Today,* June 9, 2011.

Evans, Rowland, and Robert Novak. 1992. Editorial "…But His Campaign Remains in Disarray." *Chicago Sun Times,* June 17, 35.

Exley, Zack. 2007a. What's Going On Out There? *Huffington Post*. September 26.

———. 2007b. Stories and Numbers—a Closer Look at Camp Obama. *Huffington Post*. August 29, 2007.

———. 2007c. Obama Field Organizers Plot a Miracle. *Huffington Post*. August 27.

———. 2008. "Organizing Matters: The Lesson from Hillary's NV Win." *Huffington Post*, January 19.

Fabiani, Mark, and Chris Lehane. 2000. "The Bush and Gore Description." Gore Campaign Documents, July 4.

Fallows, James. 1994. "Talent on Loan from the GOP." *Atlantic Monthly*, May 1.

———. 2004. "When George Meets John." *Atlantic Monthly*, July/August.

Farhi, Paul. 2003. "Tiny but Trusted Inner Circle Surrounds Dean." *Washington Post*, December 2, A01.

Farrelly, Jim, and James Kelly. 1976. "North: Carter Tries to Wriggle Out." *Irish Independent*, October 29, 1.

Federal News Service. 2008. "Democratic Presidential Candidates Debate." *Federal News Service*, January 5.

Fenno, Richard F. 1978. *Home Style: House Members in Their Districts*. New York: HarperCollins.

Finnegan, William. 2004. "The Candidate: How the Son of a Kenyan Economist Became an Illinois Everyman." *New Yorker*, May 31.

Fisher, Dana R. 2006. "The Problem with the Left's Model of Outsourced Grassroots Canvassing." *American Prospect*, September 14.

Fisher, Marc. 2006. "After a Nasty and Costly Race, It's All Come Back to Iraq." *Washington Post*, November 5, C1.

Fiske, S. T., A. J. C. Cuddy, and P. Glick. 2007. "Universal Dimensions of Social Cognition: Warmth and Competence." *Trends in Cognitive Sciences* 11 (2): 77–83.

Fitzwater, Marlin. 1995. *Call the Briefing!: Bush and Reagan, Sam and Helen: A Decade with Presidents and the Press*. New York: Times Books.

Forward editorial staff. 2011. "Adelson Is Gingrich's Most Prominent Jewish Backer." *Forward*, December 16.

Frankel, Jeffrey. 2003. "What an Economic Adviser Can Do When He Disagrees with the President." *Challenge* 46 (3): 29–52.

Franklin, Benjamin. 1909. *The Autobiography of Benjamin Franklin*. New York: Collier.

Frayn, Michael. 2004. *Democracy: A Play*. New York, Faber and Faber.

Freedland, Jonathan. 2008. "International: Race for the White House: Clinton Campaign Has to Deploy 'Big Dog' Bill with Care as the Democratic Contest Continues to Defy Predictions: Now Obama Has Momentum as Race Heads for Long Haul." *Guardian* (London)—*Final Edition*, January 28, 14.

Frey, Jennifer. 2004. "Dr. Phil's Advice to Candidates: Come on My Show." *Washington Post*, September 29, C01.

Frontrunner. 2001. "Bush Again Reiterates Pledge against Using Social Security Funds." *Bennet News*, September 7.

Gabriel, Trip. 2011. "In Reversal, Bachmann's Struggles Now Include Fund-Raising." *New York Times*, September 23, A23.

———. 2012. "Disdainful of Strategists, Gingrich Acts as His Own." *New York Times*, January 20.

Galbraith, John Kenneth. 1993. *A Short History of Financial Euphoria*. New York: Whittle Books/Viking.

Gawande, Atul. 2010. *The Checklist Manifesto: How to Get Things Right*. New York: Metropolitan Books.

Gay, Peter. 1984. *The Tender Passion: The Bourgeois Experience, Victoria to Freud*. Vol. 2. New York: Oxford University Press.

Gelb, Leslie H. 1991. "Foreign Affairs; Memo for Mr. Bush." *New York Times*, June 12, A27.

Gellman, Barton, and Dale Russakoff. 1999. "At Princeton, Bradley Met Impossible Demands." *Washington Post*, December 13, A1.

Gellman, Barton. 2000. "A Conflict of Health and Profit; Gore at Center of Trade Policy Reversal on AIDS Drugs to South Africa." *Washington Post*, May 21, A1.

_____. 2008. *Angler: The Cheney Vice Presidency*. New York: Penguin Press.

Germond, Jack, and Jules Witcover. 1989. *Whose Broad Stripes and Bright Stars?: The Trivial Pursuit of the Presidency, 1988*. New York: Warner Books.

_____. 1993. *Mad as Hell: Revolt at the Ballot Box, 1992*. New York: Warner Books.

Gigot, Paul. 1991. "Bush on Trade: Spirit Is Willing, Flesh Is Weak." *Wall Street Journal*, December 20, A14.

Gilbert, Craig. 2007. "Clinton's Secret Weapon in Iowa; Organizer's Success Proven in Wisconsin." *Milwaukee Journal Sentinel*, December 25, A1.

Giuliani, Rudolph W. 2007. "Toward a Realistic Peace: Defending Civilization and Defeating Terrorists by Making the International System Work." *Foreign Affairs* 86 (5): 2–18.

Giuliani, Rudolph W., and Ken Kurson. 2002. *Leadership*. New York: Hyperion.

Glenn, David. 2004. "On Death and Voting: New Studies Find That People with Subliminal Fears of Dying Choose Charismatic Leaders at the Polls." *Chronicle of Higher Education*, October 8.

Goldman, Eric Frederick. 1956. *The Crucial Decade: America, 1945–1955*. New York: Knopf.

Goldman, Peter Louis. 1994. *Quest for the Presidency, 1992*. College Station: Texas A&M University Press.

Goldman, Peter Louis, and Tom Mathews. 1989. *The Quest for the Presidency, 1988*. New York: Simon and Schuster.

Goldsmith, Jack. 2011. "How Dick Cheney Reined in Presidential Power." *New York Times*, September 15.

Goldsmith, Marshall, and Mark Reiter. 2007. *What Got You Here Won't Get You There: How Successful People Become Even More Successful*. New York: Hyperion.

Good Morning America. 1999. "Good Morning America: Dealing with Depression."

Gopnik, Adam. 2011. "The Information." *New Yorker*, February 14, 124–30.

Green, Joshua. 2002. "The Other War Room: President Bush Doesn't Believe in Polling—Just Ask His Pollsters." *Washington Monthly*, April.

_____. 2008a. "Inside the Clinton Shake-Up." *Atlantic Monthly*, February.

_____. 2008b. "The Amazing Money Machine: How Silicon Valley Made Barack Obama This Year's Hottest Start-Up." *Atlantic Monthly*, June.

_____. 2008c. "The Front-Runner's Fall." *Atlantic Monthly*, September.

Greenberg, David. 2008. "Double Negative." *New Republic*, April 9.

Greenberg, Stanley B. 2009. *Dispatches from the War Room: In the Trenches with Five Extraordinary Leaders.* New York, Thomas Dunne Books/St. Martin's Press.

Greenstein, Fred I. 1990. "Ronald Reagan. Another Hidden-Hand Ike?" *PS: Political Science and Politics* 23 (1): 7–13.

Greider, William. 1981. "The Education of David Stockman." *Atlantic,* December 27.

Grimaldi, James V. 2012. "Las Vegas Billionaire Bets Big on Gingrich." *Washington Post,* January 20.

Grove, Lloyd. 1989. "How Experts Fueled a Race with Vitriol; New Jersey Senate Candidates Stuck to Their TV Scripts." *Washington Post,* January 18, A1.

———. 1993. "The Clintons' Bad Cop; Susan Thomases Has No Official Title, but She's Sure Got Clout." *Washington Post,* March 2, E1.

———. 1998. "Guardians at the Gate; on the Front Lines at the White House, a Valiant Few Tried to Protect Clinton from Himself." *Washington Post,* September 16, D01.

———. 2008. The World According to David Plouffe. *Portfolio.com.* December 12.

Gullan, Harold I. 1998. *The Upset That Wasn't: Harry S. Truman and the Crucial Election of 1948.* Chicago: Ivan R. Dee.

Gwertzman, Bernard. 1976. "Carter Rules Out War over Yugoslavs; Says Soviet Invasion Would Pose No Threat to U.S. Security." *New York Times,* October 23.

Halberstam, David. 1972. *The Best and the Brightest.* New York: Random House.

———. 1979. *The Powers That Be.* New York: Knopf.

———. 2001. *War in a Time of Peace: Bush, Clinton, and the Generals.* New York: Scribner.

Hallin, Daniel C., ed. 1991. *The Presidency, the Press and the People.* La Jolla: University of California San Diego Extension.

Hamilton, James D. 2009. "Causes and Consequences of the Oil Shock of 2007–08." *Brookings Papers on Economic Activity* (Spring): 215–83.

Harris, John F. 2000. "For Gore, Politics vs. Policy" *Washington Post,* October 29, A01.

Harris, John F., and Dan Balz. 1999. "Gore Campaign Drops Pollster Penn; Hickman Is Hired as Part of Shake-up, Move to Nashville." *Washington Post,* October 2, A04.

Harris, John F. and Jim VandeHei. 2007. "Penn, Like Rove, Wants Intellectual Cred." *Politico,* September 6.

Hart, Peter D. 2007. "2008 Elections: The Dynamics and What's Ahead." Speech.

Hartmann, Susan M. 1971. *Truman and the 80th Congress.* Columbia: University of Missouri Press.

Hastings, Michael. 2008. "Hack: Confessions of a Presidential Campaign Reporter." *GQ,* November.

Heale, M. J. 1973. "The Role of the Frontier in Jacksonian Politics: David Crockett and the Myth of the Self-Made Man." *Western Historical Quarterly* 4 (4): 405–23.

Healy, Mark. 2008. "Who It Takes (and What They're Fighting for)." *GQ,* November.

Healy, Patrick. 2007. "Political Memo in '08 Race, the Other Clinton Steps Up Publicly." *New York Times,* December 17.

Heilemann, John, and Mark Halperin. 2010. *Game Change: Obama and the Clintons, McCain and Palin, and the Race of a Lifetime.* New York: HarperCollins.

Henneberger, Melinda. 1999. "Naomi Wolf, Feminist Consultant to Gore, Clarifies Her Campaign Role." *New York Times,* November 5, A26.

Hertzberg, Hendrik. 2009a. "A Very Merry Malaise." *New Yorker,* July 17.

_____. 2009b. "Yet More Narcissism." *NewYorker Online Blogs.* August 3.

_____. 2009c. "A Malaise Footnote (Bonus: Carter Cusses). *NewYorker Online Blogs.* July 22.

Hetherington, M. J. 1998. "The Political Relevance of Political Trust." *American Political Science Review* 92 (4): 791–808.

_____. 1999. "The Effect of Political Trust on the Presidential Vote, 1968–96." *American Political Science Review* 93 (2): 311–26.

Hitchens, Harold L. 1968. "Influences on the Congressional Decision to Pass the Marshall Plan." *Western Political Quarterly* 21 (1): 51–68.

Hoagland, Jim. 1999. "Learning on the Run." *Washington Post,* December 30. Op-ed, A31.

Hoeber, Johannes. 1966. Oral History Interview. Harry S. Truman Library Oral History Interviews, September 13.

Hoffman, David. 1986. "A Flawed Legacy;the Reagan Era Is Winding Down, and the Time Bombs—Budget Deficits and Arms Proliferation—Are Ticking." *Washington Post,* November 30, W19.

_____. 1988. "What Campaigns Tell of Leadership; Persistent, Inconsistent Bush Trusts Aides but Can Act Alone." *Washington Post,* November 6, A1.

Hoffman, David, and Ann Devroy. 1988. "The Complex Machine Behind Bush; 'Army of Ants,' Not Crusade of Ideas, Was Foundation of Campaign." *Washington Post,* November 13.

Hollitz, John E. 1982. "Eisenhower and the Admen: The Television 'Spot' Campaign of 1952." *Wisconsin Magazine of History* 66 (1): 25–39.

Horrigan, Marie. 2007. "Obama's Foreign Policy Speech Leaves Room for Debate." *New York Times,* August 1.

Hotline. 1990a. "Taxes on TV: '88 Footage Comes Back to Haunt Bush." *Hotline,* June 27.

_____. 1990b. "Print Coverage of Tax Flip-Flop: Read My Lips...I Lied." *Hotline,* June 27.

_____. 1990c. "White House-Congressional GOP 'Civil War': Who's the Boss?" *Hotline,* October 26.

_____. 1991a. "Poll Update: CBS News: War Euphoria Meets Reality." *Hotline,* January 30.

_____. 1991b. "Poll Update: Gulf Hasn't Helped Quayle Favorables Yet." *Hotline,* March 8.

_____. 1991c. "TV Monitor." *Hotline,* December 18.

_____. 1991d. "Quotes of the Year." *Hotline,* December 20.

_____. 1991e. "Bush: 'The Most Popular Man in the World.'" *Hotline,* March 1.

_____. 1992a. "Buchanan Reader: Past, Present, Future." *Hotline,* February 27.

_____. 1992b. "Perot: 'Flame in the Political Gas Tank'?" *Hotline,* March 27.

———. 1992c. "Perot: Meeting the Press Before He Faces the Nation." *Hotline*, April 13.

———. 1992d. "Perot: This Means War." *Hotline*, June 26.

———. 1992e. "California: The Ten-Gallon Shadow." *Hotline*, June 3.

———. 1992f. "TV Monitor." *Hotline*, January 9.

———. 1992g. "Quayle: 38 Million Viewers Must Be Wrong." *Hotline*, May 20.

———. 1999a. "Gore: Seeks New Issues with Brain Trust." *Hotline*, June 10.

———. 1999b. "Gore: Expectations Fulfilled?" *Hotline*, June 17.

———. 1999c. "Gore: Goes to Graceland!" *Hotline*, May 18.

———. 1999d. "Gore: Talks Scandal and Kosovo in New Hampshire." *Hotline*, April 19.

———. 1999e. "Gore: Joaquin on Sunshine." *Hotline*, April 2.

———. 1999f. "Gore: Charitable Choice." *Hotline*, June 1.

———. 2000a. "Gore: Black Gold or Exxon Valdez?" *Hotline*, September 22.

———. 2000b. "Gore: No Elian, None of the Time." *Hotline*, April 10.

———. 2000c. "Gore: Takes Dramatic Shift from WH on Elian Controversy." *Hotline*, March 31.

———. 2000d. "IA Dem Debate: Exchange a Profile in Tolerance?" *Hotline*, January 19.

———. 2003. "Clinton: No Really, Pretend I'm Not Here!" *Hotline*, November 13.

———. 2004. "Dean Post-Mortem: From Asterisk to…Asterisk." *Hotline*, February 19.

———. 2006. "Clinton: Grand Opening of a Retail Giant?" *Hotline*, December 14.

———. 2007a. "Send These Kids a Caucus E-Vite!" *Hotline*, November 26.

———. 2007b. "A Balancing Act." *Hotline*, February 12.

———. 2007c. "Iowa (1/3 Caucuses): Obama on Top." *Hotline*, November 20.

———. 2007d. "The Field: Bigger, Better, Faster, Stronger." *Hotline*, December 3.

———. 2007e. "Clinton: How to Register to Vote." *Hotline*, December 17.

———. 2007f. "Thompson: Let Me Be Everclear." *Hotline*, October 19.

———. 2007g. "For Better or for Worse." *Hotline*, November 9.

———. 2007h. "Iowa: Will Barack Rock the Caucus?" *Hotline*, October 1.

———. 2008a. "Rove: Zen and the Art of Politics." *Hotline*, March 4.

———. 2008b. "Rubbing Is Racing." *Hotline*, January 15.

———. 2008c. "Getting Vetted Down." *Hotline*, January 17.

Hsee, C. K. 1996. "The Evaluability Hypothesis: An Explanation for Preference Reversals between Joint and Separate Evaluations of Alternatives." *Organizational Behavior and Human Decision Processes* 67 (3): 247–57.

Hsee, C. K., G. F. Loewenstein, et al. 1999. "Preference Reversals between Joint and Separate Evaluations of Options: A Review and Theoretical Analysis." *Psychological Bulletin* 125 (5): 576–90.

Huffington, Arianna. 2008. "The Internet and the Death of Rovian Politics." *Huffington Post*, October 20.

Ifill, Gwen. 1992. "The 1992 Campaign: New York; Clinton Admits Experiment with Marijuana in 1960s." *New York Times*, March 30, A15.

Irish Times Staff. 1976. "Carter Cables Dublin on North." *Irish Times*, October 29.

Jacobson, Gary C. 1993. "Deficit-Cutting Politics and Congressional Elections." *Political Science Quarterly* 108 (3): 375–402.

Jamieson, Kathleen Hall. 2006. *Electing the President, 2004: The Insiders' View.* Philadelphia: University of Pennsylvania Press.

———. 2009. *Electing the President, 2008: The Insiders' View.* Philadelphia: University of Pennsylvania Press.

Jamieson, Kathleen Hall, and Paul Waldman. 2001. *Electing the President, 2000: The Insiders' View.* Philadelphia: University of Pennsylvania Press.

Janos, Leo. 1969. "The President Giveth and Taketh Away." *Time* magazine, November 14.

Jenkins, Roy. 1986. *Truman.* New York: Harper and Row.

Johnston, Richard, Michael Gray Hagen, and Kathleen Hall Jamieson. 2004. *The 2000 Presidential Election and the Foundations of Party Politics.* Houndmills, Basingstoke, Hampshire: Cambridge University Press.

Kahneman, Daniel. 2002. Nobel lecture. "Maps of Bounded Rationality: A Perspective on Intuitive Judgment and Choice."

———. 2011. *Thinking, Fast and Slow.* New York: Farrar, Straus and Giroux.

Kahneman, D. and A. Tversky. 1972. "Subjective Probability—Judgment of Representativeness." *Cognitive Psychology* 3 (3): 430–54.

Kaiser, Robert G., and John F. Harris. 1998. "White House Reaches Out on the Party Line; Conference Call Shapes Clinton Defense." *Washington Post,* September 26.

Kantor, Jodi. 2008. "Obama's Friends Form Strategy to Stay Close." *New York Times,* December 14, 2008.

———. 2009. "Back on World Stage, a Larger-Than-Life Holbrooke." *New York Times,* February 8, 2009, A1.

———. 2011. "At Harvard, a Master's in Problem Solving." *New York Times,* December 25.

———. 2012. *The Obamas.* New York: Little, Brown and Co.

Kaplan, Steven. 1993. "The Invention of Ethiopian Jews: Three Models" (Trois Approches De L' "Invention" Des Juifs Éthiopiens). *Cahiers d'Études Africaines* 33 (132): 645–58.

Karabell, Zachary. 2000. *The Last Campaign: How Harry Truman Won the 1948 Election.* New York: Knopf, distributed by Random House.

Katzenbach, J. R., and D. K. Smith. 1993. "The Discipline of Teams." *Harvard Business Review* 71 (2): 111–20.

Kaufman, Michael T. 2005. "Lloyd N. Cutler, Counselor to Presidents, Is Dead at 87." *New York Times,* May 9.

Kaufmann, Stanley. 2009. "Heroes and People." *New Republic,* February 18, 2009.

Kellerman, Donald S. 1990. "Bush Approval Rating Plummets." Times Mirror Center for the People and the Press, October.

Kengor, Paul. 2000. "The Vice President, Secretary of State, and Foreign Policy." *Political Science Quarterly* 115 (2): 175–99.

Kennedy, John F. 1960. "Transcript: John F. Kennedy on Politics." Miller Center of Public Affairs, Presidential Recordings Program.

Kilpatrick, Andrew. 1982. "Patterson Told Secret Cuban Invasion Plans to Candidate JFK." *Birmingham News*, October 24.

Kinder, D. R., and C. M. McConnaughy. 2006. "Military Triumph, Racial Transcendence, and Colin Powell." *Public Opinion Quarterly* 70 (2): 139–65.

Kinder, Donald R., Mark D. Peters, et al. 1980. "Presidential Prototypes." *Political Behavior* 2 (4): 315–37.

King, Wayne. 1976. "Rosalynn Carter, a Tough, Tireless Campaigner, Displays Same Driving Quality as Her Husband." *New York Times*, October 18, 33.

Kinsley, Michael. 1986. "In the Land of the Magic Asterisk." Review of *The Triumph of Politics: How the Reagan Revolution Failed*, by David Stockman. Sunday Book Review, *New York Times*, May 11.

———. 2000. "The Art of Finger-Pointing: Why Wait until Next Week? Let's Start Now." *Slate*, October 31.

Kirby, Emily, Peter Levine, and Karlos Marcelo. 2008."The Youth Vote in the 2008 Iowa Caucus." The Center for Information & Research on Civic Learning & Engagement (CIRCLE). January 7.

Kirkpatrick, David D. 2005. "In Secretly Taped Conversations, Glimpses of the Future President." *New York Times*, February 20, A1.

Kissinger, Henry. 1979. *White House Years*. Boston: Little, Brown.

———. 1982. *Years of Upheaval*. Boston: Little, Brown.

Klein, Joe. 1989. "Talk Politics." *New York* magazine, February 27, 28–30.

———. 2002. "The Trouble with Shrum." *Slate*, May 9.

———. 2006. *Politics Lost: From RFK to W: How Politicians Have Become Less Courageous and More Interested in Keeping Power Than in Doing What's Right for America*. New York: Broadway Books.

———. 2008. "The Incredibly Shrinking Democrats." *Time* magazine, April 24.

Kohut, Andrew. 1991. "On the Eve of '92: Fault Lines in the Electorate." *Times Mirror Center for the People and the Press*, December 4.

———. 1999. "A Clear Case of Clinton Fatigue." *New York Times*, August 5.

———. 2008. "How Young People View Their Lives, Futures and Politics: A Portrait of 'Generation Next.'" *Pew Research Center*, January 9.

Kohut, Andrew, Scott Keeter, and Michael Dimock. 2008. "Social Networking and Online Videos Take Off: Internet's Broader Role in Campaign 2008." *Pew Research Center*, January 11.

Kolb, Charles. 1994. *White House Daze: The Unmaking of Domestic Policy in the Bush Years*. New York: Free Press.

Kolbert, Elizabeth. 1996. "Dole Campaign Will Be Bringing Out Its Secret Weapon: The Candidate's Sense of Humor." *New York Times*, October 4, A25.

———. 2008. "Old Habits; How the Giuliani Method May Defeat Him." *New Yorker*, January 7.

Komarow, Steven. 1990. "Washington Today: Tax Issue Gives Gingrich His Ultimate Challenge." *Associated Press*, July 2.

Koplinski, Brad. 2000. *Hats in the Ring: Conversations with Presidential Candidates*. North Bethesda, MD: Presidential Publishing.

Kornblut, Anne E. 2003. "Dean Rivals Seek to Accentuate Positive." *Boston Globe*, November 17.

Kornblut, Anne E., and Jon Cohen. 2008. "Poll Shows Erosion of Trust in Clinton." *Washington Post*, April 16, A06.

Kornheiser, Tony. 1992. "One Toke over the Line." *Washington Post*, April 5, F1.

Krugman, Paul. 2002. "The Memory Hole." *New York Times*, August 6, A15.

Kuraitis, Jill. 2008. Leader of Idaho for Obama Savors the Big Night. *NewWest.Net*.

Kurson, Ken. 2011. "The Nuclear Option." Bookshelf, *Wall Street Journal*, November 5.

Kurtz, Howard. 1996. *Hot Air: All Talk, All the Time*. New York: Times Books.

———. 2004. "Divide and Bicker; the Dean Campaign's Hip, High-Tech Image Hid a Nasty Civil War." *Washington Post*, February 29, D01.

Lambert, Gerard B. 1956. *All Out of Step, a Personal Chronicle*. New York: Doubleday.

Lance, Bertram. 1982. Interview. Miller Center, University of Virginia, Carter Presidency Project, May 12.

Landau, Mark J., Sheldon Solomon, et al. 2004. "Deliver Us from Evil: The Effects of Mortality Salience and Reminders of 9/11 on Support for President George W. Bush." *Personality and Social Psychology Bulletin* 30 (9): 1136–50.

Langlois, Richard N. 1992. "External Economies and Economic Progress: The Case of the Microcomputer Industry." *Business History Review* 66 (1): 1–50.

Lardner, George, Jr., and Lois Romano. 1999. "Following His Father's Path—Step by Step." *Washington Post*, July 27, A01.

Latimer, Matt. 2009. *Speech Less: Tales of a White House Survivor*. New York: Crown Publishers.

Leahy, Michael. 2005. "What Might Have Been; in Which George McGovern, the Senior Member of a Rare and Burdened Tribe, Reveals Just How Long It Takes to Get Over Losing the Presidency." *Washington Post*, February 20, W20.

Lee, R. Alton. 1966. "Army Mutiny of 1946." *Journal of American History* 53 (3): 555–71.

Leibovich, Mark. 2007. "A No-Nonsense Style Honed as Advocate and First Lady." *New York Times*, October 26, A1.

Lelyveld, Joseph. 1976. "Nominees Lift Voices to Be Heard in the Land." *New York Times*, October 28, 19.

Lemann, Nicholas. 2003. "The Controller; Karl Rove Is Working to Get George Bush Reelected, but He Has Bigger Plans." *New Yorker*, May 12.

Levinson, Barry. 2008. "Hollywood Memo to McCain: 'Don't Start Shooting without a Script." *Huffington Post*, October 10.

Lewis, Michael. 2004. *Moneyball: The Art of Winning an Unfair Game*. New York: W. W. Norton.

Liberman, N., and Y. Trope. 1998. "The Role of Feasibility and Desirability Considerations in Near and Distant Future Decisions: A Test of Temporal Construal Theory." *Journal of Personality and Social Psychology* 75 (1): 5–18.

Lipset, Seymour Martin. 1993. "The Significance of the 1992 Election." *PS: Political Science and Politics* 26 (1): 7–16.

Lizza, Ryan. 2004. "Bad Message." *New Republic*, November 22.

———. 2008. "Battle Plans: How Obama Won." *New Yorker*, November 17.

———. 2012. "The Obama Memos." *New Yorker*, January 30.

Loeb, James L. 1970. Oral History Interview. Harry S. Truman Library Oral History Interviews, June 26.

London Times Editorial Staff. 1976. "Dangerous to Make Remarks That Might Aid and Succour IRA." *London Times*, October 28.

London Times Staff. 1976. "Mr Carter Explains Remarks on Ulster." *London Times*, October 29.

Lorentzen, Amy. 2007. "Presidential Hopefuls Appear in Fourth of July Parade in Iowa." *Associated Press*, July 4.

Lott, Jeremy. 2007. *The Warm Bucket Brigade: The Story of the American Vice Presidency*. Nashville: Thomas Nelson.

Lott, Trent. 2005. *Herding Cats: A Life in Politics*. New York: ReaganBooks.

Lowry, W. McNeil. 1969. Oral History Interview. Harry S. Truman Library Oral History Interviews, April 23.

Luo, Michael. 2008. "Small Online Contributions Add Up to Huge Fund-Raising Edge for Obama." *New York Times*, February 20, A18.

Lyman, Rick. 2004. "Cheney Functions as Icon as Well as Lightning Rod." *New York Times*, September 1.

Lyons, Gene. 2000. "Posturing Is Just a Part of the Show." Editorial, *Arkansas Democrat-Gazette*, March 29, B9.

MacDougal, Gary. 1988. "Memorandum for the Vice President." Gary MacDougal Papers, July 8.

———. 1990. Interview. Lyndon B Johnson School of Public Affairs, University of Texas, Presidential Election Study, June 12.

Malcolm, Andrew. 2007. "It Seems There's More to the Clinton Question Planting." *Los Angeles Times*, November 14.

Manchester, William. 1978. *American Caesar: Douglas MacArthur, 1880–1964*. Boston: Little, Brown.

Margolis, Jon. 1988. "Lack of Offensive Puts Dukakis on Defensive." *Chicago Tribune*, October 12.

Martelle, Scott. 2008. "Famed Organizer Sees History in the Making; Veteran Union Activist Marshall Ganz, Who Was There When RFK Was Shot, Is Putting His Passion to Work for Barack Obama Now." *Los Angeles Times*, June 15, 2008, A18.

Martin, Douglas. 2007. "Myer Feldman, 92, Adviser to President Kennedy, Dies." *New York Times*, March 3, C10.

Marton, Kati. 2001. *Hidden Power: Presidential Marriages That Shaped Our Recent History*. New York: Pantheon Books.

Maslin, Paul. 2004. "The Front-Runner's Fall." *Atlantic Monthly*, May.

Massa, M. S. 1997. "A Catholic for President? John F. Kennedy and the 'Secular' Theology of the Houston Speech, 1960." *Journal of Church and State* 39 (2): 297–317.

Matalin, Mary, and James Carville. 1994. *All's Fair: Love, War, and Running for President*. New York: Random House/Simon and Schuster.

Matthews, Geoffrey. 1982. "Robert A. Taft, the Constitution and American Foreign Policy, 1939–53." *Journal of Contemporary History* 17 (3): 507–22.

Mattson, Kevin. 2009. *"What the Heck Are You Up To, Mr. President?": Jimmy Carter, America's "Malaise," and the Speech That Should Have Changed the Country*. New York: Bloomsbury.

Mayer, Jane. 2008. "The Insiders: How John McCain Came to Pick Sarah Palin." *New Yorker*, October 27.

McCloskey, Deirdre N. 2006. *The Bourgeois Virtues: Ethics for an Age of Commerce.* Chicago: University of Chicago Press.

McCullough, David G. 1992. *Truman.* New York, Simon and Schuster.

McDowell, Jack S. 1983. "Press Work and Political Campaigns, 1966–1970." Oral History Interview. Bancroft Library, University of California, Government History Documentation Project: Ronald Reagan Gubernatorial Era.

McGirt, Ellen. 2009. "How Chris Hughes Helped Launch Facebook and the Barack Obama Campaign." *FastCompany*, April 1.

McManus, James. 2005. "Bluffing and the Royal Flush of Cold Warfare." *New York Times*, October 1, D7.

Mellman, Mark. 2007. "Myths and Facts in Iowa." *Hill*, October 24.

Milbank, Dana. 2001. *Smashmouth: Two Years in the Gutter with Al Gore and George W. Bush.* New York: Basic Books.

————. 2006. "The Senator's Gentile Rebuke." *Washington Post*, September 19, A2.

————. 2008. "Whose Line Is It, Anyway?" *Washington Post*, January 7, A01.

Milgrom, Paul, and John Roberts. 1988. "An Economic Approach to Influence Activities in Organizations." *American Journal of Sociology* 94:S154–79.

Mohr, Charles. 1976. "Carter Sets Out on His Final Drive; Plans Tours in Six Decisive States." *New York Times*, October 27, 85.

Mondale, Walter F. 1990. "The Lip-Reading Slogan Aside, Mr. Bush Deserves Some Applause." *New York Times*, July 3, A17.

Monmonier, Mark S. 1991. *How to Lie with Maps.* Chicago: University of Chicago Press.

Moore, James, and Wayne Slater. 2003. *Bush's Brain: How Karl Rove Made George W. Bush Presidential.* New York: Wiley.

Morgan, Dan. 1976. "Yugoslavia Begins to Overshadow Foreign Issues." *Washington Post*, October 27, A8.

Morin, Rich. 2000. "Famous for 15 Minutes." *Washington Post*, August 28, A01.

Morris, Edmund. 2001. *Theodore Rex.* New York: Random House.

————. 2004. "The Unknowable: Ronald Reagan's Amazing, Mysterious Life." *New Yorker*, June 28, 40–51.

Mosk, Matthew. 2008a. "Obama Rewriting Rules for Raising Campaign Money Online." *Washington Post*, March 28.

————. 2008b. "Consultants, Ads Cost Mega Millions." *Washington Post*, February 2, A08.

MSNBC. "Tucker." 2007. "Tucker Carlson Interview with Rep. David Dreier" (Transcript), February 15.

Mughan, A., and D. Lacy. 2002. "Economic Performance, Job Insecurity and Electoral Choice." *British Journal of Political Science* 32: 513–33.

Mundy, Liza. 2002. "Mr. President; a Gavel Stroke Away from Being the World's Most Powerful Human, He Becomes Someone's Suburban Neighbor Instead. What Is That Like? Al Gore Wasn't Telling…Until Now." *Washington Post*, November 17, W13.

Nagourney, Adam. 2007a. "The Unsure Bet of the Heir Presumptive." *New York Times*, April 15.

————. 2007b. "On Stump, Low-Key Thompson Stirs Few Sparks" *New York Times*, October 4.

Napolitan, Joe. 1986. "100 Things I Have Learned in 30 Years as a Political Consultant." Puerto Rico: International Association of Political Consultants, Inc.

Nelson, Lars Erik. 1999. "Notes from Underground." *New York Review of Books*, July 15.

New York Times editorial staff. 1901. "Approval in Boston." October 19, 1.

———. 1979. "Is There a Better Method of Picking Presidential Nominees?" December 2.

———. 1980. "Primaries 80: Once Again the System Worked Sort Of." June 8.

———. 1988. "The Republicans in New Orleans; Kean Keynote Speech: 'Seasoned,' 'Steady' Bush." August 17.

———. 1991. "China Rebukes the U.S. on a Tariff Threat." Financial Desk, December 19, 20.

———. 1992. "The 1992 Elections: Disappointment; Transcript of the President's Speech, Conceding His Defeat by Clinton." November 4.

Newsweek. 1996. Special election issue. November 18.

———. 2000a. "Face to Face Combat." November 20, 92.

———. 2000b. "Caught in Clinton's Shadow." Special edition, November 20.

———. 2000c. "Pumping Iron, Digging Gold, Pressing Flesh." Special edition, November 20.

———. 2000d. "Gore's Summer Surprise." Special edition, November 20.

———. 2000e. "George W. Wins the 'Phony War': Spring Fever: While Gore Searched for a Winning Campaign Theme, Bush Charmed Reporters and Laid Out His Agenda." Special edition, November 20.

Nixon, Richard M. and H. R. Haldeman. 1972. "Transcript of a Recording of a Meeting between the President and H.R. Haldeman: 2:20 to 2:45 P. M." June 23. Watergate Related Tapes, Nixon Presidential Archive.

Noonan, Peggy. 1990. *What I Saw at the Revolution: A Political Life in the Reagan Era*. New York: Random House.

Norrander, Barbara. 2010. *The Imperfect Primary: Oddities, Biases, and Strengths of U.S. Presidential Nomination Politics*. New York: Routledge.

Nyhan, B., and J. Reifler. 2010. "When Corrections Fail: The Persistence of Political Misperceptions." *Political Behavior* 32 (2): 303–30.

Obama, Barack. 2009. Obama Speech (Transcript). CNN.com, March 25, 2009.

———. 2011. Remarks by the President on the Economy in Osawatomie, Kansas (Transcript). *Whitehouse.gov*, December 5.

———. 2012. "President Obama's State of the Union Address" (Transcript). *New York Times*, January 24.

Oberdorfer, Don, Ann Devroy, and Stuart Auerbach. 1992. "U.S.-Japan Relations Seen Suffering Worst Downturn in Decades; Disputes since Bush's Tokyo Trip." *Washington Post*, March 1.

O'Neill, Tip, and William Novak. 1987. *Man of the House: The Life and Political Memoirs of Speaker Tip O'Neill*. New York: Random House.

Oppel, Richard, Jr. 2011. "Perry's Anti-Gay Rights Focus Is Divisive Even to Staff." *New York Times*, December 11.

Oreskes, Michael. 2008. "The Party Animal Either Plays Well or Fights Well." *New York Times*, February 3.

Orlov, Rick. 2005. "Arnold: Time to Deal Is Now; Governor Urges Accord with Dems." *Los Angeles Daily News*.

Ornstein, Norman. 2011. How to Win When You're Unpopular: What Obama Can Learn from Truman. *New Republic* (blogs). August 14.

Packer, George. 2008. "The Choice." *New Yorker*, January 28, 28–36.

Patterson, James T. 1972. *Mr. Republican; a Biography of Robert A. Taft*. Boston: Houghton Mifflin.

Paulson, Henry. 2010. "When Mr. McCain Came to Washington." *Wall Street Journal*, February 6.

Penn, Mark. 2006. "Launch Strategy Thoughts." Joshua Green Atlantic.com Collection of HRC Memos, December 21.

_____. 2007a. "Memo for Strategy Meeting." Dan Balz and Haynes Johnson Collection, September 29.

_____. 2007b. "Weekly Strategic Review on Hillary Clinton for President Campaign." Joshua Green Atlantic.com Collection of HRC Memos, March 19.

_____. 2008. "The Problem Wasn't the Message—It Was the Money." *New York Times*, June 8.

Penn, Mark J., and E. Kinney Zalesne. 2007. *Microtrends: The Small Forces Behind Tomorrow's Big Changes*. New York: Twelve.

Peretz, Evgenia. 2007. "Going after Gore." *Vanity Fair*, October 3.

Pew Research Center. 2007. "Modest Interest in 2008 Campaign News: Democratic Candidates Better Known, Even among Republicans." September 3.

Pfiffner, James P. 1993. "The President's Chief of Staff: Lessons Learned." *Presidential Studies Quarterly* 23 (1): 77–102.

Pickler, Nedra. 2007. "Bill and Hillary Clinton Urge Iowa Voters to Back Another Term in the White House." *Associated Press*, July 3.

Pinkerton, James. 2001 Interview. Miller Center, University of Virginia, George H. W. Bush Oral History Project, February 6.

Pitney, John J. 2000. *The Art of Political Warfare*. Norman: University of Oklahoma Press.

Plouffe, David. 2009. *The Audacity to Win: The Inside Story and Lessons of Barack Obama's Historic Victory*. New York: Viking.

Podhoretz, John. 1993. *Hell of a Ride: Backstage at the White House Follies, 1989–1993*. New York: Simon and Schuster.

_____. 2006a. *Can She Be Stopped?: Hillary Clinton Will Be the Next President of the United States Unless*. New York: Crown Forum.

_____. 2006b. "Giuliani '08: A Real Chance." *New York Post*, May 23, 31.

_____. 2007. "Get Real, Rudy—You're Blowing Your White House Run." *New York Post*, April 10, 31.

Pool, Ithiel De Sola. 1959. "TV: A New Dimension in Politics." In *American Voting Behavior*, edited by Eugene Burdick and Arthur J. Brodbeck. Glencoe, IL: Free Press: 236–61.

Popkin, Samuel. 1991. "Polling in Presidential Campaigns" (Transcript). Transcript of a conference session, December 5, 1991.

_____. 2007. "Public Opinion and Collective Obligations." *Society* 44 (5): 37–44.

_____. 1994. *The Reasoning Voter: Communication and Persuasion in Presidential Campaigns*. Chicago: University of Chicago Press.

Popkin, Samuel L., and Samuel Kernell. 1986. *Chief of Staff: Twenty-five Years of Managing the Presidency.* Berkeley: University of California Press.

———. 2006. "The Factual Basis of 'Belief Systems': A Reassessment." *Critical Review* 18 (1–3): 233–54.

Post Financial Desk. 1991. "Prescriptions for an Ailing Economy." *Washington Post,* December 22.

Post-Gazette staff. 1976. "Carter's Comments Here Anger British." *Pittsburgh Post-Gazette,* October 28.

Pressley, Sue Anne, and John F. Harris. 2000. "Gore Backs Bill on Elian Status; Candidate Breaks with Clinton, Favors Residency for Boy, Family." *Washington Post,* March 31.

Pruessen, Ronald W. 1982. *John Foster Dulles: The Road to Power.* New York: Free Press.

Purdum, Todd S. 2007. "Inside Bush's Bunker" *Vanity Fair,* October.

———. 2008. "Raising Obama." *Vanity Fair,* March.

———. 2009. "It Came from Wasilla." *Vanity Fair,* August.

Quinn, Sally. 1976. "Moving In and Up in Election Year Society." *Washington Post,* November 1, D1.

Radcliffe, Donnie. 1991a. "Mrs. Bush, Reaching Out." *Washington Post,* December 20, D3.

———. 1991b. "The First Lady's Yuletide House Tour." *Washington Post,* December 10, C2.

Rainie, Lee. 2008. "Online Video Audience Surges." *Pew Internet & American Life Project,* January 9.

Rapoport, Ronald, and Walter J. Stone. 2005. *Three's a Crowd: The Dynamic of Third Parties, Ross Perot & Republican Resurgence.* Ann Arbor: University of Michigan Press.

Reagan, Ronald. 1979. "On Becoming Governor." Oral History Interview. Bancroft Library, University of California, Government History Documentation Project: Ronald Reagan Gubernatorial Era.

Redlawsk, David P., Caroline J. Tolbert and Todd Donovan. 2011. *Why Iowa?: How Caucuses and Sequential Elections Improve the Presidential Nominating Process.* Chicago; London: University of Chicago Press.

Reedy, George E. 1982. *Lyndon B. Johnson, a Memoir.* New York: Andrews and McMeel.

———. 1987. *The Twilight of the Presidency: From Johnson to Reagan.* New York: New American Library.

Reeves, Richard. 1972a. "Will Ambition Spoil St. George." *New York* magazine, May 8.

———. 1972b. "Mcgovern, Nixon and the Jewish Vote." *New York* magazine, August 14.

———. 1993. *President Kennedy: Profile of Power.* New York: Simon and Schuster.

———. 2005. *President Reagan: The Triumph of Imagination.* New York: Simon and Schuster.

Regan, Donald T. 1988. *For the Record: From Wall Street to Washington.* San Diego: Harcourt Brace Jovanovich.

Reinhard, David W. 1983. *The Republican Right since 1945*. Lexington: University Press of Kentucky.

Remnick, David. 2008. The Political Scene: "Testing the Waters." *New Yorker*. November 6, 2006.

Riggs, Robert L. 1972. Oral History Interview. Harry S. Truman Library Oral History Interviews, March 31.

Roberts, John. 2004. *The Modern Firm: Organizational Design for Performance and Growth*. Oxford; New York: Oxford University Press.

Robinson, Peter M. 2000. "What Rudy Did for the GOP." *Hoover Digest*, no. 3, July.

Roll Call. 1991. "After Pa., Dole Isn't Saying If He'll Run." November 11.

Romano, Lois. 1988a. "Dukakis & the Spirit of '48; with Time Running Out, the Candidate Is Breathing Fire and Talking Truman." *Washington Post*, November 1.

———. 1988b. "Stu Spencer, Quayle's Copilot; the GOP Campaign Veteran and His Time Tested Rules to Run By." *Washington Post*, September 13.

———. 1998. "George Walker Bush, Driving on the Right." *Washington Post*, September 24.

———. 1999. "Not His Father's Campaign; New Bush Crew Irks Some GOP Insiders." *Washington Post*, September 26.

———. 2002. "Clinton Ties Put Ex-Aides in Campaign Bind." *Washington Post*, April 14.

———. 2007. "Gatekeepers of Hillaryland; the Candidate's Coterie from Her White House Days Is Back Together, All for One and One for All." *Washington Post*, June 21.

———. 2008. "Surviving the Free Fall; after a Spectacular Political Failure, the Former Top Aide to Clinton Makes Herself at Home in Obama's Camp." *Washington Post*, July 30.

Romano, Lois, and George Lardner, Jr. 1999. "Moving Up to the Major Leagues; Father's Campaign, Baseball Provide Foundation for Own Run." *Washington Post*, July 31.

Rosen, Marty. 1991. "Disgruntled Taxpayers Adopt Billionaire Hero." *St. Petersburg Times*, November 3, 1B.

Rosenstiel, Tom. 1993. *Strange Bedfellows: How Television and the Presidential Candidates Changed American Politics, 1992*. New York: Hyperion.

Rosenthal, Andrew. 1991. "Reaffirming Commitment, Bush Signs Rights Bill." *New York Times*, November 22.

Rove, Karl. 2010a. "The Girl Who Beat Up Rove: Recalling a Political Brawl (Age 9) and the Race for Student-Body Second Vice President." *Wall Street Journal*, March 13.

———. 2010b. *Courage and Consequence: My Life as a Conservative in the Fight*. New York: Threshold Editions.

———. 2011. "Boehner's Surprising Success: Time and Again the House Speaker Has Out-Maneuvered the President." *Wall Street Journal*, August 24.

Rovere, Richard. 1948. "Letter from a Campaign Train: En Route with Dewey." *New Yorker*, October 16, 79–84.

———. 1962. "Annals of Politics: New Man in the Pantheon." *New Yorker*, March 24.

Rowe, James H. 1969. "The Politics of 1948." Interview Appendix B. Harry S. Truman Library Oral History Interviews, September 30.

Royer, Charles. 1994. *Campaign for President: The Managers Look at '92*. Hollis, NH: Hollis Publishing Co.

Rusk, Dean, Richard Rusk, and Daniel S. Papp. 1990. *As I Saw It*. New York: W. W. Norton.

Russell, Don. 2003. "Cheesesteak Bites Kerry; Prez Hopeful Asks for Swiss Cheese!" *Philadelphia Daily News*, August 14.

Russert, Tim. 2006. "James Carville and Paul Begala Discuss Their Book, 'Take It Back: Our Party, Our Country, Our Future.'" (Transcript). MSNBC, February 4.

Rutenberg, Jim. 2006. "Look Ma, No Script: What That Says About Me." *New York Times*, July 23.

Rutenberg, Jim, Peter Baker, and Bill Vlasic. 2009. "Obama's Stand in Auto Crisis Shows Early Resolve." *New York Times*, April 29.

Sack, Kevin. 1991. "Cuomo Seems Closer to Decision on Running for President." *New York Times*, December 4, 9.

Safire, William. 2009. "The Cold War's Hot Kitchen." *New York Times*, July 24.

Saturday Night Live. 1991. "Campaign '92: The Race to Avoid Being the Guy Who Loses to Bush."

Schattschneider, E. E. 1983. *The Semisovereign People: A Realist's View of Democracy in America*. New York: Holt, Rinehart and Winston.

Schatz, Amy. 2007. "BO, U R So Gr8: How a Young Tech Entrepreneur Translated Barack Obama into the Idiom of Facebook." *Wall Street Journal*, May 26.

Schmitt, Eric. 1999. "A Cadre of Familiar Foreign Policy Experts Is Putting Its Imprint on Bush." *New York Times*, December 23, A22.

Schram, Martin. 1977. *Running for President, 1976: The Carter Campaign*. New York: Stein and Day.

Schroeder, Alan. 2000. *Presidential Debates: Forty Years of High-Risk TV*. New York: Columbia University Press.

———. 2008. *Presidential Debates: Fifty Years of High-Risk TV*. New York: Columbia University Press.

Schwartz, Maralee. 1989. "Take My Pollster…" *Washington Post*, June 18.

Schwarz, N., L. J. Sanna, et al. 2007. "Metacognitive Experiences and the Intricacies of Setting People Straight: Implications for Debiasing and Public Information Campaigns." *Advances in Experimental Social Psychology* 39:127–61.

Scott, Janny. 2007. "A Biracial Candidate Walks His Own Fine Line." *New York Times*, December 29, A1.

———. 2011. "In Tapes, Candid Talk by Young Kennedy Widow." *New York Times*, September 12.

Seelye, Katharine Q. 1999. "Gore Terms Clinton Affair 'Inexcusable,'" *New York Times*, June 16.

Sen, Amartya. 1999. *Development as Freedom*. New York: Knopf.

Shafir, Eldar, Itamar Simonson, and Amos Tversky. 1993. "Reason-Based Choice." *Cognition* 49 (1–2): 11–36.

Shapiro, Laura. 2010. "Washington Chronicle: The First Kitchen." *New Yorker*, November 22, 74–79.

Shapiro, Walter. 1984. "Do-or-Die Primaries." *Newsweek*, June 4.

Shear, Michael D. 2007. "Head of 'the House'; in Fred Thompson's Dining Room, Ken Rietz Helped Build a Campaign. Then the Chaos Began." *Washington Post*, November 13.

Shear, Michael D., Dan Balz, and Chris Cillizza. 2007. "Rivalries Split McCain's Team: After Months of Staff Fights, Rick Davis Emerges as the Leader of a Diminished Campaign." *Washington Post*, July 14.

Sheehy, Gail. 2008. "Hillaryland at War." *Vanity Fair*, August.

Shenon, Philip. 1987. "Contras Are Focus in 7 Investigations." *New York Times*, January 30.

Sherman, Barry E. 1990. "10 Years Ago: Jimmy Carter Makes the Gaffe of His Life." *Memories: The Magazine of Then and Now*, October, 84–88.

Shogan, Colleen J. 2006. *The Moral Rhetoric of American Presidents*. College Station: Texas A&M University Press.

———. 2007. "Anti-Intellectualism in the Modern Presidency: A Republican Populism." *Perspectives on Politics* 5 (2): 295–303.

Shrum, Robert. 2007. *No Excuses: Concessions of a Serial Campaigner*. New York: Simon and Schuster.

Shultz, George. 2002 Interview. Miller Center, University of Virginia, Ronald Reagan Presidential Oral History Project, December 18.

Sidey, Hugh. 1991. "The Presidency: Why Bush Has Trouble Firing Sununu." *Time* magazine, July 8.

Silk, Leonard. 1989. "Economic Scene; the Changes Forced by Deficits." *New York Times*, October 27.

Simon, Herbert A. 1967. "The Changing Theory and Changing Practice of Public Administration." In *Contemporary Political Science: Toward Empirical Theory*, edited by Ithiel de Sola Pool, 86–120. New York: McGraw-Hill.

Simon, Roger. 2007. "Jefferson Jackson a Warm-up for Iowa." *Politico*, November 11.

———. 2008. "The Path to the Nomination." *Politico*, August 25.

Skiba, Katherine M. 2007. "Clinton Promises Dialogue with Iowa; Universal Health Care, Ethanol among Priorities." *Milwaukee Journal Sentinel*, January 28.

Smith, Ben. 2007. "Benenson vs. Penn." *Politico*, October 18.

Smith, Dorrance. 1976. Primary Season Review. Gerald R. Ford Library, Ron Nessen Papers, July 26.

Smith, Paul. 2001. *Bagehot: The English Constitution*. Cambridge: Cambridge University Press.

Sorensen, Theodore C. 2008. *Counselor: A Life at the Edge of History*. New York: Harper.

Sosnik, Doug, Matthew J. Dowd, and Ron Fournier. 2006. *Applebee's America: How Successful Political, Business, and Religious Leaders Connect with the New American Community*. New York: Simon and Schuster.

Special to the *New York Times*. 1992. "Kerrey 'Angry' at His Adviser." *New York Times*, February 17.

Spencer, Stuart. 1980. "Developing a Campaign Management Organization." Oral History Interview. Bancroft Library, University of California, Government History Documentation Project: Goodwin Knight/Edmund Brown, Sr., Era.

———. 2001. Interview. Miller Center, University of Virginia, Ronald Reagan Presidential Oral History Project, November 15–16.

Sprey, Pierre. 2011. "Evaluating Weapons: Sorting the Good from the Bad." In *The Pentagon Labyrinth: 10 Short Essays to Help You Through It*, edited by Winslow T. Wheeler, Center for Defense Information.

Steeper, Fred. 1991a. "1992 Presidential Campaign." In *Quest for the Presidency, 1992* (appendix), edited by Peter Louis Goldman. College Station: Texas A&M University Press.

———. 1991b. "1992 Presidential Campaign: The Churchill Parallel." In Goldman, *Quest for the Presidency, 1992* (appendix).

———. 1992a. "One Measure of the Risk Factor." In Goldman, *Quest for the Presidency, 1992* (appendix).

———. 1992b. "Research Findings and Strategy: Current Status and Recommendations." In Goldman, *Quest for the Presidency, 1992* (appendix).

———. 1992c. "America's Future: National Focus Group Report." In Goldman, *Quest for the Presidency, 1992* (appendix).

Steeper, Fred, and Robert. M Teeter. 1976. "Comment on 'a Majority Party in Disarray.'" *American Political Science Review* 70 (3): 806–13.

Steinback, Robert L. 2000. "Elian Poll Signals Wake-up Call." *Miami Herald*, April 12, 1B.

Stelter, Brian. 2008a. "The Facebooker Who Friended Obama." *New York Times*, July 7.

———. 2008b. "Back to 1992: Revisiting the Clinton 'War Room.'" *New York Times*, October 13, 3.

Stephanopoulos, George. 1999. *All Too Human: A Political Education*. Boston: Little, Brown.

Stevens, Stuart. 2001. *The Big Enchilada: Campaign Adventures with the Cockeyed Optimists from Texas Who Won the Biggest Prize in Politics*. New York: Free Press.

Stone, Peter H. 2006. *Heist: Superlobbyist Jack Abramoff, His Republican Allies, and the Buying of Washington*. New York: Farrar, Straus and Giroux.

Streitfeld, David. 1994. "It's Not Easy Being Weird; Hunter Thompson's an Insider These Days. And He's Mellowing—after a Fashion." *Washington Post*, August 23, C1.

Strother, Raymond. 2003. *Falling Up: How a Redneck Helped Invent Political Consulting*. Baton Rouge: Louisiana State University Press.

Strunk, Mildred. 1948a. "The Quarter's Polls." *Public Opinion Quarterly* 12 (3): 530–77.

———. 1948b. "The Quarter's Polls 3." *Public Opinion Quarterly* 12 (3): 530–77.

———. 1948c. "The Quarter's Polls 4." *Public Opinion Quarterly* 12 (4): 754–83.

Sullivan, Amy. 2008. *The Party Faithful: How and Why Democrats Are Closing the God Gap*. New York: Scribner.

Suskind, Ron. 2008. "Change." *New York Times Magazine*, November 16.

Sussman, Barry. 1986. "Bush, Hart Lead Potential '88 Rivals; Poll Shows Them Neck-and-Neck in Presidential Trial Heat." *Washington Post,* May 26, A3.

Tarloff, Erik. 2011. "What Obama Can Learn from Harry Truman." *Atlantic Monthly,* August 16.

Teague, Lettie. 2011. "Drinking with Mike Piazza." *Wall Street Journal,* January 7.

Teinowitz, Ira. 2000. "Mad Ave. Misses the Boat on Bradley; News Analysis: Pundits Weigh In on Bradley's Bid and Why His Ads Weren't Winning." *Advertising Age,* March 13, 4.

The American Experience. 2000. "The American Experience: George Wallace: Settin' the Woods on Fire (Transcript)."

———. 2002. "*The American Experience:* Jimmy Carter (Transcript)."

The Nielsen Company. 2007. "Mitt Romney Is Still 'the Leader of the Pack' in Campaign Advertising". Nielsen News Release.

Thomas, Evan. 2009. *A Long Time Coming: The Historic, Combative, Expensive and Inspiring 2008 Election and the Victory of Barack Obama.* New York: Public Affairs.

Thompson, Dennis F. 2010. "The Primary Purpose of Presidential Primaries." *Political Science Quarterly* 125 (2): 205–32.

Time magazine. 1969. "Spiro Agnew: The King's Taster." November 14.

Todd, Chuck. 2007. "America's Presidential Idol: Rudy Obama? For Some, Vision and Leadership Trump Real-World Experience." *MSNBC.com.,* May 23.

Toner, Robin. 1990. "Washington at Work; the New Spokesman for the Republicans: A Tough Player in a Rough Arena." *New York Times,* July 31.

———. 1991a. "Political Memo after Atwater, G.O.P. Suffers Spiritual Void." *New York Times,* March 31.

———. 1991b. "Buchanan, Urging New Nationalism, Joins '92 Race." *New York Times,* December 11.

Toobin, Jeffrey. 2009. "Barney's Great Adventure." *New Yorker,* January 12, 37–46.

Trippi, Joe. 2008. *The Revolution Will Not Be Televised: Democracy, the Internet, and the Overthrow of Everything.* New York: HarperCollins.

Trope, Y. 1986. "Identification and Inferential Processes in Dispositional Attribution." *Psychological Review* 93 (3): 239–57.

Trope, Y., and N. Liberman. 2003. "Temporal Construal." *Psychological Review* 110 (3): 403–21.

Trope, Yaacov, Nira Liberman, and Cheryl Wakslak. 2007. "Construal Levels and Psychological Distance: Effects on Representation, Prediction, Evaluation, and Behavior." *Journal of Consumer Psychology* 17 (2): 83–95.

Trubowitz, Peter, and Nicole Mellow. 2005. "'Going Bipartisan': Politics by Other Means." *Political Science Quarterly* 120 (3): 433–53.

Tuchman, Barbara Wertheim. 1981. *Practicing History: Selected Essays.* New York: Knopf.

Vargas, Jose Antonio. 2007. "A Foundation Built on Small Blocks; Growing Internet Use Helps Obama to a Wide Base and a Money Lead." *Washington Post,* July 16.

———. 2008a. "Obama's Wide Web; from YouTube to Text Messaging, Candidate's Team Connects to Voters." *Washington Post,* August 20, 2008.

———. 2008b. "Something Just Clicked; an Obama Delegate's Road to Politics Began with an Online Donation." *Washington Post*, June 10.

Vavreck, Lynn. 2009. *The Message Matters: The Economy and Presidential Campaigns.* Princeton, NJ: Princeton University Press.

Verhovek, Sam Howe. 1998. "Riding High, Bush Eases into 2000 Election." *New York Times*, May 25.

Vidal, Gore. 1968. *The Late Show. New York Review of Books*, September 29.

———. 1983. *The Best Years of Our Lives. New York Review of Books*, September 29.

Viguerie, Richard A., and David Franke. 2004. *America's Right Turn: How Conservatives Used New and Alternative Media to Take Power.* Chicago: Bonus Books.

Vitello, Paul. 2008. "How to Erase That Smea…" *New York Times*, August 17.

Von Drehle, David. 2000. "A Selection That Signals Caution and Confidence; Old Hand, Not a New Direction." *Washington Post*, July 26.

Von Hoffman, Nicholas. 1981. *Know Thy President. New York Review of Books*, June 25.

Wallace-Wells, Ben. 2007. "Destiny's Child." *Rolling Stone*, February 22.

Wallison, Peter. 2003. Interview. Miller Center, University of Virginia, Ronald Reagan Presidential Oral History Project, October 28–29.

Walt, Stephen M. 1987. "The Search for a Science of Strategy: A Review Essay." *International Security* 12 (1): 140–65.

Washington Post Staff. 1991. "Trip Announcement Proves Rough Road for Fitzwater." *Washington Post*, December 18, A18.

Waterman, Richard W. 1996. "Storm Clouds on the Political Horizon: George Bush at the Dawn of the 1992 Presidential Election." *Presidential Studies Quarterly* 26 (2): 337–49.

Wattenberg, Martin P. 1998. *The Decline of American Political Parties, 1952–1996.* Cambridge, MA: Harvard University Press.

Watts, William A., and William J. McGuire. 1964. "Persistence of Induced Opinion Change and Retention of the Inducing Message Contents." *Journal of Abnormal and Social Psychology* 68 (3): 233–41.

Weinberger, Caspar. 2002. Interview. Miller Center, University of Virginia, Ronald Reagan Presidential Oral History Project, November 17.

Weiner, Ellis. 1980. "On the Campaign Stump with Yoda." *New York Times*, August 3.

Weisberg, Jacob. 1993. "The White House Beast." *Vanity Fair*, September.

Weisman, Steven R. 1981. "Reagan's First 100 Days: A Test of the Man and the Presidency." *New York Times*, April 26.

———. 1991. "Japan Irked as Bush Visit Turns into a Trade Quest." *New York Times*, December 22.

Westen, Drew. 2011. "What Happened to Obama?" *New York Times*, August 6.

White, Theodore H. 1961. *The Making of the President, 1960.* New York: Atheneum Press.

Whitman, Alden. 1967. "John Nance Garner, 98, Is Dead; Vice President under Roosevelt." *New York Times*, November 8.

Wick, Charles Z. 2003 Interview. Miller Center, University of Virginia, Ronald Reagan Presidential Oral History Project, April 24–25.

Wilgoren, Jodi, and Jim Rutenberg. 2004. "Missteps Pulled a Surging Dean Back to Earth." *New York Times*, February 1.

Will, George F. 1986. "George Bush: The Sound of a Lapdog." *Washington Post*, January 30.

———. 2006. "The Leaders We Have." *Washington Post*, October 3.

Williams, Marjorie. 1990a. "Ed Rollins, in the Worst of Times; the GOP Strategist on the Brink of the Elections." *Washington Post*, October 20.

———. 1990b. "Political Wives: Standing by Their Men." *Washington Post*, August 5.

———. 1999. "The Clinton Effect." *Washington Post*, November 28, B07.

———. 2001. "Scenes from a Marriage." *Vanity Fair*, July.

Williamson, Vanessa, Theda Skocpol, and John Coggin. 2011. "The Tea Party and the Remaking of Republican Conservatism." *Perspectives on Politics* 9 (1): 25–43.

Wills, Garry. 1992. "The Born-Again Republicans." *New York Review of Books*, September 24.

———. 1999. "A Better Way to Test a Candidate's Mettle." *New York Times*, November 10.

Wilson, Richard. 1948. "Wallace Flop and Whispers Hurting GOP: Make Dewey Restate Farm Position." *Des Moines Register*, October 17.

Wines, Michael. 1991a. "Bush Signs Transit Bill in Texas and Touts Jobs." *New York Times*, December 19.

———. 1991b. "Bush Asserts Trip Is Search for Jobs." *New York Times*, December 20.

Wolf, Jamie. 2003. "Out of Left Field; Rolling with People-Powered Howard Dean from the Highs and Lows of Spring to the Triumphs of Summer." *LA Weekly*, August 29.

Wolff, Michael. 2004. "Kerry's Karl Rove." *Vanity Fair*, August.

———. 2005. "The Power of Rove; for Spooked and Frustrated Liberals, Karl Rove Embodies Everything Evil in American Politics. How Has Bush's Top Strategist Managed to Outmaneuver and Elude Them at Every Turn? Perhaps Because He Isn't Interested in Anything but Politics: The Old-Fashioned, Down-and-Dirty, Unglamorous, Winning Kind." *Vanity Fair*, July.

Wolffe, Richard. 2007. "Clinton Fund-Raising Strategy Backfires; the Clinton Camp Pressed Donors to Give Only to Hillary. Then the Strategy Backfired." *Newsweek*, April 16.

———. 2009. *Renegade: The Making of a President*. New York: Crown Publishers.

Woodward, Bob. 1992a. "Making Choices; Origin of the Tax Pledge in '88, Bush Camp Was Split on 'Read My Lips' Vow." *Washington Post*, October 4, A1.

———. 1992b. "Making Choices; Primary Heat Turned Deal into a 'Mistake'; Disappointed Darman Offered to Resign." *Washington Post*, October 6, A1.

———. 1992c. "Making Choices: The President's Key Men: Splintered Trio, Splintered Policy." *Washington Post*, October 7, A1.

———. 1992d. "Making Choices: No-Tax Vow Scuttled Anti-Deficit Mission." *Washington Post*, October 5.

———. 1996. *The Choice*. New York: Simon and Schuster.

———. 2002. "A Course of 'Confident Action'; Bush Says Other Countries Will Follow Assertive U.S. in War on Terrorism." *Washington Post*, November 19.

_____. 2004. "Rove Revels in Democrat Kerry's Lead." *Washington Post*, April 18.

Woolf, S. J. 1937. *New York Times*, August 1.

Wooten, James T. 1976. "Carter Says He Is 'Less Open Now,' Adding, 'It's Unfortunate.'" *New York Times*, October 31, 34.

World News Digest. 2000a. "Republican National Convention: Transcript of George W. Bush's Acceptance Speech." *Facts on File*, August 3.

_____. 2000b. "Democratic National Convention: Transcript of Al Gore's Acceptance Speech." *Facts on File*, August 17.

Yang, John E. 1991. "Economic Results of Bush Trip May Not Match Expectations." *Washington Post*, December 30.

Yang, John E., and Ann Devroy. 1991. "Bush Cancels Pacific Trip; Decision Surprises Some Political Advisers." *Washington Post*, November 6.

Yepsen, David. 2007. "Obama Makes Hay at JJ." *Des Moines Register*, November 11.

York, Herbert F. 1970. *Race to Oblivion; a Participant's View of the Arms Race*. New York: Simon and Schuster.

INDEX